COMPUTERIZED FINANCIAL CONTROLS

Michael R. Tyran

Prentice-Hall, Inc. / Englewood Cliffs, NJ

Prentice-Hall International, Inc., *London*
Prentice-Hall of Australia, Pty. Ltd., *Sydney*
Prentice-Hall of India Private Ltd., *New Delhi*
Prentice-Hall of Japan, Inc., *Tokyo*
Prentice-Hall of Southeast Asia Pte. Ltd., *Singapore*
Whitehall Books, Ltd., *Wellington, New Zealand*

Library of Congress Cataloging in Publication Data

Tyran, Michael R
Computerized financial controls.

Includes index.
1. Accounting--Data processing. I. Title.
HF5679.T97 1977 657'.028'54 76-30738
ISBN 0-13-166397-6

Printed in the United States of America

To my wife Betty and children–Mike Jr., Linda, Trisha, and Tim

The Author

Michael R. Tyran, currently involved in computerized accounting and planning system consulting activities as President of Tyran Associates, was formerly Assistant to the Controller and Chief of Financial Systems Planning at the Pomona Division of General Dynamics Corporation for more than nine years. Prior to that, he was Manager of Budgets and Forecasts as well as Manager of EDP Financial Systems and Procedures at Lockheed Missiles and Space Division. He also served as Corporate Director of Management Budgets and Planning at Collins Radio Company.

He has designed, developed, implemented, and supervised a wide variety of computerized financial information systems relative to management accounting and planning at the above organizations.

A graduate of Rider College with an MBA degree from the University of Southern California, the author is the first two-time recipient of the National Association of Accountant's Lybrand Gold Medal for nationwide outstanding contribution to accounting literature.

Mr. Tyran is the author of *Computerized Accounting Methods and Controls* published by Prentice-Hall. He was elected as a Fellow in the Financial Executives Institute and included in *Who's Who in the West and America* as well as the *International Dictionary Biography*. He is presently Emeritus Life Associate of the National Association of Accountants.

ACKNOWLEDGMENTS

Special appreciation is expressed to J. D. Eiland, Controller, Pomona Division, General Dynamics Corporation, for his guidance, support, and the opportunity to pursue the development of advanced computerized systems in management accounting and planning activities.

The Benefits This Book Offers

This book will assist executive and general management, controllers, budget managers, planners, and accountants who have responsibility for managing, planning, controlling, and reporting business operations to achieve a successful venture. It provides invaluable guidelines and recommendations to EDP financial system specialists who are involved directly in the development of advanced computerized techniques to improve planning and control processes through more efficient and realistic data processing management and performance measurement. Some notable and significant benefits that can accrue from reading this book are specifically as follows:

- Shows how management dynamics can lead to advantageous manpower savings, timeliness in plan development, forecast simulation of various action decisions, and more effective operating plan revisions (pages 16-17).
- Graphically displays and describes an overview of accounting data flow and its relationship to the planning process. This flowchart will save you countless hours in determining how to proceed in making an analytical presentation and assessment of your accounting operations (page 20).
- Dispels the myth that computerization and data technology are only for the larger organizations—mini-computers and use of service bureaus have demonstrated this hypothesis as invalid (pages 16, 17-18).
- Discusses the typical planning environment and highlights the problem areas for management's attention. Correction of these deficiencies can lead to improved operations, increased effectiveness of the planning process, significant reduction in clerical effort, and increased profitability (pages 15-16).
- Highlights questions that an EDP auditor would ask, which should be the foundation of a planning system's development. It could preclude future problems for system changes and costly reprogramming (pages 29-30).
- Describes edit and audit controls so necessary to ensure the validity of mechanical input and output. Further, it provides you examples of the requirements to achieve these controls (pages 28-29).
- Demonstrates that data simulation of alternate courses of action in your planning resolution can provide cost avoidance potential of hundreds of thousands of dollars (page 32).
- Illustrates how personnel can be released from mundane clerical tasks and how their efforts can be diverted to the more important and profitable activities associated with data analysis, planning, and performance measurement (page 32).
- Describes how management decision-making can be vastly enhanced by utilizing the computer to manipulate the masses of data required to produce meaningful results for more precise planning and controls (page 32).
- Describes how ratio analyses can highlight and identify specific problem areas so that appropriate corrective action can be taken in advance of the occurrence of

adverse situations (pages 46-47).

- Describes the common planning concepts and their pro-and-con acceptability for planning activities. These guidelines will assist an organization in evaluating the methods that they currently use to determine what changes are required for more effective planning control (pages 49-51).
- Demonstrates how five weeks of four person's full time in developing one iteration of the operating plan was reduced to six hours by the employment of an on-line computerized process (page 56).
- Talks about capital expenditures and sales and profit planning—their importance and effect on return on investment and profitability and what can be done about the situation (page 52).
- Outlines various planning techniques that can be very useful in developing operating plans and assessing historical data. Illustrates their usage with chart displays that will greatly assist you in your planning activities (pages 61-66).
- Reviews current accounting systems data linkage and describes the approach to achieving data interfaces/integration in the forecast model. The discussed approach will save you countless hours of effort to achieve similar objectives (pages 74-76).
- Recommends an approach for a mechanical planning model that precludes costly experimentation and further assures you that the discussed guidelines will result in a successful model implementation (pages 82-87).
- Discusses the advantages of on-line processing and its utilization in a planning model that can save you thousands of dollars and more (depending on the size of your organization) in reducing volume reporting, making forecast changes, and improving the plan development process. This was the recorded experience in one organization (pages 77-80).
- Relates how in one organization the labor budget performance report grew to a weekly paper volume of forty feet in height which took three days to distribute. By purging obsolete data and initiating exception reporting, the size of the report was reduced to five inches in height and a cost savings of hundreds of thousands of dollars with improved controls on operations (page 103).
- Tells you how an extended work week and/or second shift could dramatically reduce manpower requirements and facilities and still maintain the necessary production capabilities (pages 89-90).
- Highlights how to control indirect manpower needs which unnecessarily erode profits and do not aid in an organization's competitive position relative to overhead rates (pages 93-94).
- Demonstrates how a computerized manpower resource and labor-pricing model will be cost effective in terms of manpower assessment and related cost reductions. Includes detailed flowcharts on various aspects of labor planning and talks about a simulation model that will be effective in control of manpower growth requirements (pages 100-103).
- Provides you with an advanced technique for ease in manpower planning and estimating. The curve spread method is computerized and efficient (pages 98-100).
- Describes how hundreds of thousands of dollars and more can be silently and rapidly dissipated through ineffective control of overhead expenses (pages 107, 120, 124-125).

- Provides you with a complete overview and background on all aspects of overhead—its control, budget development, computer-related systems, and most effective measurement of performance (pages 116-117, 120-124).
- Tells you how runaway expenses can affect profitability and pinpoints specific expenses that require constant management attention and surveillance (pages 108-111).
- Provides an insight as to the advantages and disadvantages of centralized and decentralized controls and advises which is the most appropriate for some organizations (pages 114-115).
- Highlights expense controls that can be initiated to guard against excessive expenditures that can adversely affect cash flow and an organization's competitive position (pages 124-125).
- Describes and illustrates through the use of exhibits the development of projection models suitable for forecasting fixed-price and cost-type contract sales plus their interface with, and effect on, other financial data/schedules (pages 131-135).
- Provides various statistical techniques that are guaranteed to be valuable tools for improving the analysis and projection of data. The exhibits also reflect related data that should be considered in making sales projections (pages 136-141).
- Provides an overview of sales planning requirements that will substantially assist management and the planner in developing realistic objectives resulting in increased profitability (pages 130-131).
- Discusses the impact of "what if" gaming on various data elements and financial schedules to preclude surprises when changes are made to sales projections (pages 135, 141-144).
- Highlights how centralized cash management control can improve cash flow immeasurably and result in increased profitability through the use of surplus cash in other investments. In one organization, savings, as a result of these planning guidelines, materialized into hundreds of thousands of dollars of increased profitability (page 163).
- Tells you how to evaluate the cash collection cycle and calculate formulae that will materially assist your organization in more realistic and rewarding cash planning and control (pages 149-156).
- Talks about computerization of cash forecasting and the benefits derived in terms of rapid turnaround development, substantial reduction in manual effort, improved accuracy, and capability for finite performance measurement (page 164).
- Indicates productive income opportunities through short- or long-term investments made possible by effective cash management practices (pages 164, 166).
- Debates the pros and cons of the significance of accuracy in cash forecasting. This will be of considerable interest to all organizations facing the problem of evaluating the accuracy of result determinants versus cost exposure, credit rating jeopardy, and borrowing capability (pages 166-167).
- Discusses the dynamics of cash flow planning and how an understanding of its machinations can lead to cash conservation, investment return, and profitability. In one organization, the evaluation of the time intervals between check issuance and bank clearance (as much as eight days) provided funds for interim profitable investment (pages 145-146, 164-165, 167).

- Describes a complete weekly mechanical cash forecast system with an input format, processing procedures, and the type of reporting that will permit a detailed summary evaluation of cash planning effectiveness (pages 159-162).
- Provides guidelines for controlling and managing inventory that will substantially improve the efficiency of operations and make available to management the tools for intelligent decision actions. Also provides the techniques for assessing inventory utilization performance (pages 183-187).
- Discusses automated inventory pricing methods, how they are used, the advantages and disadvantages of each, and illustrates dramatically why the appropriate selection can lead to increased profits or create problems in financial reporting (pages 174-177).
- Describes how inventory reserve planning can minimize thousands of dollars of losses from operations and why it is so vital in planning future operations (pages 178-179).
- Discusses the value of physical inventories and benefits to be obtained from reconciled records, detection of obsolete/damaged material, and determination of shortages that can affect production and delivery schedules, which can result in adverse profitability, loss of customers, and negative cash flow (pages 169-171).
- Highlights a computerized inventory planning model and the significant savings that could be achieved in manpower reduction as well as an improvement in inventory management efficiencies (pages 181-183).
- Indicates the implications of cost or market valuation, whichever is lower, and its pointed effect on financial reporting either to the detriment or advantage of an organization's operations (pages 177-178).
- Talks about the criteria for assessing bad debts and the precautions that should be taken to minimize poor risks and avoid thousands of dollars of losses resulting from bad debts (pages 193-194).
- Defines reliable methods for assessing receivable balances and their relevant effect on an organization's operations and status (pages 196-198).
- Provides the technique to be used in computerizing a billing system to expedite cash flow and improve a company's working capital through accelerated invoicing (pages 205-207).
- Describes tools and procedures for estimating uncollectible receivables to preclude surprises that could adversely affect complete operating capability as a result of purchasing power loss (pages 194-196).
- Discusses a case history on fraudulent collusion that cost one organization hundreds of thousands of dollars and describes how the losses could have been avoided through the use of some simple precautions (pages 211-213).
- Details an on-line procurement/payment system that would eliminate manual matching of documents and achieve a 90% reduction in purchase order issuance, a 50% decrease in personnel requirements in purchase/payment processing, and a 75% reduction in the purchase order/receiving files. Security and audit features required in this system are also described (pages 218-222).
- Through graphic displays, illustrates the flow of data in the accounts payable cycle and the controls that are mandatory before payment is effected (pages 213-216).
- Provides a means of evaluating the debt-paying capability of not only your organization but also of the vendor, which could be indicative of an organization's survival. Provides various ratios for vendor stability analysis (pages 223-224).

- Delineates various controls that can be used effectively in operating an accounts payable system and provides the know-how to project future cash disbursements and derive outstanding commitment balances (pages 209-211, 222-225).
- Discusses lease versus asset purchase and its effect on cash flow using an illustrative case. This approach can provide the justification for investment decisions of asset leasing versus buying. Further delineates the major advantages to be derived from leasing, which can save an organization hundreds of thousands of dollars in cash outlay and investment potential (pages 230-232).
- Highlights the importance of depreciation planning and its effect on sales, income, and property tax liability (pages 228-230).
- Indicates how property management is effected through the utilization of a computerized property data bank, which could save an organization thousands of dollars. Describes the type of financial reporting that could be achieved through the data bank concept (pages 234, 237-239).
- Outlines the various reasons that should be considered in internal asset manufacture or construction versus a costly outside investment. Describes the criteria for making comparative cost estimates with attendant influences on investment decisions (page 232).
- Describes the difference between capitalization and expensing of cost. This could have a dramatic effect on profitability and cash flow. Capitalization spreads costs over a number of periods if future benefits are expected to accrue from its utilization, whereas expense could adversely affect current operating income if the cost is improperly classified (pages 227-228).
- Describes the type of reporting required to effectively control capital asset authorization and expenditure of funds. Lack of control can have an adverse effect on cash flow and financing costs (pages 234, 235-236).
- Provides an illustration of the analysis of operational income between two product lines and their effect on total profitability which will help you in your assessment of product mix (page 249).
- Talks about the characteristics of a profitgram—its development and utilization in making sound profit projection decisions based on sales and costs forecasts (pages 243-246).
- Discusses the significance of profitability as it applies to the success or failure of a business enterprise (pages 241-243).
- Illustrates the development of net investment and the data involved in determining investment status, which is so vital to an organization's growth, stability, and success (pages 250, 252).
- Describes the criteria for judging alternative proposals for capital investment that can achieve the maximum return on resource investment (pages 242, 250-252).
- Shows how changes in product mix can maximize profitability and describes the considerations involved before action is taken to initiate this decision (page 247).
- Talks about runaway costs and specific action that can be taken to drastically reduce them with little or no effect on business operation efficiency—could lead to a savings of many thousands of dollars (page 246).
- Describes an actual case history of an organization that was rapidly deteriorating in sales and profits due to poor product quality, unprofitable operations, excessive overhead, surplus manpower, and poor management practices. Tells how a new

management team turned the situation around within a two-year period with a dramatic 35% increase in sales (hundreds of millions); 50% increase in profits (millions); 40% decrease in manpower with no effect on operations; and a whopping 45% increase on investment return (page 256).

- Reveals the type of financial ratio required to measure management and operation efficiency, the acid test, stockholders' earnings, days of sales in backlog, return on assets employed, average collection period, and many more. Ratio results provide the criteria for more effective control decisions and borrowing capacity for financing operations and growth (pages 260-261, 262).
- Describes the capitalgraph concept and use, which is sales oriented for more realistic planning. This tool is utilized for determining operating capital requirements. This model also serves as a means of rapid assessment of planning data which was developed from detailed data buildup. Includes a graphic display illustrating how to develop this capability (pages 261, 264-266).
- Tells how to develop a corporate simulator model that will lead to more efficient planning and a significant reduction in clerical effort. Through the testing of alternate courses of action, it provides management with a tool for assessing the projected results of their decisions before any costly course of action is taken. This mechanical capability could make the difference between a successful and progressive organization and operational performance mediocrity. Graphic displays are provided (pages 275-279).
- Tells how cash flow can be improved by hundreds of thousands of dollars through centralized corporate control procedures. Provides displays for two alternate mechanical approaches to planning and controlling cash disbursements (pages 266-272).
- Talks about the risk analysis technique that provides an insight to the probability of planning and achieving certain returns on investment. This result, in turn, provides the basis for selecting the most appropriate investment potential. Demonstrates how this technique can be used for effective cash management (pages 274-275).
- Discusses the use of the discounted present value in making venture/capital investments. It provides the means for making decisions for increasing profitability (pages 273-274).

Throughout the book, new and proven ideas are described relative to advanced and computerized financial planning techniques. Various effective controls are highlighted to assist you in improving operation efficiencies. Overview and detailed flowcharts of manual and mechanical planning processes and techniques are plentiful to augment and highlight data management activities. Meaningful illustrations are provided to demonstrate points of emphasis that will result in your organization's increased profitability and investment return.

This book is directed to those individuals involved and concerned with operational growth, efficiencies, stability, and progress in the financial planning and control environment. It provides you with the how-to-do-it recommendations in mechanical data processing that will substantially reduce your efforts in achieving this end. It is guaranteed to save you thousands of dollars from the employment of any one of the dozens of application techniques discussed.

Michael R. Tyran

Contents

1

Applying Financial Information Technology and Computerization for Lucrative Savings

Management's planning and control responsibilities are tantamount to a successful enterprise and they represent a mandatory function if an organization is to progress and survive in today's highly unpredictable and competitive business environment.

The projected plan of operations *must* be decisive and dynamic. Timely, intelligent planning *must* be predicated on current known facts and a thorough analysis and realistic approach to predicting future probabilities. These key requirements for planning direction will lead to business growth, profitability, and an equitable return on investment, which are the objectives of successful management.

The techniques and mechanical tools required to accomplish the development of planning and control objectives are available now, but, in many instances, appropriate management consideration, interest, and progression in fully acknowledging their utilization is unfortunately lacking. This is the dilemma that must be overcome.

TYPICAL PLANNING ENVIRONMENT

The financial operating plan sets the stage and represents the instrument for projecting the future operation climate. Realistic projections of the goals and objectives provide an invaluable planning tool as well as serve as a means of actual performance surveillance against the plan.

Some major observations relative to current characterization of the financial plan process are as follows.

- The major part, if not all, of the planning data requirements is still a manual endeavor in many organizations that involves entering and extending numbers on worksheets, performing various basic calculations, and then summarizing lines and columns over a number of time periods. This applies particularly to the case of the five-year plan development.
- Another significant and time-consuming activity is data reconciliation among various schedules and reports since similar or related values have to tie in with other data results. Typical examples—the cash balance developed from the cash flow process should be the same as the value to be reflected in the balance sheet; projected customer collections should reconcile with receivables and cash receipts; costs should be compatible with projected liabilities and cash disbursements. In all instances, data *summaries* must reflect the results of the developed *detailed* information.
- Tedious long hours are utilized in plan development and, when completed and submitted for approval, there are always last-minute changes that must be made due to revisions in operational direction or management's indecision as to the validity of end data results. This then leads to a feverish exercise in making changes to meet a deadline date with attendant errors and modifications of summary data that are not reflected in the detail—the "it will be done someday when we have the time" syndrome.
- Initial inadequate management direction and improper (if any) assignment of specific responsibilities lead to harassing and frustrating negotiations among participating functional units as to the direction of future eventualities.
- In some instances, the plan development is entrusted to inexperienced specialists in the forecasting process who do more "guessing" than relying on advanced techniques for more realistic planning.
- Then there is a lack of continual management surveillance during plan development until the end product has been submitted, which generally results in inevitable changes.
- There is also a belief in some organizations that computerization and data technology is only suitable for larger organizations, but mini-computers and service bureaus can bring this capability to even the smallest firms.

The above discussion represents the major and basic problems involved in developing a sound and realistic plan for future operations, particularly in the manual environment.

CHANGING DATA MANAGEMENT DYNAMICS

There are solutions to the dilemma discussed above which will be emphasized throughout this book on various subjects relative to improving financial planning. It could well result in many advantages such as: cost avoidance, manpower savings, timeliness in plan development, shortcuts in developing information, and successful approach to computerization in terms of system design, development, and operation. Further, it could provide a capability to test alternate courses of action, effecting changes rapidly and accurately, the use of more sophisticated techniques for advanced planning, more effective utilization of manpower, data bank capability for storage and retrieval, and the employment of on-line operations.

Data Processing Evolution

EDP operations and utilization have advanced considerably over the past few years.

Some organizations have taken advantage of this progress to upgrade their data-management activities. Noted below are some limitations of the past that have been overcome by current capabilities.

PAST LIMITATIONS	AVAILABLE TECHNOLOGY
Programming "patches" and inflexibility	System redesign and embellishment
Multi-coding language problems	Universal coding language
Magnetic tape storage	Direct-access disk storage
Slower and less versatile equipment	Advanced computer power and software
Use of data bank concept	Awareness and utilization of data banks
Little or no use of on-line operations	Increased interest and utilization of on-line operations
Large volume of paper output	Emphasis on remote station operations and exception/selective reporting
Systems grew out of necessity	Systematic analysis and scientific techniques for data development and management

Organizational Involvement

The advent of greater computer utilization has affected organizational relationships. The computer now represents the "hub" of all data processing and information requirements. Each organization provides its planning input to the total system and all user organizations have access to the data bank files for their particular data planning needs. All organizations will be originators of basic input as well as users of the information which will be program integrated so that the complete data-manipulation process will be accomplished simultaneously and the end results will reflect compatible and reconcilable data for all organizations.

Advanced Methodologies for Planning

The projection process in many organizations still reflects the lack of scientific techniques and tools for planning future operations. In these categories would be included the use of techniques such as mathematical models, linear analysis, simulation, econometric models, and correlations. These are shown on Exhibit A.

The evaluation and exploitation of these decision-making aids or tools, as they may apply to an organization's specific needs, would provide an invaluable potential for sophisticated and realistic financial planning success.

ASPECTS OF COMPUTERIZATION

Use of the computer in planning represents an advanced vehicle for the progressive organization. No other function in the financial environment is so beset with such extreme short-term deadline dates in its data development and the constant occurrence of revisions and indecisions before the finished product emerges. Manual operating plans and long-range

DECISION-MAKING PROCESS TOOLS

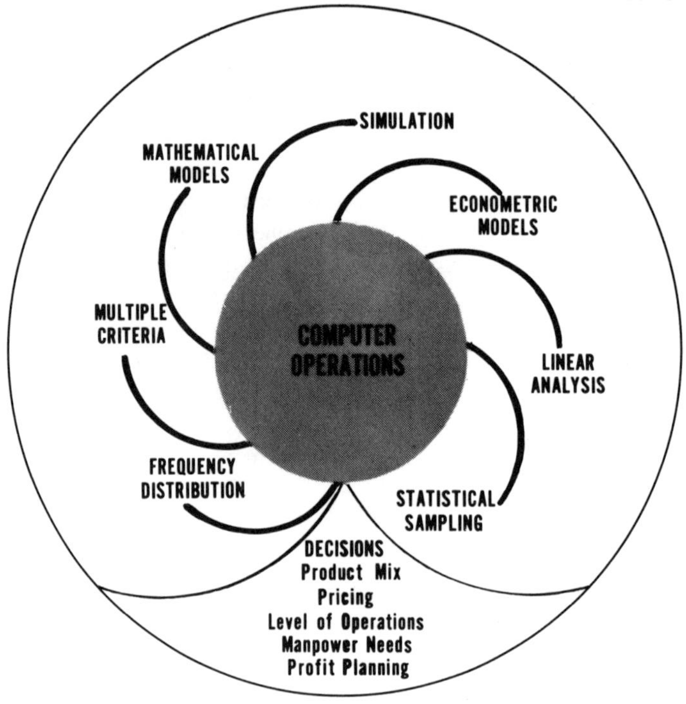

EXHIBIT A

forecasting involve a horrendous clerical effort which is unresponsive to the tempo of changing plans and the needs of management to effectively test their hypothetical courses of action. The testing of simulated courses of action cannot be overemphasized if management's decision-making actions are to assume their proper responsive role in the direction of an organization's operations. Mechanization of the planning process is a necessity, particularly in the larger, more complicated organizations in order to provide timely, detailed, and summarized projections for analysis and control. Again, this is not to infer that smaller organizations should ignore this type of capability since flexibility and timeliness in planning should be the goals of all organizations.

Planning Model Development

As a preliminary step in developing a financial planning and control model, review the real or actual data-flow environment in the accounting world. This overview will provide an insight into the source of data, what it is, how is it processed, and how it is used in management planning and reporting. This knowledge is then used to ensure that the planning model will be compatible with the reporting from the accounting system since the model must produce a similar type of information in order to effect performance measurement between actuals and the projected plan. This is not to say that the plan must reflect the gross detail which is required in accounting—journal vouchers, ledgers, work orders, and so on.

Exhibit B displays the results of such a review and provides an effective tool for the analysis of the actual data flow that is required to produce the two major finance summary schedules—the income statement and the balance sheet. On Exhibit B, note that in the actual environment the major source of information is developed in mechanical systems as indicated by the circles (files) at the top of the chart. Beneath the circles, the numbers shown represent journal voucher (JV) identifications, which journals are generated in the various systems. For example, under Sales, JV 31 in one organization is a recording transaction for fixed-price contract sales and JV 32 represents cost-type contracts. Below the JV identifiers are horizontal bars indicating the flow of the JV information to the three major data collection ledgers—general, cost, and overhead expense. From the general ledger data, a mechanical trial balance is developed to verify that the debits equal the credits which signify that the accounting records are in balance.

As further shown on this exhibit, the data then flows into the financial schedules. The account numbers are identified by name and the concerned general ledger account numbers are noted below the names. The shaded boxes represent the balance sheet accounts that are classified as assets, liabilities, and net worth or investment. The data included in a typical income statement is reflected to the right of the schedule with its account identifiers. It is noted that the net income or loss flows to the surplus account on the balance sheet; in some organizations this happens only once a year.

The white arrow (1) indicates that the cost of sales, corporate office expense, proposal and bidding, etc. are reflected as a reduction in work-in-process inventory. The white arrow (2) represents the data contained in the allocated overhead (first circle at the top). At the bottom of the exhibit, the actuals are compared to the budget for the indicated time periods. The peg strip term shown at the bottom is an identifier for preliminary schedules.

The planning model would reflect similar information and schedule development as discussed above. The flowchart of an organization's data flow, as shown above, will prove to be of considerable value as an example to other organizations in developing their planning models, as it should preclude the possibility of overlooking some vital information. Further, it shows how the information is used and what is absolutely necessary in the model to make the appropriate comparisons of planned data versus actuals.

SIGNIFICANT PLANNING CRITERIA

The detailed operating plan involves the manipulation of a mass of data in order to support a valid plan that will fulfill the requirements of management's appraisal task to determine operational direction, make resolution decisions, and assure adequate performance-measurement criteria. There are a number of considerations involved in planning the desired future operational climate. Examples of the major planning criteria utilized in the forecasting process are displayed on Exhibit C. As shown on the exhibit, projected sales volume governs the level of effort required to meet the product delivery schedules. On the other hand, the level of effort anticipated could be the determining factor in establishing the sales potential, particularly on cost-plus contracts or service-function performance.

FINANCIAL SYSTEMS DATA FLOW

(DATA SOURCE TO STATEMENTS)

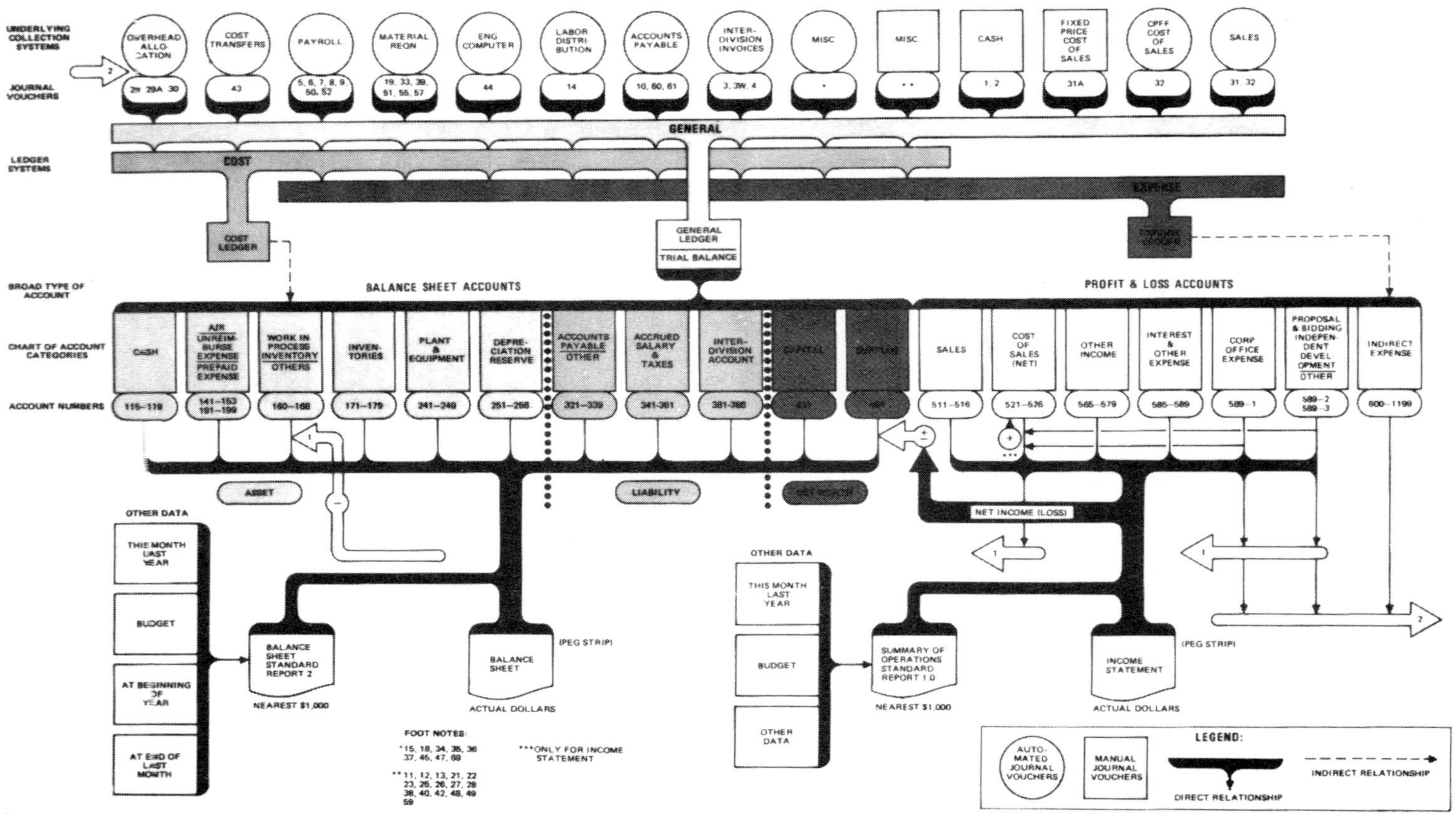

EXHIBIT B

FINANCIAL PLANNING CRITERIA

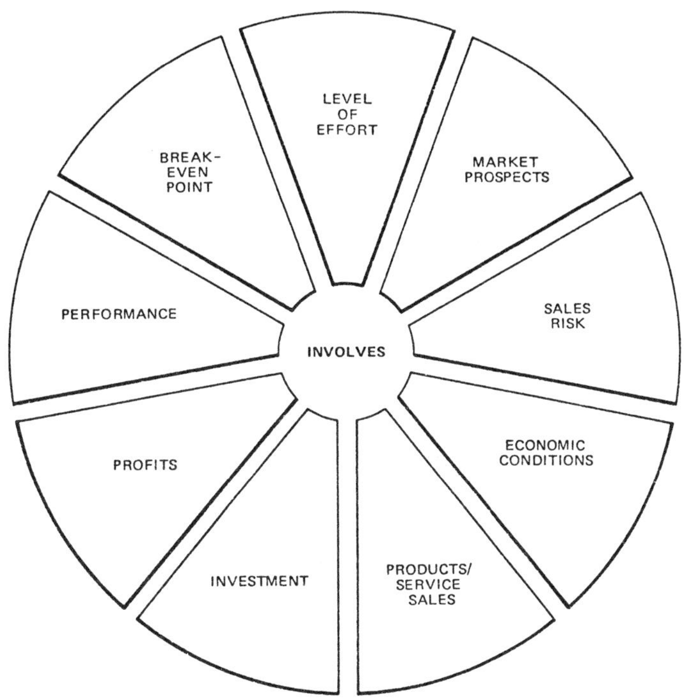

EXHIBIT C

Depending on the product and the experience associated with it, performance would indicate the learning factors to be used or, in new product development, estimated learning curve parameters. Performance results in the past are the basic and logical reference points for projecting anticipations in performance achievement.

A study of the anticipated economic conditions and related industry projections are further guidelines in the forecast process. This is particularly true when it can be associated with its direct effect on demand for products or services and the organization's growth, stability, financing, profitability, and return on investment.

A decision as to the type of product or service to be offered or exploited in the future plays an important role in an organization's planning operation. The decision could very well govern the requirement for different skills, equipment, facilities, location, financing, and other related considerations.

To price a product or service, the breakeven point must be determined in order to establish the volume required to achieve this point. It could be that the sales volume, after a market research evaluation is made, is unachievable and thereby affecting product profitability. In that instance, it would be highly impracticable to produce and market that product or service.

Profitability is one of the prime considerations in operating a business; therefore, products/project or contracts have to be assessed in terms of whether the costs and sales price can achieve this consideration. This type of evaluation must be done before action is taken to sell or produce products of doubtful success. A losing proposition based only on optimistic prospects of future price increases, without strong assurances that they will occur, can only lead to disaster in terms of profits.

Investment in additional facilities and new ventures (products, services) should be given a realistic evaluation before commitment. There are a number of methods that can be used to do this—present value of investment, market penetration potential, and so on—which will be discussed in detail later in this book.

The basic planning criteria, discussed above, should be resolved first before any attempt is made to develop the detailed data requirements for the operating plan.

SYSTEM IMPLEMENTATION CONSIDERATIONS

The computerization of the planning system, like any other system development, needs to be addressed relative to a series of activities which are involved in this type of endeavor. In the planning process, however, there are additional requirements as compared to pure accounting systems (payroll, payables, etc.). The aspects of simulation and statistical forecasting techniques must be considered. The specific steps involved are displayed on Exhibit D. The tasks are not necessarily performed in chronological order and some can be attacked simultaneously by different teams such as hardware versus software versus system design. To accomplish this task effectively requires that interface communication must be established and strongly adhered to in order that the overall requirement objectives and results will be compatible in the final analysis.

Referring to Exhibit D, the need for computerization must be established and justified as cost effective. In this instance, it is not difficult to do because of the mass of data manipulation, timeliness of data development, accuracy requirements, extent of interfaces, data bank needs for on-line operations, continual plan changes, and utilization of simulation/statistical techniques. It is practically prohibitive to do an effective planning job in a timely manner with limited manpower and at the same time achieve the objectives above. A brief description of the requirements shown in the exhibit follows.

- *Pre-system design* involves program objectives, EDP requirements, scheduling of events, and identification of specific needs of the user organizations. At this point, management approvals are required to initiate the effort based on need, preliminary cost exposure estimates, and the anticipated benefits.
- *System design* activities include reviewing and flowcharting the current system processes, establishing data source and document flow, determining overall input requirements, and resolving report output and user needs.
- *New system development* is concerned with flowcharting the proposed system, determining interface linkages, organizing the data banks, preparing detailed requirement specifications, and reviewing/resolving the new system proposals (inputs, processing, and outputs) with the user organizations.
- *Hardware/software needs* (separate endeavor by specialists) must be resolved and a determination made as to whether the required capabilities exist or must be acquired. Also, at this point a pro and con analysis is made to determine whether the effort and equipment

PLANNING SYSTEM IMPLEMENTATION CRITERIA

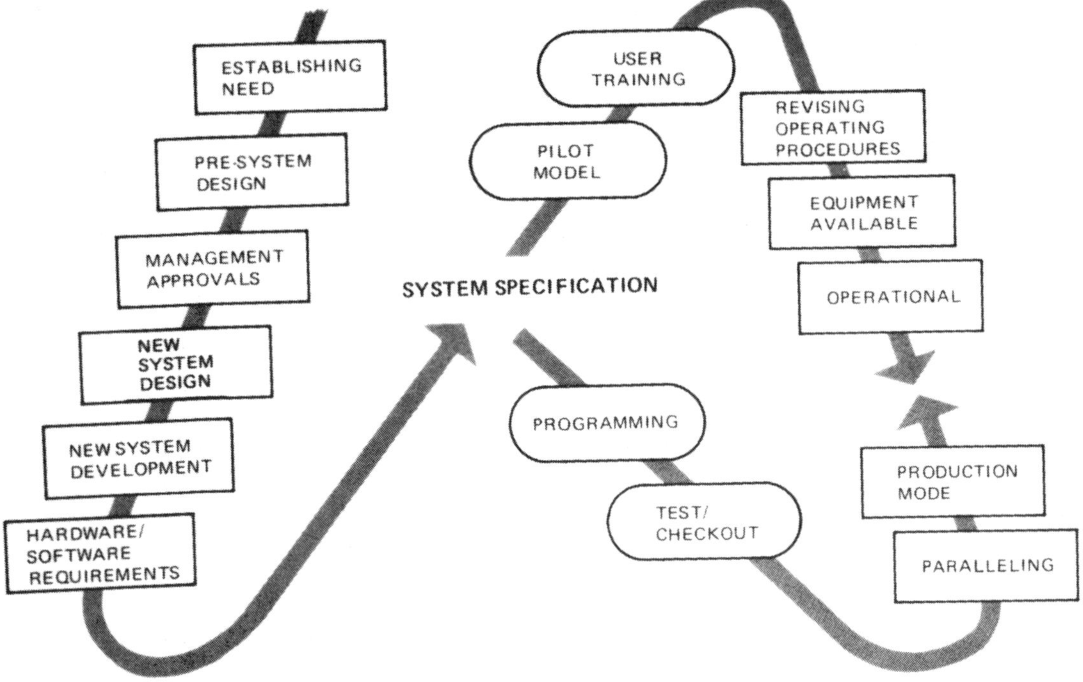

EXHIBIT D

to be utilized will be from in-house resources or outside service bureaus. In many instances, it has been determined that service bureaus are more expedient, less costly and complicated, and involve minimal politics, particularly when the necessary EDP system/programming talent or computer power is unavailable or inadequate.

- *The programmers*, with the aid of the systems analysts, review the requirement specifications, expand data instructions in much greater detail, develop logic charts, prepare economic justifications, establish estimated completion dates for the processes involved, and obtain user and management approvals to proceed before starting the coding process.

After completion of the system coding requirements, the next steps involve test and checkout of the logic to verify that each program and the aggregate operation will perform the processing tasks required. The paralleling operation involves the comparison of the manual operation outputs to that developed in the mechanical environment. Upon achieving successful results from the paralleling check, the system is ready for the production mode. At this point, system and processing documentation as well as the phase-out of the current system and the phase-in of the new system schedules are reviewed and approved by the users and the concerned management.

As a separate endeavor before the production mode, a pilot model is developed for training the users in revised data flow procedures and system support needs. They are also instructed in the operation and usage of remote (terminal) station equipment for the on-line process. When the above activities have been completed, the mechanical planning system is then ready to be placed in the operational mode.

The procedures described above are all necessary in implementing a computerized planning and control system. Depending on the specific needs of the organization and the desired degree of sophistication, there may be additional needs or shortcuts to the current activities involved. It has been determined, however, that adherence to the sequence of events described above will result in the implementation of a successful venture.

PROGRAM INTERFACES/INTEGRATION

A planning model involves varied interfaces that must be resolved and incorporated into an integrated program flow. Exhibit E illustrates a typical overall program currently in existence which interfaces the development of the investment account with the balance sheet and also includes the cash flow, income statement, and backlog data. A description of the exhibit's data integration flow is discussed below.

- *Investment Balances.* The beginning net investment balance (prior period's ending balance) is combined with corporate office payments (savings plan, retirement, group insurance, payroll taxes, etc.) and the net interdivision/intercompany transactions. Year-to-date pretax profit, derived from the consolidated contract file, is combined with the year-to-date cash (surplus) deficit which is obtained from the cash flow system. This value is combined with the amount above (beginning net investment balance plus corporate office payments plus net interdivision/intercompany transactions) to obtain the period ending net investment balance which flows to the balance sheet development.
- *Backlog Balance.* The beginning backlog balance is combined with projected new business (direct input) to obtain total backlog. This value is reduced by the projected sales (from consolidated contract file) to obtain the ending balance. The dashed line signifies that the ending balance becomes the next period's beginning backlog balance.
- *Balance Sheet.* Current assets are comprised primarily of the cash balance (cash flow system), projected accounts receivable and inventory balances (from the consolidated contract file) and prepaid expenses (direct input). The capital assets (from the capital expenditure/status system) is combined with the current assets to obtain the projected total assets.

  Accrued salaries and wages are derived from the mechanical labor forecast system and combined with accounts payable (developed in a separate program) to obtain projected current liabilities. If there were long-term obligations (generally direct inputs), they would be combined with current liabilities to obtain total liabilities.

  Total liabilities are combined with investment balances (developed above) and average investment (times 1½%) and netted against profit from operations to obtain pretax profit. The tax rate (direct input) is applied to the pretax profit. The calculated provision for taxes is subtracted from pretax profit to obtain net income. The year-to-date pretax profit from this system flows into the investment program.

The built-in data program interfaces among these systems permit uninterrupted processing throughout the planning process. The automatic balancing of the balance sheet and cash

MECHANICAL FINANCIAL FORECAST SYSTEM
(Program Integration Flow)

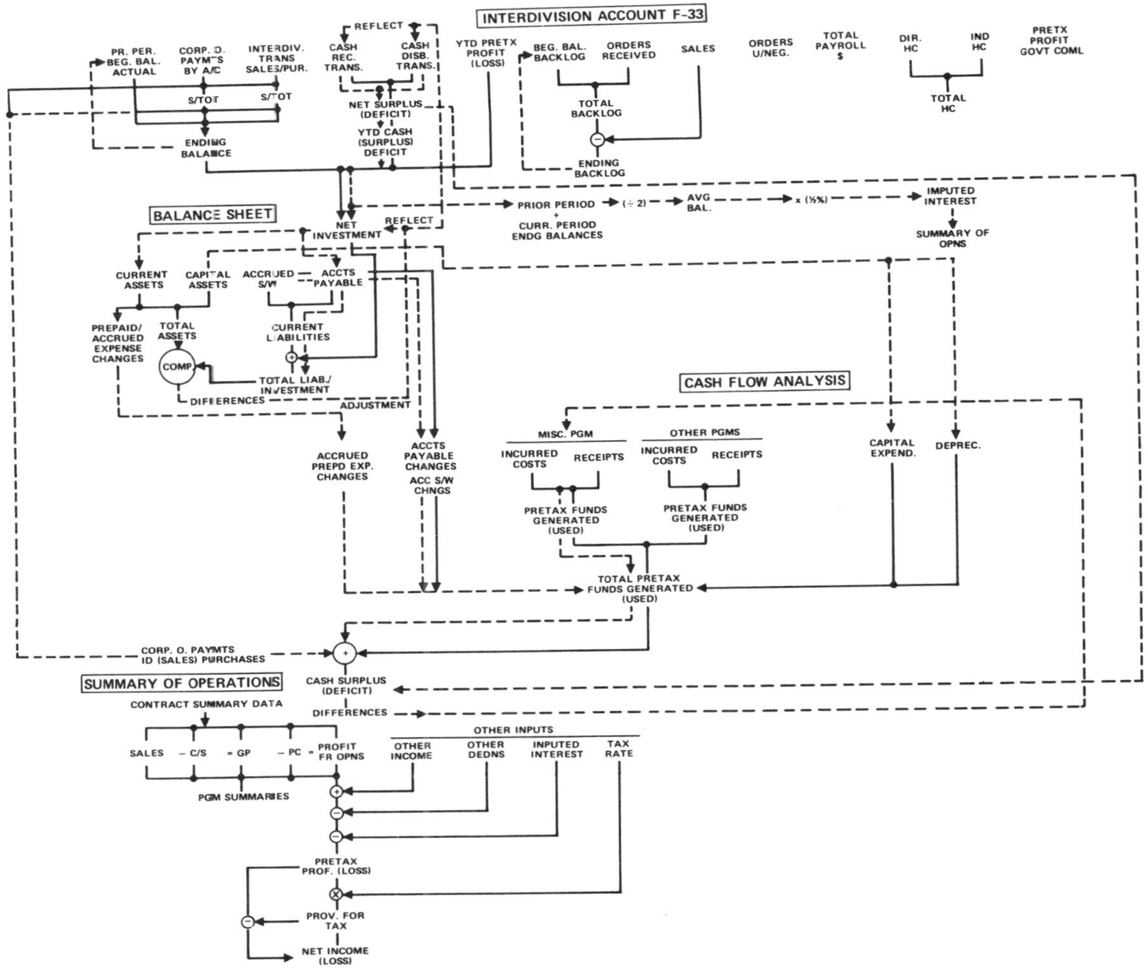

EXHIBIT E

surplus/deficit balance are very desirable features in that the manual effort to perform this task becomes unnecessary. Program integration permits rapid development of projected data and change capability with minimal clerical activity.

FACTORS INFLUENCING PLANNING CHANGES

After the detailed data has been prepared and summarized into the primary financial schedules, it is forwarded to management for review and approval. More often than not, changes are required because of the following considerations:

- Various new developments have occurred since the start of the planning and development process cycle—gain or loss of contracts, contraction or extension of the product delivery schedule, product obsolescence due to the availability of more advanced or versatile competitors' products, unavailability of financing to develop the new anticipated products.
- The plan results generated indicate that projected manpower, for example, involves the expansion of facility requirements which may or may not be practical due to cost and financing problems.
- The sales values might indicate that the manpower is too great or insufficient to accomplish the projected production activity. Further, it may not be realistic in terms of anticipated business and/or projected economic conditions.
- The profit from operations might indicate an overoptimistic outlook based on past experience, or, conversely, management may choose to make it conservative as a hedge on possible adverse future business conditions.
- The projected overhead could indicate that it required changes due to competitive requirements or its influence on net income goals. Further, it could very well be a management decision to establish cost control goals that represent lower expense projections than historical trend and experience had indicated.

Any and all of the above factors could very well influence management in recommending revisions to the projected plan. Using the manual system, it was difficult if not impossible to accomplish this task in the detail and depth required.

OPERATING PLAN EVALUATION

In addition to the factors influencing plan changes discussed above, there may be others directly concerned with the initial goals and objectives. Management will want to test the data based on certain decision-making criteria as displayed on Exhibit F. A brief description of their importance follows the exhibit.

- *Return on Investment*
  This statistic is very important, particularly to top management and the stockholders. It indicates whether the assets employed will be sufficiently effective to yield an adequate return on investment. It governs the availability of earnings for distribution as dividends and also to meet other potential investment requirements.

DECISION-MAKING CRITERIA

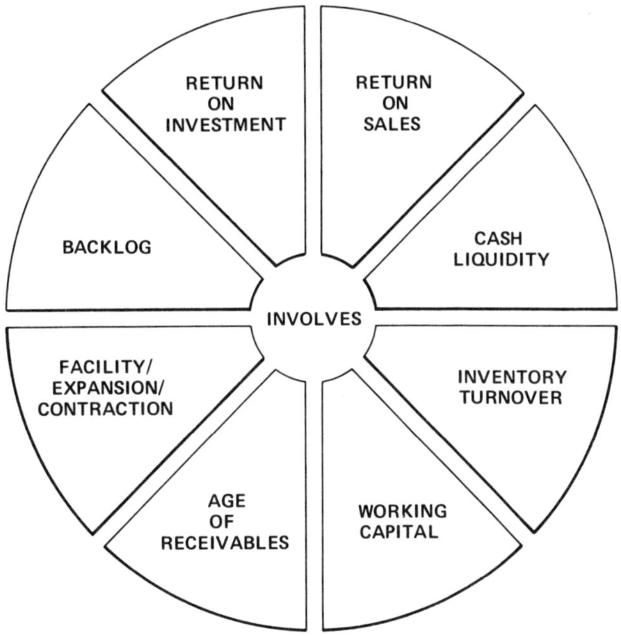

EXHIBIT F

- *Cash Liquidity*
  This type of assessment, commonly known as the "acid test," reveals the organization's immediate solvency and liquidation status.
- *Inventory Turnover*
  This statistic indicates the effectiveness of inventory utilization. It answers the question of whether the projected inventory balances are excessive in relation to cost of sales or sales volume.
- *Working Capital*
  This data provides an insight into the projected status of working capital. It represents the increases and decreases in cash flow and availability of funds to effectively support the organization's operational requirements.
- *Age of Receivables*
  When the accounts receivable is developed, it represents the lag period of projected sales which indicates predicted customer-owed outstanding balance by time period. This data is compared to historical experience to verify the reasonableness of the balances as compared to sales volume.
- *Facility Expansion/Contraction*
  Management's review of the operating plan will reveal whether the input into the system reflects the data developed separately in the capital expenditure budget. The two sets of data should be similar.

- *Backlog*
  The backlog is reviewed to determine whether it is sufficient to accommodate the projected sales volume. If it is less than the sales, an adjustment would have to be made to the sales volume since they cannot exceed the current orders on hand plus future anticipations. The other possibility is that the marketing group would have to adjust their anticipated business volume figures or make an all-out effort to increase sales.

In the evaluation of the plan, management must make the necessary decisions as to what has to be done if the criteria discussed above do not coincide with their anticipated objectives. In subsequent chapters planning criteria will be discussed in greater depth.

EDIT AND AUDIT TRIAL CONTROLS

Although accurate input is important in both manual and computer systems to provide reliable management reporting, it is of paramount importance in the latter since the computer does not automatically discard erroneous input as a person can do. Since the processing is done within the computerized system at extremely high speed, reliance must be placed on system logic for adequate edit and audit controls to preclude and/or reject the processing of irrelevant, inaccurate, and extraneous data. The computerized system logic must be formulated so that the program monitor can properly identify erroneous data and reject it before it is used in the data banks for ultimate reporting.

Edit Control Considerations

This type of control is performed internally within the system. It is concerned with data which, on the input format, must be entered in specific fields:

1. Appropriate and selective identifiers as to length of the field, alphanumeric designation, and possibly a maximum/minimum code number range (contract codes 100-500, for example; if an inputted number is less or greater than the specified range, it is rejected).
2. Program codes to identify input to a specific program such as:

   COSMULTI—Cost-type contracts
   CASHMULTI—Cash flow
   BSMULT—Balance sheet

   Program codes to process data (manipulate or update) would be the same designators as above except they would be preceded by an alpha sign (α). Retrieval of selective data by line number or production of the report would be signified by a dollar sign ($) prefix to the above codes. Any type of identifier can be used as long as it is built into the logic program. The above codes merely represent examples in one organization.
3. Length of fields in a record must be specific for an identifier, data element, description, amount, and so on.
4. Record fields would also be controlled by the entry of an alphanumeric character or both. If the field were designed as "alpha," all numeric characters would be rejected, and vice versa.
5. The transaction designator would be edited as to its validity code and utilization. For example, (1) would indicate addition, (2) would be subtraction, (3) would be multiplica-

tion, and so on. These are predesignated in the system. The unfortunate situation, however, is that the program cannot judge whether the transaction function is correct but only whether the transaction identifier is valid.

6. The edit control also requires the appropriate data bank identifier and line and column location of data for retrieval. If any of these three inputs is incorrect or lacking, the request for information will be rejected.

Audit Controls

This type of control is concerned with the monitoring and validating of data input and output. The audit can be visual at the terminal device to ensure that all of the input being entered fulfills the field requirements of the input format such as data identifiers or dollar amounts. The audit can also be performed by retrieving a listing of the input and checking this data against the original input. There is also a control on the number of line items that have been inputted versus the contents on the input sheet, which is to ensure that all of the data have been entered. If input data is unacceptable for any reason due to control procedures, an exception report is outputted with the rejections.

Audit Trails

In order to achieve an effective mechanical planning system, consideration must be given to the establishment of audit trails in the data flow so that information can be traced from its input source or development to the final utilization point. Examples of audit trails are as follows.

- Manpower is translated into direct and indirect hours and dollars. Labor dollars are reflected in overhead and cost of sales as well as in accrued salaries and wages (balance sheet) and a cash disbursement (cash flow).
- Capital expenditures are reflected as a cost commitment (accounts payable), a cash disbursement when paid (cash flow), and an addition to gross property (balance sheet).
- Material, other direct cost and overhead are included in product costs (income statement), inventory, accounts payable (excluding indirect labor) on the balance sheet and as a cash disbursement.
- Sales and profits are translated into receivables (balance sheet) and cash receipts (cash flow). Profits are also reflected in the investment account (retained earnings or surplus on the balance sheet).

If audit trails are properly established, it becomes a fairly simple task to analyze, determine, and explain the causes for the end result numbers in the various summary schedules. This capability provides a rapid means for isolating situations that require corrective action.

CHECKPOINTS FOR EDP AUDIT REVIEWS

In the development and implementation of computerized systems (including planning and controls), consideration must be given to certain criteria that could be subject to criticism by a financial audit review team. No attempt is made to list all the possibilities, but certain major points are highlighted below as guidelines.

- Are original source documents retained for a sufficient period of time?
- Does the program provide for adequate exception listings and are they controlled?
- Are the appropriate fields of information controlled?
- Are exceptions corrected by those who prepared and are responsible for the input?
- Is the master file checked for duplicates at each update?
- Are control totals automatically compared within the computer rather than manually?
- Have controls been established to ensure that all transmitted data has been received by the receiving facility?
- Are tests for redundancy made after each read or write instruction?
- Are control totals compared as soon as possible to prevent further processing of erroneous data?
- Are programs always tested after being changed by a patch to determine the integrity of the balance of the program's operation?
- Are predetermined totals used as much as possible and subtotals cross-footed?
- Are the programs adequately documented?

Some of the points mentioned above are also a part of the edit and audit control processes. Sufficient attention to the above considerations in the planning model's implementation will yield very tangible savings in avoiding programming changes in the future and providing the controls necessary to achieve an efficient operating system.

In summary, the discussion in this chapter has been directed toward the various aspects involved in the financial planning and control model. It highlighted the problems and deficiencies of a manual system and the advantages of a computerized system in terms of savings and operational efficiencies. The discussion provided the criteria for planning, decision-making aids, and other technology required to achieve an effective planning environment. Guidelines for edit and audit controls were included to validate input, computer processing, and output. Compliance with the checkpoint questions in EDP audit reviews will ensure the development of a sound mechanical system and an efficient data processing environment.

2

Statistical Techniques for Optimal Computerized Financial Planning

The techniques to be described in this chapter will provide invaluable guidelines to successful analysis and evaluation of results from operations. These tools are described as to their utilization in analysis, control, and planning processes. Some of the techniques are commonly used in some organizations, but others have yet to have their effectiveness recognized in the business environment.

OPERATION RESEARCH AND COMPUTERIZATION

In today's progressive business climate, the emphasis is being placed on the employment of advanced techniques and tools to solve complex business problems. Business management is looking to scientific methods to assist them in their problem-solving and decision-making processes. Operation research (OR) is becoming a familiar term in certain business practices since it represents a systematic approach to establishing sound business criteria for managing the business. Its usefulness is based on techniques that are involved with mathematics, statistics, models, probabilities, simulations, correlations, and so on.

Data Analysis

Management decisions are based on data observation assessment, whether it be external or internal. Operation research methods provide the techniques to determine the validity and accuracy of data and its utilization in business planning. The significance of data is not readily recognizable in groups of numbers but is considered in terms of business requirements to meet goals and objectives. Data should be well defined, properly associated, and arranged in an understandable and meaningful form for comprehension, utilization, and communication.

There are two general types of data analyses that are used in business which can be classified as vertical or horizontal in nature. In the vertical analysis, data results are measured on a numerical or quantitative relationship that exists among the data items at a certain point in time. For example, on the income statement you would relate the magnitude of costs and profits to sales. On the balance sheet you would associate current assets to current liabilities and their composition, return on investment, and status of cash and property.

In the horizontal type of analysis, consideration and evaluation is given to the increases or decreases in data item behavior over periods of time. For instance, horizontal analysis would answer the questions: Did inventories, receivables, sales, cash, investments, etc. increase or decrease between months and why? Can the situation be remedied in the future or were there extenuating circumstances? The answers are very important in future planning and decision-making.

Statistical Analysis for Data Significance

Employment of statistical methods is considered to be a science in the more comprehensive understanding of data as it applies to business operation and management. These techniques provide the means for the proper collection of numerical data and for arranging it in a way that makes logical sense. Data is presented in a form that provides the capability to focus attention on significant data behavior and, hopefully, its association with problem areas. Each data set is evaluated in terms of observation and effect on other data sets (sales versus net income). Data significance is measured in terms of its relevance and variability.

Computerization of Operation Research Techniques

As has often been said, the business of management is managing never-ending changes and problems due to internal or external forces. Management science is a prerequisite to effective business strategy as demonstrated by its planning capabilities. In order to effectively accomplish the management and planning processes, we must use the capability of computerization. Therein lies the answer to scientific business problem solution. It provides the required flexibility and speed to accomplish the tasks involved. Through the use of the computerized approach, masses of data can be manipulated and simulations can be performed for testing and providing alternate courses of action without the costly exposure of actual experimentation. It provides timely and accurate data for assessment, exception reporting, validation of data relationships, the probabilities of event occurrence, and it improves operation planning through rapid data collection and evaluation.

In the current business climate, management is faced with centralization, decentralization, and mergers. Business planning must be flexible, compatible, and function oriented. Computerization provides the means for advanced planning, reporting, and control. Results can maximize the probability of an organization's success. Last, but not least, it releases people for data analysis and business management from their involvement in the mundane tasks of data collection and developing the requirements for planning.

VOLUME-COST-PROFIT RELATIONSHIP

Generally, costs vary with sales volume and is classified as a dependent variable as opposed to sales, which is an independent variable, because increased sales volume cannot be achieved without a proportionate increase in costs (labor, material, and expenses). Under some circumstances, the increases vary directly and proportionately to increased volume, whereas in other situations they may vary directly but not in the same relative proportion because of their nature. For example, if production is increased, it does not necessarily mean that indirect support (planners, accountants, supervision) would increase in the same proportion. There are also cases where costs do not vary at all because they are of the fixed type such as rentals (unless expanded facilities are required), property taxes, and security guards.

Determining Cost Trends

Cost-volume relationship plot points are established based on historical actuals. Based on sales, costs have been incurred as displayed on Exhibit A. Using the regression analysis approach, a cost trend line is drawn on the chart. A statistical formula can be derived that is indicative of the historical cost trends and an extension of the line can be drawn (dashed line on the exhibit) to represent projected costs at a higher sales volume. For example, at a sales volume of $2.8 million, the costs appear to be approximately $2.6 million. Dividing the total costs by total sales volume indicates that costs represent 92% of the sales dollars and 8% is attributed to profits. Multiplying sales at any point on the trend line results in cost values (on the exhibit—$2.0 million sales times 92% equals $1.84 million in costs).

Development of Sales and Profit Trends

Historical sales values, like costs, can be plotted and a trend line drawn; or the profit margin percentage can be applied to the costs which results in profit dollars. These values added to costs will result in sales data to plot the trend line. The actuals reported on this exhibit were only used to plot the points for the cost line. For the projected periods of increased volume, the sales were extended and the difference between sales and costs represented profits. This type of planning can be very effective and provides a basis for evaluating the results from the detailed projection process. A graphic display further indicates a trend line for analysis and determination of its applicability for future planning.

EVALUATION OF TRENDS FOR PLANNING CRITERIA

Trends play an important role in the analysis and planning processes because they indicate, based on historical experience, the direction of specific data which may characterize future operational projections. Trend information can be reflected in absolute dollar values, percentages (increases or decreases) from the selected base year, ratios, and/or graphics. The selection of how the types of data are to be presented is therefore varied and dependent upon what is being measured and which method provides management with the maximum insight into future anticipations.

VOLUME - COST - PROFIT RELATIONSHIP

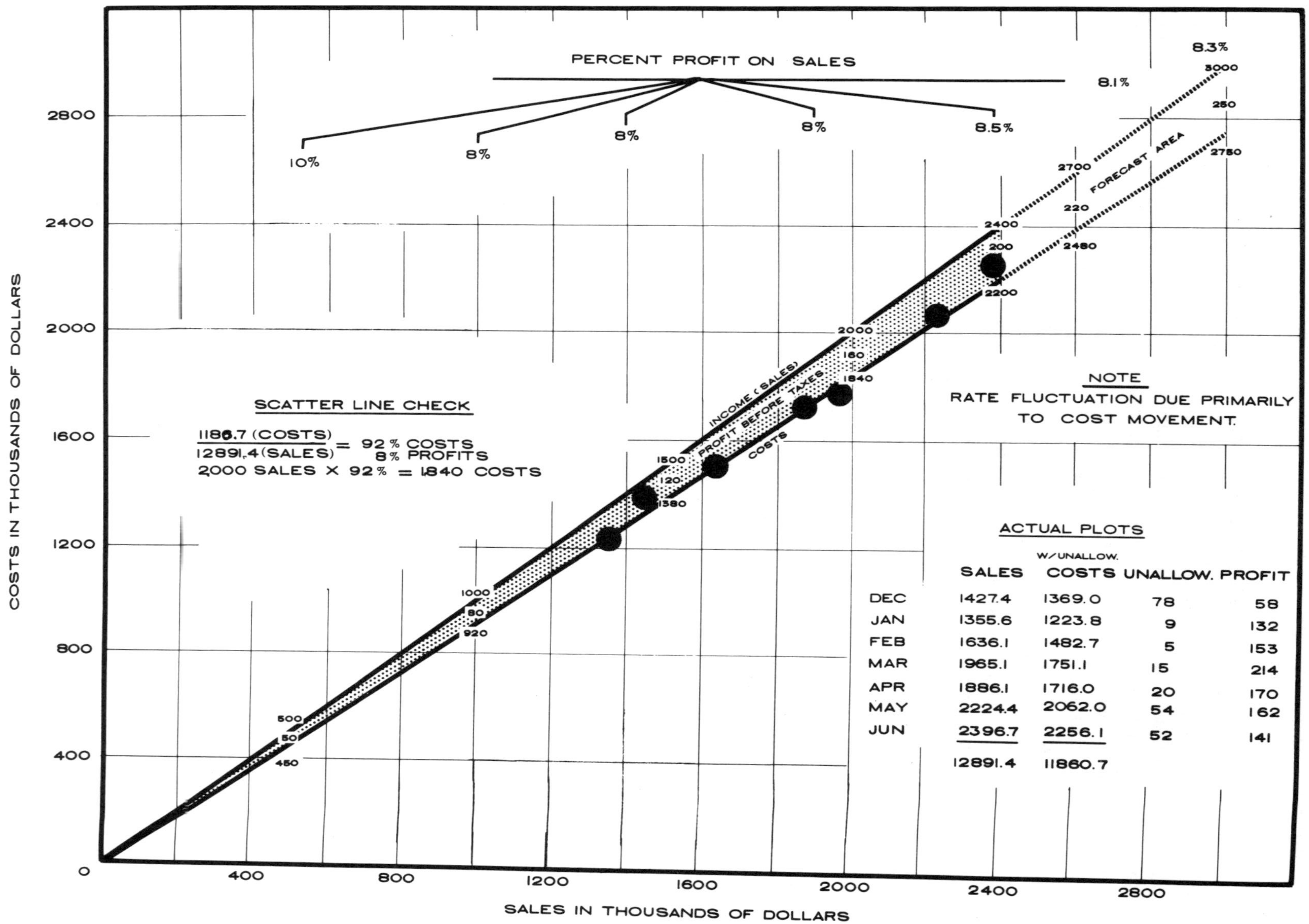

EXHIBIT A

Utilization of trends yields the greatest benefits if the data compared is relevant so that two or more data sets can be assessed at the same time, such as costs to sales, receivables to collections, payables to disbursements. In other words, the intent is to correlate data in such a manner that meaningful information can be derived for analysis and the decision-making projection process.

To illustrate the above comments and also to be able to discuss this subject in more tangible terms relative to trend utilization, the following specific data will be used. It represents results from operations and projections ($000s).

		Annual/Annualized				
Actuals	Sales	Costs	Profits	%	Collections	Average Receivables
1	50,000	44,000	6,000	12	45,000	5,000
2	80,000	72,000	8,000	10	69,000	11,000
3	100,000	90,000	10,000	10	88,000	12,000
4	75,000	69,000	6,000	8	68,000	7,000
Projections						
5	90,000	84,000	6,000	6.7	82,700	7,300
6	100,000	92,200	7,800	7.8	90,000	10,000

	Absolute Dollar Value & Percentage Rate Changes Successive Year Increases (Decreases)									
Actuals	Sales*	%*	Costs	%	Profits	%	Collections	%	Receivables	%
2	30,000	60	28,000	64	2,000	33	14,000	31	6,000	120
3	20,000	25	18,000	25	2,000	25	19,000	28	1,000	9
4	(25,000)	(25)	(21,000)	(23)	(4,000)	(40)	(20,000)	(23)	(5,000)	(42)
Projections										
5	15,000	20	15,000	22	0	0	14,700	22	300	4
6	10,000	11	8,200	10	1,800	30	7,300	9	1,700	23

*Calculations—The absolute dollar values represent the differences between successive years (80,000 − 50,000 = 30,000). The percentages were derived by dividing the differences by the prior year value (30,000 ÷ 50,000 = 60%).

Analysis and Planning Observations

Although the absolute value changes indicate substantial changes, they do not represent the dramatic significance that is achieved by the present changes and their comparison to other relevant data. Some questions that arise immediately from the assessment of the above are as follows:

- What caused the drop of sales, costs, and profits in the successive fourth year as compared to the second and third years? Particularly, why were the profits 40% less?
- Although sales and costs were projected higher for the fifth successive year over the fourth year, why was there no increase in profits?
- Projected sales and costs for the successive sixth year were less than the fifth year; why were the profits forecasted at a 30% increase?

- Why did receivables show an increase of 120% in the second successive year but a drop to 9% in the third year?
- Although sales decreased 25% in the fourth successive year, why did receivables drop 42%?
- Why did collections show an increase of 28% in the third successive year, whereas receivables showed only a 9% increase but a whopping decrease from the 120% increase in the second year?
- Are the projections for the fifth and sixth years too optimistic based on the fourth year's performance—new products or market penetrations?

The above type of review is healthy and necessary to evaluate the progress of the organization over a period of time and provides the opportunity to assess the planning projections in light of past history. The conclusion is that both absolute values and percentages are necessary for a detailed and intelligent evaluation of financial operation results and the establishment of plans for the future. In some instances, the problem with using percentages is that the size of the base may unduly distort the increase/decrease deviations. An answer to this dilemma may be to use the same base year in evaluating other years, either actual or projected. This is illustrated and described below.

TREND RATIO EVALUATION

Using a Base Year for Variations (VAR) and Comparisons (COMP)

	Percentages									
	Sales		Costs		Profits		Collections		Receivables	
Actuals	VAR	COMP	VAR	COMP	VAR	COMP	VAR	COMP	VAR	COMP
1	—(Base Year—100%)—									
2	60	160	64	164	33	133	53	153	120	220
3	100	200	105	205	50	150	96	196	140	240
4	50	150	57	157	0	0	51	151	40	140
Projections										
5	80	180	91	191	0	0	84	184	46	146
6	100	200	110	210	30	130	100	200	100	200

Calculations

The first year was designated as the base (index) year, but in actual practice any year could have been used. The *variation percentages* were calculated by dividing the succeeding year dollar value differences from the base year by the base year values. For example, the 60% variation in the second year was the result of dividing 30,000 (80,000 − 50,000) by 50,000.

The *comparison percentage* of 160% in the second year was obtained by dividing each succeeding year by the base year (80,000 ÷ 50,000 = 160%). You will note that in each case the comparison percentage is 100% greater than the variation percentage, which is logical in that the variation percentage reflects differences and the comparison percentage represents the total value.

Observations for Data Analysis

- Although the sales and costs reflected variations of 100% in the third year, profits only increased 50%.
- In the fourth year sales increased 50% but profits had no increase—probably due to the 57% increase in costs.
- In the second year receivables increased 120% and collections 53%, but in the third year collections increased 96% as opposed to 140% in receivables.
- In the fifth year projected receivables showed a 46% increase and collections 84%—could be overoptimism.

The above observations permit a thorough analysis of planning data against historical experience. As actuals become available, they can be readily compared to the planning data to determine how effectively the projections are materializing based on actual results.

Graphic Display of Trends

Although a great deal can be determined by number analysis, graphic displays provide almost an instant visibility of data trends. They are particularly conducive to management's use because the trend variations can be more rapidly assessed. There are two common types of graphic display—arithmetic and ratio. The arithmetic methodology generally shows absolute values, whereas the ratio or rate charts are best employed to show the rate and/or trend of changes. The ratio charts are plotted on semilogarithmic paper. An example of the arithmetic display is represented by Exhibit A above.

Computerization of Trend Data Development

Many organizations either have or are striving for mechanical processing of actual data as well as projection development. In the mechanical system files, any set of data can be extracted to develop trend lines, ratios, variations, and so on. With minimal clerical effort, trends can be updated monthly for evaluation. The output can be in the form of absolute numbers, percentages, and graphic displays. Actuals are compared to projections on the same time period basis. This capability lends itself to constant tracking of information and provides detailed visibility for making plan changes if and when appropriate.

REGRESSION ANALYSIS POTENTIAL

This type of analysis is concerned with establishing the *nature* of the association between two variables. It is expressed in terms of a mathematical equation and provides the capability to forecast one variable based on the assumption or knowledge of the other variable's predictable behavioral pattern. The variables are identified as independent (predictable) and dependent (data to be developed from its association to the independent variable). The relationship can be linear (representative of a straight line) or curvilinear when a curve more effectively describes the data relationship. The line of regression is also identified as the method of least squares wherein the sum of the squared vertical distances from each point to the regression line is minimized.

Scattergraphs

The scattergraph is one of the most common tools used for regression analysis. This technique consists of plotting the data on a graph wherein the x-axis is identified with the independent variable and the y-axis is symbolic of the dependent variable. The character of the plot points indicates whether a valid and definite association between variables exists or not, whether there are possibilities of a relationship between the variables if the data was "cleansed" by removing erratic components from the data totals, and also whether the plot representations are linear or curvilinear.

Examples of the types of relationships that can characterize scattergraphs are illustrated as follows:

A B C

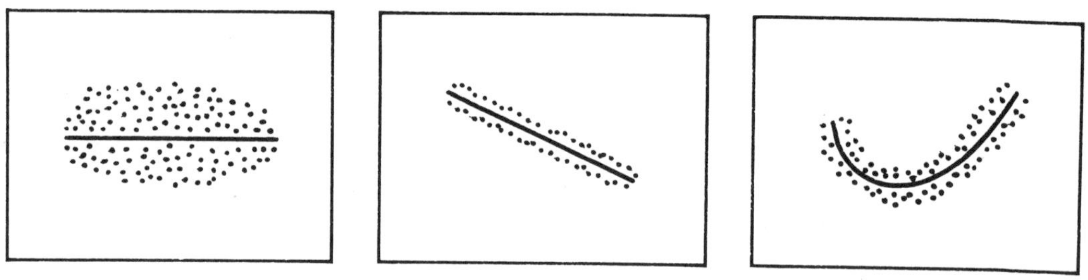

Invalid Relationship | Useful Relationship (Linear) | Useful Relationship (Curvilinear)

In Example A there is definitely no relationship as the points are scattered in every direction indicating that the variables are independent of each other and therefore further pursuit to establish a valid association would be a waste of time. This diagram could be representative of prepaid expense relationship to sales.

Example B illustrates a good relationship that has potential for the projection process as it indicates the direction of the trend line as well as the degree of variables' association. It could well be representative of costs and sales since the volume of sales would cause costs to fluctuate accordingly.

Example C also indicates good possibilities because the line is curvilinear in nature. This line could be representative of the association of sales and profits. During an adverse economic climate, both sales and profits turn downward; then, as business improves, both variables turn upward. This could also happen when operation efficiencies are achieved.

Development of the Regression Formula

Observation of the plot points reveals the association of the variables but this relationship must be defined or expressed in a mathematical formula in order to be useful for making projections. Therefore, a representative line must be drawn in order to develop a definite equation. This can be done in two ways—arbitrarily drawing a line of best fit or solving a statistical equation to determine the line fitting. To arbitrarily draw the line, you manipulate a transparent straight edge until you find a line position that reflects the closest position to all of the plotted points. This is not a scientific procedure, however, and the results could lead to errors in projection.

Using the statistical approach, you would solve the following equations:

Sum of Y = [Number of observations × (a)] + [Sum of X × (b)]
Sum of XY = [Sum of X × (a)] + [Sum of X^2 × (b)]

Let us assume the following simplified data for equation development wherein "X" is representative of the independent variable and "Y" is an identifier for the dependent variable. Nine observations will be used, but for greater accuracy it is far better to use at least two years of historical experience eliminating any points with major deviations.

No. of Observations	X	Y	XY	X^2
1	10	30	300	100
2	20	40	800	400
3	30	60	1,800	900
4	40	50	2,000	1,600
5	50	100	5,000	2,500
6	60	90	5,400	3,600
7	70	100	7,000	4,900
8	80	120	9,600	6,400
9	90	110	9,900	8,100
Totals	450	700	41,800	28,500

Solving for the equation (note above formula):

Data Substitution

700 = 9a + 450b
41,800 = 450a + 28,500b

Eliminating (a)

41,800 = 450a + 28,500b
35,000 = 450a + 22,500b
6,800 = 6,000b
b – 1.133

Substituting (b) in the first equation to obtain the value for (a):

700 = 9a + 450b
700 = 9a + (450 × 1.133 = 508.85)
–9a = 509 – 700 or 191
a = 21.11

Substituting the results of (a) and (b) in the formula

Y = (N × a) + (b × X)
Y = 21.11 + 1.133X

The 21.11 value above represents the fixed portion of the formula and the 1.133X is the variable application factor. The application of this equation to any of the data under "X" should provide an approximation of the "Y" value projection.

In summary, regression analysis is extremely helpful for making projections or other future estimates. Knowing the independent variable, the dependent variable can generally be effectively approximated. Past experience has demonstrated that sound correlations usually exist in the business environment between sales and costs or profits, receivables and collections, payables and disbursements, sales and receivables, costs and payables, direct labor hours and dollars.

Computerized "canned" programs generally exist in any organization that has computer operations capability or, if not, they are readily available from service bureaus. These programs are commonly used with effective results. The input into the system only consists of "X" and "Y" variables, and in seconds the results are known in the form of equations, coefficient of correlations (measurable accuracy of association in percentages), and a graphic display of the plotted lines and regression line.

CORRELATION TECHNIQUE

The prime objective in the use of correlations is to determine the *degree* of association between variables. The relationship can be considered to be causal in nature if the two variables are influenced by the same external force. Reduction in seasonal sales generally reflects a decrease in costs and profits. A rise in receivable balances implies a reduction in collections which is often due to the customers having problems in making their collections for some reason or another. A correlation can exist even though the two variables do not necessarily affect each other.

The degree of association is the quantitative measurement of the closeness of the points on the scattergraph to the regression line. The most common measures of the association are the coefficient of correlation and its square, which is identified as the coefficient of determination.

The *coefficient of correlation* measures the strength of the variable relationship. It may range from a value of +1.00 (a perfect positive correlation), through 0 (reflecting no relation), to a −1.00 (indicating a perfect negative relationship). The coefficient of correlation, of course, is only one criterion in determining the association of two variables. As discussed above, under regression analysis the use of the regression line is a necessary process in order to establish the slope and intercept of the line that will minimize the squares of the value distances from that line. The coefficient of correlation can be obtained by using the following formula:

$$r = \frac{\text{Sum of } XY}{\sqrt{(\text{Sum of } X^2) \times (\text{Sum of } Y^2)}}$$

The *coefficient of determination* factor indicates the relative degree between variables. It is calculated by squaring the result of (r) developed above. It signifies the proportion of the variance in Y which is determined by the reduction of the variance as expressed by knowledge of the X factor.

Correlation techniques have a wide range of utilization in business as well as in other sciences. In business it is generally assumed that the relationship between variables is linear, so that a change in one variable results in a similar magnitude of change in the other. Some common applications are the measurement of direct labor hours or dollars to overhead expense, sales, and costs; industry trend in specific product sales to an organization's projection of sales, investment and percentage return, receivables, and cash flow.

Costs Versus Progress Payments

To determine the correlation between costs and progress payments, twenty-six time periods were used to plot the various points displayed on Exhibit B. The data represents true actuals in one organization. The regression line was statistically derived by using the formula discussed under regression analysis. As shown on the exhibit, three points (black circles) were developed by use of the equation (cost times .3627, minus $1.763 million). The formula was applied to three cost values—$75, $90, and $135 million. After plotting the point locations, the regression line was drawn. The slope of the line was calculated to be .3627 and the intercept is represented by the −$1.763 million value. The degree of data association (coefficient of correlation) was determined to be .987, which indicates almost a perfect degree of association. The coefficient of determination (square of .987) was calculated to be .974.

It is noted again that regression analysis and correlations do not reveal causality between two variables. A separate study was conducted to determine the reason for the major deviation of some points and it was learned that in some periods there was a greater availability of funding for progress payments based on costs. The points below the trend line reflected periods of limited funding.

Sales Versus Delivery Collections

Exhibit C displays another example of the degree of association between two variables. This exhibit also indicates an almost perfect correlation. The data was developed mechanically. The slope of the line was determined by multiplying the sales volume by the variable factor of .4436 and deducting $1.062 million from that value. The correlation coefficient was calculated to be .999 and the coefficient of determination is .998. This correlation indicates that delivery collections are highly predictable based on projected sales and therefore would be used for the planning process.

BREAKEVEN POINT ANALYSIS

The breakeven point represents that point of activity (sales volume) at which total revenue and expenses are equal; in other words, zero profit. There are a number of influences that can affect the location of this point such as changes in unit price, product mix, volume of productivity, variable or fixed expense, increase in labor or material costs.

Utilization of the Technique

This process is very important in the overall planning of an organization's operations. This is particularly true when it is anticipated that there will be a reduction in profits due to price or volume reductions or increased costs.

COSTS vs PROGRESS PAYMT CORRELATION

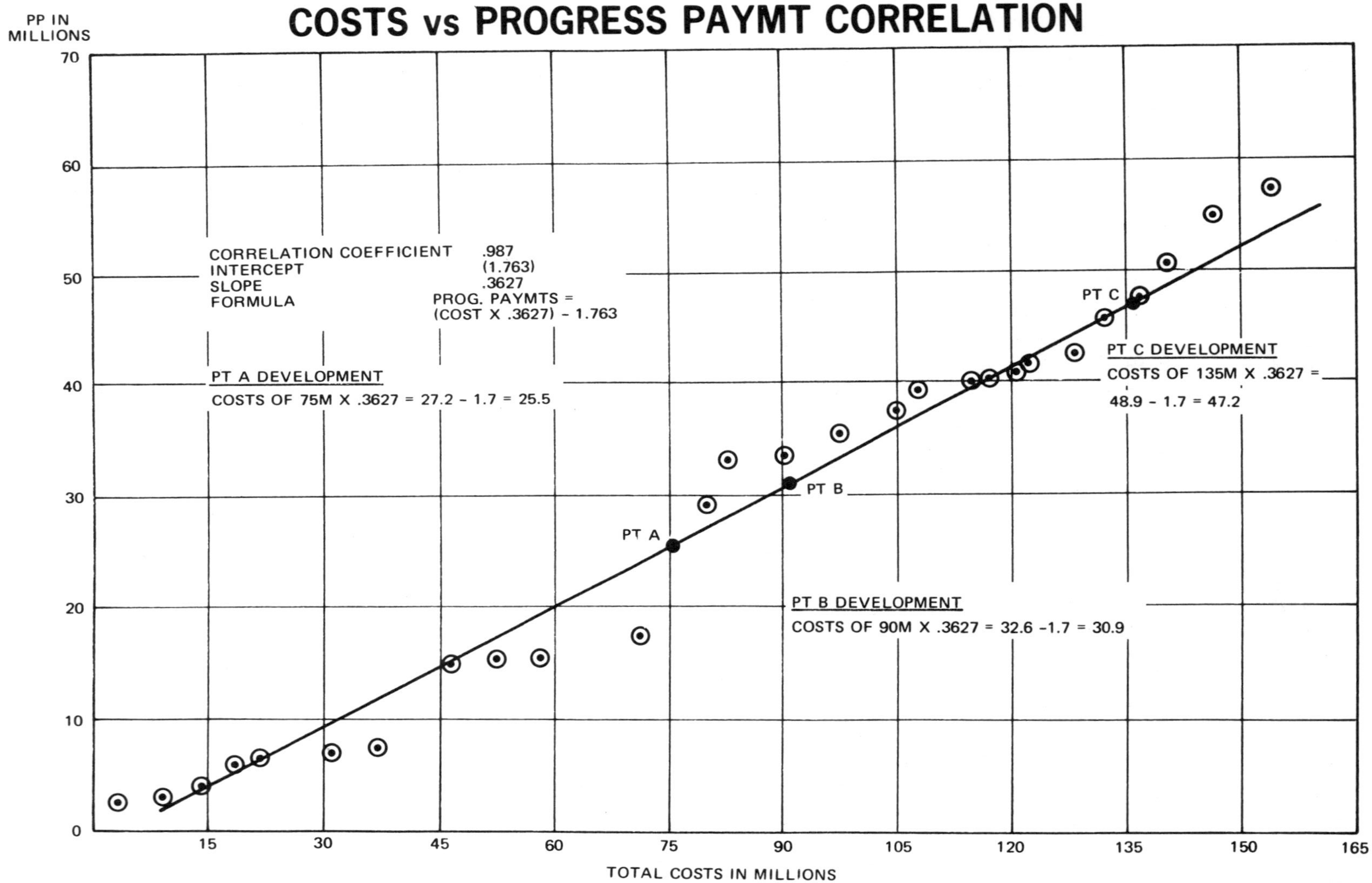

EXHIBIT B

SALES vs DELIVERY COLLN CORRELATION
FIXED PRICE CONTRACTS

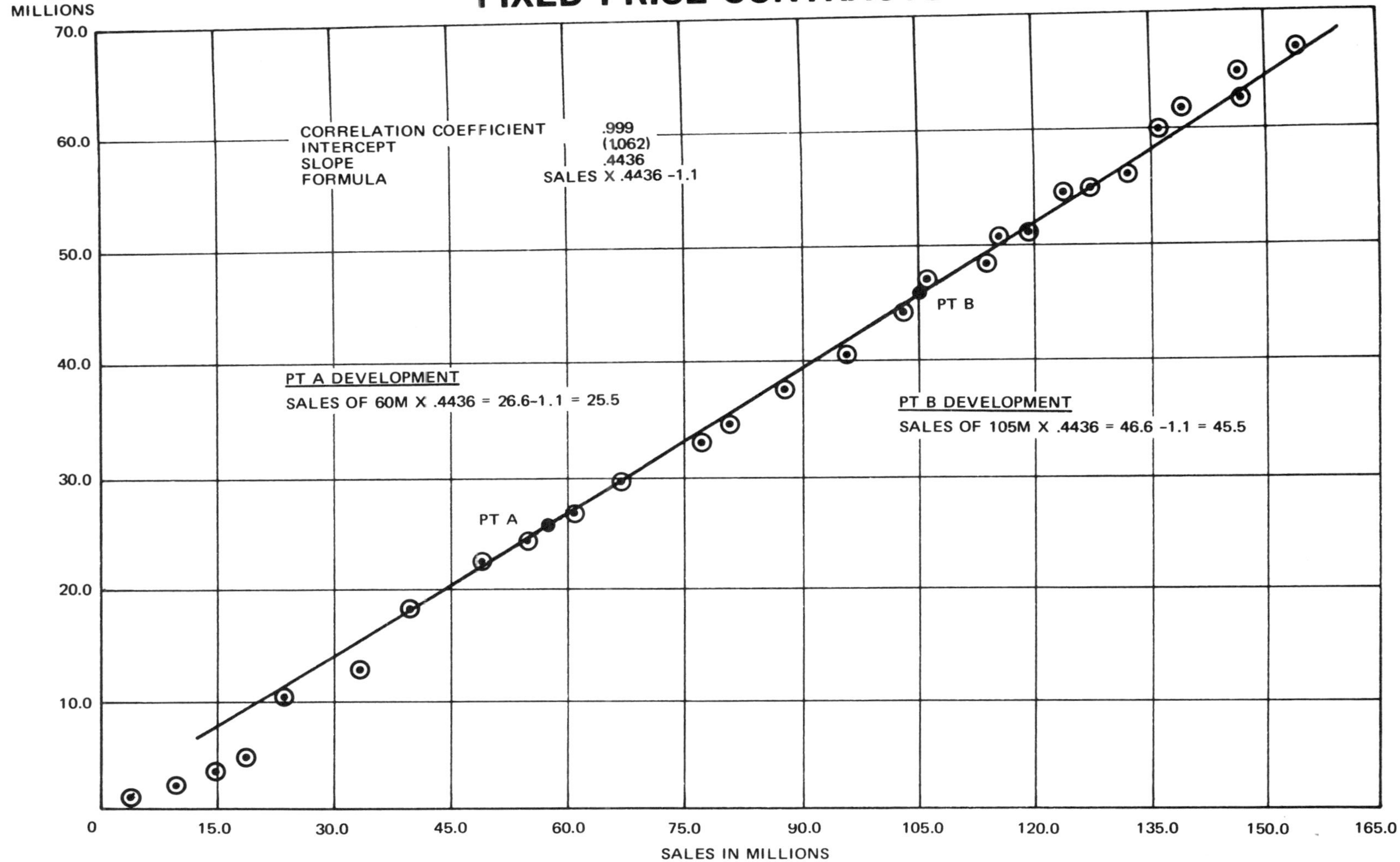

EXHIBIT C

Breakeven point utilization can be used to determine the price level required to produce a particular profit when the sales volume declines or costs increase. It is useful in determining the volume of sales required to meet profit requirements. This technique can provide the basis for intelligent decision-making relative to price or volume changes.

Development of the Breakeven Point

A typical illustration of a common graphic breakeven chart is shown on Exhibit D. Any changes in volume or costs in the illustration would result in a change in the breakeven point location. On Exhibit D the breakeven point is at 400K units at a cost of $200K. Any output below the point would reflect a loss; any output above the point, a profit. The breakeven point is mathematically computed as follows:

Sales (S) = Breakeven Point
(FE) = Fixed Expense
(VE) = Variable Expense

S = $100K (FE) + 50% (VE) − 100 ÷ 200 = 50%
100%S − 50% = $100K
50%S = $100K
S = $200K

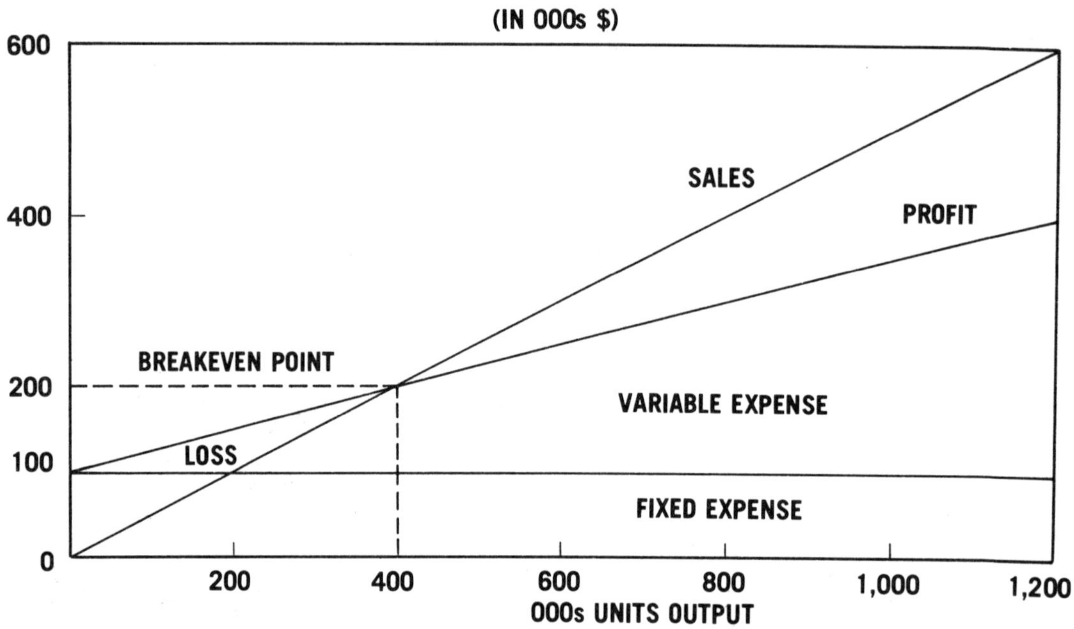

EXHIBIT D

There are any number of variations of the formula that can be used to achieve different objectives. Expenses can be increased, profits can be designated, and so on. Two examples are noted below.

Sales Required to Increase Costs (FE) by $20K	Sales Required to Achieve $100K Profit before Taxes
S = $120K + 50%(VE)	S = $120K + 50%(VE) + $100K
100% S − 50%(VE) = $120K	100% S − 50%(VE) = $220K
50% S = $120K	50% S = $220K
S = $240K	S = $440K

In the above discussion, expenses were classified as variable (vary with production expense—labor, material and other costs) and fixed (generally do not vary with output). In the latter group you would include taxes, rentals, corporate office expense, and the like. Further, these expenses can be either cash or noncash as in the case of depreciation.

Exhibit E displays another version of the breakeven chart which also includes the cash designations, income taxes, and net income. For purposes of constructing this chart, the following information was used at three output levels.

Units of Output	5,000	10,000	20,000
Variable Expense	$10,000	$20,000	$42,000
Fixed Cash Expense	10,000	10,000	10,000
Subtotal	$20,000	$30,000	$52,000
Fixed Noncash Expense	5,000	5,000	5,000
Total	$25,000	$35,000	$57,000
Taxes	Calculated at 50% of the profit in each case.		

Using a sales price of $5,000 per unit of output, the chart shown in Exhibit E evolves. This display represents a useful management tool for evaluating cost impact on sales and cash breakeven points. It shows the effect of changes in sales volume as well as highlights areas for cost reduction attention. Although the chart may reflect certain inaccuracies at volumes below or above the range for which the estimates were derived, its usefulness exceeds its limitations as a significant planning technique.

RATIO UTILIZATION FOR PERFORMANCE MEASUREMENT

The development and use of financial ratios is another important tool for analysis, planning, and performance measurement. A ratio represents the quotient of two numbers where the first number is divided by the second. In the case of proportions, it indicates the equality of ratios where one set of numbers is equal to another set. For example, 6 to 30 and 5 to 25 indicates that both ratios are 1/5. Ratios can be reported in the form of whole numbers, percentages, or fractions.

Trend Versus Structural Ratios

Financial ratio analysis is a common practice in most progressive organizations. Ratios are useful in determining trends and changes in financial data of an organization over a period of time and also in comparing the differences among companies and/or similar industry results.

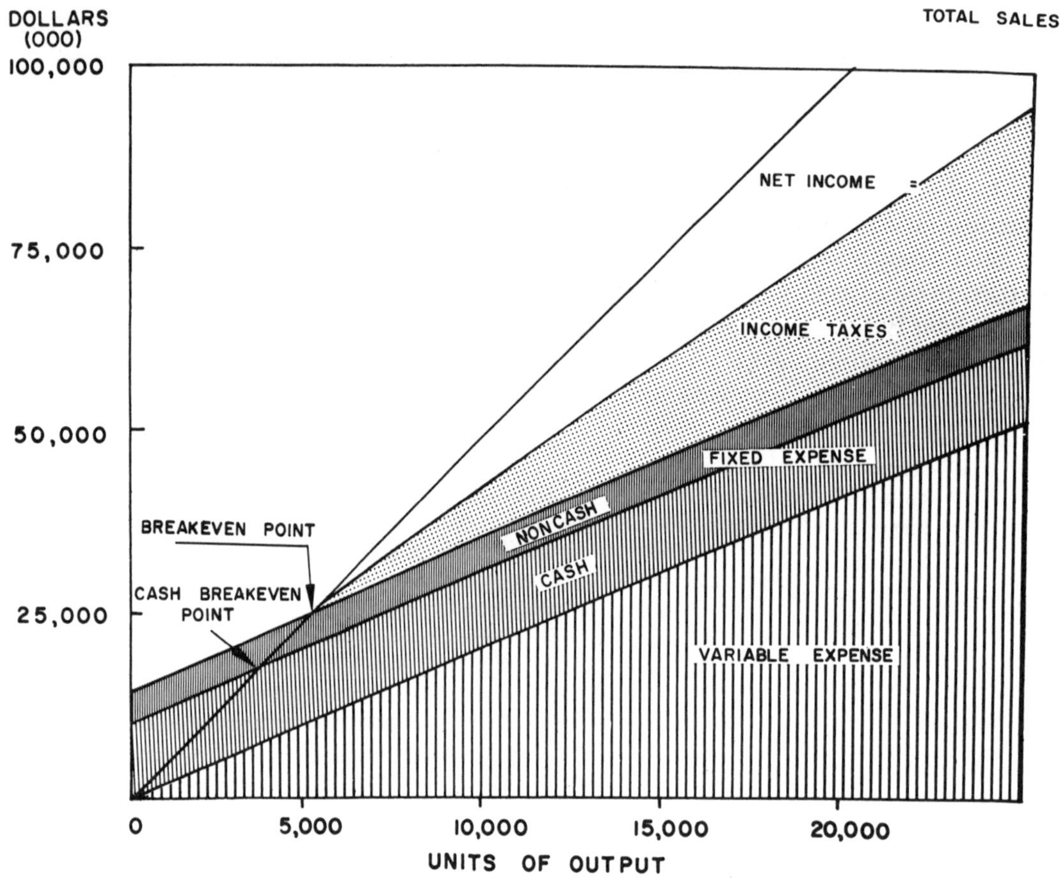

EXHIBIT E

Trend ratios are used to determine which data items have increased or decreased over time periods and the rate of the change. *Structural ratios* are concerned with the measurement of the relationship between relative items at particular points in time which represents the status in a given period. It is often highly desirable to make a comparison of several points in time in order to determine progress and/or acceptable performance. Further, the analysis may reveal problem areas where the deviations are trending in an adverse manner.

Evaluating Ratio Results

In most instances, the calculation and observation of one ratio has little significance in itself and therefore many and varied ratios provide a more valid and comprehensive insight into the results of operations. After determining the type of analytical ratios required, the next step is to evaluate them in terms of their significance. Based on past experience, the analyst and/or management must make a determination as to whether the results are satisfactory and indicative of an organization's planned progress or whether they point to problems that require investigation as to causes.

Structural ratios are also identified as operation ratios. This type of ratio (vertical in nature) includes the analysis of ratios between data sets in one statement, such as the balance sheet; however, items are also used from the income statement (for example, the net income from the income statement to calculate the return on investment).

Levels of Analysis for Determining Ratio Influences

If the ratio deviations are determined to be of major magnitude, a detailed analysis should be performed to reveal the specific cause for the differences. To conduct this type of investigation, it is necessary that consideration be given to the review of the structural ratio itself, ratio trends, evaluation of the variables that contribute to the ratio data elements, and possibly the effect from certain aspects of the operations that could influence ratio performance.

In analyzing receivables to sales, there are a number of possibilities that could create ratio differences such as increase in sales but no change or even a decrease in receivables; increases and decreases in sales and receivables but not in the same relative proportion. The following procedural method would be an effective tool for a thorough and effective evaluation of variations between periods (the same process is recommended for other ratio analyses).

- *Structural Ratio*—Sales to Receivables
- *Trend Ratio*—Measure of Sales and Receivables individually
- *Variable Analysis*—Sales (price and volume)—Receivables (aging)

Performance Ratio Analysis

In measuring performance, there are certain common and comparative ratios that effectively disclose operation and financial status results. Some of the primary ones are noted as follows:

- *Percentage of Net Income to Sales.* Revenue from sales is predicated on sales volume and price, while net income is primarily influenced by the associated costs required to achieve the sales.
- *Return on Net Investment.* A significant influence would be the reassessment and use of capital asset replacement values which would reflect a lower return.
- *Current Assets to Current Liabilities.* This is a common ratio but it could be greatly influenced and distorted by reducing inventories and receivables at month end which would be offset in the surplus account and thus the result would be a higher ratio.
- *Turnover of Working Capital.* Sales divided by working capital indicates the number of times working capital is turned over in a given time frame. Increases in turnover reflect efficiency in working capital employment.
- *Inventory to Cost of Sales.* This ratio is calculated by dividing inventory balances by the average daily cost of sales. It is indicative of the number of days costs are reflected in inventory. An excessive number of days would reflect a greater investment in inventories.

In conclusion, this chapter has been concerned with the various techniques that can be employed to improve operational controls, measure performance, determine deviations from the operating plan that necessitate corrective action, and provide the basis for intelligent and rewarding future planning. Hundreds of thousands of dollars in cost avoidance can be achieved by utilizing the capabilities above, which provide the means for data assessment, establishment of appropriate data relationships, and testing of alternate courses of planning before costly redirection action is taken.

3

Utilizing the Computer in Financial Decisions That Establish Profitable Operations

Financial decision-planning is an inescapable activity which, in essence, translates the projected operating plans and objectives into quantitative monetary expressions. It provides a systematic approach to resolving the guidelines for future operations in terms of the specific requirements of accomplishing the planned tasks and management's operating direction. The overall major considerations in financial planning are particularly concerned with the economic outlook, manpower and production, capital expenditures, profit goals and, quite importantly, the source of funds to accomplish the above, as well as the most effective utilization and disbursement of those resources.

COMMON PLANNING CONCEPTS

In general, there are four basic methods that are employed in the financial planning philosophy. The terminology and description used below may vary somewhat among organizations, but the processes still remain, in context, the same. In many instances, organizations may not be aware of their planning activities in terms of definitive terminology or identification. In reality, planning can reflect a combination of two or more of the methods described below.

Mechanical Process

The conclusions used in this type of planning are predicated primarily on historical experience with little or no evaluation of past and current causal factors that made certain result eventualities happen as they did. A typical example is where planners conclude that particular operating or financial events in terms of data results are moving downward (production, sales, inventories, etc.) because of the current trend indicator in that direction or the rate of increase has leveled off, then the planners are prone to projecting the future in a similar vein. The same type of concept also applies to conclusions based on the assumption that a series of data (resulting from operations) is presently above or below its long-term trend line, then the resultant expectation is that the future events will result in the return of operations to the original trend level.

This is a naive planning approach because previous statistical and historical relationships are projected for the future without a complete analysis and investigation of the specific event occurrences that influenced the deviations and direction of the operating results. This type of planning could lead to impractical or inadequate plan development and subsequent dire effects on operational results.

Knowledge of Plans for Future Action

If specific and valid operating plans and events can be determined in the early stages, prior to their occurrence, then it is often possible to predict certain future results. This type of planning, in effect, is a function of summarizing the anticipated effect of the plans currently in existence. For example, if management were contemplating the purchase of a new building or equipment in a specified future period, indicated costs, financing, location, and so on can be effectively analyzed before the economic effects are felt.

The problem with this type of forecasting is that it is impossible to outguess all of the possible eventualities that may occur. For example, in the case above of purchasing a building, poor sales, profits, and cash flow could make it impractical or impossible to make the purchase as scheduled. Financing from the outside could be impractical because of the unforeseen high interest economy. Unanticipated strong competition or product obsolescence might have a serious adverse effect on the proposed building venture. This type of planning is not sound without a thorough analysis of possible events that may occur in the future and their impact on what were considered to be firm future actions.

Opinions and Expectations

This type of planning is contingent on the reliability of management's experience and judgment relative to the future business outlook and environment. It is generally classified as the "seat of the pants" approach to the prediction process. In past uncomplicated business practices and organizations, the single controlling entrepreneur generally used this method effectively since advanced techniques had not surfaced in use or importance. This planning represents a nonscientific, nontechnical approach to the dynamics of projecting future events based on past history event causes and effects.

In this highly competitive business environment, a successful operating plan cannot be achieved with this method since its basic characteristic is an intuitive feel for future events rather than a thorough analysis of business influencing factors. Current computerized techniques could be used to verify the validity of anticipated expectations with relative probabilities or indicated alternatives with a greater potential for successful planning.

Causal Predictions

This planning approach is by far the most effective approach since it involves many specific techniques that have one prime objective in common. Basically, an attempt is made to determine and isolate causes for the deviations and fluctuations in the data element series to be projected. The causes are measured and evaluated to ascertain whether similar events will prevail in the future. This method provides a realistic rationale to be used in justifying the judgment used in the planning process.

The above approaches to planning are used in varying degrees among organizations. Experimentation with the results of their utilization should reveal the method with the greatest potential for reliability.

BASICS OF PLAN DEVELOPMENT

There are various types of planning criteria which are used and classified according to their objectives in the development of the operating plan. They represent important segments and support for evolving the future overall plan of operations. Some of the prime forecasting activities are described below.

Economic

This type of planning deals with external forces outside of a company that could conceivably influence probabilities or result in future events that would affect an organization's operations, competitiveness, or even survival. Through research and analysis of government agencies, trade/industry and other economic indices and trends, certain measurable determinations can be made of the anticipated future economy and market conditions that could affect an organization's operations.

Economic planning is concerned with the business climate as a whole—growth potential or decline, trend of the gross national product, extent and direction of projected government expenditures (particularly Department of Defense procurements as they affect defense contractors), availability of financing with the associated interest rates, commodity prices, fuel consumption, employment trends, population and location predictions, outlook of union negotiations, availability of raw materials, foreign trade probabilities, world economy, seasonal variations, and so on. The effect of the above considerations on an organization's operations in terms of products or services must be determined. This planning is a dynamic force on an organization's posture and progress because of the many inherent intangibles that could occur such as labor strikes in associated industries, international strife, or change in national leadership which could adversely affect sales and profits. Management and its economic planners must weigh the pros and cons of the projected economic assumptions and set forth their findings in objective business operation and strategy guidelines. These premises then become the basic philosophies to be employed in the development of the operating plan. External force effects are often extremely difficult to assess unless valid correlations have been established between the projected occurrence of the above events and their relationship to an organization's operations.

Marketing Activity Projections

This type of forecasting is concerned with estimating product/service performance volume and dollars for the projected periods. The process involves a survey of type of products (both currently in production and those anticipated from new developments), new market penetrations, type of customers, territorial sales, unit prices, and anticipated competition. Product (service) sales trends are predicated on various economic indicators (discussed above), as well as projected customer demands. The rate of economic growth or decline trend in related industries as a whole is very helpful in this type of projection, as is the knowledge of the organization's proportionate share of the total market.

Production Planning

The product production plan must reflect needs to fulfill the anticipated customer sales demand in terms of volume, limits to estimated costs in the sales price determination, and ability to meet the delivery schedule. This planning must consider manpower skills and number, facilities, and equipment needs. Further, it encompasses production scheduling (current products and new developments), raw materials, component part purchases, outside production, supplies, learning curves, subcontracting, indirect support, and quality control. In essence, this plan delineates the requirements to achieve the estimated product output to meet the anticipated customer demand on a scheduled basis.

Capital Expenditure Planning

This is another important facet of the overall operating plan development. It involves the participation of all departments of the organization since facilities (acquisition or improvements), machinery, equipment, furniture, and fixtures must be determined to meet the aggregate and specific requirements of the operating plan objectives.

In the final analysis, management is responsible for assessing relative needs and allocating funds to provide the requirements. Too little in fund commitments is just as detrimental as too much. Insufficient funds for facilities would prevent meeting operational requirements, whereas too much would result in idle, nonprofit-producing expenditures that could seriously affect profitability and create adverse cash flow problems. Therefore, it behooves operating organizations to carefully plan capital expenditure needs with detailed justification to preclude unwarranted cost impact, which involves top management's active and direct participation in the review and approval/disapproval cycle.

Profit Planning

Profit planning is one of the most important aspects in the aggregate operating plan. It predicts anticipated profitability and affirms those products with the highest potential of return on the investment. It considers both the direct costs (labor, overhead, material) associated with the specific product production as well as the indirect support expenses (labor, supplies). Other costs such as general selling and administrative expenses, research and development, proposal and bidding, interest, and taxes are also considered in the assessment of total costs in relation to the selling price in order to determine the anticipated profitability status. Profit goals must be conservatively set and the necessary controls established to ensure profit requirements, which is a necessity if progress and survival is to be achieved. Knowledge of cost-volume-profit relationships by specific products is of inestimable value if an organization is to control effectively and intelligently its flow of resources. Because of the importance of this subject, a chapter has been included in this book to discuss profitability in depth.

ORGANIZATIONAL PARTICIPATION

Financial plan development is all encompassing since it embodies the combined thinking and participation of all functions and responsibilities of an organization's operations. It starts with predicting a customer's product requirements and/or developing and marketing a new product. Engineers' efforts are involved in new innovations, designs, and pilot production. Production manpower and facilities are utilized in manufacturing various products in specified quantities to meet scheduled delivery dates. The Quality Assurance Group is responsible for the inspection of the products produced and determining if they will meet the required specifications. Industrial Relations becomes involved in the selection, training, and manning of the necessary skills categories. Accounting provides historical records and other data concerned with billing the customer and the receipt and disbursement of funds. Last, but not least, an efficient, multi-tiered management is necessary to provide the guidance and direction of the organization's operations through their varied decision-making processes.

The business entity and its planning, therefore, includes all organizations and entails the five basics of an organization's operations—management, manpower, money, machinery, and materials, but not necessarily in that order.

Delegation of Control Responsibility

To achieve the most effective control for operational plan success, task responsibilities must be delegated to the lowest supervisory levels of the functional organizations. This delegation requirement is obvious because it is at this level (leadman, supervisor, chief, manager) that supervision is directly involved in the detailed operation efficiency and output as well as the effective utilization of the resources being committed. Higher echelon management cannot be reasonably expected to become involved in great detail at the expense of the myriad of other major decisions that must be made to run the organization at the composite levels of operation.

Successful experience has demonstrated that control can be most effectively achieved through the employment of two diametric forces working and driving toward the same objectives—top management *down* involvement and lower hierarchy management *up* participation and responsibility. Eventual goals must be thoroughly understood and compatible. Both approaches should complement each other to achieve the objectives. As an example in the production area, machine hours are projected at the lowest level relative to the type of operator required and his cost, the kind of operation to be performed, the number of hours of machine utilization, and the operator's effectiveness. This data is further associated to specific cost centers and summarized to department and division totals. Planning data and performance evaluation should always pyramid through successive levels of management hierarchy in order that all concerned have the opportunity to participate in the development of a successful operating plan.

Plan Coordination Control

The coordinating aspect of long-range financial planning should be assigned to a centralized planning group whose major tasks would include the coordination and assembly of the plan segments into a cohesive total plan. They must report to the top executive in order that they can be constantly aware of any changes in management's outlook into the future that govern new judgments they must reflect in plan submissions. This group's responsibility must include the authority to seek and obtain the necessary capabilities and resources required to initiate and implement the planning and operating requirements. Their tasks would be vastly improved in accuracy and timeliness, with minimum clerical effort, through the employment of computerized techniques discussed throughout this book.

FINANCIAL PLAN REQUIREMENTS

Planning of any type or of any time duration involves a number of basic criteria that are definitive in establishing certain goals and objectives and a projected means of achieving them. In a business enterprise, the objectives for business operations must be specifically defined. The future business environment and associated circumstantial relationships must be established. Management must define the appropriate policies and guidelines to provide initiative and direction in meeting the future projected plans. Management's literal plans, determinations, and judgments must be translated into quantified or monetary probabilistic expressions that can be readily and effectively communicated and interpreted to provide the basic requirements for performance measurement. Time schedules for accomplishing the tasks must be established in order to achieve an orderly flow of events on a timely basis. Responsibilities must be appropriately delegated. Each of these considerations and others are important in ultimate goal accomplishment.

FINANCIAL PLAN OVERVIEW

The data requirements for premised projection guidelines, as noted below, are inputted with other basic data into the computer. Through program specifications, the data is manipulated to produce segmented information (right side of Exhibit A) for use in various support and summary schedules. Exhibit A displays a detailed plan overview of the type of inputs and outputs that are involved in the development of the annual operating plan.

As noted on Exhibit A, the following components of the operating plan are highlighted:

- Status of contracts or commitments (firm/potential)
- Type of contractual/sales order coverage (fixed price, cost plus)
- Projected percentages to calculate gross margin, funding, liquidation

FINANCIAL PLAN OVERVIEW

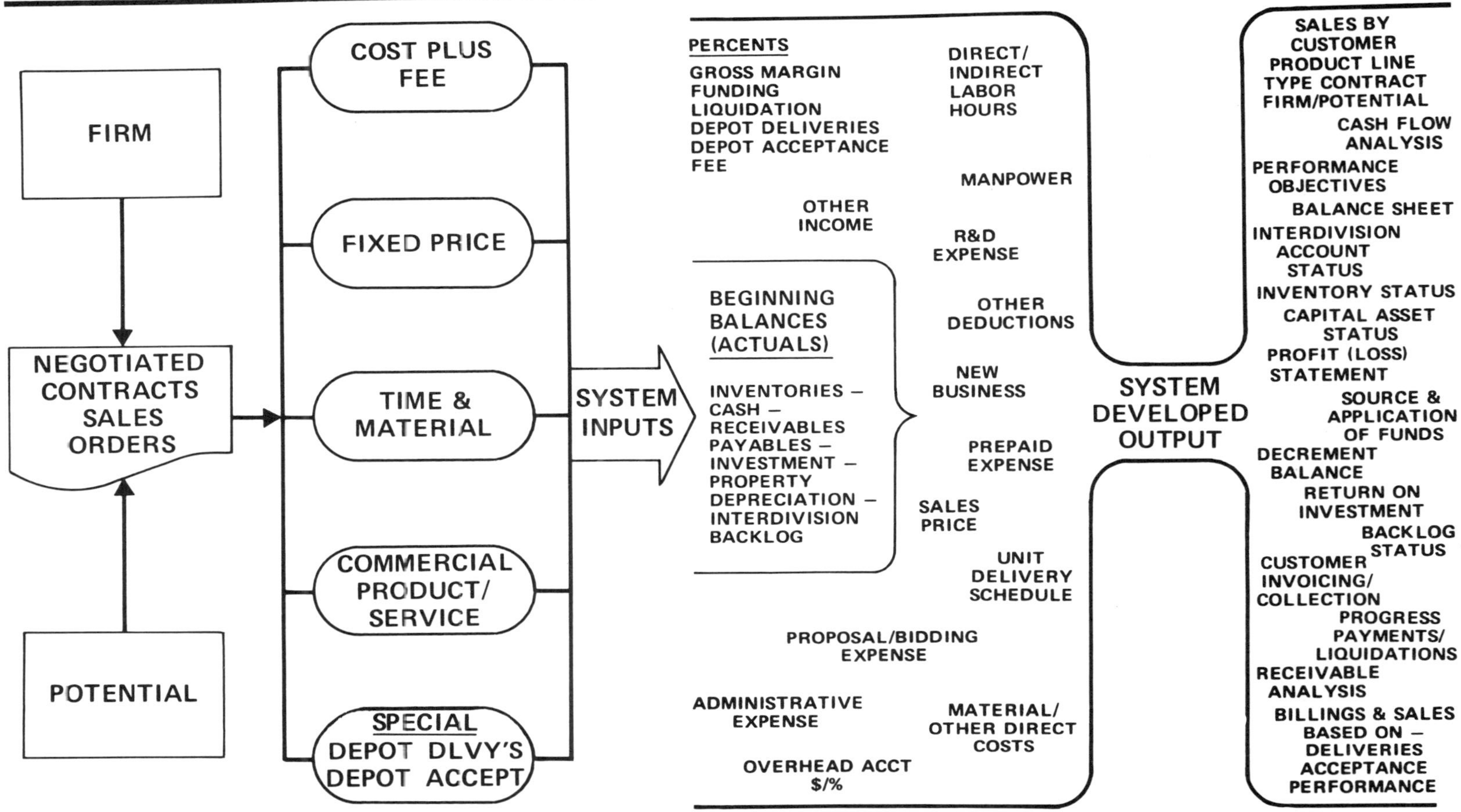

EXHIBIT A

- Actual beginning balances derived from the accounting records
- Various other inputs as shown on the exhibit that are developed in satellite subsystems, which are management edicted or part of contractual agreement
- The output is extensive and varied as shown to the right in the exhibit

On-Line Processing

When the basic input data such as sales or costs by contract, profit rates, and other required information has been resolved, it is entered via an on-line terminal device into the system. For approximately fifty contracts in one organization, it took about fifteen hours of terminal time to enter the detailed data. Summaries of this information are available in a matter of minutes and changes can be effected immediately before the decision is made to produce the top financial schedules. The contract detailed schedules and certain summaries, because of the volume involved, are batch processed and available in about six hours. In the former manual environment, the above process required five weeks of four person's full time.

Disk Storage

The contract detail is maintained on disk storage until all facets of the plan have been resolved and approved. This permits last-minute changes based on top schedule results and permits concerned management to review the data and make final decisions on new business developments—delay or acceleration of product deliveries, changes in product price, or profit manipulation.

DECISION AND CONTROL CYCLE

Financial planning as well as decision-making can be basically classified into three major categories or levels of activity—operational, tactical, and strategic.

The operational category is characterized as representing the real world such as that concerned with engineering and production. It involves labor activity and schedule performance, cost accumulation, product pricing, payroll, general ledger transactions, and so on. Decisions are concerned with the physical business operations. Planning is on a relatively short-term basis.

In the tactical area, the concern is with the utilization of resources and the results as reflected on the summary financial statements. The management level is control oriented and actual performance is measured against the budget plan. Variances are analyzed and corrective action initiated. Middle management has the major involvement in this category.

Strategic planning and decision-making involves top management whose major concern is the future in terms of business growth and expansion, profits, financing, project selections, solvency, economic outlook, and long-term investments. Each level of activity has its responsibilities, authority, and participation in the development of a comprehensive and realistic operating plan. Exhibit B displays the cycle of events that must occur to develop and finalize an operating plan. As shown on the exhibit, the premises are predicated on basic forecasts such as future business outlook, organizational growth, and capital expenditures.

COMPUTERIZED FINANCIAL PLANNING
DECISION AND CONTROL CYCLE

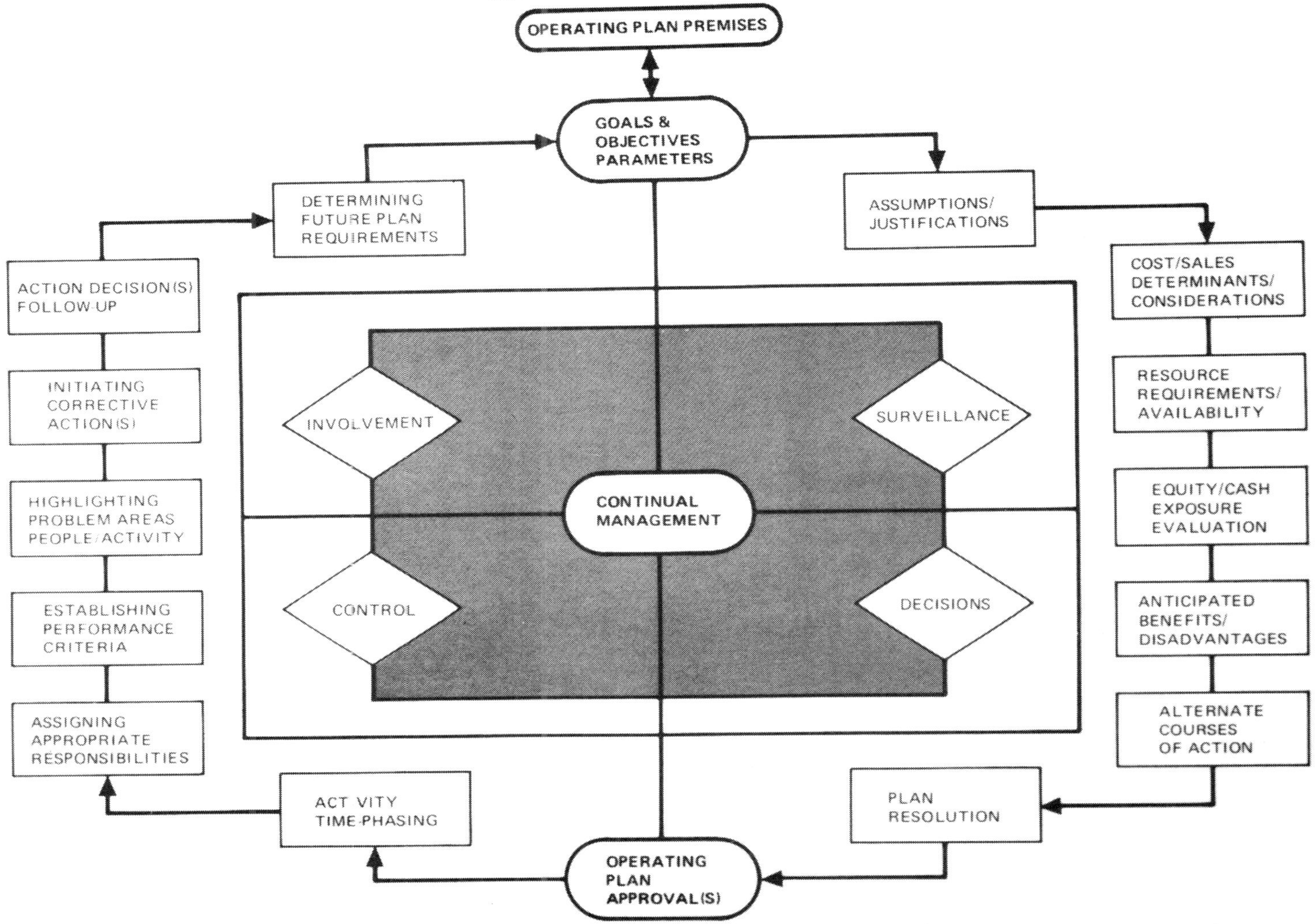

EXHIBIT B

Top management is involved at this level and the goals and objectives permeate from the top down.

Assumptions and justifications are translated into cost and sales, resource requirements, cash exposure, and so on, as shown on the right-hand side of the exhibit. Alternate courses of action are tested and the proposed plan resolved for management approval. Throughout this process there is continual management involvement, where appropriate, and decisions made to make changes or proceed in the direction of the initial objectives.

Post-Plan Approval

After the plan has the necessary approval, the activities (engineering tasks, production) are time-phased into scheduled events of proposed accomplishment. Responsibilities are delegated to various management levels for implementation and surveillance of the progress of the activities. Actual performance is measured against the planned operations as shown on the left side of the exhibit. Variances are identified as to being people- or activity-caused. Corrective action is initiated and a follow-up is maintained to ensure compliance with the decisions made to alleviate the adverse situations creating the problem. Based on the results of the operating plan and performance, this criteria is utilized as basic input, with changes as required, in the development of the next operating plan objectives. A successful execution of the plan must involve all levels of management to achieve the necessary controls and provide guidance and decisions along the path and time of the plan's existence.

DECISIONS INVOLVED IN PLAN DEVELOPMENT

The annual budget plan represents a short-span management tool over a defined period of time which encompasses the details of an operational/functional/financial plan. Its objective is to propose attainable goals and the means to accomplish them in the near future—generally, a year. The planning objectives are translated into financial data so that a common communication link is established among the various concerned organizations for the purposes of interpreting the intent and understanding of the overall projections. Its development must conform to the essentials in the accounting system from which data will be used to measure actual performance against the plan.

Prior to initiating plan development, specific criteria are outlined by management to serve as the basic philosophies and directions to be taken by the personnel who will be directly involved in planning the details. These management premises are predicated on the longer range operational goal and objective planning results. The specific guidelines included in the premises, but not necessarily restricted thereto, are described below.

Manpower Level

Direct and indirect headcount is initially projected by the various organizations based on their requirements to achieve their specific objectives. The headcount is identified to functional organizations, contracts, products, special projects, as appropriate. The composition and extent of the manpower level is reviewed by varying management tiers and must be approved by management before utilization in the plan development.

Level of Effort

The extent of this activity is based mainly on research, engineering, and production requirements and also includes the indirect support needs. Manpower is translated into hours of activity and is priced according to employee classification and wage rates.

Sales Goals

There are various considerations involved in projecting sales. It begins with the marketing forecasts which include the current backlog of unfinished business, pending results of contract/sales order negotiations, new product and customer anticipations, related industry projections, and historical sales trends. Sales volume is segregated into firm and potential, and is classified as to product, contract, project, sales order, and customer.

Research and Development

No organization can progress or long survive if it does not plan and expend funds to improve their products to meet competition. It must invest in new developments to supplement or even replace certain of its current products due to the inroads of possible obsolescence and/or diminishing customer demands. This is the price an organization must pay to stay in business, progress, and increase profitability.

The marketing (sales) organization is the most logical source of this information based on customer contact and demands and, further, knowing their competitors' products' sales potential and/or plans. Research engineers are another likely source for possibilities that lend themselves to product enhancements or new exploitations. Management, however, has the final decision to make relative to the direction and extent of this effort since market demand, source of funds, and profitability prospects are the prime considerations in their decision-making process of planning resource expenditures.

Capital Expenditures

Capital expenditure asset plans are derived from the long-range plan, taking into consideration company objectives relative to growth and expansion, new developments requiring different machinery and equipment, rearrangements, facility relocation, and so on. This derived budget is detailed to specific items or tasks by organization. Detailed justification is a necessity. A composite listing is made of all the requests requiring capital expenditures. After a thorough review and verification of the justifications, the projects are given priority by time period for fund expenditure. Depreciation factors are provided to determine the period expense write-offs after acquisition.

Operating Cash Levels

Based on historical experience, the organization designates the amount of cash required to operate its business. This amount is kept to a minimum so that the excess can be more profitably employed in other types of investments. Whenever a short cash position occurs, short-term financing is effected by prearranged float fund availability from the bank. The projected cash balance is derived by adding the beginning cash balance to the anticipated receipts and deducting the anticipated cash disbursements. Generally, the cash balance is equivalent to the total of one week's payroll and accounts payable commitments.

Property Leasing

Leasing is contingent on long-range objectives. Before this decision is made, studies are conducted to determine the relative advantages of lease versus buy considerations. This is an important management decision since it can involve borrowing and financing criteria, adverse cash flow, or poor utilization of personnel and facilities if it were determined that the make decision was the most judicious action to take.

Unallowable or Disallowance Costs

Primarily, defense contractors are involved in this type of contingency. Based on historical experience and previous negotiation results with the customer, it can be determined that certain expenses or portions thereof will be disallowed, thereby influencing profits. The projected amount is generally computed as a percentage of total overhead and distributed to contract/sales orders based on their expected utilization of direct labor hours. Typical examples of this type of costs are excess amortization, interest expense, portions of research (irrelevant to the contract), management incentive plan, and nonpertinent travel and entertainment. Disallowances apply only to cost-type contracts.

Fee Rates/Profit Margin

On government contracts, fees are negotiated on cost-type contracts and applied to costs as a percentage to obtain sales (fees plus costs). This type of contract is based on the performance of certain tasks such as project research. On fixed-price contracts, a total price for the task or product is negotiated and the projected fees are included in that price. This type of contract has a profitability risk; if the estimated costs are exceeded, the projected profits are reduced accordingly. On fixed-price incentive contracts, profitability can be increased if work performance, delivery schedules, and so on, on the contract exceed the negotiated goals.

On commercial products/services, management establishes the profit margin that is required to conduct their operations profitably. The price margin included in the sales price is based on return on investment requirements, past experience, competition, and what the customer or market would be willing to pay for the product or services.

Projecting Lag Intervals

A lag period represents a time interval between the occurrence of certain events and is particularly important in the cash flow process. Based primarily on historical experience, a time projection determination is made between the accrual of costs and cash disbursement outflow and the time interval between customer invoicing and cash receipts from the customer. In other words, as you perform effort on a product, task, or service, you accrue costs for labor, material, and other expenses. After the cost accrual, there is a time interval between recording your liability and paying the employee or vendor. In the case of labor, generally one to two weeks pass before a cash disbursement is made. In the case of the vendor, the disbursement period is variable, but four to six weeks is generally representative.

Cash receipts can also be quite variable. On government fixed-price contracts, a progress payment is made, which is based on the percentage of work performed, deliveries, and funding availability. This is a complicated procedure that will be specifically addressed in a subsequent chapter.

On cost contracts, you invoice the customer as soon as you perform the work and pay the employee and vendor. Cash receipt could be approximately two to three weeks after the invoice submittal. On a commercial account, cash receipt is generally thirty days after invoicing. A shorter time span could be encouraged with a discount incentive or a longer period arranged upon agreement with the customer. The value of a computerized system here is that you can change or experiment with time intervals and obtain rapid results as to what happens to cash flow when payments or collection cycles are delayed or accelerated.

ANALYSIS TECHNIQUES FOR DECISION PLANNING

There are various decision-planning techniques that are adaptable to computerization in assisting operating and executive management in their projection activities. Some of the more universally employed methods for planning and decision-making include simulations, correlations, mathematical models, risk analyses, and scenarios. Depending upon an organization's objectives and requirements, these techniques provide a means of reducing the burden of developing detailed and summary planning data and further provide the capability for incorporating scientific procedures in their projection processes. Following is a short discussion of the individual merits of the computer techniques mentioned above and how they can be most effectively employed.

Simulation

A simulation model represents a gaming technique of substituting alternate values in the operating plan to determine what happens as a result of these action decisions. The planners (more likely management) experiment with testing alternate courses of action in order to resolve the most suitable future plan of operation.

The data experimentation can be in the form of fees or profit margin percentage revisions and/or increasing/decreasing sales, research, elements of cost, or overhead. This is accomplished through inputs into a mechanical simulation model which recomputes the originally developed data and provides the results of the data manipulation. The simulation model must be interfaced with the basic mechanical operating plan model so that any change that is made will be reflected throughout the forecast plan.

This technique provides a responsive capability for experimenting with the initial and subsequent business operation assumptions. It does not provide all of the possible infallible results, but rather simulates the results of the change actions taken.

SIMULATION MODEL
Income Statement Manipulation

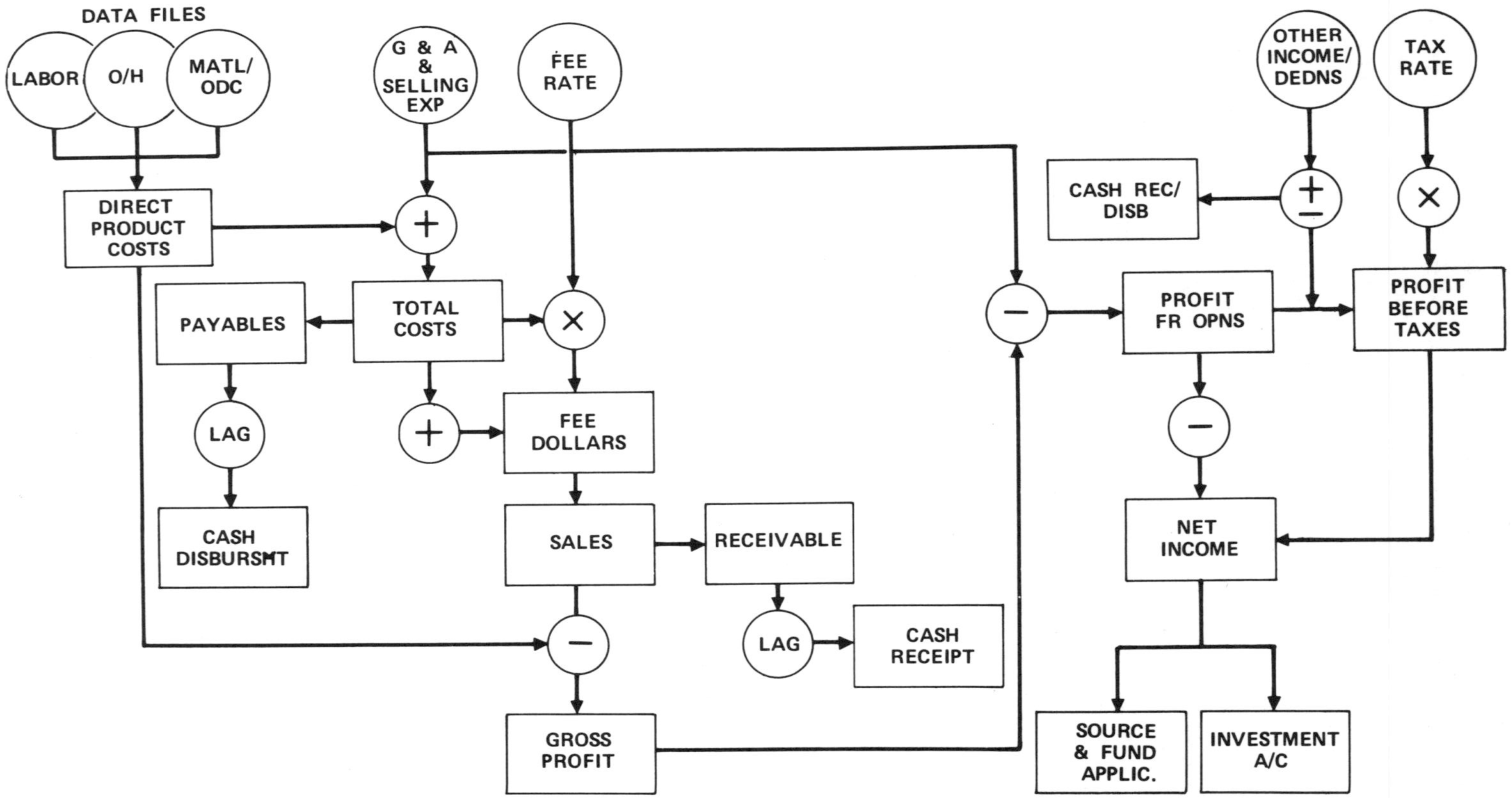

EXHIBIT C

Exhibit C displays a typical income statement model in which changes in the basic data result in changes to sales and receivables, profits and investment, costs and payables, cash receipts and disbursements, and the fund statement. Having reviewed the effect of their proposed revisions, management is now more able to make an informed decision as to whether their alternate decision is acceptable or further changes are in order. Simulation is a very effective tool for finalizing the most realistic plan for future operations and it saves time and costly labor to provide manually the answers required.

Correlation

This technique is used to establish the relationship between two variables. Fluctuation of one variable generally implies the movement of the other. Some notable examples would be sales versus costs, costs and payables, sales and receivables. The objective of this technique is to provide reliable factor correlations, based on historical association, so that through the projection of one set of data, the other set can be readily predictable.

It should be recognized that extenuating circumstances in the future such as delayed receipts or payments, escalating costs, or margin markdown could affect the validity of future expectations. Exhibit D illustrates the relationship of sales, costs, and collections on cost-type contracts over twenty-seven periods of time. Suffice it to say that in this case the relationships are significantly close to effect planning predictability through factor application. A month-to-month visibility, however, would reveal wider variations for analysis which would highlight seasonal fluctuations and other unusual circumstances that caused the values to deviate from the norm.

Mathematical Model

This planning technique offers unlimited capability, particularly when the data volume is large and its manipulation excessive to derive a relationship between two sets of data. This process provides a rapid means of calculating the missing data requirement based on a historically recognized relationship as shown on Exhibit E. This display is based on the regression analysis of sales to costs correlation. A mathematical formula is developed by which sales times a developed factor, less a fixed value generates the cost data. From the plotted points and the line of intercept through the points, this display indicates the close relationship between these two data elements. The correlation coefficient of 1.00 indicates a perfect relationship of the data.

Risk Analysis

This is another invaluable tool that is often used to determine the risk exposure involved in profitability and/or stockholders' investment status if certain decisions are made relative to probabilities and consequences involved in make-or-buy decisions, changes in operating plans, long-term debt commitments, capital acquisitions/expansion, product mix redeterminations, magnitude of research and development activities, or customer requirements. In the computerized process, the decisions can be readily tested using various alternatives and the anticipated risk exposure rapidly ascertained.

CUMULATIVE SALES, COSTS, COLLECTIONS
COST TYPE CONTRACTS

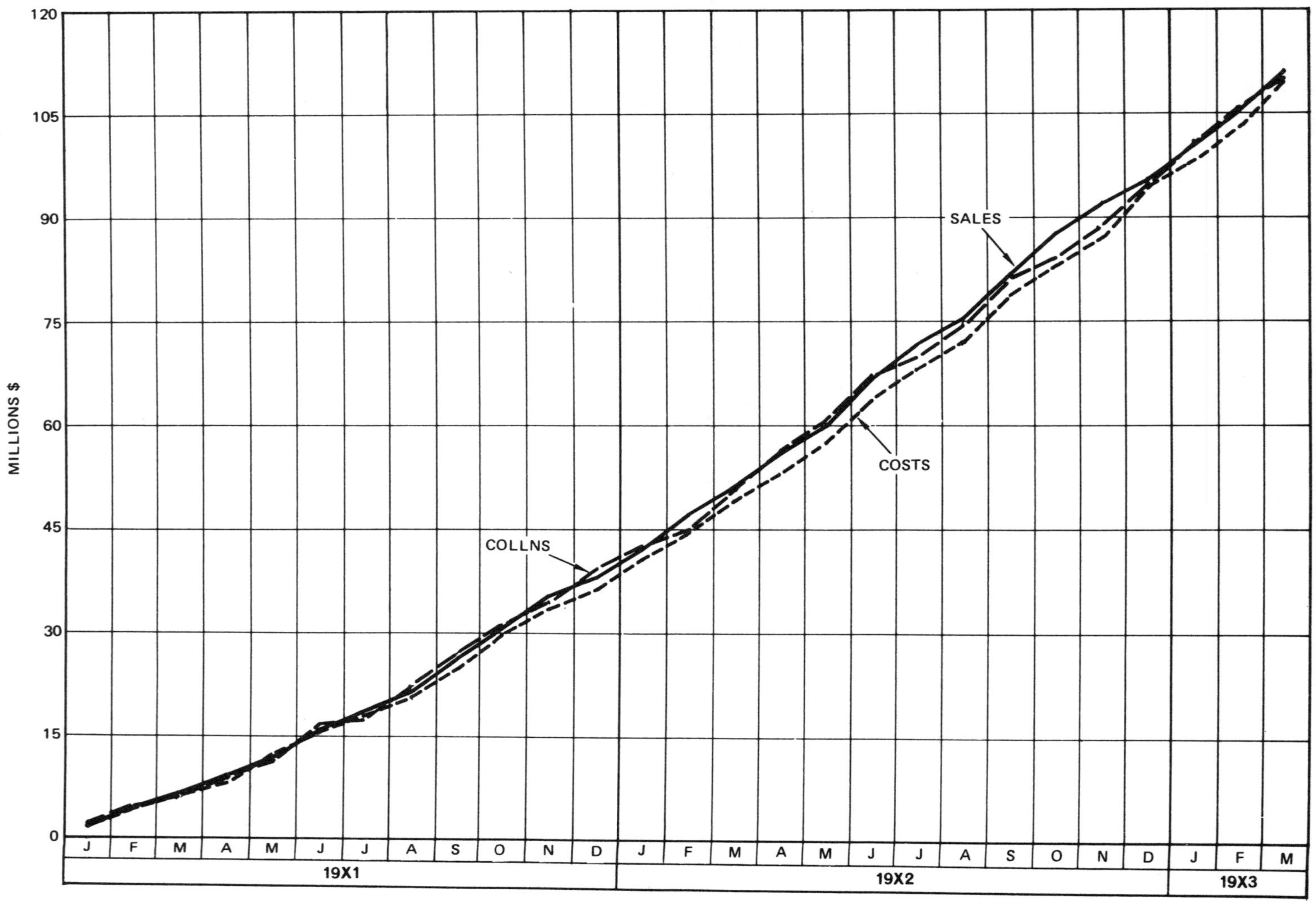

EXHIBIT D

TOTAL SALES TO COSTS CORRELATION
FIXED PRICE CONTRACTS

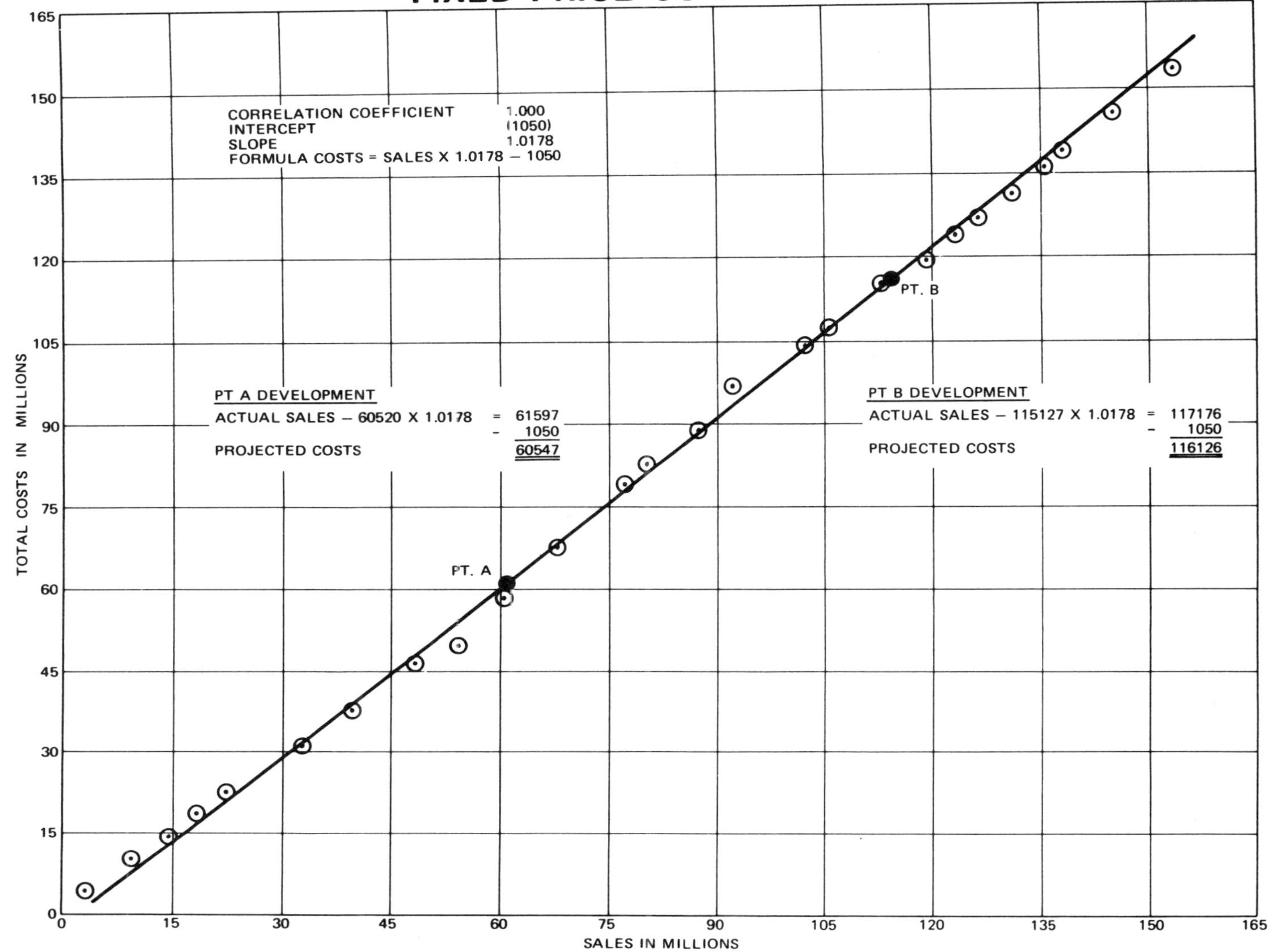

EXHIBIT E

It is noted that this process involves the establishment of the probability values for event occurrence and distribution of input variables. It considers certain uncertainties associated with the inputs. Rates of return are determined for each data set. Levels of approximate risk are established based on historical experience and analysis. This planning technique permits greater visibility of anticipated and pending future risks and represents a rational approach to decision-making. A further discussion of this subject is included in chapter 14.

Scenario

As the name implies, this is another procedure employed for developing probable future results based on a predicated sequence of events. It represents hypothetical patterns of thinking as would be reflected in theatrical plays and enables an organization to establish, simulate, and test alternative courses of action in a quantitative model. Scenarios provide management with an analytical approach to planning that supports, affirmatively or negatively, the results of current decisions that will affect future operations.

For example, if the sales projections were changed, you would have to reflect the effect in costs, profits, or both. Revising the sales picture also influences the inventory and receivables balances. Cost changes affect the payables balance and cash disbursements. Profit changes influence return on investment and sales. The whole chain reaction of events through a change in any data set can be viewed through the use of the scenario technique, which is quite similar to the simulation method. It represents a demonstrable means of verifying the preliminary decision approach.

Organizations should explore the various aspects of the above techniques for possible utilization and computerization to determine which could be of most benefit to their planning requirements. Each has a particular purpose to serve, and the potential to aid realistic planning is immeasurable to an organization's progress. It should be emphasized, however, that models do not make decisions but are used to provide the necessary data that serve as a basis for realistic decision-making since their output reduces the risk of poor or incomplete data.

CONSIDERATIONS IN PLANNING DECISIONS

The criteria involved in effective decision-making is based primarily on the evaluation of various probabilities that may occur in the future relative to the planned goals and objectives. As can be readily understood, there is no sure way to achieve exactness or assurance that the decisions made will materialize as planned because of business complexity and the uncertainties of the future.

Utilization of the various planning models discussed above provides a means for testing alternative actions and does give a measure of decision security due to the more scientific approaches to planning. The use of models lessens the risk of poor decisions since they temper projections with past realities. Models also provide data results on the relativity of probability occurrences, particularly when they employ the optimistic, pessimistic, and median approaches to forecasting the future.

Requisites of a Successful Model

The success or failure of decision-planning models depends on the adherence to certain basic principles that are requisites to a model's utilization. The primary considerations are noted below.

- Models should be constructed to reflect the actual business environment in terms of cause and effect of events.
- Models must be appropriately tested in the real environment in order to validate their usefulness in producing effective data results.
- Models should be developed by competent and knowledgeable personnel who understand management philosophy, problems, and objectives in using a model for planning purposes.
- Management and the users must know basics and principles upon which the model has been or will be built and its utilization in the planning-decision process.
- Top management must have confidence in the chosen model's capabilities to provide the kind of assistance required for their decision-making.
- There must be assurance that the historical input data used in the model development and testing was valid, representative, and reliable.
- There must be concurrence and understanding that the model provides data for planning and decision-making and that it was not intended to force judgment and decisions.

Affirmative verification of the above criteria for the development and use of models will provide the answer to their usefulness and effectiveness as an aid to planning decisions.

In summary, planning and decision-making must be synonymous with objectivity. There must be unanimity in understanding what and how data is to be manipulated, as well as what is expected in the end results. Success in predicting future eventualities requires a knowledge of the various advanced planning techniques and then selection of the appropriate ones most compatible with a particular organization's needs in the business environment. Decision planning is one of the most important aspects of establishing a successful plan for future operations.

4

Slashing Costs and Tightening Control Through the Use of a Computerized Financial Planning and Control Model

A successful and effective computerized planning and control system must have, as one of its major requisites, data integrity; otherwise, confidence by management and the user will be lost relative to its processing and reporting capabilities. Further, it could lead to the abandonment of this valuable mechanical tool and the return to archaic manual activities.

SYSTEM PLANNING CONSIDERATIONS

The objectives of a planning and control model are to ensure that data input validity is constantly maintained and that the procedures employed in data-processing manipulation will yield the expected results according to the development plan with minimal clerical effort. There are a number of basic considerations involved in establishing the appropriate planning controls which are noted as follows.

- Determination of the type, source, sequence, and collection of raw data for input.
- Establishment of appropriate input formats and procedures for data entry.
- Development of processing logic and testing to assure that the output results will reflect the planned reporting requirements.
- Establishment of standard procedures outlining tasks and responsibilities in system operation.
- Construction of the system in modular form so that it can be easily and rapidly changed to

reflect new requirements. System modularization also provides the capability of running a portion of the system for selective data rather than processing the complete cycle, which is costly.

- Use of sequential processing logic so that data from one program can automatically be used in a subsequent module without interruption.
- Inclusion of appropriate sorting capabilities so that various reporting outputs can be achieved.
- Establishment of adequate checkpoints in the system to verify that the input has been correctly entered in the required sequence/format.
- Establishment of adequate audit trails to effectively trace the flow of data from the initial input, through its manipulation, to its ultimate use in reporting.
- Use of capable personnel to operate the system. They must be knowledgeable of detailed system operation, instinctively know when something is wrong during the data-processing operation, and have the expertise to remedy the situation rapidly.

THE OVERVIEW APPROACH

In developing a financial planning system and establishing the necessary controls, the initial approach should be to flowchart the broad requirements in the aggregate so that the direction and objectives of the system effort is understood and approved by the concerned management relative to fulfilling their requirements. Detailed system segmentation often does not provide the proper perspective on which to base go-ahead decisions. Development of the detail falls in the realm of trained data-processing technicians in conjunction with the prime users responsible for the detailed data development who are aware of the specific management requirements.

Exhibit A displays one type of system overview that has proven to be effective in system approval and implementation.

Selective Inputs

As shown on the exhibit, there are certain unique major schedule input requirements that cannot or are impractical to be developed in a computerized system and therefore must be direct inputs. Some notable examples are depreciation factors, interest expense, long-term debt, backlog, and beginning balances. Certain selective input results from management decisions, such as research and development projected expenditures and other types of input, is contained in the accounting records relative to beginning account balances for the balance sheet. Selective actuals are merged into the forecast system via magnetic tape file input that is developed in the accounting mechanical system. This file is also used on a monthly basis to compare actuals to plan, and to derive the variance report to ascertain performance status.

DESIGNING THE SYSTEM

In order to design an effective projection model, there are certain preliminary basic requirements that should be given due consideration before the development effort is under-

SYSTEM OVERVIEW SUMMARY

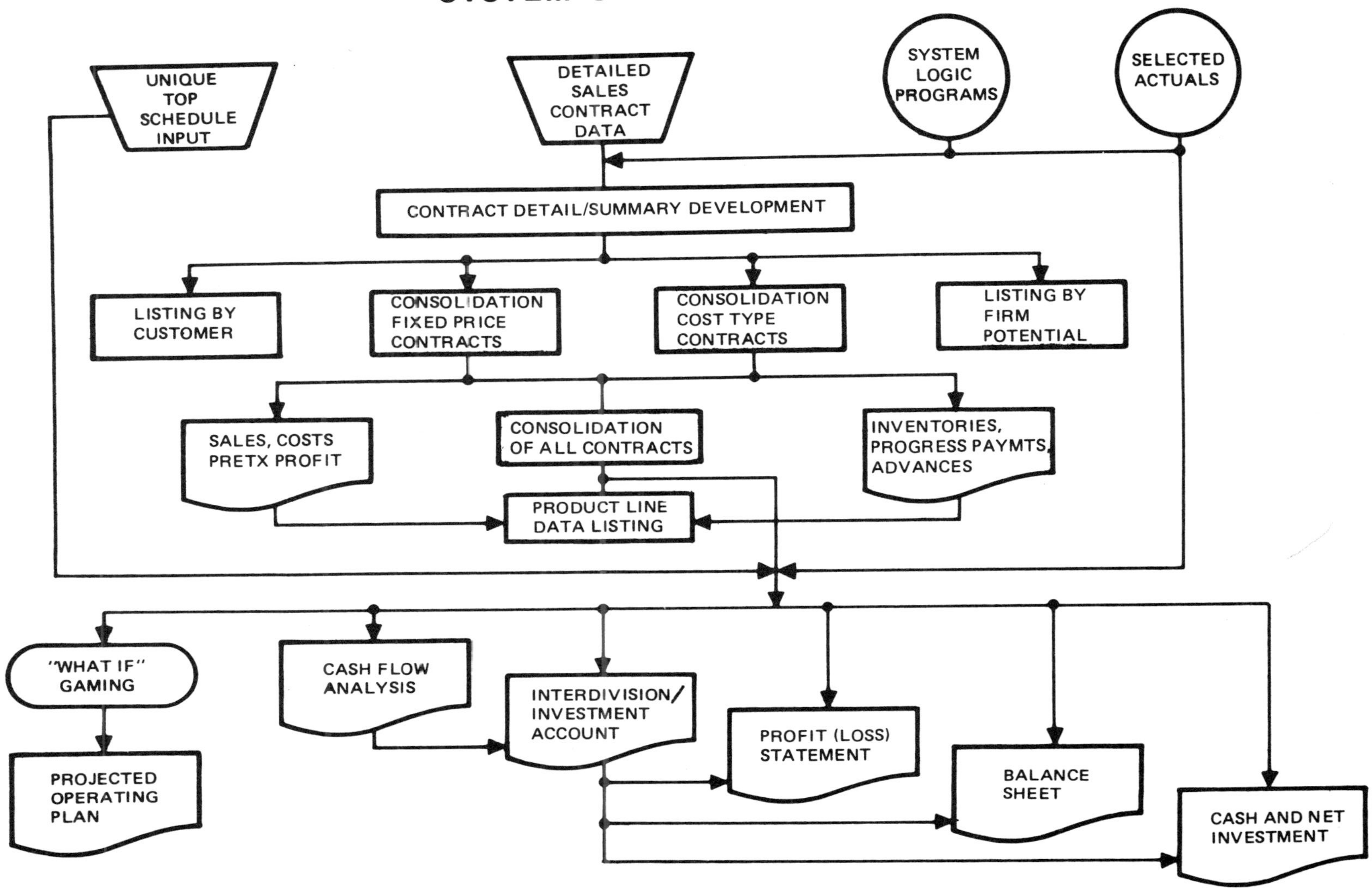

EXHIBIT A

taken. Developing a model could be a costly endeavor, particularly in complex structured organizations with their attendant information needs.

System Development Considerations

The following questions lead to the development of some major guidelines in making the decision to undertake system development:

- Is there a definite need that can be justifiably supported in terms of cost effectiveness and/or other measurable and tangible benefits?
- Do the necessary capabilities exist in terms of trained technicians to do the task and are there sufficient and effective computer power and facilities available?
- Has a study been made to decide whether the effort and information processing should be done in-house or through an outside service bureau—pros and cons?
- Does the concerned management understand the implications of the venture relative to its advantages and disadvantages?
- Is there any current capability that can, with few changes, be adapted to achieve the proposed computerization objectives?
- Have the various participating organizations and proposed users been contacted to determine their reactions?
- Has all of the risk exposure potential been explored to preclude surprises in the future—in other words, has the proper homework been done?

After a careful review of the above determinants and after obtaining management approval to proceed, the next course of action is to establish the criteria involved in designing the framework for the effort to be performed.

OPERATING PLAN REQUIREMENTS

In developing the financial planning model, a flowchart is prepared to show a composite of the operating plan needs. The flowchart is then "exploded" into detailed segments so that no required information has been overlooked before the programming effort is initiated.

An example of the type of flowchart required is displayed on Exhibit B, which shows the data elements involved in the organizational financial plan, briefly highlighted below.

- Sales and cost of sales (lower right of the exhibit) data flows to the income statement where the difference between the two data elements represents gross profit. Although period costs (R & D and G & A expenses) are not reflected on the exhibit, they are in the system and their reduction to cost of sales results in profits from operations as shown. Other income and deductions are netted against the operational profit to obtain pretax profit. Taxes are deducted from pretax profit to obtain net income.
- Direct and indirect manpower projections are translated into hours and, with a wage/salary rate application, labor dollars are computed. Direct labor dollars become a part of direct product costs and indirect labor dollars flow into the overhead expense group.
- The facility plan provides the anticipated property acquisitions which are combined with the gross property on the books. Depreciation factors are determined and applied to gross

ORGANIZATION FINANCIAL PLAN
Data Flow

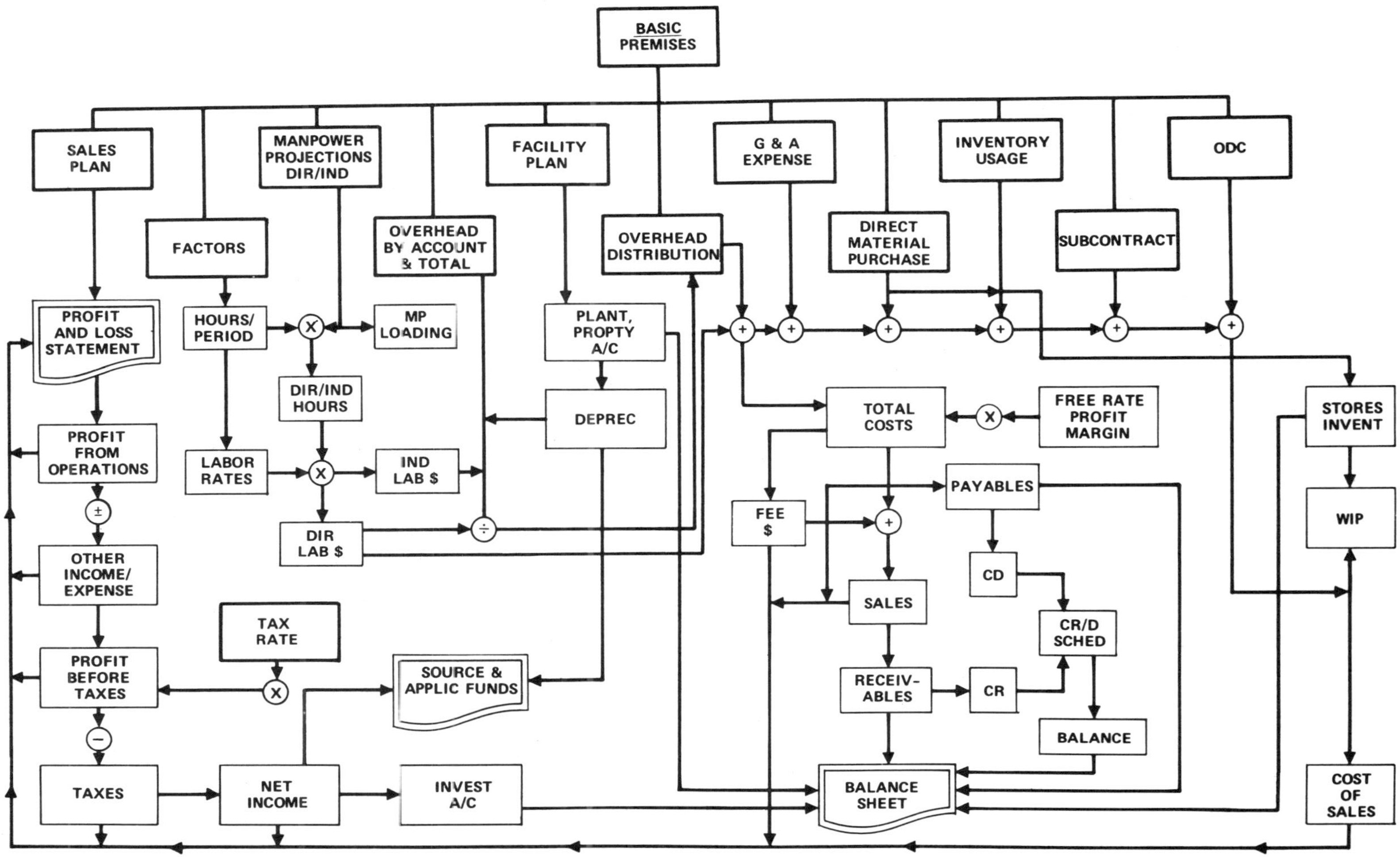

EXHIBIT B

capital asset categories (mobile equipment, furniture, fixtures) to obtain the depreciation expense which is reflected in both the overhead schedule and the fund statement. Depreciation expense is also added to the prior depreciation reserve balances and the sum total is reflected on the balance sheet as a reduction to gross property for deriving net property balances.

- Overhead is projected by account and organization and the total when divided by the direct labor hours or dollars results in an overhead rate. This rate is used to distribute overhead to contracts based on dollar/hour activity.
- General and administrative expenses are projected and translated into a rate, similar to overhead above, and applied to direct labor hours or dollars for distribution to the contracts.
- Projected direct material costs and inventory usage from the Material Planning Group are combined with forecasted subcontract activity and ODC (Other Direct Costs—travel, computer usage, outside production) and classified as Direct Material and ODC cost element in the cost of sales.
- As noted on the exhibit, sales can be provided by the sales plan or computer developed if total costs and profit margin percentage is known. On fixed-price contracts, the total sales price is utilized, whereas on cost contracts, the sales value is built from costs plus margin. Sales data flows to receivables and cash receipts.

The above discussion is an overall view of the projection model. Since other chapters contain more specific detail, no further elaboration is necessary at this point.

DATA SYSTEM INTERFACES

As indicated earlier, all of the current procedures and systems in the actual environment must be reviewed and the interfaces determined in order to ascertain what is available in the form of information that will provide the source of raw data for mechanical system input. A determination must be made as to how the data flows and is utilized. Further, it must be known what actual files will have to be tapped for actual data to compare with the projected information.

An insight to this type of review and the preparation of an appropriate flowchart is displayed on Exhibit C. There is a myriad of interfaces in the actual operational environment that include both financial and nonfinancial systems. Nonfinancial systems are represented by the shaded circles (representing files) and the clear circles represent the automated financial systems. It is noted and emphasized that in the projection world the interfaces are far less complicated because of the hierarchy of data elements involved. The concern in projections is with costs, sales, and inventories starting at the contract and organizational levels. Performance measurement is also based on that level of data summary. There is no involvement with journals, ledgers, or registers.

Actual Environment

For better comprehension of the data flow on Exhibit C, a description highlighting a few of the processes follows.

FINANCIAL SYSTEMS DATA LINKAGE

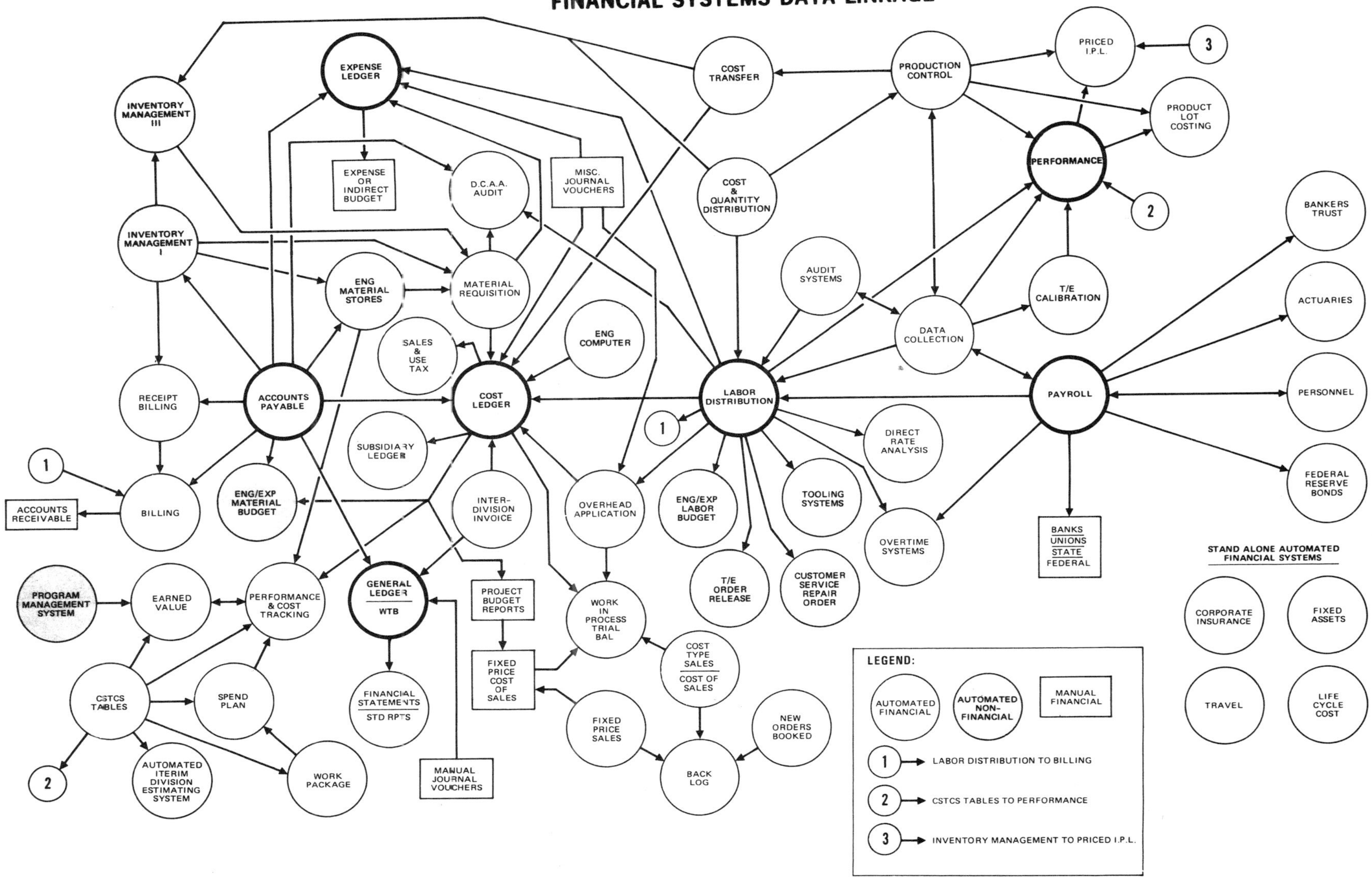

EXHIBIT C

- The expense ledger, for example, has input from accounts payable, labor distribution, material requisition, and miscellaneous journal vouchers (adjustments and other special entries). Its output is the basis for performance measurement and development of an expense budget.
- The cost ledger receives input from overhead application file, computer usage, material requisition, accounts payable, interdivision activity, cost transfers, miscellaneous journals with output flowing to sales and use tax, detailed subsidiary ledger, project budget reports, performance and cost tracking system, and work-in-process trial balance.
- The payroll system derives data from the personnel file (classification, wage rates, organization) and the labor data collection system. Its output goes to labor distribution, bankers trust (stock plan), actuaries, personnel, bond issues, overtime system, and governmental agencies.
- The labor distribution system obtains data from the mechanical data collection file, payroll, and labor audit system. Data is outputted to various other systems and files of which billings and overhead application are the primary ones.
- The general ledger/working trial balance system which is used to produce the top financial schedules (income statement, balance sheet) derives its data from accounts payable, cash flow, receivables ledger, manual and mechanical journal vouchers, and interdivision invoices.

This exhibit indicates the intricacies of the accounting, performance, and other reporting systems. Each file, represented by a system, has its role in the integration environment. The main purpose of this exhibit is to demonstrate a step in the financial planning process that must not be overlooked if one is to understand the flow of planning data, its interfaces, and the requirements for computerization. The planning process must interface with the actual environment systems in order to merge with certain data that will be required for performance measurements such as labor, overhead, and material.

DATA BASE CONCEPT

A data base, often referred to as a data bank, is characterized by file record locations that serve as depositories for various types of information that can be rapidly accessed, changed, updated, and retrieved. Controls are established to safeguard data integrity and preclude its availability to anyone who does not have a need to know. Input changes and updating can *only* be made by those designated individuals who have that responsibility. This control is established by assigning code entry identifiers to the personnel who operate the system. Individual terminal station codes are changed periodically to preclude information compromise. Key executives usually have privileged access to all data.

Data Bank Organization

Data banks can be organized for various (individual and/or collective) levels of data such as contract, organization, manpower, hours, wage rates, labor dollars, accrued salaries/wages liability, and employee payments; or one data base which would include all of the labor related information, for example. Each item of data is assigned a unique field location.

A contract file would contain the following: its number identification and description; terms and conditions; monthly, yearly and cumulative-to-date sales; elements of cost; profit rates, and dollars—both actual and *planned*.

In the instances cited above, the developed information is sorted, summarized, and transferred to summary files that are used for producing top financial schedule output—income statement, balance sheet, and cash flow.

Data files must be organized in sequential modular form so that the data flow can be readily summarized to a hierarchy level of data needs without interrupting the processing cycle. Exhibit D provides an actual environment insight as to the data flow from the basic input through the computer-processing cycle to the type of reports being prepared. Each of the report files is considered an individual data bank so that selective data can be accessed or changed for simulation purposes, although direct linkage of these files permits the flow of data between them as appropriate or required. You will note on this exhibit that the computer processes are defined. Budget and plan data is an integral part of the system. Since the data files provide information for multi-reporting requirements as shown on the exhibit, it is necessary that they be organized and integrated in a manner conducive to varied reporting needs.

On-Line Data-Bank Processing

In order to take advantage of advanced computer techniques as well as to enhance the capabilities of a planning and control system, the on-line approach is very effective and rewarding in changing, updating, and retrieving information. The on-line terminal is a tool that is employed to accomplish this endeavor. It provides an instantaneous capability to input directly to the computer as well as retrieve selective data or summaries. Simulation of alternate planning decisions is readily achievable. Exhibit E illustrates how this is accomplished.

As shown on this exhibit, basic data is entered via the terminal by accounting/planning organizations. The computer's teleprocessing monitor manipulates and directs the data in accordance with the edit and audit requirements of the data-collection program. If the data is invalid due to nonexistent identifiers and codes or improper field formatting, it is rejected back to the monitor for transfer to the terminal location for analysis, correction, and reentry. Valid data, using the backlog planning system as an example, proceeds through the processing cycle to update the master file records. This information resides in its data bank and the appropriate summary data required is transferred to the integrated data base. The data is now available for retrieval through on-line inquiries by the terminal stations. Audited information input is transmitted back to the remote stations in the form of tabulated listings on the terminal for visual audit confirmation and reference purposes. The process is the same for all types of data involved in planning requirements and the day-to-day actual environment.

FINANCIAL INFORMATION INTEGRATION

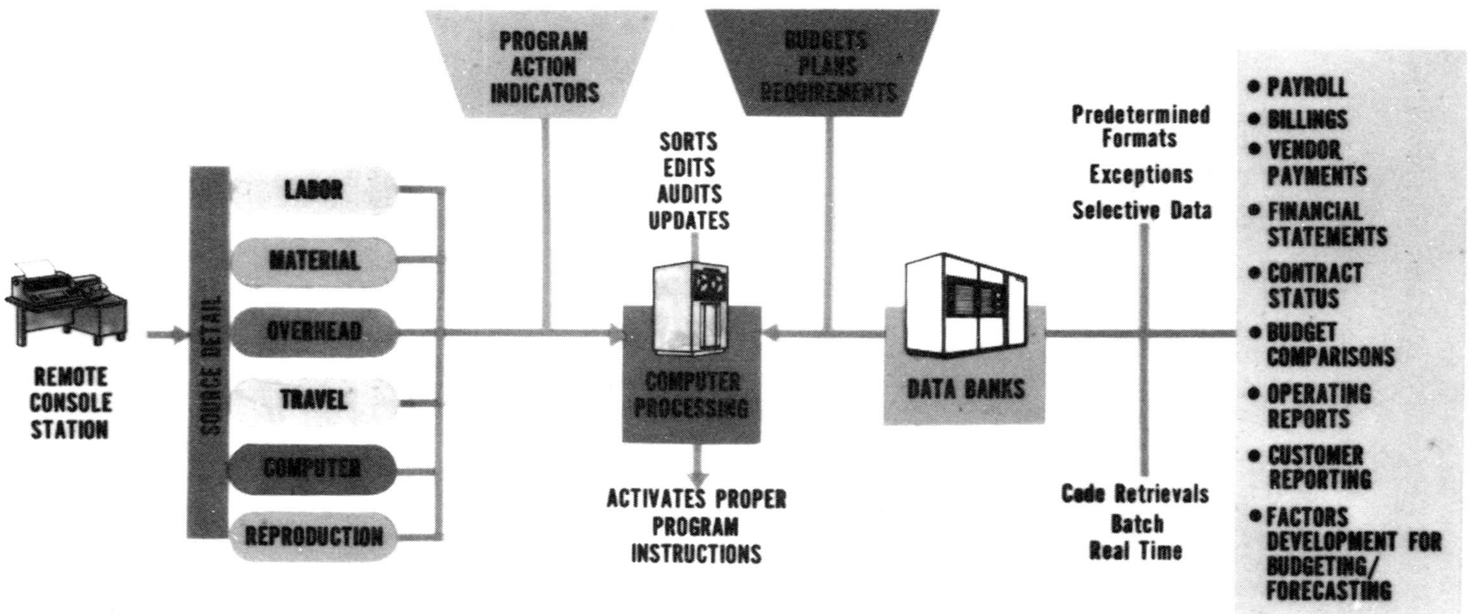

EXHIBIT D

BACKLOG DATA PROCESSING & COMMUNICATION ONLINE APPLICATION

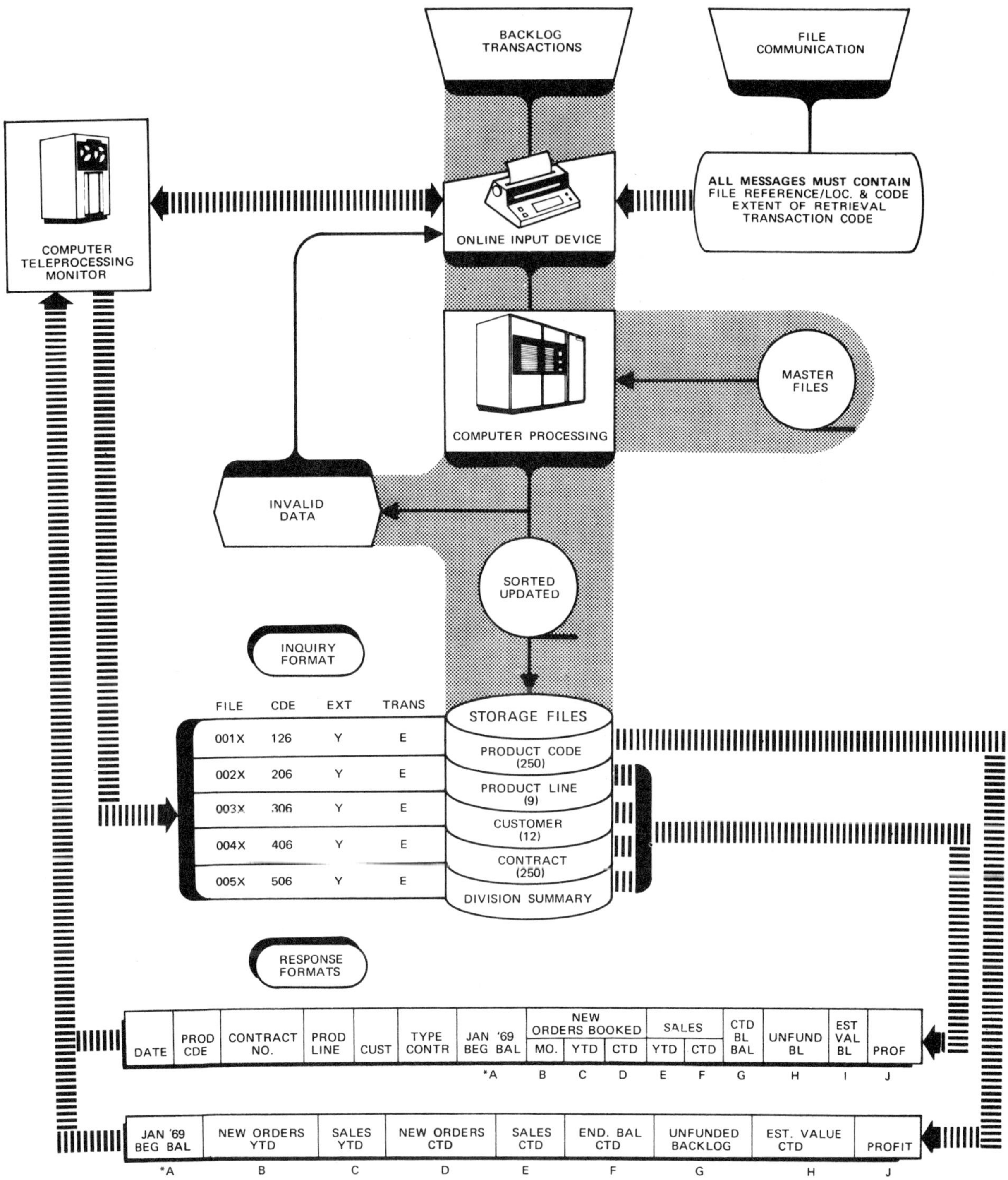

*REFERENCE SUB;DESIGNATION REFERENCE FOR SPECIFIC ITEM RETRIEVAL, CHANGE, ETC.

EXHIBIT E

EXHIBIT F

Demonstration of an On-Line Operation

Exhibit F depicts a demonstration of the on-line operation by the author (right of picture) to the Controller of General Dynamics, Pomona Division, J. D. Eiland (center of picture) and the Assistant Controller, Jim Comyns. The operator is Peggy Gibbs, a secretary, who learned to operate this system effectively in a very short period of time, thus demonstrating that trained specialists are not necessarily required.

In the above operation, a 1040 terminal device was used for inputting and retrieving information. There is a telephone linkage to the computer which is located fifty miles from the terminal. After contact is made with the computer by dialing its number, a high-pitched sound is heard, which means communication has been established. Then the telephone receiver is placed in a coupler to maintain computer linkage.

This was an on-line demonstration of a planning system. As the Controller indicated various changes to the sales and profit plan, the data was inputted by the operator in a prescribed format and the results were immediately retrieved. This mode of operation provides instantaneous results and substantially reduces clerical effort and voluminous paper output. The operation is simple and cost effective. Further, it will decrease and/or eliminate the amount of physical (manual) control required to monitor information validity from its source to the ultimate usage output.

PRODUCT/PROJECT PRICING

In order to ensure adequate controls in the planning process for projecting statistically reliable product/project costs, the effort must be initiated at the lowest level of organizational detail. Based on predicted firm or anticipated sales (deliveries/effort), the concerned organizations—in many instances at the cost center level—prepare an estimate of time (manpower/machinery) that will be required to perform the tasks involved in meeting production schedules and/or performing certain contractual services (for example, research and development).

In the initial stage, the forecasts are concerned with the effort and materials involved in production—the quantity of individual parts, component and complete assemblies, subcontract needs, and the like. The results of this planning provide detailed information as to manpower requirements (number, time-phasing, and type of classification), materials (type and quantity), and the indirect support (manpower, supplies, maintenance) necessary to augment the direct effort and costs involved. Manpower needs and costs are summarized by task to the project/product level within an organization. The projected manpower plan requirements are submitted to varying levels of management for review and approval for incorporation into the overall plan.

The above discussion has been primarily addressed to production needs, but similar requirements are being simultaneously developed by other organizations (engineering, procurement, marketing) within the business enterprise.

Organizational Participation in the Forecast Plan

In the engineering area, effort and costs have to be projected for research, design, and development of new products; changes in contract specification requirements; current product or service enhancements; possible pilot production, and other related activities. In quality assurance, the concern is with the manpower needed to perform the inspection requirements as well as the equipment required to test the performance or quality of the product in terms of contractual specifications. Plant engineering must provide its cost for facility maintenance, repair, and inspection of facilities as well as the effort to be involved in new machinery/equipment installation.

Various administrative organizations (marketing, accounting, planning, purchasing) must also provide input into the forecast plan. Research and development, proposal and bidding expense, and corporate office allocations must also be considered since this type of indirect expenses must be allocated to the cost of the product/project.

Other Forecast Plan Considerations

As indicated earlier, various controls are exercised concerning the validity of project direction and costing by varying levels of management. Direct manpower is carefully scrutinized as to need. The indirect to direct manpower ratio must meet the planning requirements of upper management not only to meet competitors' proposals but also to assure projected profit requirements. Direct material requests for purchase are evaluated against inventories to preclude unnecessary inventory buildup. Forecasted overhead expense by individual account and organization is reviewed and analyzed in depth to ensure that the overhead rate per direct labor dollar (or hour) is in line with competitive quotes and/or does not overprice the product or service to be sold. Further, overhead represents a measure of managerial efficiency in the conduct of their operation/function.

Project costing then entails the combination of the elements of cost (direct labor, overhead, material, and other direct costs) and, subtracting this value from product/project sales, will result in gross profit. In some contracts, sales values are developed by applying a gross profit percentage plus 100% to total costs to derive sales.

In the computerized planning process, basic control parameters are entered as input to the system, and, if the projections indicate discrepancies or departure from the initial plan goals and premises, exception reports are outputted to reflect this situation (such as indirect to direct ratios). Then it is the function of management to take the appropriate corrective action.

SALES AND PROFIT SIMULATION MODEL

Having developed project costs in the controlled environment, the next concern is sales and profits from operations. For this type of planning, a mechanical simulation model will be very effective in resolving the aggregate projection plan. It provides a rapid tool for analyzing the total sales and profit outlook for the organization and permits the testing of alternative decision actions from an overview standpoint.

Data Manipulations in the Sales Model

Exhibit G displays three different methods involved in sales, cost, and profit manipulations. In the first example on the left of the exhibit (representing a cost-type contract), sales, fee percentage, general and administrative expense (dollars or application factor), and disallowances (dollars or percentage) represent the initial projected data. Costs and profits must be derived from this basic data.

As shown on the exhibit, the mechanical processes are as follows:

- Projected sales are divided by 100% plus the fee percentage to obtain total costs which are subtracted from sales to obtain fee dollars.
- General and administrative expenses are deducted from total cost resulting in cost of sales.
- Cost of sales subtracted from projected sales equals gross profit.
- Gross profit less G & A expenses equals profit from operations.
- An alternate way of obtaining profit from operations is to deduct the G & A expenses and disallowances separately from fee dollars.
- Controlled manipulation of data can be achieved in this application by changes in sales, fee rates, G & A, and/or disallowances.

In the center example (representing a commercial product operation), total costs, profit margin markup, and G & A and selling expense have been individually projected. Sales and profit must be determined. The process is as follows:

SIMULATION MODEL

Income Statement Manipulation (Projections)

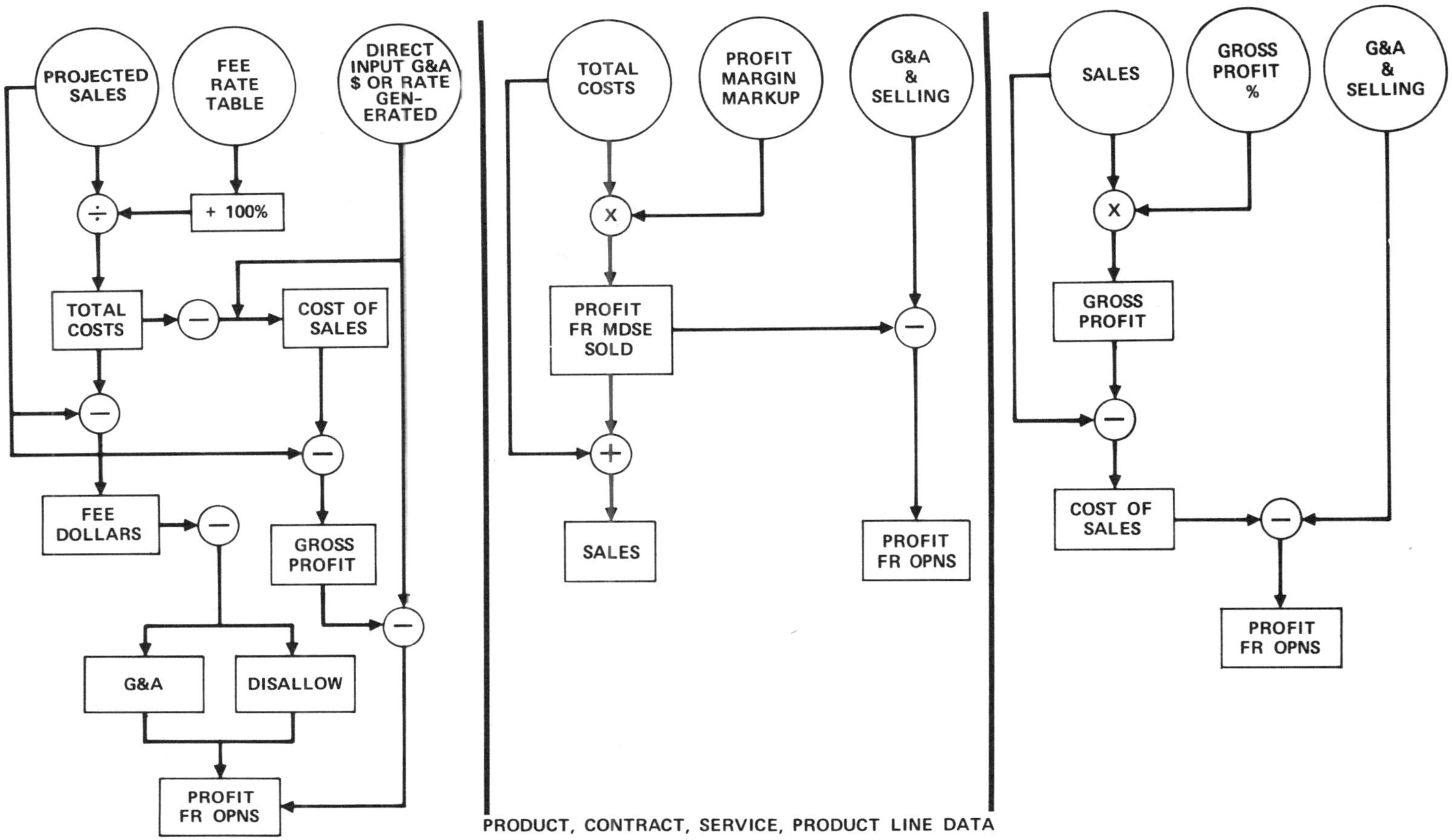

EXHIBIT G

- Profit margin markup percentage is multiplied by total costs to determine projected profit from merchandise sold.
- Total costs plus the above profit results in projected sales.
- Profits less G & A and selling expense results in profit from operations.
- Controlled manipulation of data can be achieved by changes to total costs, margin markup percentage and/or G & A and selling expense. It is noted that in the detailed satellite model to support this model, changes can be made to any one or more elements of cost (labor, overhead, material), individual product margin markup, or to individual G & A or selling accounts.

The example on the right of the exhibit can be representative of a fixed-price contract in which sales have been negotiated and the gross profit dollars is a part of the sales price. Cost of sales and profit from operations must be developed. The process is as follows:

- Sales multiplied by the gross profit percentage will yield the gross profit dollars.
- Sales less gross profit equals cost of sales.
- G & A and selling expense deducted from the cost of sales results in profit from operations. It is noted that disallowances are not considered in this type of contract because total sales price is negotiated. Overrun in estimated costs in the negotiated fixed-price sales contract adversely affects profits.
- Controlled manipulation of data can be achieved by changes to sales, gross profit percentage, and G & A expense. These changes are made at the contract level since each contract is projected separately.

The major advantages of this type of model are that it contains the capability of manipulating the data at the product, contract, service, product line, and organizational levels; and it permits revisions to the operating plan based on testing alternatives of management decisions as to the direction in which they seek to operate the segments (product, contract) of their business. The simulation model is a sophisticated approach to realistic planning.

BALANCE SHEET GAMING MODEL

The balance sheet symbolizes the financial status of an organization at a point in time. It is concerned with the assets, liabilities, and net investment. The data developed from the operation cycle of the business is ultimately reflected in the ending balances of the balance sheet. This statement reveals to management, the stockholder, credit agencies, banks, and governmental organizations the company's utilization of resources, outstanding debt, and net worth. It depends on a number of subsidiary systems for its input. The data reflected in this schedule indicates the type of controls required to improve an organization's financial status.

Exhibit H flowcharts the type of data reflected in the balance sheet and its source. A simulation model can be developed to test alternate decisions for reflecting changes to data developed in subsidiary systems without initially changing the details. A description of the process follows.

SIMULATION MODEL
Balance Sheet Gaming

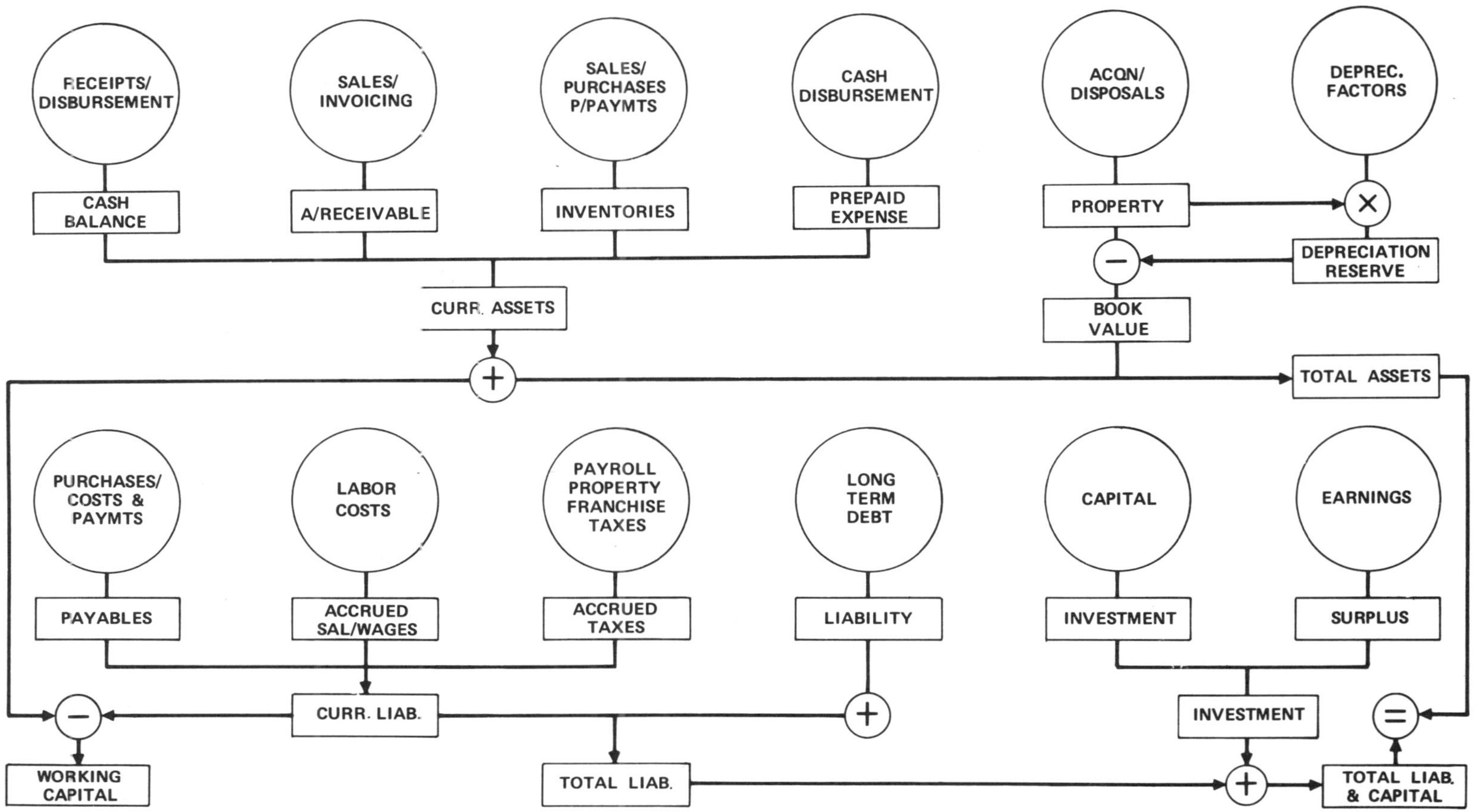

EXHIBIT H

Assets

- The cash balance is generated in the cash flow system on a time-phased basis. The beginning actual balance plus anticipated cash receipts from projected customer billings, advances, borrowings, and other sources are combined to provide the total projected cash available. Cash disbursements reflects the projected expenditures for accounts payable commitments (lagged), accrued salaries/wages, capital expenditures, interest expense, advances to vendors, and so on. The difference between the total anticipated receipts and the disbursements added to the beginning balance then represents the cash balances anticipated during the projection periods.
- There are various types of receivables—customer, employee, miscellaneous other. The prime receivables in a business organization are those concerned with invoicing the customer for product deliveries or services performed. This data is obtained from a subsidiary system that develops anticipated receivables predicated on sales by project, contract, and customer.
- Inventories include work in process, materials and supplies, and finished goods. This data is developed in a satellite system in which beginning balances are combined with purchases and reduced by usage (reflected in cost of sales) to determine the period ending balances. Progress payments (reflected on the exhibit) has recently been reclassified to a form of receivable rather than part of inventory.
- Prepaid expense is generally a direct input into the system since it is a type of recurring expense that can be readily projected by time period. Included in this category of prepaid expense assets are real and personal property tax, lease expenses, state franchise taxes, income taxes, utilities, insurance, and the like. Each period, expenses increase or decrease depending upon advance payments of utilization of the expended value of the asset.
- The summary of the above four major and common assets (but not restricted to these as there are others such as marketable securities, accrued income) derive a projected total current assets.
- The capital expenditure budget, which is time phased, is projected separately and is combined with the beginning balance (generally by property classification type in the subsidiary schedules) to obtain total gross property by period. Generally, manually developed and projected depreciation factors (based on property life and type of depreciating method—straight line, double declining, etc.)—are applied to gross property either on an item or major classification basis to obtain depreciation expense. The period expense combined with the original depreciation reserve is used to reduce gross property acquisition costs to obtain net property (book value) balances.
- The combination of current asset, net property, and other long-term assets (such as investment in subsidiaries) results in total assets.

Liabilities

As shown on Exhibit H, purchases of material, subcontracting, overhead items, capital additions, and other miscellaneous direct and indirect expenses are considered accounts payable commitments, and, when reduced by projected (lagged) cash disbursements (from cash flow), result in accounts payable balances. The accounts payable detail is obtained from subsystem development.

Labor costs represent projected direct and indirect labor dollars. Upon cost incurrence, the accrued salaries/wages liability is created. This liability is lagged to derive a projected cash payment in the cash flow system and the accrued salaries/wages balance is accordingly reduced.

Projected accrued taxes are developed in other subsystems and flow into the balance sheet as a liability until anticipated to be paid. When payment is made, it is reflected as a forecasted cash disbursement and expensed through overhead.

The sum of the above commitment balances is identified as current liabilities. Long-term liabilities are generally a direct input into the planning process and are governed by management edict as to when payment will be made. Current and long-term debts are combined to obtain the total projected liabilities.

The combination of net investment (beginning balance) plus net income or surplus (year to date basis or annually) results in the ending net investment balance or stockholder's equity. The sum of the total liabilities and ending investment balance become the balancing criteria to be matched against total assets.

In the simulation model, the capability exists to determine the variance between assets and liabilities plus investment (if any) to make the appropriate adjustment to either side of the equation mechanically in the selected balancing account (receivables, inventories, payables). Generally, accounts payable is used since it is usually the most unpredictable projection to make accurately.

The statistics outputted in this system include not only working capital but also return on total assets employed and the ratio between current assets and liabilities. Other ratios are discussed in a subsequent chapter.

Pitfalls in Planning System Mechanization

Computerized financial planning systems, as well as others, have not, in many instances, been given proper recognition when decisions are made to utilize data-processing resources. The reasons are varied and may often be valid depending upon the decision-maker. Some notable obstacles are as follows:

- Greater emphasis is placed on the hardware aspect and its use for day-to-day routine activities because of the more immediate return on the costly computer investment and related requirements (software).
- Haste in implementing systems without a thorough design to include future anticipated data needs of the user—there exists the requirement for rapid results in system implementation to justify computer capability acquisition.
- Changing environment and organizational requirements.
- Incomplete knowledge of computer usage capabilities.
- Inexperienced personnel who inadequately define the data requirements or were not properly advised of the complete user needs.

The above pitfalls can be overcome by sound computer resource planning procedures. It has been proven that a mechanical planning system particularly is cost effective and leads to a more realistic development of a financial operating plan which, in turn, governs or directs the efficiency, control, and profitability of an organization's operations. Further, this type of capability lends itself successfully to changing business climate decisions.

In summary, the financial planning and control system using a computerized model approach is a powerful tool to assure validity of data input, manipulation, storage, and retrieval. Use of data banks and program integration provides the opportunity for sequential data flow and file updates in logical uniformity. Management is provided data requirements with minimal cost and data handling to meet the changing business environment. On-line operations is the most advanced technique in information processing. The approach to system design guidelines and the various considerations involved provide the reader with a means to implement this type of capability in a short time span and aids in precluding a costly approach and expensive experimentation.

5

Computer-Aided Manpower Resource Planning and Pricing

The basic, major essential in all organizations, large or small, is the manpower resources required to perform the necessary tasks or services (direct and indirect) and also the various hierarchy of management to guide, control, and manage the business enterprise. The tasks require various skills (depending upon the complexity of the organization) to achieve the multitude of responsibilities for accomplishing the organization's goals and objectives. All of this talent must be properly organized in order to function in a compatible manner that will augment other efforts.

MANPOWER RESOURCE PLANNING

Planning manpower requirements is a vital function in any successful organization in that it is a major determinant in the ability to achieve production and sales goals. All organizational levels participate in this forecast process since they are all involved, either directly or indirectly, in meeting the organization's planned objectives for the future.

Criteria for Controlling Manpower Costs

All levels of supervision must be concerned and directly involved in manpower projections because of its extreme importance in the organization's operations. Generally, the personnel making the projections are unduly optimistic as to their needs and tend to overestimate their requirements, which can have an adverse effect on costs and profits. Management control must be exercised. Close scrutiny must be given to the indirect personnel needs specifically because of their impact on overhead costs and rate. Also, the projections may be disproportionate to management's prime manpower control tools—the ratio of indirect to direct personnel.

Manpower planning should be carefully viewed from the standpoint of employee costs and facility requirements. It may be more cost effective to utilize an extended work week or overtime than to hire more people, particularly during periods of increased seasonal demands, because employee benefit costs have increased so dramatically in the past few years and have become a major expense in payroll costs.

Due consideration must also be given to projected manpower that will exceed facility capacity because this will mean the need for additional investment in facilities and equipment which may not be cost effective. It would be more desirable and practicable to consider a second shift that could be expanded or contracted as required with minimal increase in investment outlay. Since the projections reflect firm and potential business as well as new product or service development, caution should be the guideline in a too rapid manpower growth because some of the projected potential business may not materialize or new products may not gain the size of the market anticipated to offset the manpower expansion.

MANPOWER AND PRICING PROJECTION MODEL

An overview of a computerized manpower and pricing system indicating the process and reports produced is displayed on Exhibit A. Manpower development is shown on the left side of the chart, whereas the right side is concerned with determining hours and dollars. A highlight review is given below.

The first step that occurs in the development of a direct and indirect manpower forecast occurs when Long Range Planning or Marketing, depending upon organizational structure and responsibility, provides the operating organizations with projection guidelines. The forecast parameters are by contract within product line as to the sales delivery schedule and level of effort identified to firm and potential business. Included in the guidelines is the effort required for interdivision sales, proposal and bidding, and research and development. The Financial Budget organization provides other parameters to the projecting organizations such as organizations associated with various project budget centers (PBC) and contracts linked with product lines as well as hour factors (equivalent manpower conversions) by period and the anticipated overtime percentage by contract and/or PBC.

The functional projecting organizations develop, from the above, their estimates of direct and indirect manpower requirements, which are forwarded through various levels of management and, upon approval, go to the Budget Group and top management for review, resolution, and final approval. If changes are required, they are forwarded to the functional organizations for manpower revisions and/or negotiation.

When the projections have been resolved, the data is inputted into the computer program by the Budget Group with additional information (labor rates, percentage of indirect to direct labor) which is manipulated in terms of calculations, sorting, and summarizing to meet the needs of the various reporting requirements shown at the bottom of the exhibit. Manpower projections are converted to midpoint averages for conversion to labor hours and gross payroll dollars. The reason for midpoint averages is to minimize the effect of manpower fluctuations between the beginning and the end of the period.

DIRECT AND INDIRECT MANPOWER DATA FLOW
PROJECTION MODEL

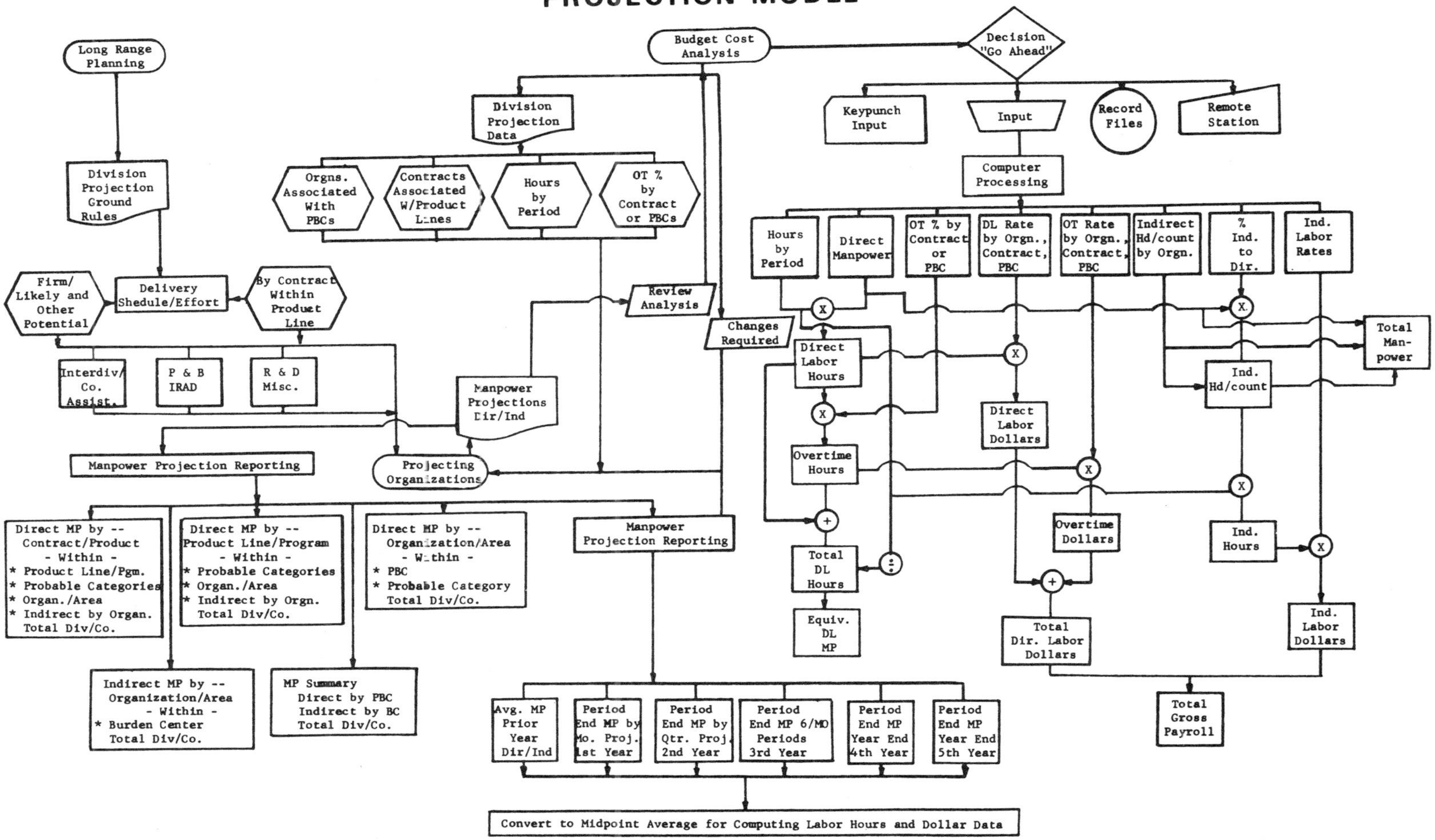

*Sub Totals

EXHIBIT A

The mechanical system is a complete entity within itself which permits changes in input as required in order to finalize the projections. Many of the points highlighted above will be elaborated upon later in this chapter.

PROJECTION PLANNING PARAMETERS

The Budget Group provides the following detailed information to the functional organizations simultaneously with the Planning Group's guidelines.

Format for Manpower Input

Projected manpower input will be entered as indicated below. Hierarchy summary information will be prepared in a similar format mechanically.

ORGANIZATION MANPOWER INPUT

<table>
<tr><td colspan="6">DEPARTMENT
DESIGNATION ____________</td><td colspan="4">SUBMISSION
DATE ________</td></tr>
<tr><td rowspan="2">PROGRAM/CONTRACT
OR PRODUCT LINE</td><td rowspan="2">PRIOR
ACTUALS</td><td colspan="2" rowspan="2">FIRST-YEAR
PROJECTIONS</td><td colspan="2" rowspan="2">SECOND-YEAR
PROJECTIONS</td><td colspan="3">ANNUAL AVERAGES</td></tr>
<tr><td>3rd YR</td><td>4th YR</td><td>5th YR</td></tr>
<tr><td>FIRM
____
____
____
POTENTIAL
____
____
OTHER
____
________</td><td>Last Three Months of Preceding Year</td><td>By Mo.</td><td>Annual Avg.</td><td>By Qtr.</td><td>Annual Avg.</td><td></td><td></td><td></td></tr>
<tr><td>SUBTOTAL
PLANNED DIRECT*
TOTAL INDIRECT
GRAND TOTAL</td><td colspan="8">*Indicates anticipated staffing level in the event that this level should vary from the arithmetical total of the direct manpower projection. This may be necessary in order to smooth the curve to be consistent with normal fluctuations and also to conform to manpower levels planned by management.</td></tr>
</table>

The above data format provides for uniformity and consistency in the projection process in submitting manpower data which is derived from converting level-of-effort requirements and identifying this information to specific contract, program, and/or product line. The form further simplifies summaries of organizational unit projections.

Definition of Business Potential Categories

To ensure that all organizations are properly classifying the future business endeavors, the following definitions are provided.

Firm Business — All current authorized work including work assignment requests to the extent expenditures have been authorized.

Potential — All programs having a substantially high probability of "win"; particularly, follow-on efforts to firm business.

Other — New business potential having less than a substantially high probability of "win."

Department Designations

A listing is provided that indicates departments associated to functional groupings such as Engineering, Operations (support, tooling, factory, plant engineering), Quality Assurance, Material (support, procurement), and others as required. Identifications are necessary in order to properly summarize department manpower projections in their specific functional groups.

Program and Contract Groupings

A listing is provided that identifies projects to programs/contracts and is also associated with specific product lines to achieve necessary consistency for the summation process.

Manpower Conversion Factors

Projecting organizations are also provided with the different types of labor factors that are used in converting manpower to hours. This is required to ensure consistency in the conversion process. There are basically three common methods by which labor hours can be computed based upon the specific projection need and usage:

- In PROPOSAL ESTIMATING, the interest is in *average equivalent man*, which is calculated by multiplying the number of workdays in the year by eight hours a day and dividing by twelve for the monthly average hours of work.
- In COST-TO-COMPLETE FORECASTING, the interest is in *equivalent man*, which is calculated by multiplying number of actual workdays in an accounting month by eight hours per day. Many organizations use 4-4-5 monthly weeks in each quarter.
- In the third instance, the interest may be in derived *actual headcount* as commonly used in MANPOWER FORECASTING, TRACKING, or INDIRECT BUDGET FRINGE COMPUTATIONS. The calculations performed would be historical average productive hours per man per day, times the number of workdays in an accounting month. The productive work hours per day factor approximates 7.4 in most organizations, but does not hold true for all organizations. Traditionally, there are less productive hours per person in manufacturing than in engineering due to idle time, machine breakdown, waiting for materials, or other slowdowns.

Indirect Manpower

To determine the indirect manpower projections, the organization or the Budget Group would use a percentage ratio of indirect to direct headcount for computer computation. This ratio is generally a management edict to meet certain and definite cost-control goals. If the direct manpower changes, then the indirect would also change in order to maintain the same relative proportion of indirect to direct that was originally planned. This ratio is one of the major controls used by management in establishing a competitive overhead rate.

LABOR HOURS DEVELOPMENT FORECAST

Midpoint Headcount

After the manpower projections are developed and approved, the next computerized process is to calculate midpoint manning which is by organization, project/contract, and period. It is segregated into direct and indirect manpower. The mechanical program can calculate midpoint and/or month-end manning depending upon need and usage.

- If given the period-end headcount, the process is to add the beginning and ending head-counts and divide by two, which results in the midpoint manpower count—used primarily for labor hour development.
- If given midpoint headcount, the computer calculates the period personnel by taking one-half of the combined total of the previous and subsequent period headcount projections—primarily used for performance analysis and reporting.

The midpoint personnel count is used because the average hours per person and period factor is already in the computer reference file and its application must be made to the average midperiod headcount in order to compute more realistic and representative labor hours by period.

Direct Productive Hours

Productive hours represent the time spent by direct personnel in performing functions specifically identified with the product. There are instances where indirect personnel also perform direct functions and, in those cases, their hours worked are included in the direct hour category. This information is also reflected in the manning forecast in equivalent heads. The average hours factor is entered in the computer reference file. The factor is based on historical experience with the average person working approximately 7.4 hours out of the total of 8.0.

Unproductive Hours

The .6 hour difference of unproductive time is attributed to average time off for sickness, vacation, holidays, conference attendance, coffee breaks, idle time, tool problems, machine repairs, and so on. This time differential is priced and charged to indirect costs.

Labor Hour Development

The computer calculates the straight-time productive direct hours by performing the arithmetic function of multiplying the midpoint headcount by the daily average hours factor. The result represents total direct hours worked per day. As indicated above, the computer reference file contains the total projected workdays in a period to which is applied the hours factor per day to obtain the total straight-time direct hours by period.

The above computation is made for each contract and is then summarized into program and organizational totals. Organizational totals are at various levels—cost centers, departments, project budget, and burden centers. Computation of the indirect hours follows the same pattern as for the direct hours, but is not identified to contracts, only to organizations.

Direct-Hour Activity Distribution

In some organizations it is necessary to further segregate direct labor hours into research and development (R & D) as differentiated from operations or manufacturing effort. Planners make projections of the representative percentage of their activity which is R & D and the difference represents the manufacturing activity. The forecast is based on historical experience, contractual requirements, and operating plans. These percentages are applied to the direct contract hours by period to obtain the distribution into the major categories of R & D and operation hours. A more realistic approach is to develop the percentages by individual contracts, which would make the data more finite and accurate. The reason for the most realistic split is that there could be a significant difference in contract costs because the R & D rate per hour is greater than that for manufacturing.

Overtime Projections

The overtime factor is based on past history statistics, requirements of contract delivery and service performance, production problems, and government approval. The developed factor is entered into the computer and applied to the direct labor hours to obtain the direct overtime projected hours. The output report will display the total straight time, direct overtime, and total projected productive hours. Direct overtime hours are used to generate the overtime premium hours which are included as a part of the overhead expenses.

LABOR HOUR CONVERSION TO DOLLARS

The actual historical direct and indirect rates are assimilated and calculated by individual organization and period mechanically. Generally, two years of past history is used to assess rate trends. Merit increases are analyzed as to the time of occurrence and amounts plus management's anticipated plans for the projected periods. Overtime premium is naturally excluded in straight-time rates. Using the least squares statistical approach, the computer calculates the application formula (using the hours and dollars relationship). When the projected rates have been developed, they are carefully evaluated as to their reasonableness by graphically plotting them against previous historical periods, they are studied as to their relationship to customer-negotiated wage-rate constraints (government business), and finally they are reviewed by the appropriate management for approval. Many organizations use "cluster" rates for pricing hours. These rates are based on averages for certain types of functions, cost centers and tasks, or a combination of suborganizations for ease in application. They are frequently used in proposal bidding rather than in the actual budgeting process since they represent broader estimates of labor costing rather than a planned control.

COMPUTERIZED LABOR PROJECTION MODEL

The mechanical labor planning model reveals its versatility as displayed on Exhibit B. This exhibit indicates the sequence of events as they occur in the mechanical process. It shows the flow of data to hierarchy summaries. In the early part of this chapter the basic steps of this process were discussed. This exhibit, however, shows the supplemental flow of data after its development. It is this part of the model that will be discussed below.

- The developed direct labor dollars flow into inventory as the projected direct labor costs are presumably incurred. When the customer has been invoiced, the labor costs are retrieved from inventory into the cost of sales.
- The indirect labor dollars also flow into inventory as part of the overhead costs which are also reflected in the cost of sales.
- The direct and indirect labor costs incurred represent total payroll dollars which represent accrued salaries and wages on the balance sheet until paid. Upon payment, labor costs represent a cash disbursement.
- When the customer has been billed, the labor costs are reflected in the receivable account. When the customer pays his invoice, the labor costs included in the accounts receivable become a part of cash receipts.

As changes are made to any of the basic data starting with manpower, the computer redevelops the new data in a matter of minutes. The mechanical process is a great time-saver with extreme accuracy in data development.

OBJECTIVES OF A COMPUTERIZED LABOR MODEL

Due to the various processes involved in projecting manpower, its pricing and required association, to a number of organizational units, products, services, or contracts, a mechanical model is ideal to reduce clerical effort, provide flexibility in making changes rapidly, and provide the types of reporting and performance measurement capabilities necessary in a sophisticated projection process. The specific objectives to be fulfilled are outlined as follows.

- To identify, sort, and summarize manpower data in various classifications to achieve user requirements.
- To provide a rapid means for making additions, changes, and deletions to forecast data as required to meet varying demands of business conditions; this process would be accomplished on-line through the use of terminal devices.
- To perform the various calculations required for translating manpower into hours and dollars and vice versa.
- To achieve selective reporting on-line without voluminous paper printout.

DEVELOPMENT OF MANPOWER & LABOR COST PROJECTIONS

Initial Premise Projections

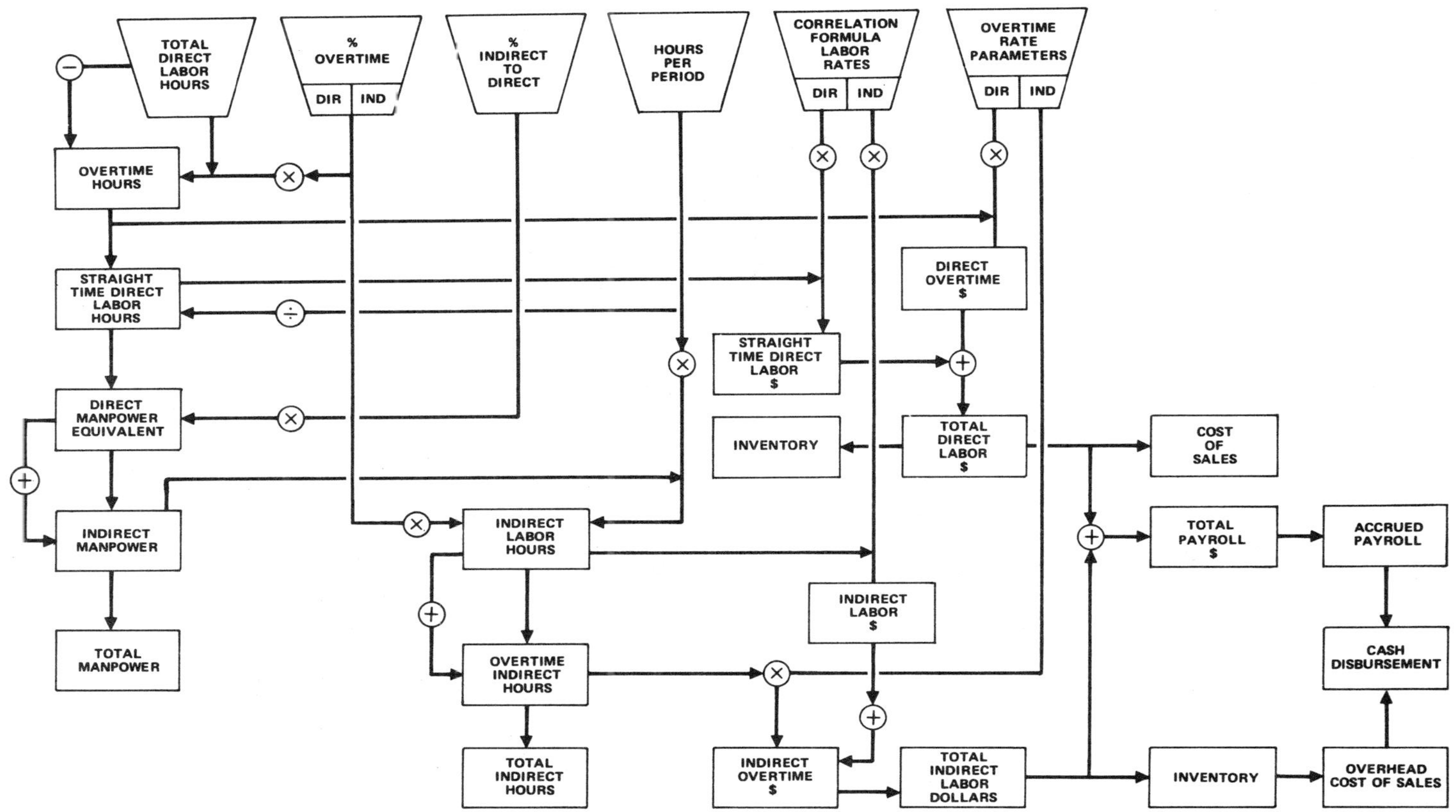

EXHIBIT B

- To project manpower by using a "curve spread" technique, particularly on new or anticipated projects/contracts.
- To accommodate any number of projected time periods (long-term forecasts) with the capability of adding monthly actuals and roll forward the current forecasted data in the system.
- To incorporate table files for data reference and data printout as well as to structure the various reports.
- To allow for computer-generated chart displays by time period and organization, program, various categories (direct, indirect), and summary totals. The data used for the plot line constructions will also be printed at the bottom of the report.
- To permit the mechanical data output to be used in an integrated projection system as a basis for developing overhead, cost of sales, accrued salaries and wages, and disbursements.

The objectives outlined above for achievement in a mechanical process will dramatically improve an organization's planning endeavors and provide rapid development and access to data for product pricing. It will also place the organization in a more competitive position because of the rapid turn-around time in changing their product price proposals and testing alternate situations (increasing/decreasing manhours on a task) and obtain the effect on their projected profits.

CURVE SPREAD TECHNIQUE

Consideration should be given to the use of the curve spread capability in mechanically generating manpower projections, particularly for future periods. It is based on the principle of bulk task resource values (hours) being proportionately distributed using a task curve that will fit anticipated future performance. It is based on historical experience and contract requirements.

The curve spreads are represented by mathematical table factors for calculating labor values that are mechanically converted to manpower requirements for accomplishing the task or projects. A graphic display of the curves is shown on Exhibit C. You will note that there are unit as well as cumulative curves showing respectively effort versus approximate percentage of span time, and percentage of effort versus percentage of time. Although the straight-line curve is not shown, it is simply the distribution of the total amount of the task over the number of periods involved; the value would be the same for each period.

Examples of the predetermined and inputted common curve factors to match the display on the exhibit are noted below.

FACTORS FOR EXHIBIT CURVES

CURVE	TIME PERIODS 1	2	3	4	5	6	TOTAL TASK PERCENTAGE
C	.075	.185	.240	.240	.185	.075	100.0
D	.029	.175	.296	.296	.175	.029	100.0
E	.012	.092	.200	.280	.278	.138	100.0

TIME CURVE SPREAD OF EFFORT

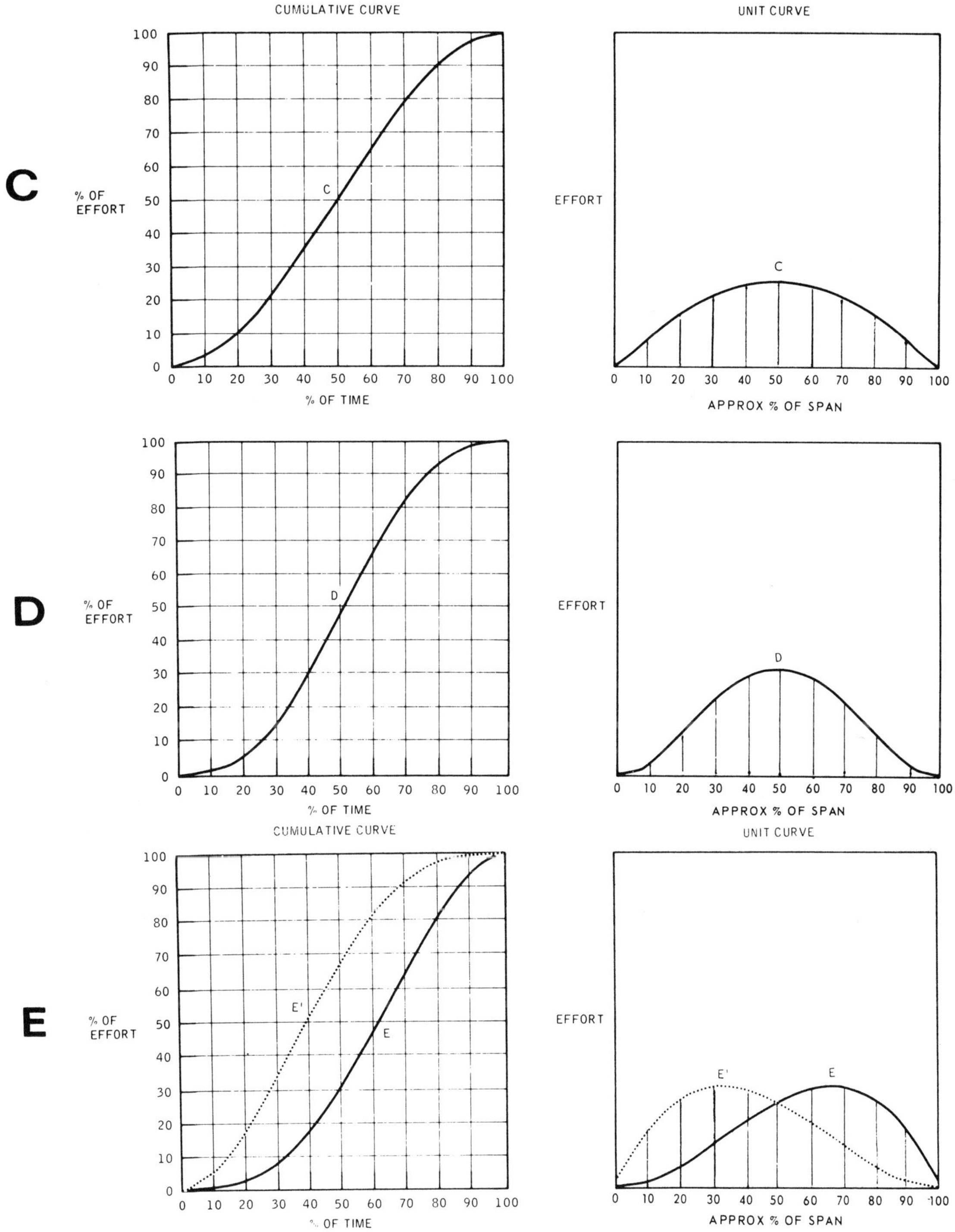

EXHIBIT C

Significance of the Curves

The above standard factors represent the percentage of the total task to be performed during each of the six time periods. For example, if the total hours required in "D" above were 1,000, then the number of hours projected to be expended in the fourth period would be .296 times 1,000, or 296 hours. Assuming a simplified 40-hour work week per man effort, the translation into manpower would be 7.4 persons required to accomplish the task in the fourth period.

Since the factor table is identified by each curve and series of time periods in the computer file, any type of curve can be readily selected and the appropriate factors applied to the total effort value for spreading performance over given time spans which are translated into manpower resource requirements. Using this technique, much clerical effort is reduced. It provides a more rapid means of visibility for projections, making changes, and testing the effect of alternate results from varied curve selections. It definitely gives an organization a competitive edge on bidding time and price on contract performance.

EFFECTS FROM MANPOWER REVISIONS

As an example of what happens to the overall operating plan forecast when the direct manpower projections are changed, Exhibit D was prepared for illustrative purposes. The revision action sets off a chain reaction of data element changes which, in turn, affect a number of summary financial schedules. Direct manpower changes affect direct labor hour activity and dollar costs. A change in labor costs affects the inventory balance and cost of sales. A revision to cost of sales requires a decision as to whether the sales, profits, or both will be affected. The projected accrued payroll balance is affected as well as cash disbursements. If a change is made to sales, the receivables are affected as well as cash receipts. A change to profit affects both the return on sales and investment.

Changing direct manpower generally always changes indirect manpower, particularly if a planned indirect to direct ratio is to be maintained. Revision to the indirect manpower forecast is reflected in the indirect labor costs which, in turn, affects the accrued payroll liability, cash disbursements, total overhead expense and rate.

A significant increase or decrease in manpower projections may necessitate a larger facility or contraction thereof. Expansion would mean fixed-asset investment, which would result in changes to cash disbursements, property status, depreciation, source and application of funds. Profits could be affected, which changes return on investment and the income statement.

Exhibit D provides a perceptive overview of the dramatic effect of manpower changes and demonstrates the need for a simulation model to view the results of changes before action is taken to initiate them.

LABOR SIMULATION MODEL

As an overview example of the simulation process relative to manpower and cost gaming, Exhibit E was developed. As shown on this exhibit, if manpower projection is the

EFFECT OF CHANGES TO PROJECTED DATA

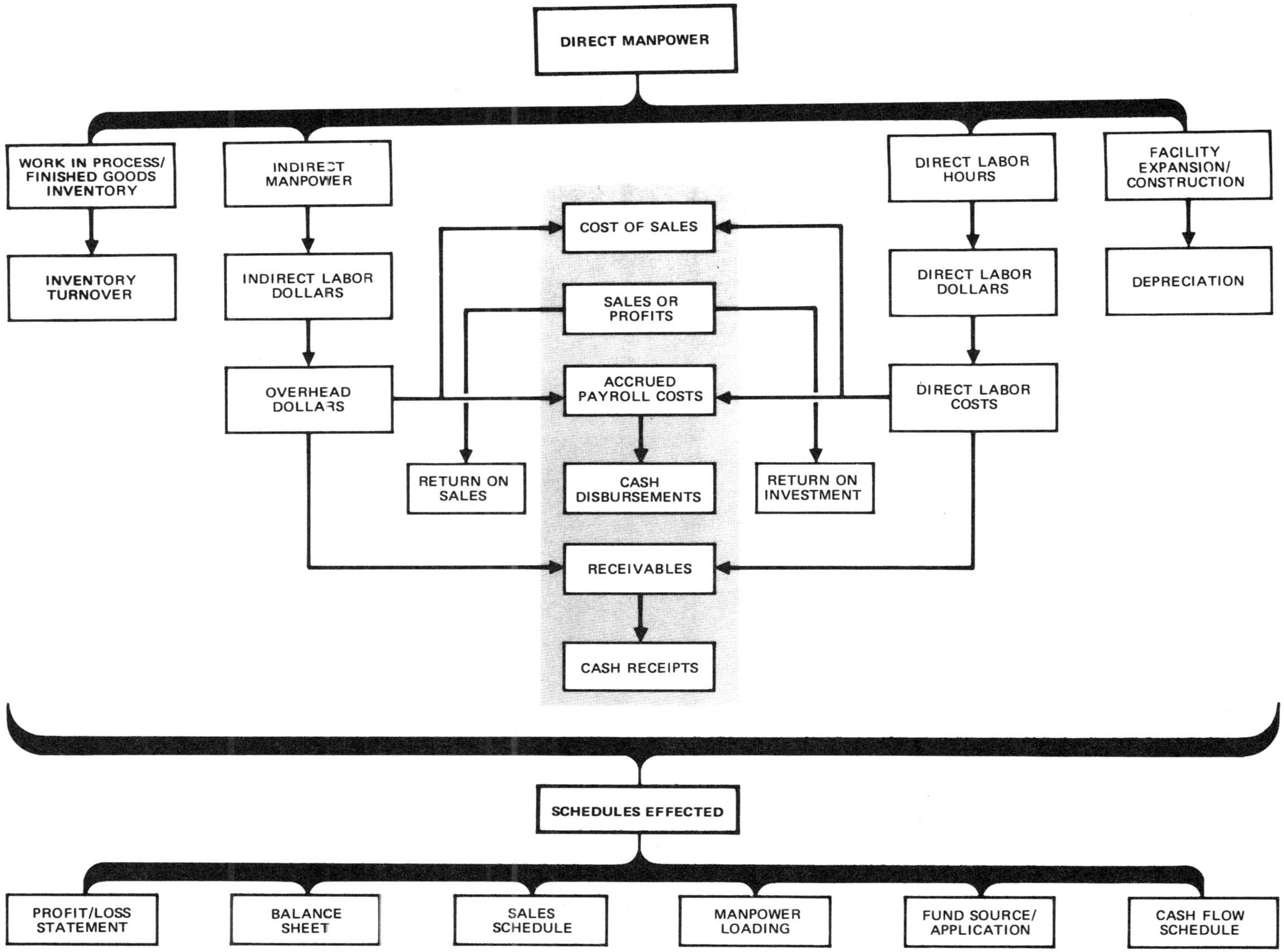

EXHIBIT D

SIMULATION MODEL
Manpower & Pricing Gaming

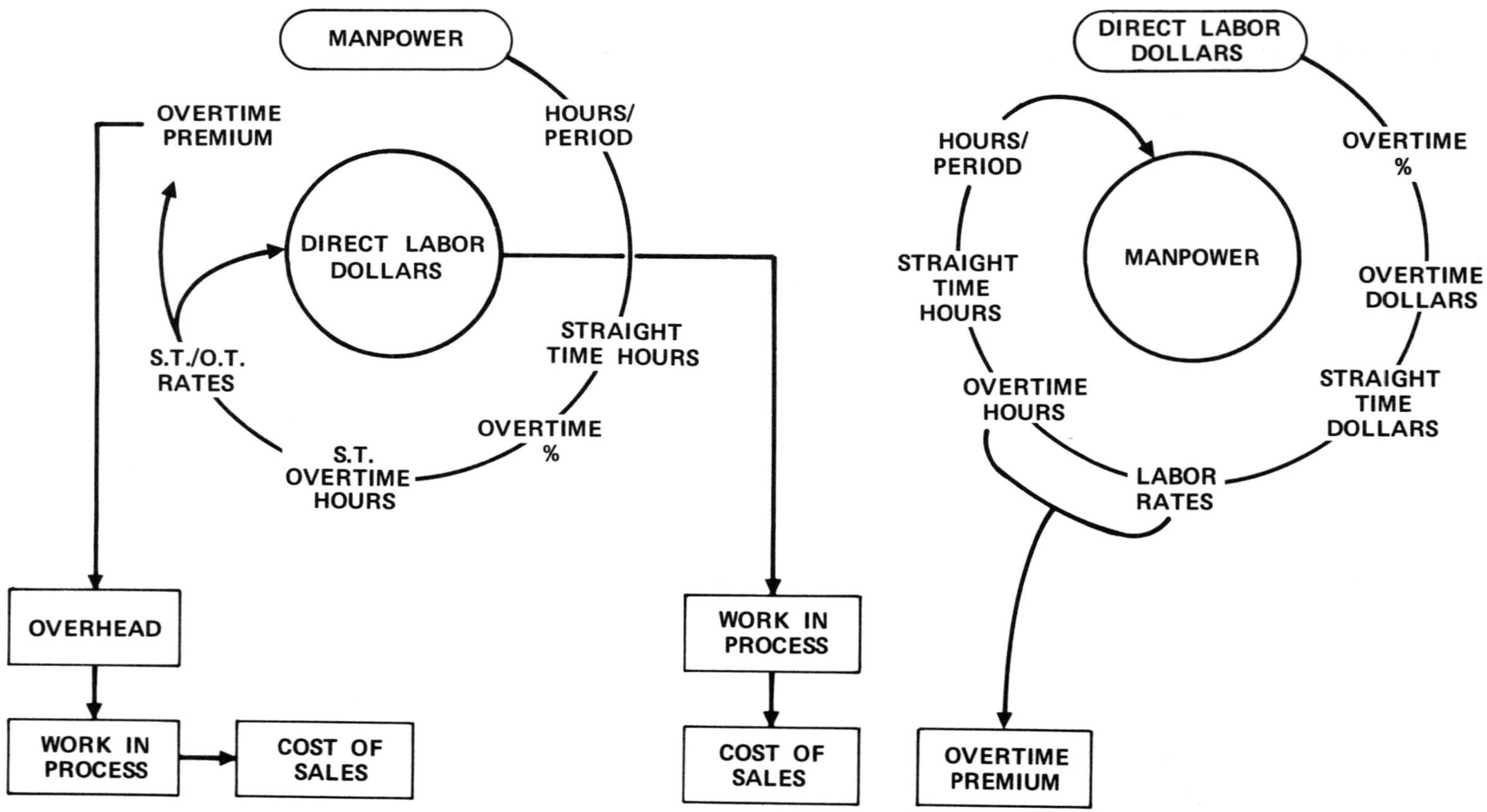

EXHIBIT E

start point for development or simulating changes, they are converted into straight-time hours and a factor is applied to determine the anticipated overtime hours. Using projected rates, the hours are converted into direct labor and overtime dollars. As noted on the display, changing labor dollars and/or overtime affects the overhead, work-in-process inventory, and cost of sales. Other changes to projected data elements are discussed above under "Effects from Manpower Revisions."

If changes are to be initiated in direct labor dollars, then the effect must be determined on projected manpower requirements. As shown on the exhibit, the reverse process is used to that described above for manpower changes. Overtime has to be recalculated as well as the hours activity volume. Using the reference file factors, the hours are converted and time spread to determine manpower by periods. The effect of the changes must then be reflected in other data elements as described above.

The paramount point to be stressed for the gaming process is that any factor (overtime percentage, number of workdays, productive hours/day) of the major projection (manpower or direct labor dollars) can be easily changed and the results reflected throughout the forecast with little manual intervention.

LABOR COST FLOW AND USAGE

In the actual environment, the development and flow of labor data has a very important impact on a number of other systems. Exhibit F gives an overview of a mechanical system and its utilization. There are a number of audits made and controls established to assure the validity of the data.

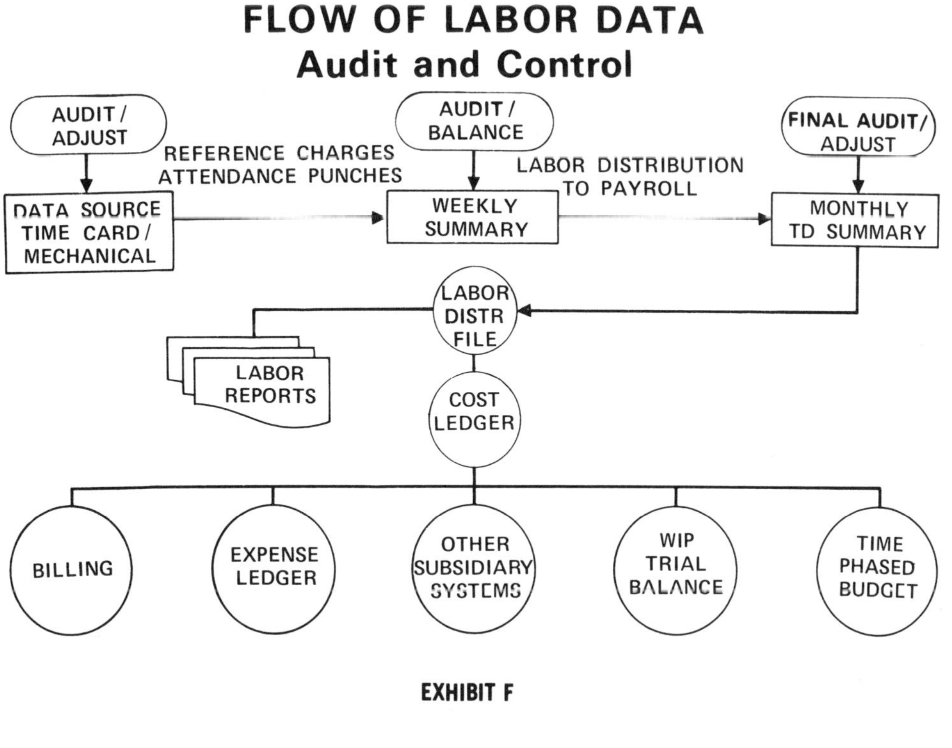

EXHIBIT F

As displayed broadly on this exhibit, the following processes occur:

- The two sources of labor input are (1) manual timecard data is keypunched into the mechanical system and (2) is obtained from the mechanical data collection and recording terminal devices. A manual audit is performed on the timecard and the mechanical data is audited internally in the system to verify organization numbers, work orders and contract numbers, and reconciliation of the hours worked.
- The mechanical system collects, sorts, and summarizes the data by organization, work order, contract, PBC, etc., for weekly reporting. An audit is made to ensure that labor distribution and payroll records are in balance.
- A final audit is performed at month end and adjustments are made before the monthly reports are processed.
- The labor distribution file is used as the data source for detailed and summary reports and the cost ledger requirements.
- As shown on the chart, labor is utilized in billing the customer; indirect labor flows into the expense ledger where it becomes a part of the overhead rate, is used in the work-in-process trial balance, is entered into the time-phased budget system for performance reporting, and also is used in various subsidiary systems such as contract and task analysis reports, estimating systems, and organizational labor status.

In the forecast environment described in this chapter, the labor cost data element has similar utilization as above but the processing differs somewhat from that described for the actual manual process. For example, labor hours and dollar projections are generally based on manpower projections in totals rather than collected and projected on an individual basis, which is the case with actuals. The actual and projected systems must be compatible in order to achieve the required performance reporting mechanically.

PERFORMANCE ANALYSIS AND REPORTING

As actual data becomes available at the end of each period, it is entered (either manually or by program interface transfer) into the projection system (sorted and merged) for comparison to the operating plan data. As indicated previously, both sets of data must be compatible for reporting and analysis requirements. The levels of summation to be compared are as follows from minor to major sorts:

- PBC, Contract Code, Program, Department
- Department, Contract Code, Program, Category, PBC
- Department Contract Code, Program, Category, PBC, Division
- Contract Code, Subprogram, Program
- Program, Division
- Department, Contract Code, Program, Category, Type of Contract
- Department, Contract Code, Program, Category, Burden Center (Indirect Reporting)

The format of the report would be as follows.

DIRECT LABOR HOURS

	CURRENT PERIOD			YEAR-TO-DATE		
DESCRIPTION	FORECAST	ACTUAL	VARIANCE	FORECAST	ACTUAL	VARIANCE

Reported separately in the same format would be direct labor and overtime dollars and indirect hours and dollars. The reports would be distributed to the responsible management, an analysis would be made of the variances, and, if major, corrective action would be taken to preclude future discrepancies or changes in the projection plan may be required.

Exception/Selective Performance Reporting

The computer program should include the capability to output only those reports or selective data where the variance is of certain prescribed magnitude deviation (greater or less) from the projected plan. This would reduce not only printed paper volume but also would greatly lessen the analysis task as attention would only be necessary to be directed toward major deviations from planned operations.

The author was exposed to a good example of what could happen with volume output in one organization. A weekly time-phased (labor) budget performance report grew to a stack of paper output forty feet high. It took three days to burst and distribute the report to the concerned organizations who found it impossible to evaluate in the short time span before the next report was due. It was a costly operation—ineffective and useless reporting for timely decision-making. The changeover to exception and selective reporting resulted in the reduction of this report to a five-inch thickness with same-day distribution; its review and analysis was completed by the following day for corrective action purposes. There are other instances of this same type of inefficient reporting that needlessly cause organizations to expend hundreds of thousands of dollars uselessly on high-volume paper output from which little or no benefits are gained.

A capability must also exist to call out of the file records specific data or reports of the sorts required, preferably through an on-line system. This type of operation saves time, paper, and requires little effort for data analysis since the inquiry would be for specific information that would reveal problem areas. On-line operations provide the means for instantaneous changes and data retrievals. Many organizations are directing their efforts toward this objective.

Mechanical graphic displays of forecast versus actual manpower and labor cost data are highly desirable to evaluate rapidly and visually specific data deviations by period. This type of reporting readily reflects problem areas because of the dramatic line trend comparisons.

In conclusion, there are many benefits to be derived from a computerized manpower planning and control system. Some of the major advantages are indicated below.

- Provides the means for dramatically reducing costly high-volume paper output and inefficient reporting
- Permits rapid access to operational problem areas, which provides the basis for corrective action
- Ideal for various simulation exercises before finalization of the projection plan
- Drastically reduces clerical processing effort associated with sorting and re-sorting of data, calculations, and summations
- Provides capability to move contract data between the probability categories rapidly and accurately
- Allows for frequent interval projection updates
- Permits effective performance measurement and planning and control of manpower utilization and costs

6

Systematic Overhead Analysis and Control with Computer Power

In today's business environment, management is placing far greater emphasis on, and giving more attention to, overhead expense and control. Management has become increasingly aware that hundreds of thousands of dollars can be silently and quickly dissipated if the proper surveillance is not given to the management of overhead expenses. Attention must not only be concentrated on the volume dollar expenses, but also on the smallest expense accounts that belie the significant outgo of cash over a period of time.

Further, there has become a more pointed acknowledgment that overhead expenditures can well govern an organization's competitive product or service price position, cause extreme profit dilution, create cash flow problems, and influence gross inefficiencies in managing and operating activities. Overhead control is a necessary evil if an organization is to survive and exploit its growth potential.

ASPECTS OF OVERHEAD EXPENSE

Definition

Overhead is defined as those indirect expenses that cannot feasibly be identified to a specific product or service cost contribution. It represents expired costs that are related to given fiscal period (a write-down of income). Further, because of incurrence for common or joint objectives, overhead expense does not realistically fit the criteria of a direct cost (product or task identifiable).

Classification of Overhead

There are two main classifications assigned in describing types of overhead—factory overhead, and selling and general administrative expense.

Factory overhead encompasses all factory costs other than direct labor and direct material. These indirect expenses cannot be identified specifically or charged directly to units of production, particular jobs, tasks, or product lots. This overhead is reflected in the cost-of-sales summary on the income statement.

Selling and general administrative overhead is broadly defined as general overhead. Selling expenses are incurred in the activities associated with selling a product or service. General administrative expense is associated with the costs incurred in managing a business and its general administration activities. These expense accounts are segregated from the cost of sales (product cost) so that they can be readily identifiable for individual analysis and control. They are further classified as period costs which represent expenditures in a given period of operation. They cannot be identified and do not contribute directly, except arbitrarily, to the end product.

EXPENSE GROUP CATEGORIES

Exhibit A displays seven prime categories of expense that are included in factory overhead. These classifications may vary among organizations but nevertheless are considered typical in grouping overhead expenses. As noted on this exhibit, the various groups of overhead are summarized to an overall organizational total which is used for computing the overhead rate. The rate is developed by dividing the total expense by either direct labor hours or dollars, which represent the two most widely accepted determinants in rate calculations. The rate is the basis for applying overhead to direct labor hours/dollars as they are expended. This is a very necessary procedure in costing the product or service as it is being produced or service performed. The specific expense accounts associated with these major groupings are displayed on Exhibit B.

Category Descriptions

Indirect salaries and wages represents factory employee costs that cannot be directly identified to the specific production or assembly of a product and its components. The various types of labor involved are reflected in Exhibit B. This expense is controllable by management edict through the establishment of an indirect to direct labor ratio standard and enforcing adherence. Appropriate standards are established through job analysis and the specific requirements of the support labor needed. One well-known West Coast firm was able to dramatically reduce its indirect to direct manpower ratio from 65% to 45% (a whopping 20% decrease) through the use of standards.

Fringe benefits are factory employee expenses that are associated with their earnings and activities. These expenses represent about 30% of the direct labor dollar costs and are the company's contribution to the employees' welfare benefits. Controlling manpower growth will result in substantial expenditure reduction in this expense category.

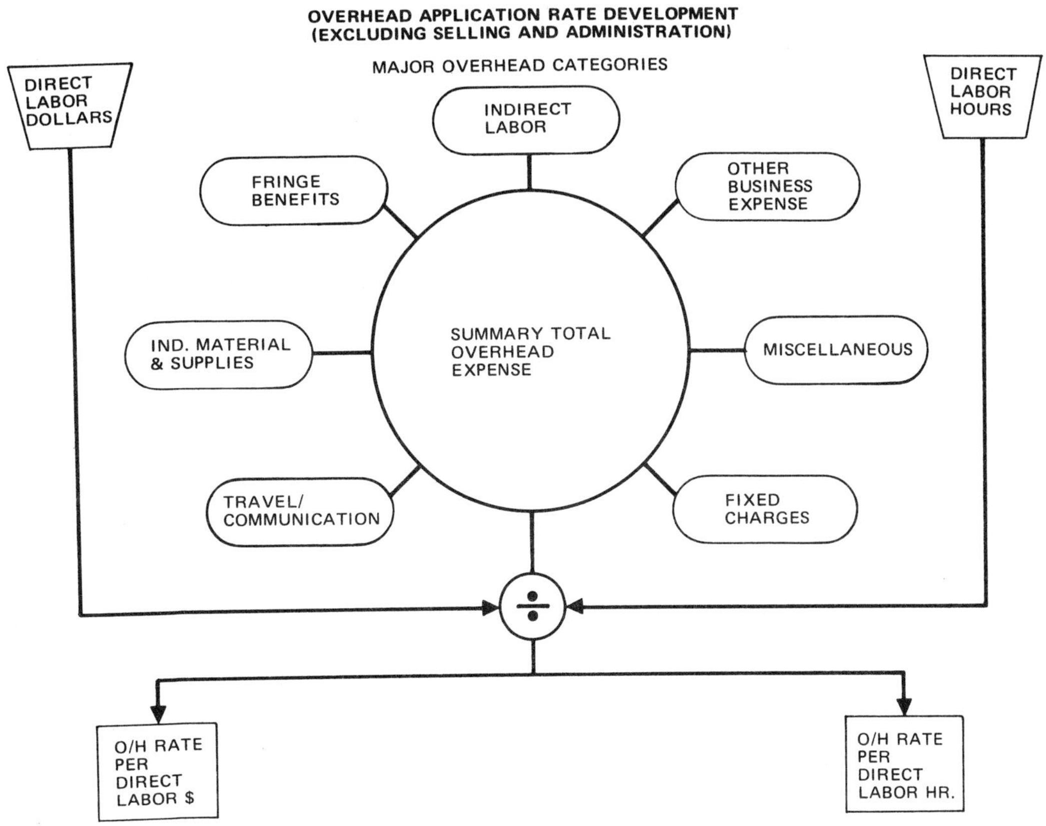

EXHIBIT A

Indirect material and supplies represents the cost of material and supplies that are not associated with the end product. This category includes maintenance supplies, lubricants, office and janitorial supplies, as shown on Exhibit B. Proper employee training, constant supervision surveillance, and the elimination of spoilage will provide significant dollar-realization reductions in this group.

Travel and communication is generally unidentifiable to the factory end product or service but are, to a degree, essential expenditures in operating a business. Unnecessary or duplication of employee travel to the same place at the same time has a major bearing on the magnitude of these expenses. For example, in one major organization on the West Coast, a detailed travel cost analysis revealed that there were over ten individuals attending the same seminar in New York City (from various suborganizations of the company). That was only one incident, but the aggregate cost of other such travel, it was discovered, was in the high thousands of dollars—inadequate surveillance was the problem!

Fixed expense represents costs that are fairly predictable and constant. They involve depreciation, taxes, rent, and insurance, as shown in the lower portion of Exhibit B, and generally fall into the uncontrollable classification.

DETAILED OVERHEAD EXPENSE ACCOUNTS (WITHIN MAJOR CATEGORY)

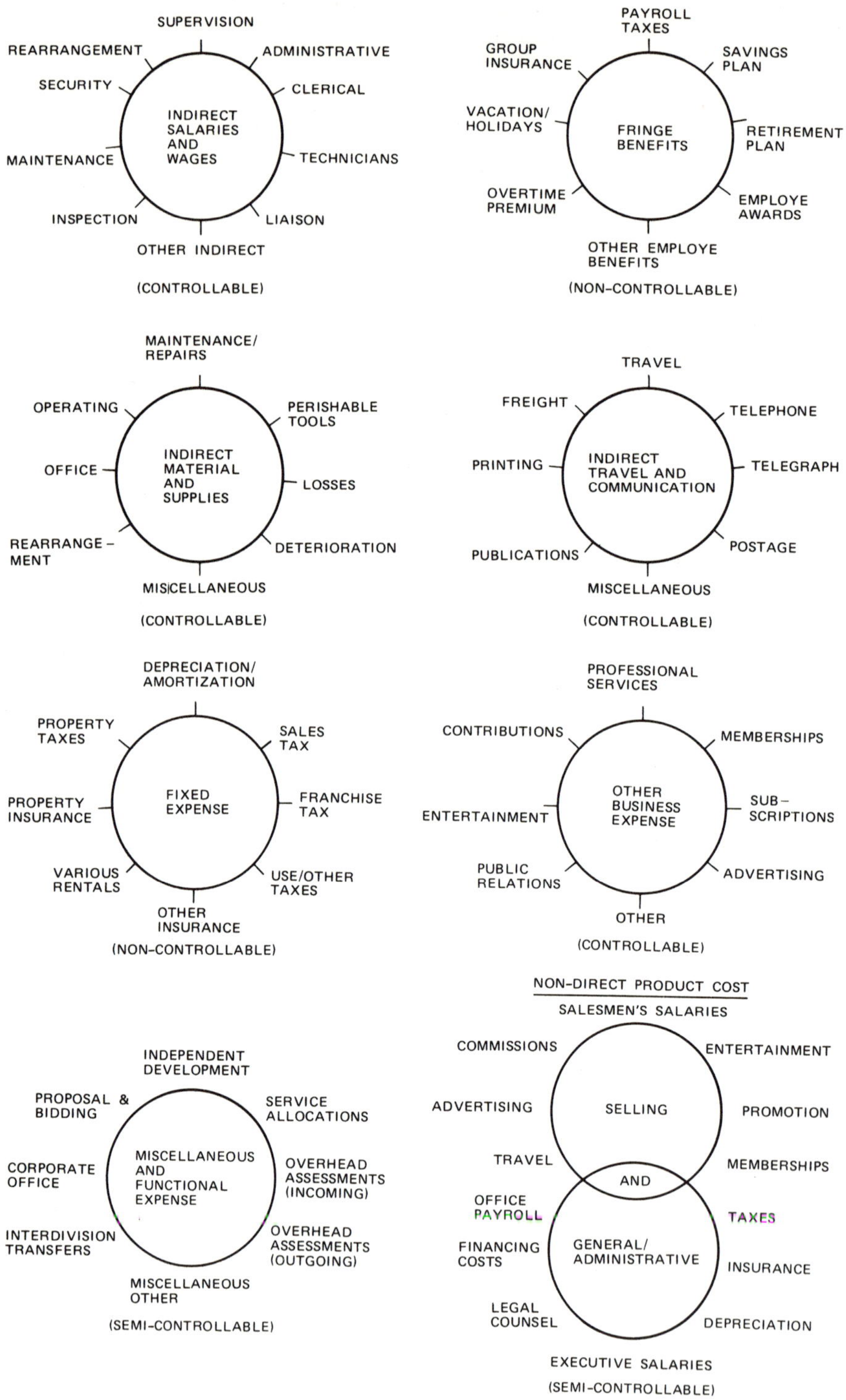

EXHIBIT B

Other business expense represents various services and miscellaneous expense as shown on the exhibit. The use of professional consultants involves outlays of thousands of dollars—many times needlessly! The exercise of appropriate management control is the only answer to significant reductions in this expense category.

Miscellaneous expense is the cost involved in interdivision transfers (pertinent to loaned employees), contract bid or proposal expense, and independent research—a catchall category. The magnitude of the expenses can be readily controlled through management discretionary decisions, particularly regarding expenditures for independent research activities.

Nonfactory Overhead

Selling expense represents the costs associated with making sales to customers. It consists of salesmen's salaries, commissions, advertising, and other related expenses, as shown on Exhibit B. This category often represents runaway expenses if management's constant vigilance is not maintained. Salesmen are generally known for their lack of or limited interest in the price paid in making a sale. They must be made accountable for the return on dollars expended to effect their sales.

General and administrative expense is cost incurred in managing and administering a business. The detailed expense accounts are noted on the above exhibit. One of the major contentions of the operating organizations is that administrative expenses are far too excessive in terms of the value of the services rendered to them. One of the prime causes can be attributed to building "people empires" to support supervisory/managerial roles and importance in the business environment. Top management's constant attention is a must to achieve conservatism in the price it pays for administration and the burden it places on the operating organization which is trying to make a profit.

OVERHEAD DATA FLOW CYCLE

An overview of expense data flow from cost incurrence to financial statement reporting is displayed on Exhibit C. The accumulation source of the expenses is represented by cash purchases, vendor credit invoices, write-off of prepaid expense (rent, taxes) as expended, accruals, and supply inventory usage. As expenses occur, recording journals are prepared to indicate charges to specific expense accounts and contra-credits to asset or liability accounts.

The data flows to the expense and general ledgers for summation and the results are reflected primarily in the income statement and balance sheet.

Cognizant management's attention to and interest in the expenses being incurred at the responsible-source spending level will lead them to question the need, and then establish the necessary corrective control measures to prevent any future indiscriminate expenditures. This action will definitely lead to attendant overhead dollar savings.

EXPENSE VARIABILITY

There are three common classifications relative to expense variability, which are identified as *wholly variable, fixed* (nonvariable), and *semi-variable*. In order to set standards

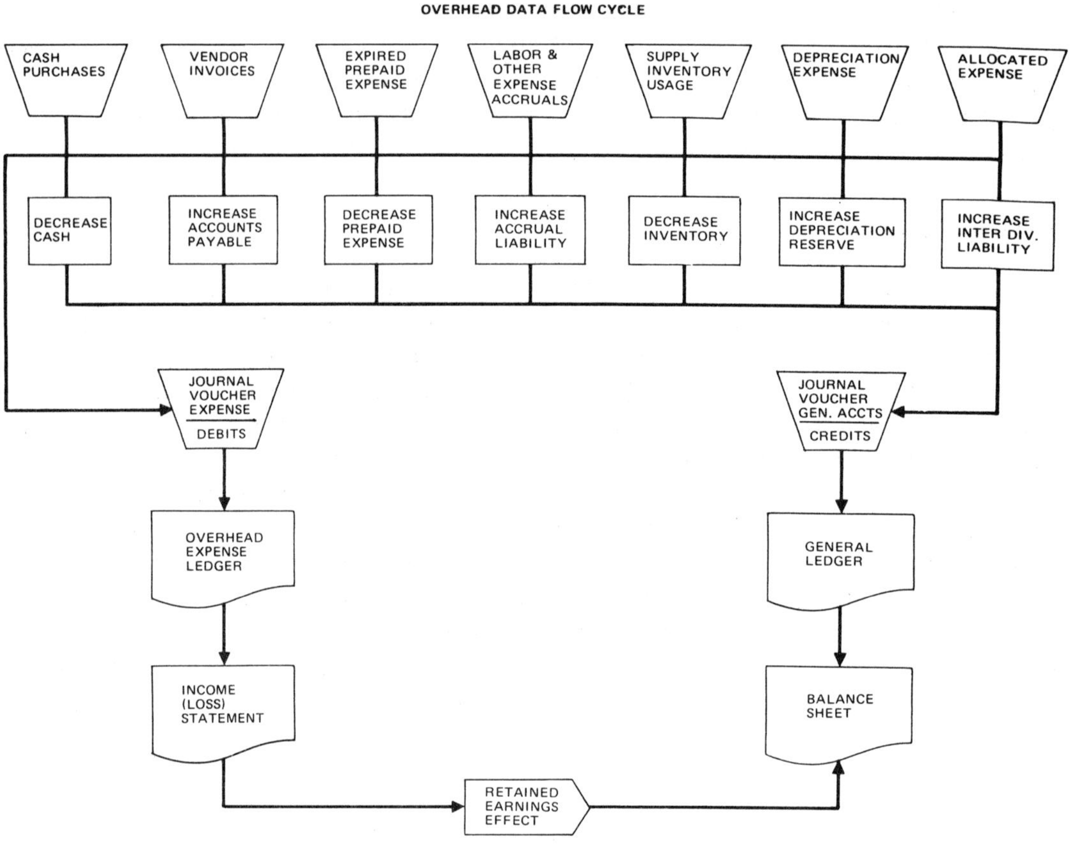

EXHIBIT C

and develop overhead budgets, expenses must be thoroughly analyzed to determine the appropriate category for each expense account. Sometimes this is a difficult segregation to make because, under certain circumstances, the classification can change due to varying operating conditions or requirements.

Wholly variable expense tends to vary directly with volume changes, generally in a straight-line relationship. If the volume doubles, then the expense doubles. There are very few expenses represented in this category but they could include such costs as power, supplies, lubricants, travel, and others associated directly with production activity and sales effort. An illustration of this expense is shown graphically on Exhibit D.

Fixed or nonvariable expense is relatively constant or stable in total regardless of production volume or other index changes such as labor activity. This expense represents a cost commitment to depreciation, supervisory salaries, rent, taxes, and the like. A graphic illustration is shown on the above exhibit.

OVERHEAD EXPENSE CLASSIFICATIONS

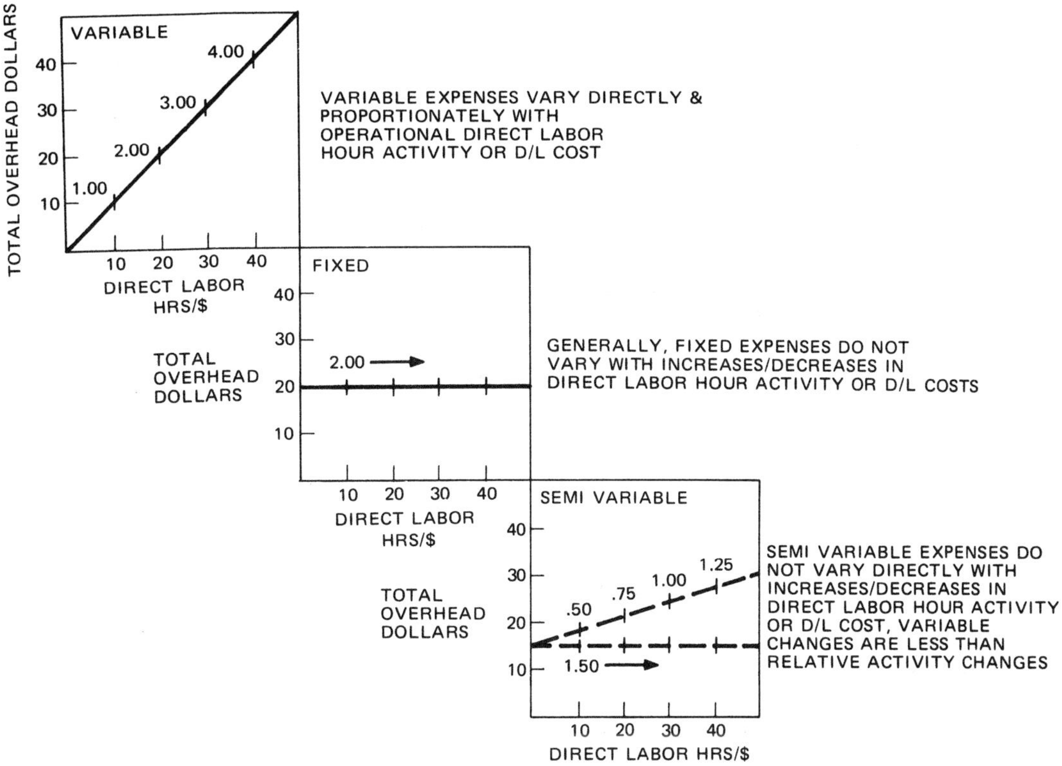

EXHIBIT D

Semi-variable expense tends to vary somewhat with changes in activity but does not vary proportionately. It represents both a partly fixed and variable expenditure combination. Supplies, indirect labor, maintenance, clerical costs, and so on are typical examples of this expense category. Exhibit D displays the fixed/variable lines.

CONTROLLABLE VERSUS NONCONTROLLABLE EXPENSES

Responsibility accounting requires that expense or cost centers be established and that each expense be classified as to whether the expense is controllable or noncontrollable. The overhead expenses incurred in a responsibility center are those associated with accomplishing the mission or tasks assigned to that organization.

The segregation of expenses provides management with a useful tool in distinguishing between those costs that can be controlled through some action on their part as opposed to those over which they have little or no influence.

The establishment of a standard cost system is a systematic means used to identify that part of an overhead expense that is controllable through supervision responsibility. Emphasis is therefore mandatory toward determining the appropriate standards so that analyses can be performed for assessing performance in each responsible center.

Controllable Expenses

A *controllable expense* is one in which a supervisor of a responsible cost center can significantly influence a cost incurrence through some action on his part. The term "significant influence" is used because rarely does any one individual have complete control over all factors that govern the magnitude of an expense incurrence. Controllable and uncontrollable expenses (although not absolute) are identified on Exhibit B.

It is noted that controllable expenses are generally not the same as fixed or variable expenses in that the fixed or variable expense changes are relative to volume or activity fluctuations and the fixed expenses have been established as a standard based on experience. Controllable expenses, however, are closely allied with semi-variable costs in that they can be influenced and controlled to a major degree. Controllable expenses would be indirect labor, business expense, and travel and communications.

Noncontrollable Expenses

Noncontrollable expenses represent the type over which there is little or no significant influence by responsible management. These expenses have generally been committed or predetermined in advance based on experience and known criteria (depreciation policy). This expense category includes rent, insurance, taxes, allocated costs, and electricity.

In some cases, uncontrollable expenses can be converted to controllable expenses by changing the emphasis of responsibility as, for example, in eliminating allocated service costs. This is accomplished by charging the organization for *only* their specific usage of services or utilities. Separate utility meters, for example, would provide exact costs for water, gas, and electricity. Changing purchasing policies may be the solution in some cases where it may be cheaper to buy various components from an outside source rather than build them inplant.

DECENTRALIZED VERSUS CENTRALIZED EXPENSE CONTROL

A recent trend to effect more responsible and efficient control over expenses is to delegate responsibility to lower levels of management (responsible centers) for making decisions relative to controllable expenses. For example, a shop foreman is in a better surveillance and judgment position to have significant influence over the use of operating supplies, overtime, idle time, and other operational expenses.

In the centralized control organization, decisions are made by the hierarchy level of management. These individuals are not directly involved in or daily exposed to direct operations and therefore are generally not in a position to know the specific problems associated with affecting cost control. Using generalized statistics to indiscriminately control expenses can only lead to problems in the production schedule, an inferior product, poor cooperation, and other operating inefficiencies.

The decentralized control system has additional advantages in that it creates better understanding on the part of lower-level management of the goals and objectives for controlling expenses. Further, it stimulates lower supervision to become personally involved in improving cost controls in a manner that will not be detrimental to his operations.

DETERMINING RATE APPLICATION PROJECTIONS

As actual indirect expenses are being incurred and recorded for entry into the expense ledger and allocation to work-in-process accounts, an equitable overhead rate must be determined in advance to apply the burden to direct labor hours as they are expended on specific jobs, products, or services. The labor index is used because it is more closely allied with overhead expenditures than any other standard criterion. Based on historical experience and analysis, an application rate is developed for this purpose (total overhead divided by direct labor hours), as noted on Exhibit A.

Since costs are collected in cost centers and summarized to department and burden centers, it is far more realistic for control purposes to apply overhead at the burden center level. The aggregate total rate may not be representative of the individual burden center operations.

A burden center is defined as an area of functional responsibility that includes in the aggregate similar associated activities and services as a collection medium for accumulating costs and controlling expenses. The administration burden center would include top management, industrial relations, controller organization, contracts, marketing, and procurement. The engineering organizations included in that burden center would be engineers, standards and calibrations, design and development, and manufacturing technology. Manufacturing would include operations and production control, production engineering, factory production, and experimental manufacturing.

The suborganizations of a department are organized as cost/expense centers. A department could have one or more cost centers depending on the nature of the tasks to be performed. In larger organizations particularly, cost centers are necessary for equitable charging of applicable costs to jobs or products and also will permit evaluation performance of individual supervisors who have been made accountable for certain costs.

Burden Center Rates

Exhibit E displays the process of developing various burden pool overhead rates for the segregated organizational operations. As noted on this exhibit, these rates are used for many purposes other than applying current application burden. The rates are used for such activities as planning, customer billings, estimating, and costing the products. For more stringent control in measuring performance, cost center and department overhead rates are considered relative to those expenses over which their supervision has cognizant influence.

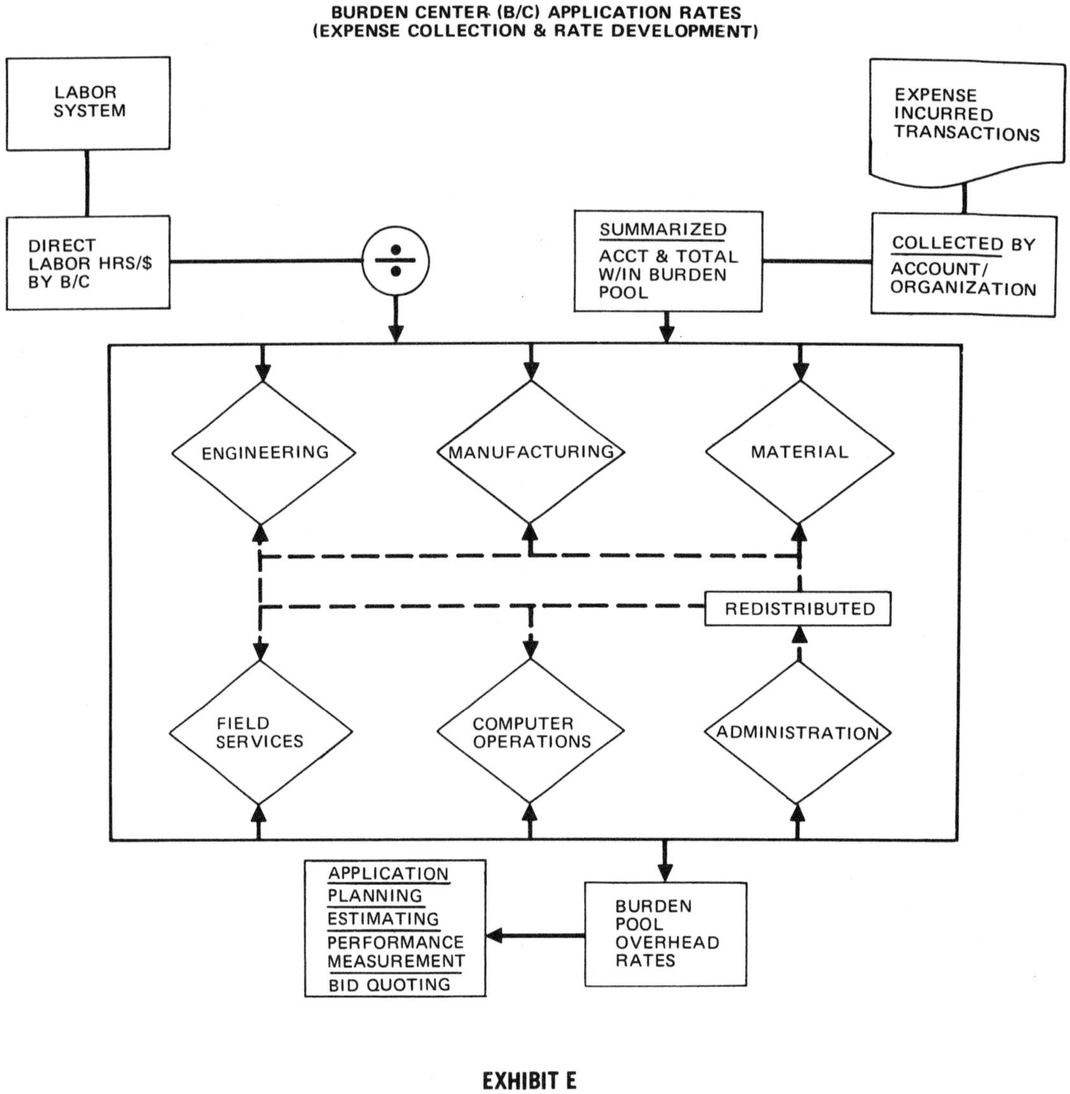

EXHIBIT E

AN OVERHEAD ANALYSIS TECHNIQUE

There are many methods that can be used in analyzing and projecting overhead rates—past experience correlations, statistical formulae plus the anticipated future plans of operation.

Scattergraphs are commonly used to establish the correlation between two statistical data series. The historical data can be plotted mathematically by using the least squares method to derive a representative trend line or by fitting the appropriate trend line by inspection. The linear equation employed is y = a + b. The "b" represents the slope of the line and "a" is the "y" intercept point. Overhead dollars (y) is the dependent variable and direct labor hours (x) represents the independent variable. This technique will reveal both the degree and type of association.

The relationship between overhead dollars and direct labor hours is illustrated on Exhibit F, which also shows the fixed rate as well as the total. The major feature of this type of analysis is that fixed and variable rates are developed separately at varying volume (labor-hour activity) levels. As noted on the exhibit, the rates decrease as volume activity increases.

For planning, pricing, and budgeting, this analysis technique is very effective in measuring actual performance. Variances can be rapidly analyzed and immediate action taken to correct problem areas or revise the criteria for future projections if the current rates are not achievable.

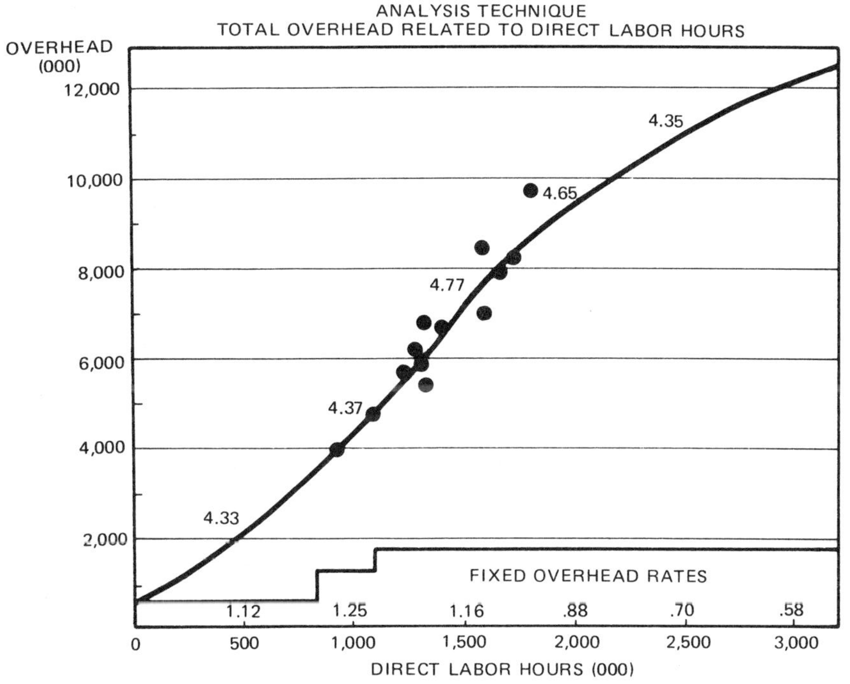

EXHIBIT F

OVERHEAD VARIANCE ANALYSIS

The difference between the applied or budgeted overhead and the actual incurred expenses represents the variance from actual. Variance analysis is initially performed at the aggregate organizational level, and then by individual expense account within cost center, department, and burden center. The differences are analyzed in depth to determine the type of variance—*volume, efficiency,* or *spending* in order that the cause and responsibility can be determined and the appropriate action taken to correct the problems.

Volume Variance

This variance results when there is an over- or underabsorption of overhead due to the labor-base activity being higher or lower than anticipated, with the resultant effect on the magnitude of the overhead dollars. Volume variances represent the criterion of whether or not the level of activity was achieved during a given period of operation.

Overhead costs vary with volume but not in the same proportion. Generally, overhead rates/hour are *higher* at *low* volumes of activity versus being *lower* at *high* levels of activity (note Exhibit F). This is due to the fact that even at low levels of activity, an organization is still incurring fixed as well as a certain amount of necessary variable costs such as maintenance supplies.

In many instances, the supervisor is responsible for variances (volume) because of his failure to obtain the anticipated standard volume due to his inability to keep products moving through his department as originally planned. This situation could result from excessive idle time, spoilage, or poor planning. On the other hand, the activity changes may have been due to the inability of the sales force to achieve their sales quotas.

Efficiency Variance

This variance represents the difference between the overhead budget dollars *projected* for a certain level of activity and the overhead budget *allowed* for the actual activity in terms of direct labor hours. This is often due to poor planning and projection of unachievable overhead goals.

Spending Variance

This variance represents the difference between budgeted overhead and actual expenses. Generally, the supervisor is responsible for spending variances, but there could very well be extenuating circumstances over which he may not have had any control such as excessive repair and maintenance on equipment due to its age or obsolescence.

Computing Overhead Variances

Exhibit G illustrates the procedure used in computing the various types of overhead variances. A description of the computation process follows.

The *favorable volume variance* of $100 is due to the actual activity being less than standard. The 900 standard hours multiplied by the standard overhead rate of $1.00/hour equals $900. The value of $900 less the actual hours at standard rate of $1.00/hour, or $800, results in $100 of favorable volume achievement. This situation could have resulted from efficiencies in operation due to operator training, new or improved equipment, production bonus incentive plan, or new innovations in operating procedures.

The *efficiency variance* is calculated by subtracting the budget allowed for the actual hours of activity of $840 ($950 ÷ 900 hours equals $1.05 × 800 hours) from the standard budget actual hours (800) × $1.00 standard rate/hour, or $800, which results in an unfavorable variance of $40. Variances of this type are attributed to standard activity hours being set

COMPARISON OF ACTUAL & BUDGETED HOURS
VARIANCE ANAYSIS

PERTINENT DATA

ACTIVITY HOURS WORKED	STANDARD ACTIVITY HOURS	STANDARD HOURS PRODUCED	STANDARD OVERHEAD RATE
800	1000	900	$1/HR

CONTROLLABLE OVERHEAD	BUDGET - FOR 900 HRS	ACTUAL-HOURS 800	CONTROLLABLE VARIANCE
SUPERVISORY SALARIES	$ 300	$ 300	$–
INDIRECT LABOR	200	230	(30)
SUPPLIES	150	180	(30)
OTHER BUSINESS EXPENSE	100	80	20
TRAVEL/COMMO	100	120	(20)
S/TOTAL	$ 850	$ 910	$ (60)
NON-CONTROLLABLE OVERHEAD			
DEPRECIATION	$50	$50	–
TAXES	30	30	–
INSURANCE	20	20	–
S/ TOTAL	$100	$100	$(60)
TOTAL OVERHEAD	$950	$1010	$(60)
OVERHEAD APPLIED 900 HRS X $1		900	
TOTAL OVERHEAD VARIANCE		$110	

VARIANCES

VOLUME	(900–800)	=	100	FAVORABLE
EFFICIENCY	(800–840)	=	(40)	UNFAVORABLE
SPENDING	(840–1010)	=	(170)	UNFAVORABLE

EXHIBIT G

too high thus the higher budget dollars; or the actual hours worked were far less than anticipated for the reasons explained above under the efficiency variance.

The *spending variance*, as shown on Exhibit G, is calculated by subtracting the total overhead actual of $1,010 from the budget allowed for the standard hours of $840 (above calculation). The result of this calculation is an unfavorable variance of $170. Since the actual expenditures exceeded the budget allowance, it can only be assumed that the budget was set too low or there were inefficiencies in operations, poor planning, or supervision apathy.

It is noted that the total unfavorable variance of $210 ($40 plus $170) less the favorable variance of $100 results in a net unfavorable variance of $110.

Major Causes for Variances

There are many conditions that can contribute to overhead variances, as noted below:

Volume	Efficiency	Spending
Differences in number of calendar days in month	Poor or no instructions to employee	Overbuying
Decrease in sales volume	Excessive idle time	Price changes
Excessive facility space	Poor labor performance	Changes in operations
Labor activity increases/ decreases	Excessive material spoilage	Improper material usage

Variance Control Responsibility

The responsibility for monitoring and controlling overhead expenditures, in terms of standards and budget limits, lies with the individuals who are assigned the authority to control spending. Controlling overhead is also largely dependent on the setting of realistic standards that are achievable and, further, close adherence to spending limitations.

Volume variance responsibility is often difficult to place because it may involve a number of individuals within a given organization. A thorough study of why and where the variances are occurring should result in alleviating this problem. Some volume variances cannot be controlled because of external conditions such as decreased customer demand for a product or service.

Efficiency variance responsibility is fairly simple to determine since the individual in control (supervisor or foreman) is the one charged with maintaining an efficient operation and should establish the appropriate controls at the problem source.

Since variances occur due to a variety of causes, it is imperative that they be isolated in their component parts for intense analysis.

OVER/UNDERABSORBED VARIANCES

It is not possible to predict an application or projected rate that will coincide exactly to the actual expense results from operations; therefore, a variance will generally occur.

Overabsorbed Variance

If the applied overhead is less than the actual expense incurred, then the condition is described as "overabsorbed," and the variance is commonly recorded as a deferred credit on the liability side of the balance sheet.

Underabsorbed Variance

If the applied overhead is less than the actual expense, the result is described as *underabsorbed or unabsorbed* overhead, and the variance is recorded as a deferred charge on the asset side of the balance sheet.

Disposal of the Variance

The over- or underabsorbed variance is generally charged or credited against the period by an adjustment to the cost of sales (overhead element of cost) account. Another method would be to apportion the difference to various inventory accounts or, if it is a minor amount, keep it in your records until such a time that it becomes a major amount for write-off. It could be that future periods would offset the amount.

PROJECTION OF CATEGORY GROUP EXPENSES

Based on a thorough analysis of group expenses over a period of three or more representative years, a computerized forecast model can be developed. The model would provide the means to predict future overhead costs. The *analysis technique*, previously discussed, would be the initial step in developing the model. This process involves the determination of trend lines and formulae through the use of a bivariate data (overhead and labor) as illustrated on Exhibit H. After the formulae are developed and tested for the various expense groups, they are applied to the independent variables to obtain the overhead projections.

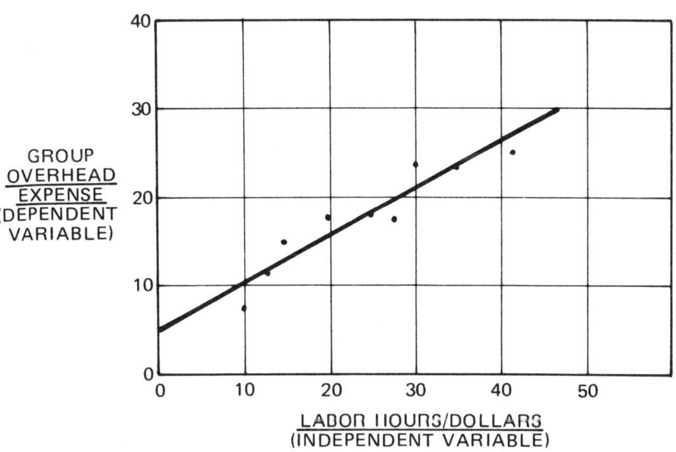

EXHIBIT H

The Projection Model

Exhibit I displays an effective projection model that can generally be used by most organizations in some relative degree. Correlations and other relative criteria are needed in making future predictions. As you will note on the exhibit and the discussion following, the procedure involved is described.

Indirect Labor

Using a projected manpower level by type of employee, the headcount is then converted into indirect labor hours (hours per period × manpower). Average wage rates by job application are applied to the hours to obtain indirect labor dollars. An excellent correlation formula for obtaining indirect manpower projections is their relationship to direct headcount, which is more realistically stable and predictable.

Fringe Benefits

These expenses are derived by multiplying total manpower (direct and indirect) by the correlation formula represented by "B1" on the exhibit. Holidays and vacations are projected separately because they can be known fairly specifically.

Supplies/Expensed Material

Direct labor hour or dollar relationship is used in projecting this expense group. This is represented on the exhibit as "B2."

Travel/Communication

This expense group is projected on the basis of total headcount relationship to historical data and is represented on the exhibit as "B3."

Other Business Expense

Total manpower projections are to establish the relationship with this expense which is represented on the exhibit as "B4." This is a reliable correlation.

Fixed Expense

This type of expense can be predicted very accurately based on past experience and known future events in terms of expense commitments.

DETAILED EXPENSE ACCOUNT PROJECTIONS

Using the correlation technique described above, the individual expense accounts (shown on Exhibit B) can also be accurately predicted providing the appropriate independent

OVERHEAD FORECAST DEVELOPMENT
Projection Model

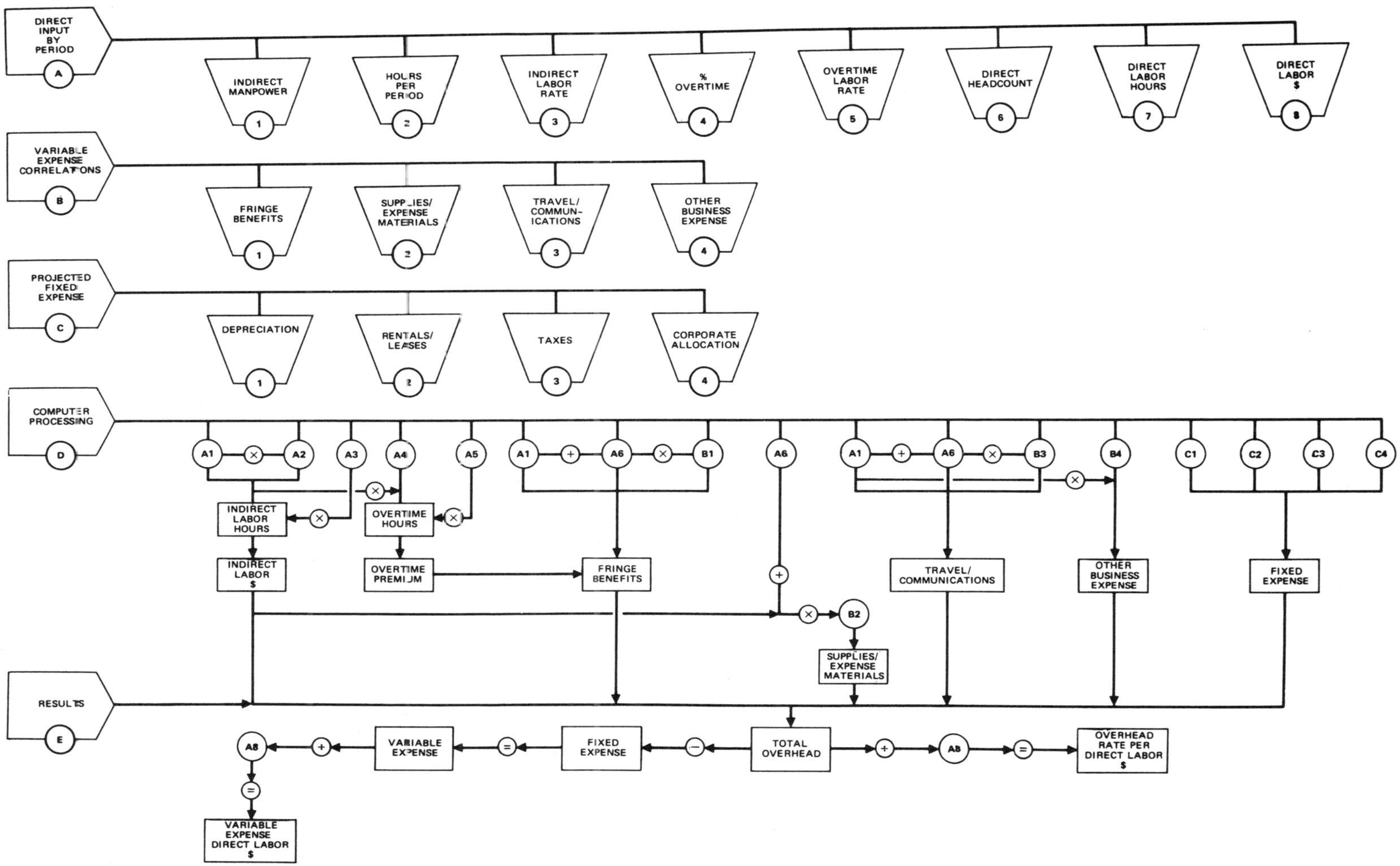

EXHIBIT I

variable is used in establishing the relationship. To do this effectively, a series of alternative tests should be made that will reveal the most reliable independent variable to be used.

This testing process can be performed mechanically since it is a common computer program. The results can be further expressed as to the degree of relationship between the two variables by determining the coefficient of determination and correlation (the square root of ''determination'').

ESTABLISHING EXPENSE CONTROLS

There are a number of approaches that can be used to effectively control overhead expenses. The main requirement is management's will and determination to provide the proper guidance in establishing controls and then taking the appropriate actions when there are deviations from their established plans.

- Determine what expenses are controllable versus those that are noncontrollable through a detailed study of historical data. Segregate the expenses as to their variability in order to establish the focal control points of responsibility.
- Assign specific responsibility for maintaining constant surveillance to individuals who have been given the authority to control.
- Budget at the detailed expense account level in order to achieve the most effective analysis of variances.
- Establish an effective system for collecting data and reporting on actual performance results on a timely basis at the end of each operational period.
- Provide reports at the lowest level of the organization so that the responsible individuals will be aware of *all* variances that affect their operations.
- Require responsible organizations to report monthly to the appropriate management the causes for the variances and their plan for corrective action. A follow-up should be performed.
- Establish a flexible budget system in those instances where there are extreme fluctuations in activity volume. This tool is predicated on volume changes and establishment of standards at various levels of activity.
- Use correlation studies and other statistical techniques in analyzing expenses and their relationship behavior under varying conditions.
- Consider computerization for expense processing and projections. The concentration of manpower utilization should always be on the analysis of overhead behavior and direction rather than the clerical aspect of compiling data and the recording variances. Then, too, mechanization lends itself readily to playing the ''what if'' game under varying operating conditions.

OVERHEAD BUDGETING AS A CONTROL VEHICLE

The overhead budget serves as a very useful means to control overhead. The following points represent the major advantages of a budget control process:

Clearly defines spending objectives
Establishes expense goals at varying levels of activity

Reveals weaknesses in personnel, supervision, and operational performance
Reflects management's policy for future operations
Provides a means and incentive for effective and efficient operations
Deviations from the budget provide an insight to problem areas
Represents a tool for measuring budget versus actual performance

In summary, overhead expense is a major criterion in the establishment of a competitive and profitable product/service price. With proper planning, appropriate attention, and adherence to the governing rules of control, any organization can save *thousands of dollars* of overhead expenditures, which may mean the difference between profitable growth and survival or losses and eventual dissolution.

7

Computerizing Sales Forecasting for Dramatic Payoff

The management planning process establishes the significant guidelines for the future operating environment. No organization, large or small, can successfully operate in the competitive business climate without a realistic operating plan to govern the directional and operational course of action in achieving progress and profitability relative to projected goals and objectives. One of the basic preliminary forecast developments required for the income statement is sales, which, in turn, provides the major input for the projection of cash flow, balance sheet, investment status, and other subsidiary financial schedules.

INFLUENCING FACTORS IN SALES PROJECTIONS

The sales forecast, involving products or services, is predicated on a number of basic economic internal and external parameters, somewhat controllable and noncontrollable, that can affect the validity and/or achievement of sales projections. The most general influencing considerations are noted as follows, some of which may not be applicable to all organizations.

- Verification of current backlog on hand and determination of its validity.
- Competitive status of product/service price and quality.
- Resolution of future customer demands/needs for specific product/services.
- Determination of potential of new developments.
- Availability of skilled technical competency in product development.
- Resolution of sales and profitability of appropriate product mix projections.
- Capabilities of marketing organization to achieve sales objectives.
- Assessment of competitors' future strategy as to price, quality, and new developments.

- Availability of production facilities and manpower to accommodate projected sales volume.
- Evaluation of similar industry trends associated with organization projections.
- Business economic outlook and its possible effect on the organization's operations.
- Trend of the gross national product (GNP).
- Sufficient working capital to maintain growth.
- Organization policies and procedures limitations.
- Government budget and funding limitations.
- An organization's growth/decline trends.

Each of the above factors has its unique role in affecting sales projections of a given organization. Only through thorough analysis and study can it be determined where emphasis should be placed on those factors that can have a decided effect on resolving an organization's sales projection validity.

AN OVERVIEW OF PLANNING REQUIREMENTS

Sales forecasting is primarily based on an organization's overall planned goals and objectives. The organizational plan must be translated into representative dollar values that will reflect successful growth potential as well as profitability. The forecasting process utilizes the application of evaluation and judgment to known facts and conditions to estimate probable eventualities. The planning cycle represents a rational and realistic approach to forecasting future operations. It must minimize the effect of internal and external forces resulting from business complexities due to competition, technological advancements, government legislation, and other future economic uncertainties.

The complete sales and income forecast cycle involves input from various organizations based on management direction. The concerned criteria involved are discussed below.

Sales Forecasts

Generally, the marketing organization is responsible for the future prediction of the sales outlook. They base their planning on past experience trends, anticipated customer needs, economic conditions, market intelligence, new product developments, current undelivered commitments, and various statistical techniques. Their projections are in terms of units of sales (required for inventory and production planning) and product mix associated with contracts, sales orders, and customers. Units must be translated into dollar values. Projections for services (research and development, consulting) are in terms of level of effort (hours expenditure), which is converted to dollars.

Sales projections are segregated as to the type of known or anticipated commitment —cost plus fixed fee, fixed-price contracts and incentives, commercial, time and material. This is very important as each type of sales agreement has its own peculiar characteristics in the detailed data development process. For example, cost-plus contracts involve a projection of costs with fee application to obtain sales. Fixed-price contract sales are negotiated with a projected fee rate and total costs are derived by dividing sales by 100% plus the fee percentage. Commercial sales are predicated on priced product delivery units (includes profit margin) or priced services to be rendered.

Production/Inventory Planning

The sales projections are disseminated to various concerned organizations for their planning and development input to the overall operating plan. The Production organization must dissect the sales plan in detail to determine what should be produced in terms of type and quantity of parts, subassemblies and assemblies, to meet sales objectives. An assessment must be made as to production capacity and ability to meet the time schedule of delivery and/or effort performance.

Decisions are required for manpower and skill needs. Labor utilization and material requirements must be scheduled. Machinery and equipment needs must be evaluated. Indirect support (manpower, supplies) must be projected. Work-in-process and finished-product inventory balances must be analyzed to determine the actual production requirements for the projected time periods. Consideration must be given to scheduling even workloads that lend themselves to maximum efficiency in utilizing manpower resources, equipment, and material. Also, this procedure provides for a predictable, steady flow of production results.

Grass Roots Involvement

At the cost center and department levels, direct and indirect manpower needs must be projected and priced by period based on the number and type of personnel translated into hours (work hour factor × manpower × rate per hour). Certain controllable overhead expenses must be determined for the projection, such as utilities expense, operating supplies, maintenance, repairs, overtime, and scrap losses. Input from operating organizations is based on the anticipated level of effort required to achieve the production goals.

Material Planning Function

This group is concerned with the direct material budget and requisitioning process. Unit part production needs are converted into raw material components based on the production budget. Inventories are evaluated to determine the material purchase requirements, which are based on multiplying the number of pieces in each part by the appropriate measure of length, size, weight, and/or type of each material required. This can be in the form of raw materials, parts, assemblies, and the like. Average length of the production cycle must be considered in scheduling material purchase receipts. Consideration must be given to storage capacity and the maintenance of inventory levels at a minimum to preclude increased investment, property taxes, insurance, obsolescence, and handling costs. Then, too, there are possibilities of product changes requiring different needs.

Financial Budget Group's Contribution

This function is concerned with providing the operating organizations with the basic ground rules for their budget preparation. They project and disseminate work hour factors, wage rates, time periods involved with the number of workdays per period, and other pertinent statistics.

They are also concerned with the development of gross margin, capital expenditures, depreciation, overhead rate development, cash flow requirements, and product mix profitability. Further, they assemble the projected data submitted by the other organizations, summarize it, and analyze the results in terms of meeting management's aggregate planned objectives. Budget change requirements are negotiated with the submitting organizations when and as necessary. Various schedules are prepared for management review and approval.

In summary, therefore, it is obvious that the sales forecast triggers a series of events that affect all organizations in the development of the financial operating plan. Sales projections (based on reasonable costs and profits) and their achievement are the backbone of an organization's potential growth, profitability, and successful operation.

COMPUTERIZATION OF SALES PLANNING

Computerizing the development of a cost and sales model can be highly rewarding, particularly in those organizations having a significant volume of information to develop and report. The model can be ultrasophisticated or relatively simple, whichever is appropriate to meet the needs of an organization. Its major attributes are that it is a dynamic tool for planning operations, developing related data for other financial schedules, testing alternate courses of action, and providing rapid performance reporting that results from plan versus actuals comparison. It is a rapid means of accessing file data and making changes with immediate results.

Program Logic Statements

In the mechanical process when the system needs have been resolved, there are certain logic statements that have to be formulated for data processing. Each data statement must contain the following information in the teleprocessing operation.

- Line Number Reference—Signifies the location and manipulation of specific data in the file records.
- Data Description—Describes the data name in the file records, such as unit quantity, sales price.
- Operation to Be Performed—An identifier indicates the type of function to be performed—add, subtract, divide, compare.
- Print Instruction—Indicates whether the data in the files will be required as a printout report.
- Line and/or Column Totals—Specifies whether certain totalling will be required—line totals across time period, column totals, or no totals as in the case of balances (balance sheet).

An example of the instructions described above is as follows:

<u>37</u> <u>Gross Profit Dollars,</u> <u>3</u>, <u>1</u>, <u>1</u>, <u>1</u>, <u>21</u>, <u>24</u>

The above statement says that in order to obtain gross profit dollars located on line <u>37</u>, multiply function <u>(3)</u> lines <u>21</u> (gross profit percentage) by <u>24</u> (sales dollars). Print <u>(1)</u> data, line <u>(1)</u> total, and include in column <u>(1)</u> total. It is noted that line numbers 37, 21 and 24 above were assigned in the actual program logic; they would be different among organizations depending on program logic construction.

Sales Projection Data Identifiers

Certain predetermined and assigned identifiers are also required for each contract/sales order in order to achieve various types of data sorting and summations within the computer. The identifications are dependent on the expressed needs of an organization and are highly abbreviated to reduce detailed input each time. Typical examples of symbols used for association to specific file records/description are illustrated:

- "PL"—designates product line; "PLA"—product line A; "PLB"—product line B.
- Contract/Sales Order Code—four-digit numerical number (could be alphabetical). The number is associated to the actual contract number.
- Contract/Sales Order Status—"F" for firm business; "P" for potential.
- Contract/Sales Order Type—"C" for cost-type contracts; "F" for fixed price; "O" for commercial.
- Customer Type—"M" for military; "C" for commercial; "F" for Foreign.

An example of the input message is: <u>PLA 1212 F C M</u>. Reference to the above will indicate message interpretation. Data sorts are performed by categories shown above. The processes in the computerized models to manipulate the data will be discussed below.

COST-TYPE CONTRACT SALES MODEL

A mechanical cost-type contract model is displayed on Exhibit A. As discussed above, sales data development interfaces with many other aspects of the overall operating plan projections. This type of contract is negotiated on the basis of level of effort in terms of cost plus fixed fee. It can also include incentive provisions. The two sources of input shown at the top of the exhibit involve the reference to the data record file and direct input via the terminal device.

Sales Development

From mechanical subsidiary system developments, the direct elements of cost (labor, overhead, and material) are extracted and summarized, by contract initially, and represent contract *cost of sales*.

G & A (general and administrative) expense factor is applied to direct labor dollars to obtain G & A expense, which is added to the cost of sales to obtain total costs. A fee rate is applied to the total costs to derive the fee dollars by each individual contract since the fee rate generally is different for each contract.

The projected disallowance rate (based on historical experience) is applied to the direct labor hours to obtain the disallowance dollars (certain expenses are unallowable—wholly or in part—such as entertainment or advertising). The projected fee dollars is reduced by the anticipated disallowances to derive the adjusted fees, which, when added to the total costs, represent the sales projections.

CPFF COST AND SALES FLOW
PROJECTION MODEL

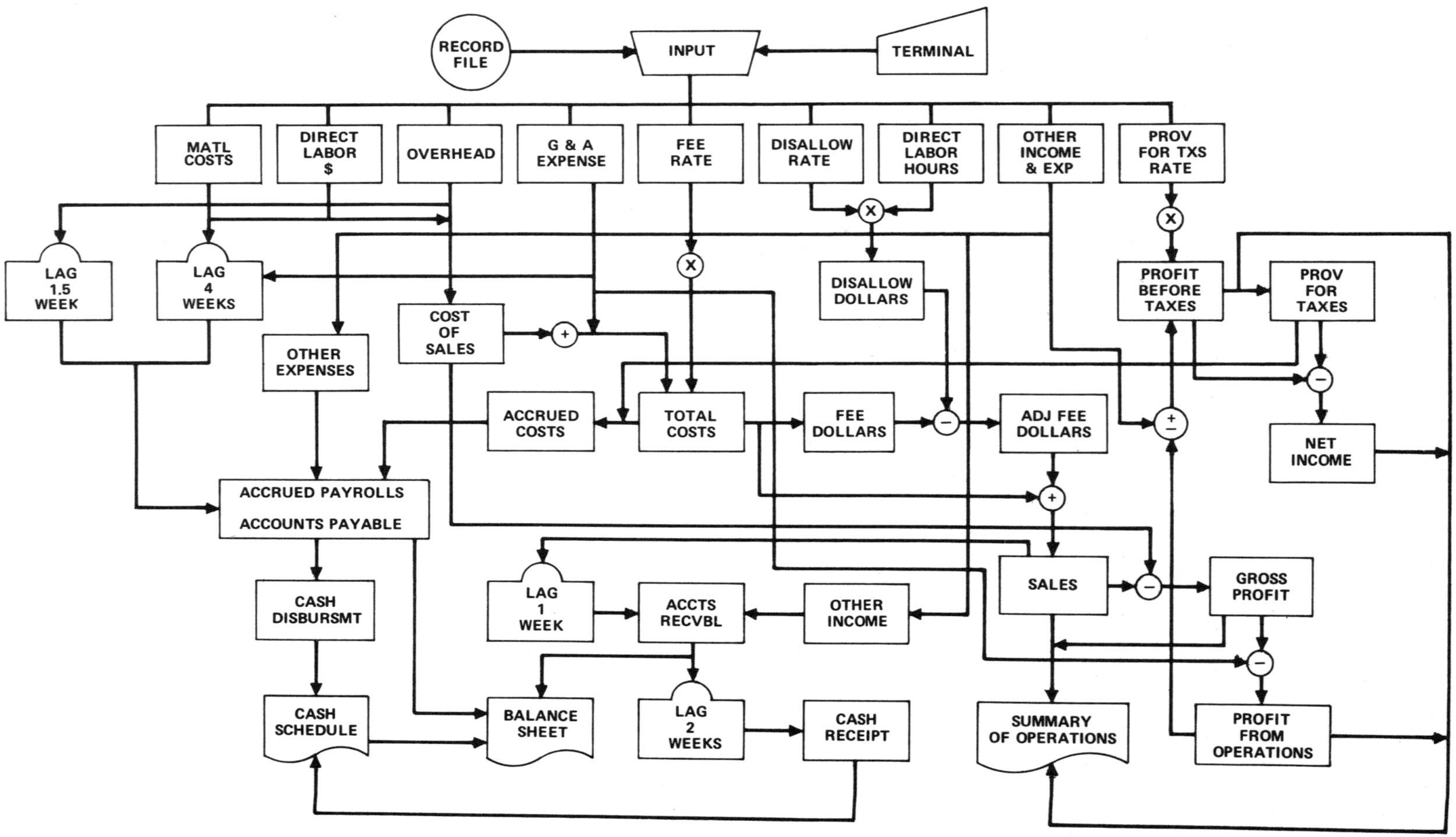

EXHIBIT A

The organizational summary would be the consolidation of the above developed contract data. Subsequent data for the income statement is developed after the contract consolidation process above.

Income Projections

The difference between sales and cost of sales represents gross profit. G & A expense is subtracted from the gross profit to derive profit from operations. Other income (royalties, etc.) and deductions (loss on sale of fixed assets, interest expense, etc.) are netted against profit from operations to obtain pretax profit. An inputted tax rate is applied to pretax profit to obtain the provision for income taxes and its deduction from pretax profit results in net income.

Data Reflection on the Balance Sheet

Accrued but unpaid direct and indirect labor costs represent accrued salaries and wages on the liability side of the balance sheet. Direct material costs, overhead, and other committed expenses are classified as accounts payable liabilities. Sales and other income projections are represented as assets on the balance sheet until they are liquidated through cash receipts.

Effect on Cash Flow

After applying a lag-time factor based on past experience, accrued payroll (1.5 weeks from cost incurrence to payment) is paid and thus becomes a cash disbursement. Accounts payable is lagged four to five weeks before the cash disbursement is made. Accounts receivable and other income is lagged anywhere from two to six weeks (depending on type of business and customer negotiations) before a projected cash receipt is achieved. It is noted that these effects on the balance sheet and cash flow are only those resulting from the income statement. Other input into those schedules are derived from other sources such as the capital expenditure budget, borrowings, or investments.

FIXED-PRICE CONTRACT MODEL

A fixed-price contract is negotiated on the basis of total sales price and/or in units with a price per unit. The price includes the gross margin. The contract may also contain incentive provisions that could increase profit based on certain negotiated performance criteria such as accelerated development and/or deliveries, improved efficiencies in operation, or advanced product quality and enhancements. It is noted that the sales price is predicated on projected cost detail estimates and profit margin.

Generally, fixed-price contract data is more complicated to project than cost-type data because they involve progress payments, greater susceptibility to funding limitations, inventory status, liquidation of holdback computations, and final payment is withheld until depot deliveries are made. Further, if the negotiated costs are exceeded, the resulting difference has to be absorbed from profits.

Sales and Total Product Cost Development

Having a projected and negotiated delivery schedule, fixed-price sales are obtained by multiplying units of delivery by price per unit. Adding 100% to the anticipated fee rate and dividing this value into the sales price results in total product costs.

Period Cost Determination

Period costs are representative of those expenses that will be absorbed in a given period. They include general and administrative expense (G & A), research and development, proposal and bidding expense, and corporate office allocations. A developed application rate is applied to direct labor dollars to obtain period costs.

Cost of Sales and Profit Forecast

Period costs are deducted from total costs to derive cost of sales. In order to determine the composition of the elements of cost in the cost of sales, correlation formulae are used in satellite systems to predict direct labor and overhead dollars (these costs are more readily predictable than material costs due to the timing in material receipts and probable price differentials). Reducing cost of sales by direct labor and overhead, the material dollar forecast is obtained. It is noted, however, that the Inventory Planning and Control Group has also developed material projections in great detail; these values are compared to the values above and the actual forecast in the operating plan is resolved. Based on past experience (if not provided by the Planning Group), fairly reliable factors can be developed to ascertain and segregate other direct costs and subcontract costs from the total material costs. All of this information is required in reconciling the detailed actuals to the planned projections.

Therefore, sales less cost of sales will result in the projected gross profit. Sales less total costs (includes period costs) will provide profit from operations. Profit from operations can also be derived by deducting period costs from gross profit. The balance of the calculations is similar to those described for cost-type contracts for use in the income statement. The effects on the cash flow schedule are more complicated due to progress payments and other factors and are described in detail in chapter 8.

COMMERCIAL PRODUCT PROJECTION MODEL

Many of the features discussed for the cost-type and fixed-price projection models can be utilized for commercial product sales as well. The factors influencing sales projections are similar to those discussed at the beginning of this chapter.

Product Pricing

The component parts of a commercial product are assessed in terms of labor effort involved to perform the tasks required for producing the "bits and pieces" for a finished part required to complete the product entity. Material costs must be calculated and projected into the future based on anticipated prices for raw materials or components. Indirect support costs must be evaluated and projected over specified time periods. Unlike government business, selling and advertising expenses are a major contribution to the cost of doing business.

Unit costs can be projected based on standard and/or historical actual costs. In many commercial organizations, the cost of sales can be readily projected by applying a percentage to the sales price based on historical experience and adjusting for known or anticipated differences between the past period results and the future period expectations.

Sales Projections

As discussed earlier in the chapter, products are segregated into product lines, firm or potential, and customer. Salesmen and territories are important considerations in performance and sales projections and are associated to quota goals for each hierarchy of sales management. There is generally more leeway in adjusting sales price to achieve certain objectives as compared to firm negotiated contract prices in government business.

The salesman is very often called upon to submit future sales estimates for his territory since he is closest to the anticipated customer needs; however, inherent salesman optimism must be tempered by management judgment and experience because of the latter's optimistic overview perspective.

TECHNIQUE OF SIMULATION MODELING

An integral part of a computerized financial forecast model should encompass a mechanical simulation capability interface so that various decision-making alternatives can be tested to determine their impact on various aspects of the operating plan objectives. A properly constructed simulation model affords a number of distinct advantages that could mean the difference between a very aggressive and progressive climate as opposed to one of latent and mediocre performance. Its major attributes are highlighted as follows:

- Reflects changing operating/economic conditions and/or business climate through rapid and selective input and other manipulation of data.
- Provides advanced warning of future possible eventualities resulting from new findings or market intelligence that could affect future operations and performance.
- Permits timely decision-making and action to lessen and/or avert anticipated adverse operating events through changes in the original operating plan direction.
- Significantly reduces clerical effort to effect changes on a more responsive time schedule.

The significance of the simulation technique approach is that it is an artificial, symbolic model paralleling the actual projected derivation of data that signifies the performance and planning of an organization's operations. The model is developed by using basic logic formulae as the basis for measuring performance in the actual or planned environment. Some common and universally used formula examples would include the following for operation assessment:

- *Operation Efficiency*—measured by the return on sales, which is calculated by dividing net income by sales.

- *Investment Utilization*—provided by return on investment, which is developed by dividing annualized net income by the average investment.
- *Management Efficiency*—represented by capital turnover, which is derived by dividing sales by assets employed.
- *Liquidity Status*—measured by the ratio of current assets to current liabilities.

Undelivered Sales Commitment Simulation

An illustrative example of the use of the simulation process is reflected on Exhibit B. It displays what happens to the business backlog status as new orders are received and customer deliveries are made or performance accomplished. A description of the processes involved follow:

- As new customer commitments in the form of contracts and sales orders are received, they are inputted into this mechanical satellite system.
- In the history file, there is maintained the prior period's sales, new business, and backlog data. The new orders received above are added to the prior period's commitment total.
- As current deliveries/performance are accomplished, the values are invoiced to the customer and represent sales. The sales are reflected in the income statement and also entered as receivables.
- The history file is adjusted to reflect the new input. The computer generates a new backlog (undelivered sales) balance by adding the prior period's ending backlog balance to the combined orders booked and subtracting the sales to obtain the ending backlog balance.
- The results developed above are compared to the budget plan for each of the data items (sales, new business, and backlog) and variances are computed. If the differences are major, corrective action is initiated to determine the cause.

Simulation models are effective planning and decision-making tools. They provide an ideal means to finalize (in a controlled environment) an appropriate operating plan without the costly experimentation of actual action implementation before the fact.

STATISTICAL TECHNIQUES FOR PROJECTING SALES

There are various statistical techniques employed in sales forecasting. Some may be relevant to some organizations but not appropriate to others. Experimentation with and analysis of historical data should reveal those that are pertinent to an organization and/or specific industry. A few of the more common methods will be discussed briefly (since they have been described in other chapters of this book). These techniques are concerned with trends, least squares, and correlations.

Historical Trends

Based on historical data, trend lines are plotted over a period of time, either on a monthly or cumulative basis, to indicate the direction, growth, or decline of the sales volume (units or dollars). Exhibit C illustrates the plotting of cumulative data for twenty-seven time periods. Although data other than sales is reflected on this exhibit (work-in-process costs,

SIMULATION MODEL

Undelivered Sales Commitments—Product or Service

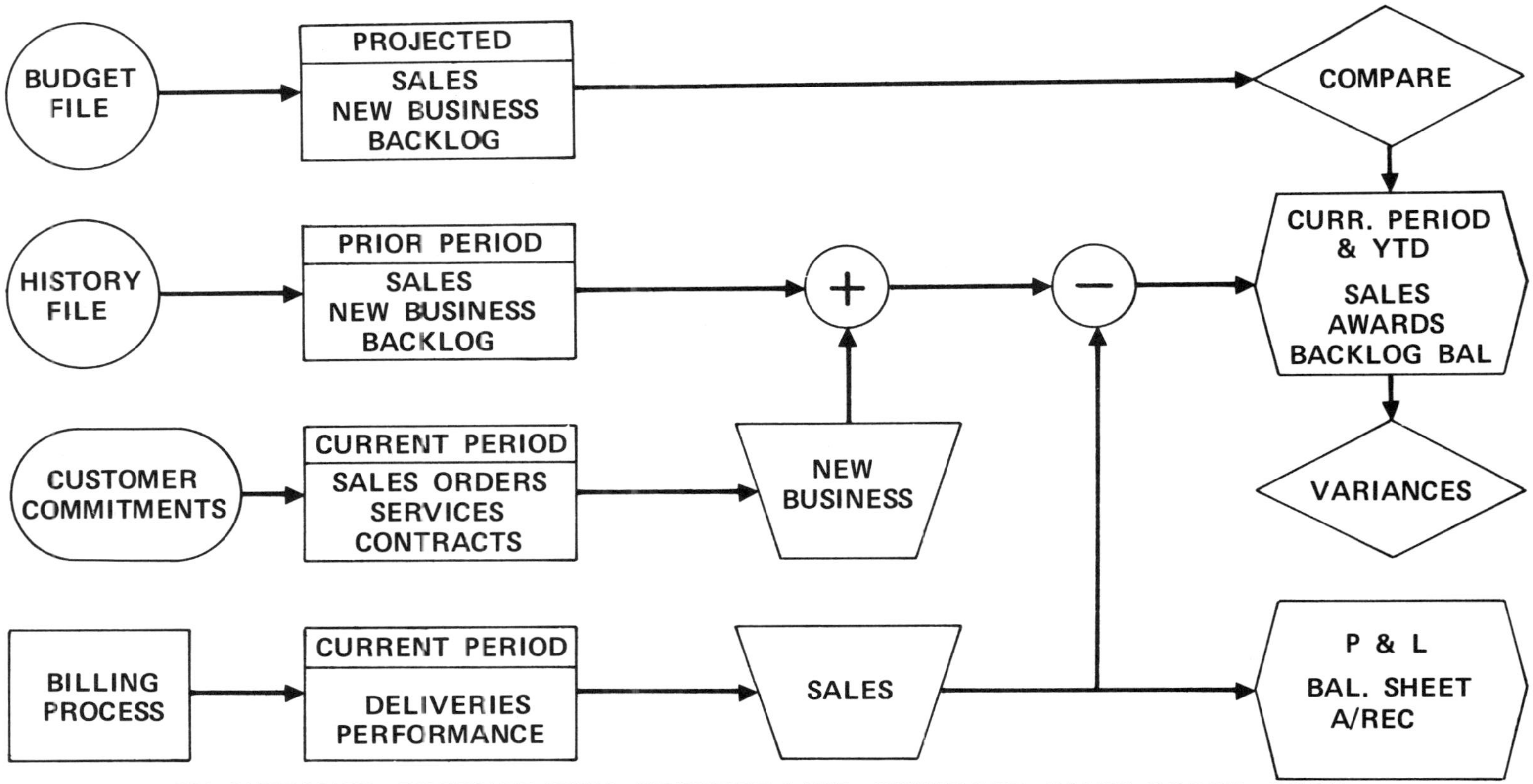

BY CUSTOMER, PRODUCT ITEM, PRODUCT LINE, CONTRACT, SALES ORDER, ORGN., CONTRACT TYPE

EXHIBIT B

CUMMED SUMMARY OF SALES, WIP COSTS, COLLECTIONS FIXED PRICE CONTRACTS

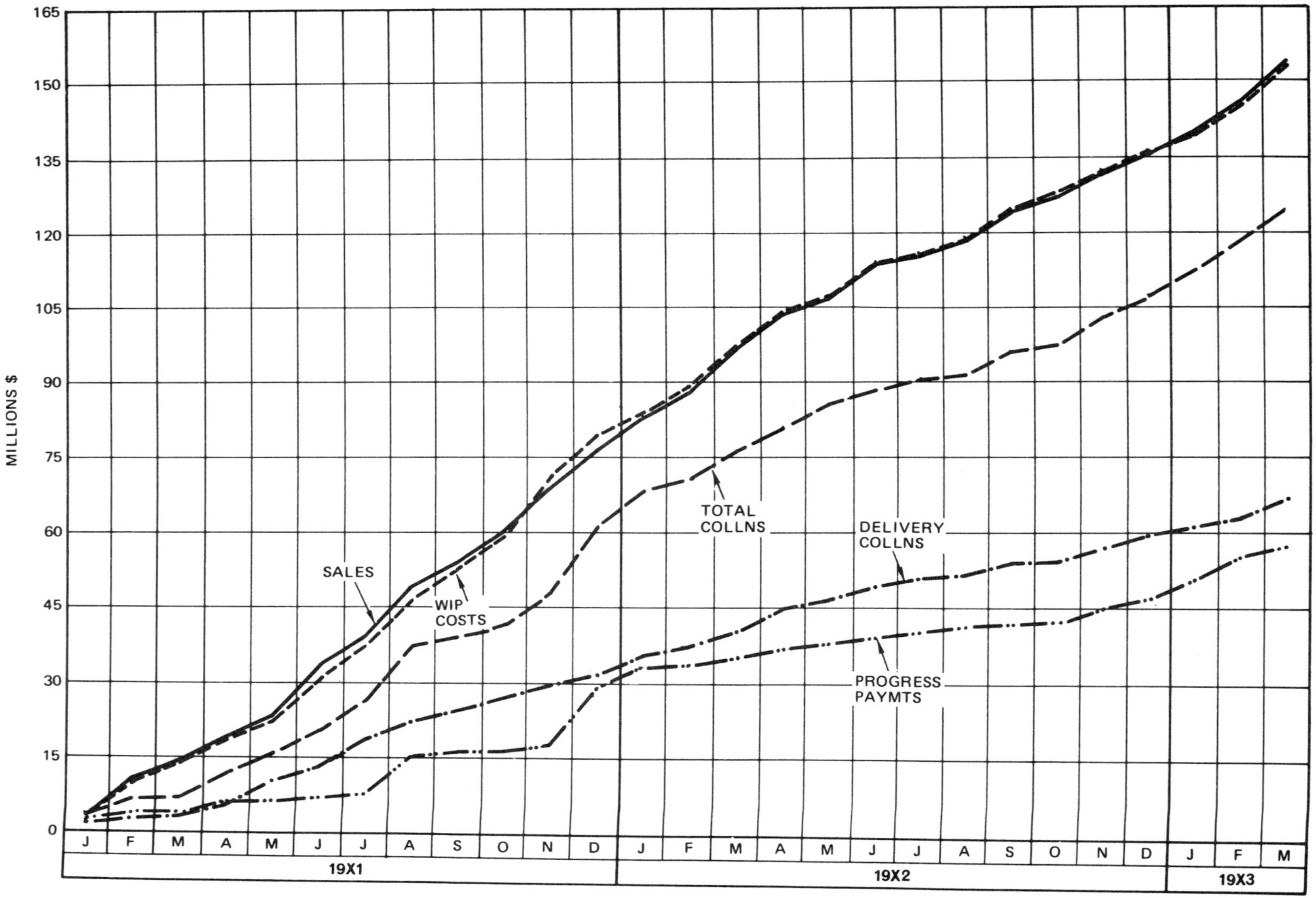

EXHIBIT C

collections, etc.) for comparative purposes of establishing various relationships, attention will only be directed to the sales trend line.

This display reveals that the organization is enjoying steady growth with the passage of time, but that growth was decreasing by individual year. The trend pattern can be measured by calculating the percentage differences by period of time. For example, in December 19X1, cumulative sales for the year were $80 million versus $137 million at the end of 19X2. The growth pattern reveals that the sales of 19X2 were actually declining from 19X1 since the 19X2 sales were $80 million versus $57 million in 19X3 ($137M − $80M) and this represents 71% of the 19X2 sales ($57M ÷ $80M). The next step in this evaluation process is to develop a formula for the sales projections regression line that would indicate a declining trend. This process is described in chapter 2.

Another approach to plotting a sales trend line is to do it by year, which is shown on Exhibit D. This type of display reveals that the sales for 19X1 were in fact $80 million as compared to $57 million at the end of 19X2. The chart also indicates that at the end of the first six months the 19X1 sales were 57% of the total sales volume for the year; whereas in 19X2, 65% of the sales were achieved. This definitely reflects a decreasing sales direction.

Month-by-Month Plotting

There are other types of trend line plotting, but one of the more useful would be month by month, which would more clearly focus on seasonal variations, cost influences, and economic effects (unemployment, strikes, GNP). Trend line evaluation is a rewarding exercise in making sales projections provided they are properly analyzed and interpreted relative to an organization's specific situation.

Least Squares as a Projection Tool

The least squares method is similar to that described for the scattergraph in chapter 2. It involves the plotting of dependent and independent variables in order to fit a straight line to irregular lines or curves. The least squares method establishes a most probable relationship between "X" and "Y" for a known historical period. If conditions in the past caused this relationship, and it is *assumed* that the same situation will be characteristic in the future, then this method for projection purposes is considered valid.

The least squares method becomes a particularly valuable and realistic projection tool for sales forecasting when an organization's sales can be significantly correlated with industry trends, economic climate, population growth, defense budget spending, and allied industry directional trends. For example, an upswing in the automotive industry would certainly indicate a relative demand for tires, metal, glass, and parts. Increased shoe production would indicate requirement for leather (soles and uppers), rubber heels, and shoelaces.

Generally, the most difficult task is to establish a reliable criterion that will assist in developing sales projections or verifying the data that is otherwise developed and independent of the association relationship.

It is noted that if a couple of points deviate radically from the normal pattern because of a possible differential in sales price or another factor, these points should not be used or else

SUMMARY OF ALL FIXED PRICE CONTRACTS
SALES, COSTS, TOTAL COLLNS, PROGRESS PAYMTS & DELIVERY COLLNS

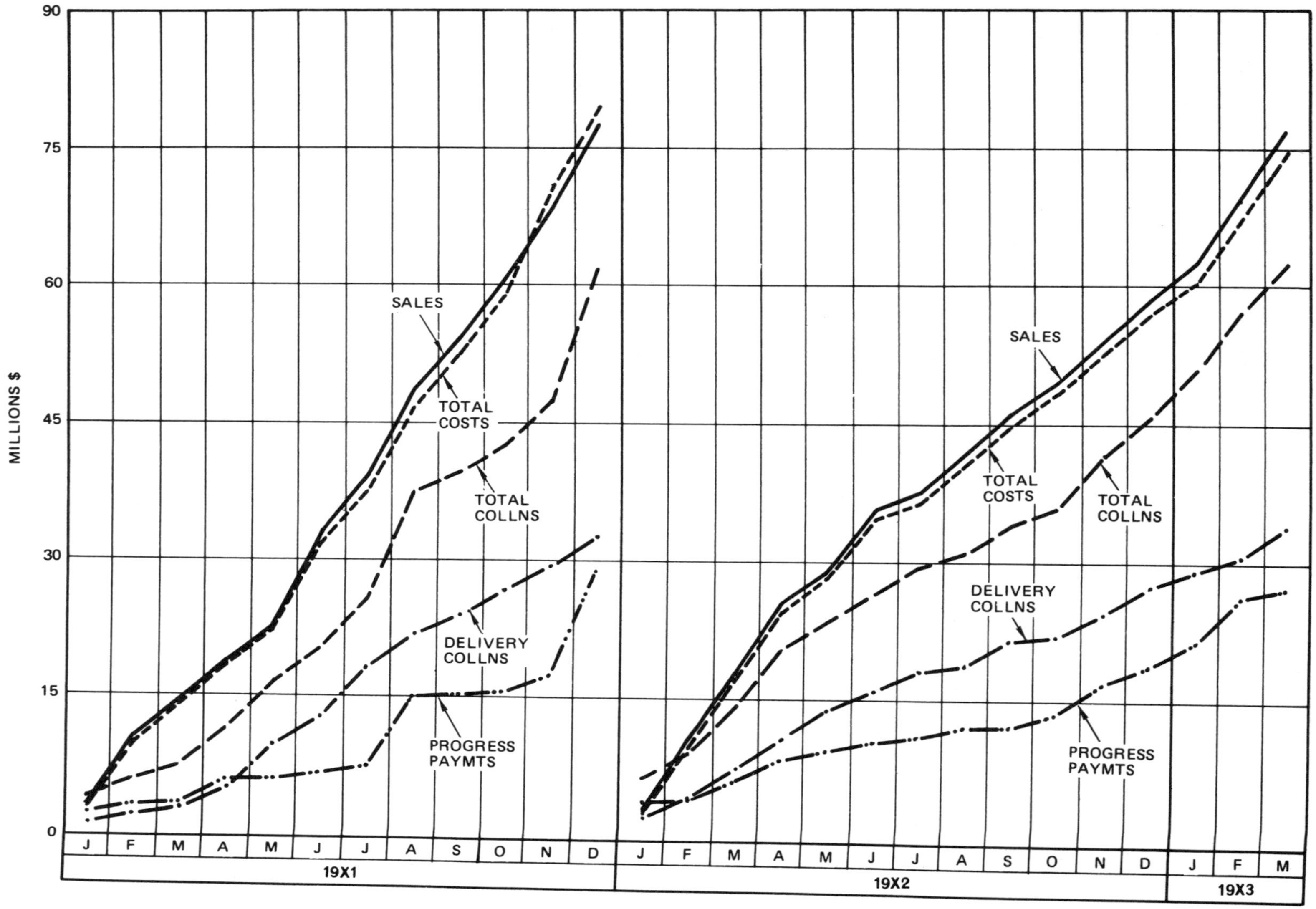

EXHIBIT D

adjusted, otherwise the line and equation will reflect an unreasonable distortion. Good judgment is a necessary criterion to successful use of the least squares method.

Use of Sales Correlation

Correlation is the historical association or relationship between two variables that is translated into an equation for projection purposes. Exhibit E reflects the relationship between sales and total costs. As noted on the exhibit, the points are plotted by period and the regression line intercept is drawn based on the location of two calculated points (black circles). The equation used to develop the formula—costs equal sales times the factor 1.0178 less $1,050—is expressed as follows:

$$Y = Na + b\Sigma X$$
$$XY = aX + b\Sigma X^2$$

Y represents total cost values by period
N indicates the number of time periods used
X signifies the sales values by period

Using actual sales for two different time periods, points A and B are plotted to determine the regression line as shown on the exhibit. The correlation between sales and costs is perfect, as evidenced by the coefficient of 1.000 shown at the upper left of the chart.

For rapid projections without using the equation, costs can be approximated visually by selecting a sales value, noting its intercept on the regression line, and determining the value on the vertical axis. For example, $75M sales would indicate costs slightly higher than sales. This is possible on fixed-price contracts because sales are not booked until final delivery is made—progress payments are billed in the interim.

Sales Versus Delivery Collection Correlation

Another example of the correlation technique is displayed on Exhibit F. The same principles govern as discussed above for Exhibit E. In this case also, the coefficient of correlation indicates almost a perfect line fit of .999. The first four points on the exhibit were not considered in the calculations because it was determined that they were not representative of the actual relationship climate.

"What If" Gaming

After the sales and related data is developed, management usually decides to test various alternatives such as changing the volume or product mix of the sales, assuming different cost and sales prices, or experimenting with different profit goals. This simulation exercise (described earlier in the chapter) permits them to finalize, interjecting judgment factors, the projected operating plan. Computerization of the process definitely lends itself to this activity because of rapid data manipulation, inherent accuracy, and immediate results. The effect on various schedules and the overall operational plan is rapidly ascertained without tedious, time-consuming manual effort.

TOTAL SALES TO COSTS CORRELATION FIXED PRICE CONTRACTS

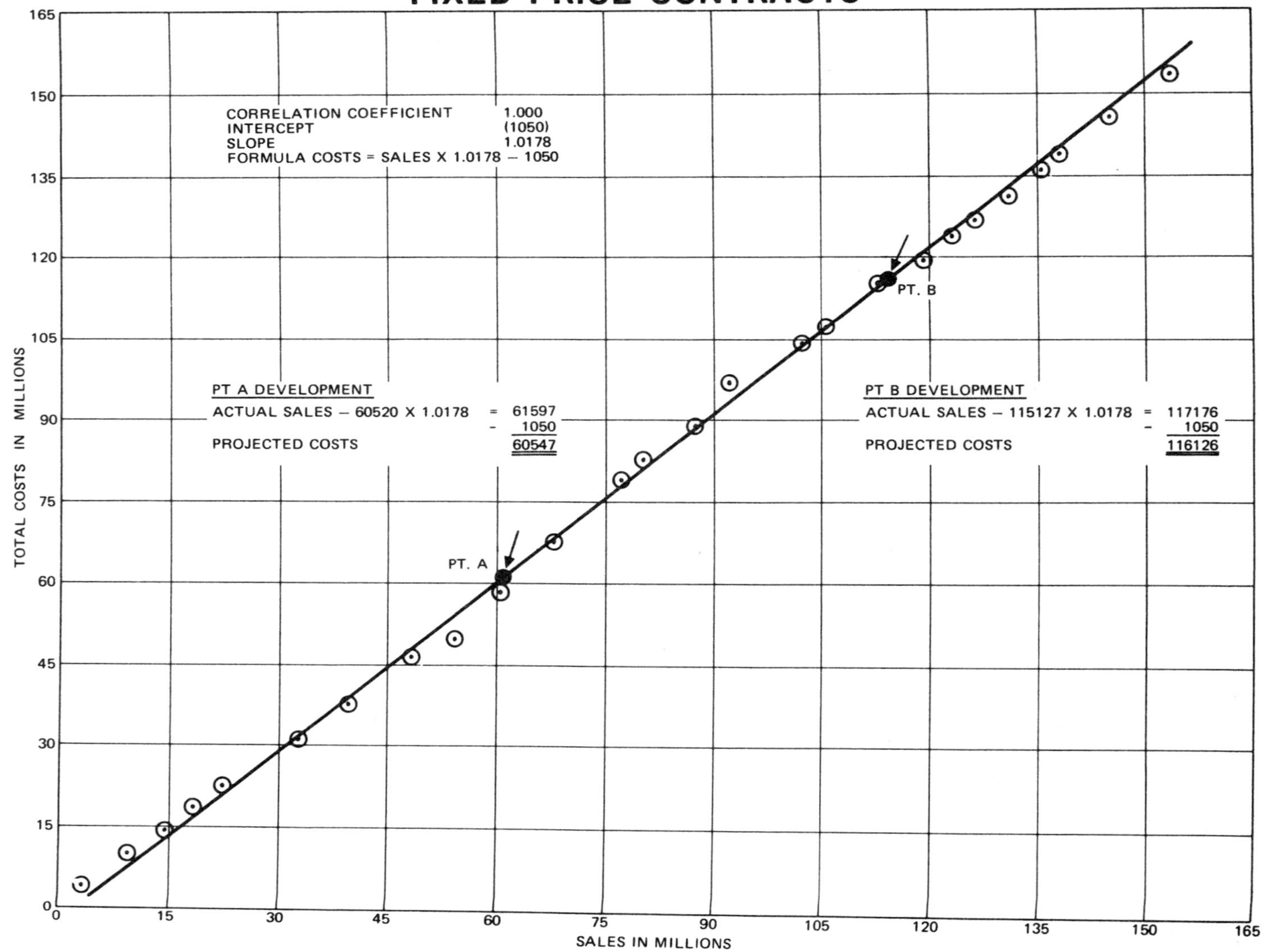

EXHIBIT E

SALES vs DELIVERY COLLN CORRELATION FIXED PRICE CONTRACTS

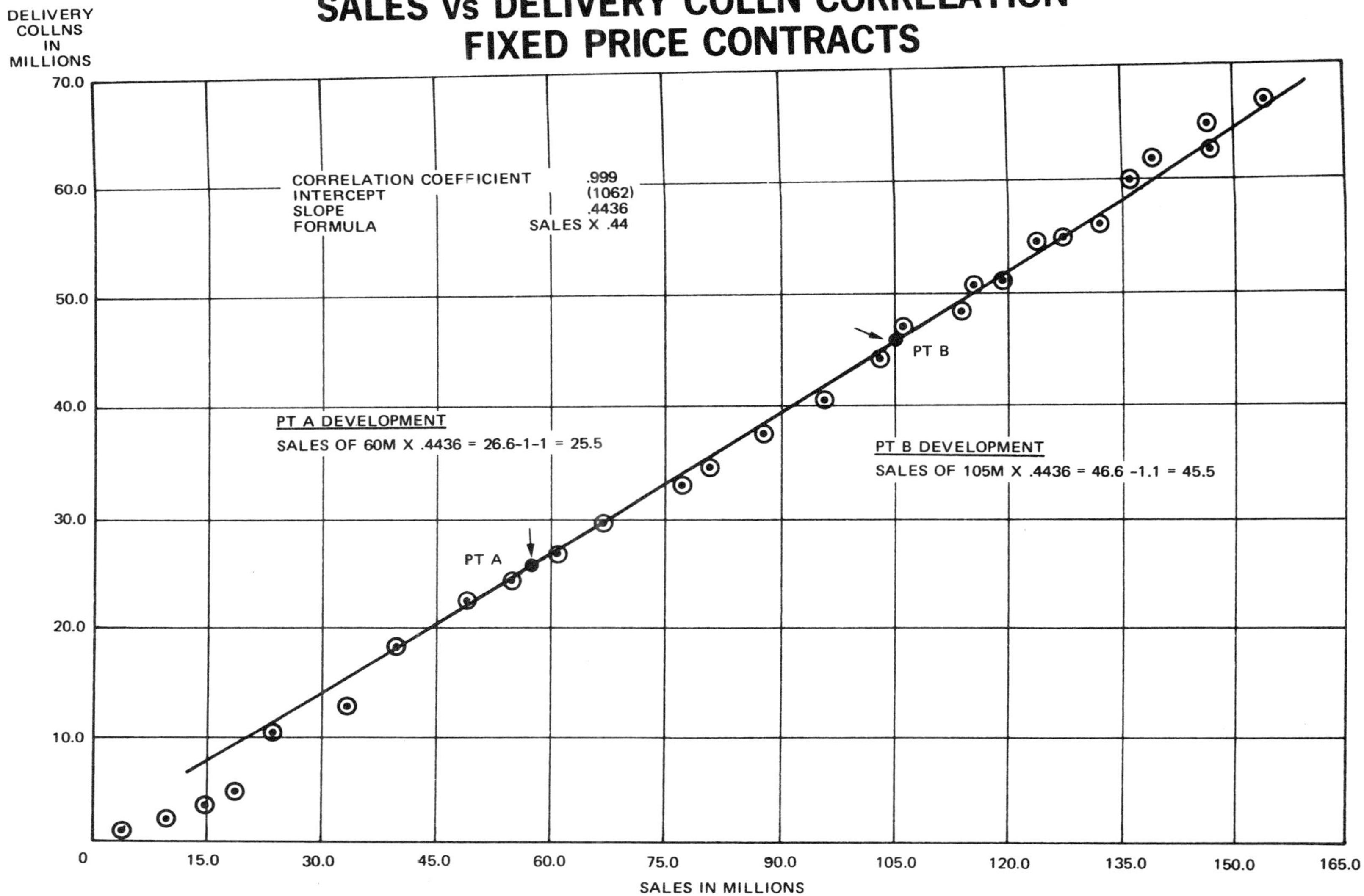

EXHIBIT F

An illustration of what happens and its effect in the gaming process when changes are made to sales projections is noted below:

Increase or decrease will occur to—	Schedules that will be affected—
Inventories	Income statement
Cost of sales	Balance sheet
Total product/service costs	Source and application of funds
Undelivered business backlog	Cash flow
Assets (receivables)	Backlog status
Liabilities (payables)	Inventory status records
Profitability	Receivables register
Investment	Sales order/control summaries
Financial performance ratios	Procurement requirements

The schedules in the right column are not intended to line up with the data on the left. The above change effect is very dramatic and emphasizes the need for computerization.

PERFORMANCE MEASUREMENT AND CONTROLS

After the sales projections have been formalized and approved, the next most important effort is to monitor actual results against the plan. In the mechanical process, this is accomplished by feeding the resulting actuals into the projection records where a matching process occurs and variances generate. The differences are calculated by individual contract/sales order, product line, customer, firm or potential, and organizational totals. This type of comparison permits a detailed analysis of varied aspects of the projected sales plan. Major deviations are investigated. Results are communicated to the concerned management for action decisions that could affect product marketing practices, advertising/selling budgets, new product developments, capital expenditures, and production scheduling.

Controls are therefore contingent on constant surveillance of actual performance against the operating (budget) plan. It is an effective management tool in ascertaining deviations from the plan.

In conclusion, the development of a realistic sales plan is one of the most important functions in the planning process because of its impact on manpower, production, purchasing, inventory levels, cash flow, and the income statement. Utilization of computerized techniques and processes, as discussed above, will aid immeasurably in improving an organization's sales planning practices and profitability.

8

Boosting Cash Flow and Profitability Via the Computer

Cash or its equivalent is what makes it possible for the wheels of industry to turn. Without cash turnover, the basic objectives of a business enterprise, such as research, production, service performance, or product sales, could not be achieved. The term "cash" represents a monetary liquid asset resource that can be expended immediately or in a short time interval from internal organization sources (petty cash, traveler's checks, office safe), bank deposits, pre-negotiated bank "floats," short-term marketable security receipts, or anticipated collection of near-term receivables.

DYNAMICS OF CASH FLOW

The cash flow process involves all inflow of cash receipts and outflow of cash disbursement transactions that occur or are planned within an organization over a given period of time. The difference between the two sets of data (increases or decreases) plus the net beginning balance represents the ending balance. The balance in the actual world is a positive value but it could be negative in the forecast process as a result of data development.

In the actual environment, you cannot disburse more than you have available—except temporarily—with the known assurance that the disbursement will be covered by a receipt of funds before the disbursement cycle is consummated (the time span involved in a vendor payment check being cashed and clearing the bank). For example, a check mailed from the West Coast to the East Coast may involve as much as an eight-day time span before funds are required to cover it.

Cash flow schedules provide the means for evaluating historical experience in terms of specific items of cash receipts relative to those concerned with physical disbursements. Past experience provides the basic criteria for projecting future anticipations by comparing previous or actual operational requirements and their effect on cash flow utilization and source replenishment with that of the projected operational goals.

It is noted that revenues and expenses are not cash items in the true sense of cash terminology. Revenues from sales or other sources represent customer commitments (receivables) until paid, which occurs after a time period interval. Expenses are generally commitments to pay and do not become a cash disbursement until paid; in the interim they are classified as accrued salaries and wages, accounts payable, and so on.

An example of cash disbursement data flow is reflected on Exhibit A. The exhibit indicates the various overhead expenses and their flow to disbursements and the balance sheet. Although depreciation is an expense, it does not represent a cash disbursement since it is a transaction write-off periodically against capital assets. Because of the many various types of expenditures, the complexity of projecting cash disbursements cannot be overemphasized in order to achieve effective cash planning.

CASH PLANNING DETERMINANTS

The projected operating statement sales and cost buildup provides the primary and basic data for projecting the detailed cash receipts and disbursements. The process of forecasting cash can entail a simple process or can be very complicated depending on the complexity of an organization's operations and transactions. There are other criteria that have an impact on cash planning. These are concerned with the gain or loss on the sale of surplus capital assets, royalty/interest income, borrowings, loan repayments, issuance of capital stock, or purchase of their own outstanding stock. Relative to other cash disbursements (excluding operational requirements), cash outlay may be necessary for acquisition of new capital assets for asset replacement due to obsolescence or inefficiency, interest expense, payment of dividends, and investment in the acquisition of securities and/or subsidiaries.

CASH FLOW ANALYSIS DEVELOPMENT

There are a number of ways to project cash mechanically depending upon the procedures employed in an organization. A method used in one organization is described below.

The objective of a cash flow analysis process is to develop the cash surplus or deficit resulting from operations and the inclusion of other pertinent data, as reflected on Exhibit B. As shown, the projected summary of contract cost of sales incurred is netted against the anticipated cash receipts (collections) to obtain the pretax funds generated or used by product line and organization totals.

Other data requirements are obtained from various satellite systems as follows:

- Capital asset expenditures and depreciation are obtained from the capital asset budget/status system.
- Changes in payables represent the difference between two period ending accounts payable balances. For example, if January's balance was \$5,000 and February's balance was \$6,000, the \$1,000 difference would represent a minus value or funds used. The balances

ULTIMATE USE OF OVERHEAD EXPENSE CATEGORIES

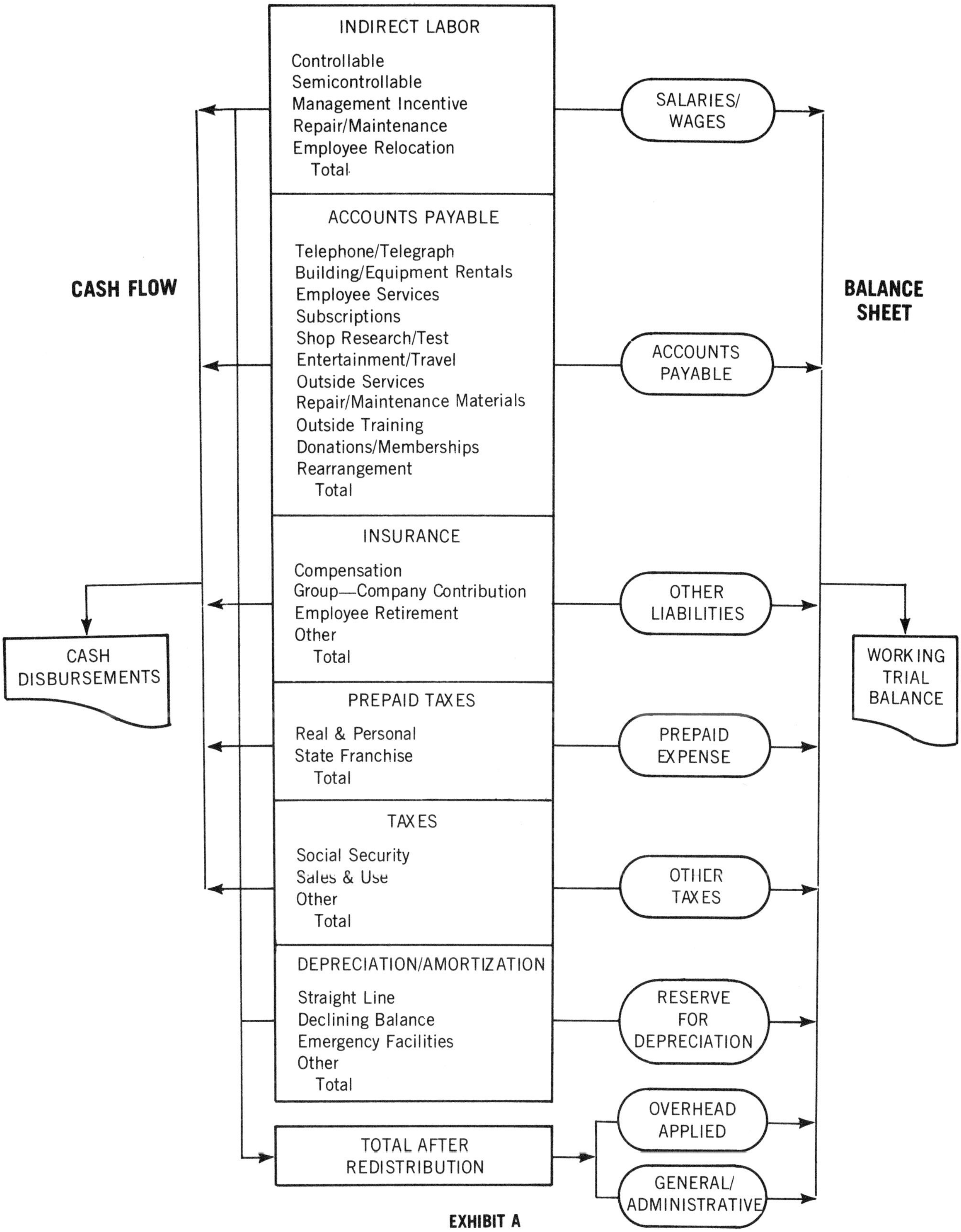

EXHIBIT A

CASH FLOW ANALYSIS DEVELOPMENT

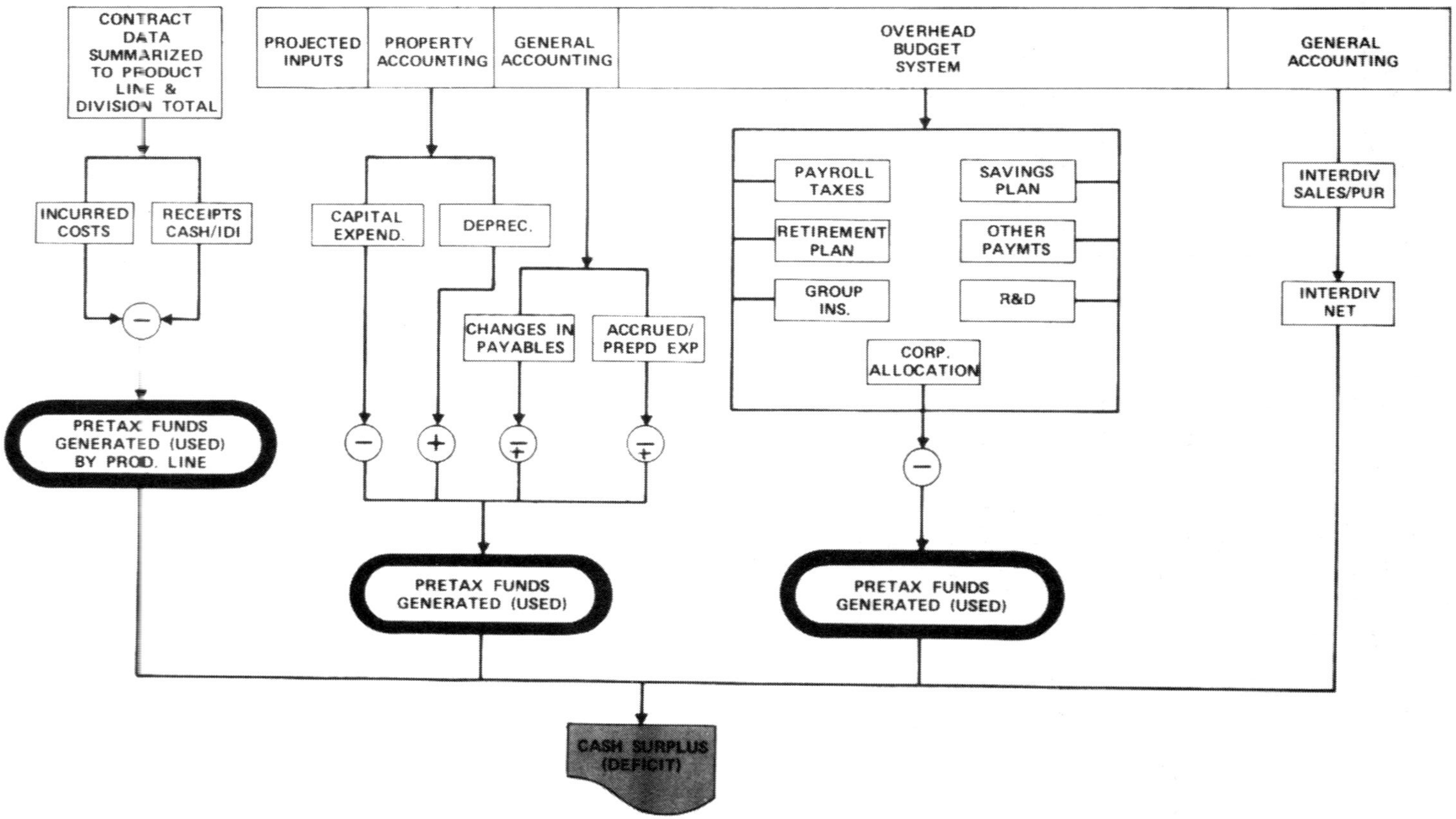

EXHIBIT B

are obtained from a cash disbursement program wherein the beginning payable balance is added to the period's incurred costs and a time-lag factor is applied (note discussion on accounts payable liquidation in this chapter) to derive disbursements and ending payable balances.

- Prepaid expense is a direct input based on historical experience.
- The mechanical overhead system provides the corporate office payments which represent funds used.
- Projected interorganization sales and purchases (direct input negotiated with other organizations) are netted to obtain either a positive or negative amount.

The combined total of the items described above represent cash surplus or deficit for the period.

Because of the number of major programs and forecast time periods involved in this type of analysis, computerization lends itself effectively to reduce the time-consuming effort of doing the task manually. Further, any changes that are required can be rapidly reflected with minimal manual effort.

MECHANICAL DEVELOPMENT OF CASH RECEIPTS

An example of cash receipt development from basic detail is displayed on Exhibit C, which indicates the composition of the cost accruals, commercial sales, miscellaneous receipts, and fixed-price contract progress payments (governed by contractual holdbacks).

As shown on the exhibit, the following processes occur:

- Direct labor dollars are combined with overhead and general and administrative expense to derive total inplant costs (by cost-type contract or in total).
- Total inplant fee dollars are divided by the inplant costs which results in a fee percentage per cost dollar.
- One hundred percent is added to the fee percentage and applied to labor, overhead, and material to obtain inplant accrued costs and fee (sales) dollars by contract.
- Projected subcontract (internal and external) sales are lagged five weeks (based on past history) to derive anticipated subcontract receipts. Profit is included in the sales price.
- Commercial sales are lagged one month and represent a receipt, whereas anticipated cash sales require no lag period. Profit is included in the sales price.
- Collections on fixed-price contracts are received at specified intervals of time, based on certain negotiated criteria, during the course of contract performance.
- Reimbursement is predicated on total contract value—80% of the costs incurred are collected as progress payments and the balance is received upon delivery of the product to the depot and its acceptance by the customer. Since funding limitations are also set, the progress payment is governed by the overall funds available.
- Net holdback, in reality, represents a type of uncollectible receivable until the above criteria have been met. Profit is included in the fixed-price contract negotiated sales price.
- Expenditures for government-owned facilities are generally reimbursed in about two weeks after invoicing the customer.
- The summary of the projected collections represents total cash receipts.

It is noted that the time-lag interval between cost incurred and sales relative to collections is

COMPUTERIZED PLANNING
DATA FLOW OF COSTS & SALES TO CASH RECEIPTS

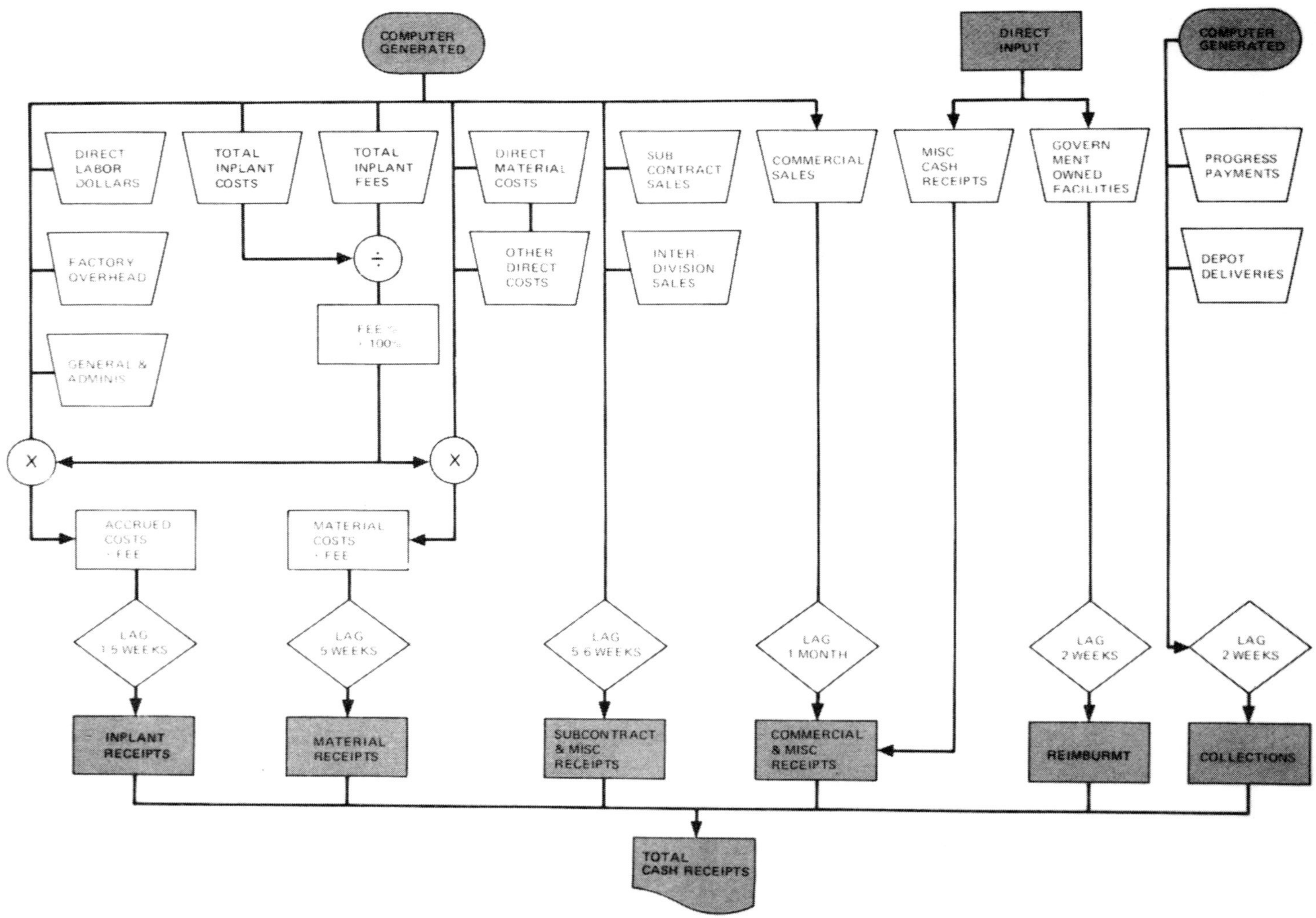

EXHIBIT C

based on a study of historical experience or highly predictable other known or negotiated facts. The collections are initially developed at the contract level and summarized to organization totals since some contracts may have individual criteria for projecting results.

The planning process discussed above can be accomplished either manually or mechanically. Particularly in complex organizations, the computerized process is recommended because of the mass of data to be manipulated, accuracy and timeliness requirements, rapid change capability, and reduced cost of development.

AVERAGE CASH COLLECTION CYCLE

The average collection period is the elapsed time interval between cost/sales invoicing and the physical cash receipt or collection.

Developing the Collection Formula

Using two to three years of historical data, divide each month's ending receivable balance by the average daily sales in that month to obtain the amount of days' sales uncollected at month end. The purpose for utilizing two to three years of monthly experience data is to be able to analyze and determine the cause for any unusual fluctuations that may have occurred in a given month of the year. This type of evaluation will lead to more reliable planning on a month-to-month basis. Adjustments could be made then to reflect unusual seasonal differences, funding problems, larger number of workdays in a month, heavy vacation periods resulting in reduced operation activity and cost incurrence, or invoicing peculiarities. The factor developed above should be translated into a percentage for ease of application in the mechanical projection cycle.

Application of the Formula

In determining the projected collections by period, the beginning receivable balance would be combined with the forecast period sales and the percentage developed is applied to the combined total above to derive the ending receivables balance. By subtracting this calculated value from the total of the beginning receivables balance and the sales, the result would represent the anticipated cash collection for the period. Illustrations of the above procedure are shown below.

(1) *Monthly History*

Sales—\$60,000; Ending Receivable Balance—\$40,000; Number of Calendar Days Used—360.

CALCULATIONS

a. Average daily sales equals \$2,000 (\$60,000 ÷ 30 days)
b. Uncollected days of sales equal 20 (\$40,000 ÷ \$2,000)
c. Percentage of uncollected sales in month equals .6667 (20 ÷ 30)
d. Ending Receivables Balance equals \$53,336—
   (BB \$20,000 + \$60,000 × .6667)
e. Cash collections equal \$26,664 (\$80,000 − \$53,336)

(2) *Annual History*
Sales—$720,000; Ending Receivables Balance—$40,000; Number of Annual Calendar Days Used—360.

CALCULATIONS
a. Average daily sales equals $2,000 ($720,000 ÷ 360)
b. Uncollected days of sales equal 20 ($40,000 ÷ $2,000)
c. Percentage of uncollected sales in month equals .6667 (20 ÷ 30)
d. The balance of the process is similar to that shown in illustration (1) above.

Using the first method is preferable because monthly data fluctuations require a different factor for each month to make the forecasting results more realistic. In order to translate the monthly uncollected sales into sales weeks represented by receivables, you would merely divide the 20-day factor developed above by the 5 workdays in the week to obtain 4 weeks of uncollected sales.

(3) *Collections Based on Receivables Turnover*
Historical data indicated annual credit sales of $720,000 and the sum of the monthly ending receivable balances for the year were $540,000.

CALCULATIONS
a. Average monthly receivables balance equals $45,000 ($540,000 ÷ 12 months).
b. Rate of turnover equals 16 months ($720,000 ÷ $45,000).
c. Single turnover equals $1^1/_3$ months (16 ÷ 12).
d. Month-end receivables balances would be collected in 40 days (30 + ⅓), which means that ⅓ of the balance is projected to be collected in the following month.

CASH COLLECTION CORRELATIONS

Sound collection projections are based on a thorough analysis of historical data in order to determine significant correlations among the concerned dependent and independent variables. Unusual variations in given periods of time must be evaluated to determine the reasons for deviation in data performance.

In government business, but not necessarily restricted thereto, some of the reasons that plague the collection forecasting endeavors are attributed to unusual or abnormal circumstances such as

- Late deliveries (affecting delivery collections)
- Funding constraints or unavailability at the time required (affecting progress payments)
- Customer delays in processing invoices

Each of these circumstances can significantly affect the validity of the projected collection data.

In other cases, the situation may occur in specific months of the year as a result of the following:

- Funding availability caused by fiscal budget transition to the new year budget allotments (new funding on government projects becomes available after July 1)
- Vacation periods (summer months particularly), which creates reduced production activities and shipment delays

- Seasonal delays in raw material deliveries thus slowing production and collections
- Weather conditions that create delays in deliveries

The above extenuating circumstances must be considered and analyzed before an attempt is made to develop and establish valid correlation formulae.

Correlation Significance

Exhibit D illustrates the relationship, on an annual cumulative basis, among sales, costs, delivery collections, and progress payments. It is noted, however, that monthly plotted data would reveal more significant variations for analysis. As shown on the exhibit, the trend lines for both years are compatible. Sales and cost lines run practically together with the difference representing the lag interval between cost incurrence and the actual billed sales values. The difference between sales/costs and collections is attributed to the time intervals between billing the customer and the cash collection, as well as holdbacks on fixed-price contracts.

It is noted that in 19X1 there was an upswing in progress payments starting in mid-July and November that was analyzed as being caused by new and increased funding availability and follow-on contract additions. The use of graphic displays often reveals relationships among data that often cannot be easily discerned by evaluation of figures.

PROJECTED INVOICING AND COLLECTIONS

Fixed-price contracts and, in many instances, commercial sales orders can involve progress or partial payments on total cost and effort expended, and the delivery billings are based on the actual delivery of a product or performance of a service. The mechanical process used is displayed on Exhibit E.

Progress Payment Collections

The progress payment limit by period is developed by subtracting the prior period limit from the current period limit. The limit is based on funding limitations and the percentage of incurred costs that can be billed as a progress payment. A collection lag factor (generally 15-30 days, translated into a percentage of 50-100) is applied to the limit to establish the value for the current progress payment (PP) lagged. A lag factor is next applied to the current PP lagged to obtain the prior billing lag. As shown on the exhibit, the PP limit less current lag and plus prior billing lag will result in projected PP collections.

The most effective way of explaining the lagging (time interval) process among billings, receivables, and collections is illustrated below in which a 50% lag is assumed.

	000s $ by PERIOD					
	1	2	3	4	5	6
Invoice Billing Amount ($)	10	12	14	16	20	
A/R Current Lag (Billing × .50)	5	6	7	8	10	
Prior PP Billing Lagged (½ Billing Forward)	0	5	6	7	8	10
Billing/Delivery Collections	5	11	13	15	18	10

SUMMARY OF ALL FIXED PRICE CONTRACTS
SALES, COSTS, TOTAL COLLNS, PROGRESS PAYMTS & DELIVERY COLLNS

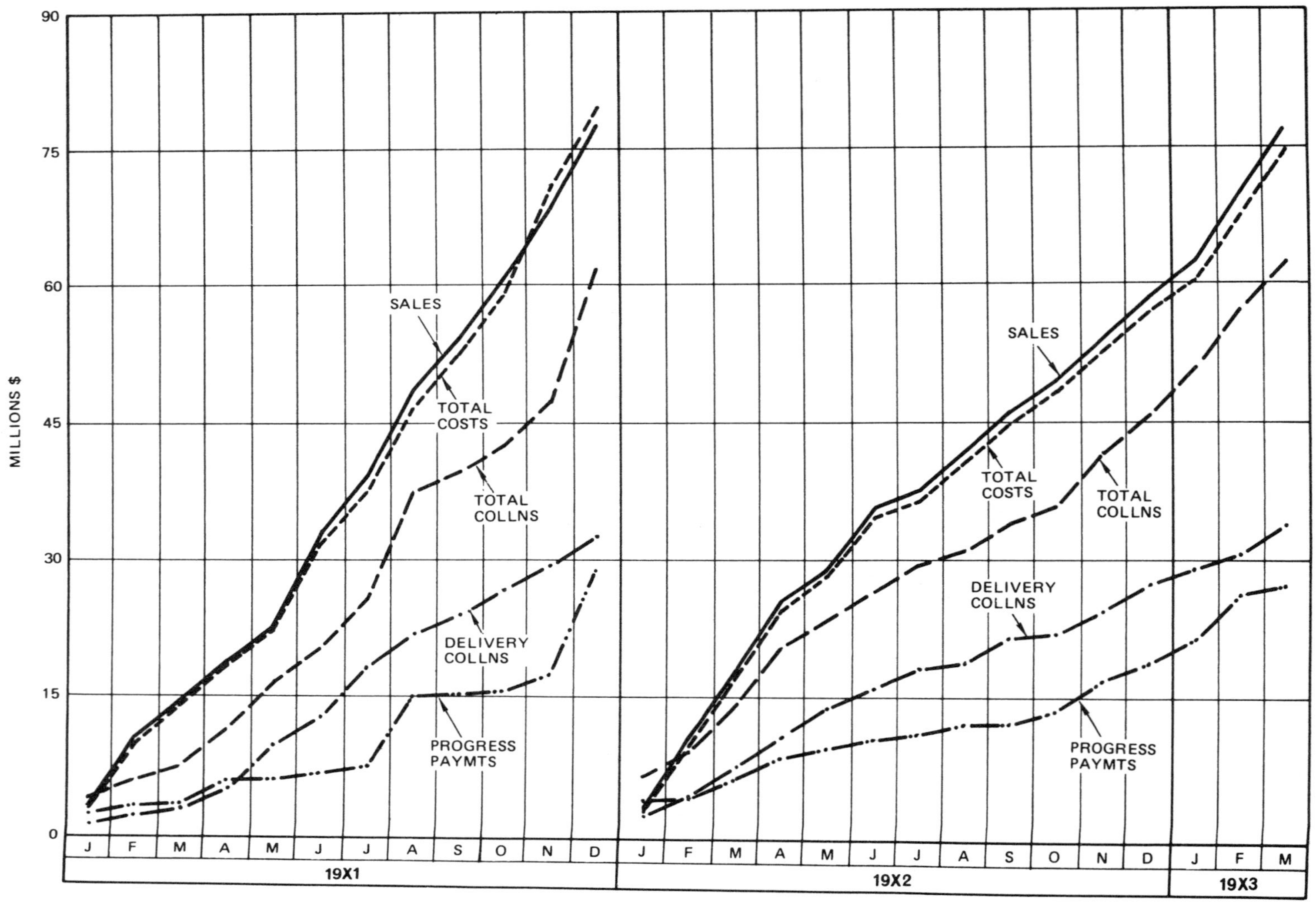

EXHIBIT D

CUSTOMER BILLINGS AND COLLECTION DEVELOPMENT

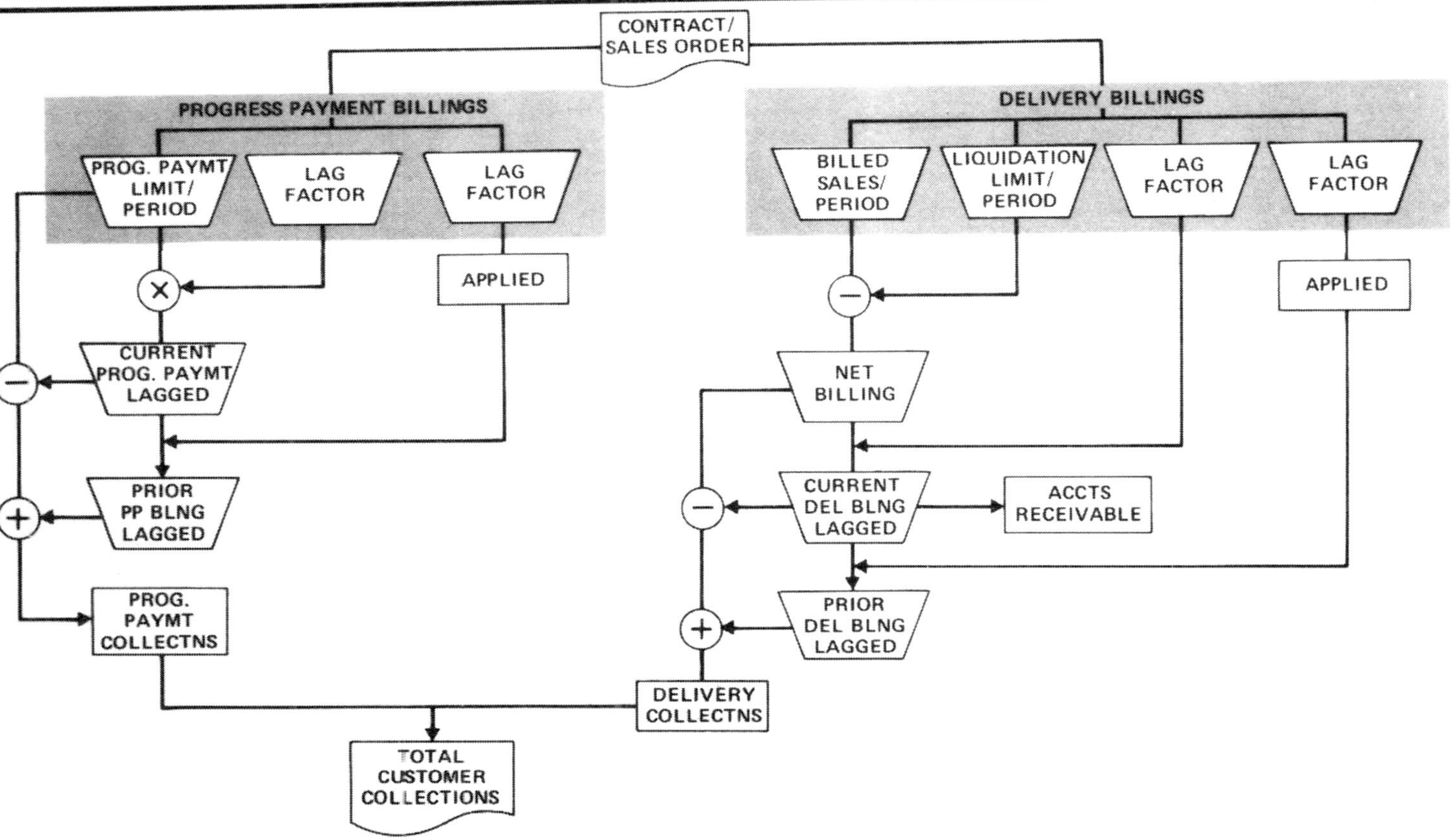

EXHIBIT E

Delivery Billings

The billed sales by period less the liquidation limit (contractually negotiated and developed by applying the percentage factor to sales), shown on Exhibit E, provides the net billing amount. The lag process, illustrated above, is used to obtain projected delivery collections. The combined total of the progress payments and deliveries represents the projected customer collections.

CASH DISBURSEMENT PLANNING

Cash disbursement planning is more difficult to achieve than collections planning because of the greater detail of cost accruals and other liability commitment items and the varying degree and disparity in the accrual/disbursement time lags. A few notable examples of lag differences are as follows, but they may vary among organizations due to the type of business, customer, and payment policies.

DISBURSEMENT TYPES	TIME INTERVAL BETWEEN ACCRUAL/LIABILITY AND DISBURSEMENT
Dividends	1 Month
Subcontract Costs	6 Weeks
Inplant Material Costs	4-5 Weeks
Labor and Overhead	2 Weeks
Special Government Facilities	2 Weeks
Employee Withheld Income Taxes	1 Month + 1 Week
State Disability Insurance	1 Quarter + 1 Week
FICA	1 Month + 1 Week
Comprehensive Insurance	2 Months
Franchise Tax	Expensed Monthly
Real & Personal Property Taxes	Expensed Monthly

Using the lagging process discussed above, the accruals can then be translated into cash disbursements by applying the lag factors by individual cost item.

In many uncomplicated organizations, an average lag for total costs can be developed for determining the time interval for the cash disbursement cycle. It cannot be overemphasized that a thorough analysis of historical experience relative to the cash disbursement cycle will aid considerably in attaining effective cash flow planning.

Cash Disbursement Forecast Development

There are a number of methods used for cash disbursement planning. They vary among organizations depending on their individual needs, the size and complexity of an organization, type of operation and customer. A proven computerized system will be discussed below. It was tailored for one type of organization but there are segments included that would be applicable to many organizations.

Mechanical System Inputs

a. Direct labor dollar total by period
b. Indirect labor dollar total by period
c. Employee deduction percentage of gross payroll dollars
d. Total organization overhead by period
e. Total depreciation expense by period
f. Direct labor dollars by contract
g. Material and other direct costs by contract
h. Corporate office payments
i. Fixed-asset additions
j. Interdivision purchase
k. Direct labor hours by contract and organization total
l. Material and other cost rate per direct labor hour

Most of the data shown as input above is developed in satellite systems and transferred mechanically to the cash planning system.

Processing

Net Payroll Dollars

- Relate indirect labor dollars to the direct labor (inputs (a) and (b) above) to obtain percentage of indirect labor to direct.
- Apply above percentage to direct labor dollars by period and contract (input (f)) to obtain indirect labor dollars by contract and period.
- Combine direct and indirect labor dollars to obtain total gross payroll dollars by period.
- Apply employee deduction percentage (input (c)—approximately 20%) to total payroll dollars to obtain payroll deductions, which are then subtracted from gross payroll dollars to derive net payroll dollars by contract.
- Summarize the contract net payroll dollars, apply lag factor, and the payroll disbursement is calculated.

Overhead Development by Contract

- Subtract total depreciation expense (no disbursement involved) and indirect labor dollars (inputs (b) and (e)) from the total overhead (input (d)) to obtain an adjusted total overhead (payable/disbursement purposes). Indirect labor falls under the accrued salaries/wages category.
- Divide the adjusted overhead by total direct labor dollars to obtain the adjusted overhead rate.
- Apply adjusted overhead rate to the contract direct labor dollars (input (f)) to obtain the adjusted overhead dollars by period and contract.
- Summarize the above contract overhead dollars which should reconcile to the adjusted total overhead above. This value is lagged for payable and disbursement purposes.

Material and Other Direct Costs by Contract

- This is either a direct input (g) or it can be developed by contract on the basis of direct material rate per direct labor hour (input [(k) × 1]).
- If the cost is to be developed by rate application, the total projected material and other

costs (input (g)) is divided by the total direct labor hours (input (k)) to obtain a rate per hour if not given.
- The rate per hour above is applied to the contract direct labor dollars to obtain the contract material dollars by period.

Lag Application for Projecting Disbursements
- Lag contract payroll dollars two weeks (40% in five-week months and 50% in four-week months) to obtain the projected disbursements for payroll. The balance represents accrued salaries and wages.
- Lag the contract overhead dollars two weeks to obtain the overhead disbursements. The balance represents accounts payable.
- Lag the contract material and other direct costs four weeks (80% in five-week months and 100% in four-week months) to obtain the projected disbursements for material and other costs. The balance represents accounts payable.
- Summarize the above disbursements by contract and organizational totals.

Other Disbursements (Division Level)
- Corporate office payments can be a direct input (h) into the system. If data represents expenses, then a four-week time lag will convert this data to a disbursement cycle.
- Capital asset expenditures are inputted on a disbursement projection basis.
- Interdivision purchases are a direct input since they are developed in conjunction with other organizations. The input is on a projected cash disbursement basis.

Total Cash Disbursements

The summary of the cost element and other disbursements above will result in total cash disbursements by period which is used in the cash flow process.

Lag Factors in Percentages

In order to facilitate the lagging process, percentage application factors were developed by dividing length of lag period by the number of weeks in the projected accounting periods. For more precise forecasting, the lag factor should be different for four- and five-week months. A lag factor table in percentages is illustrated in chapter 10.

LIQUIDATION OF ACCOUNTS PAYABLE

Accounts payable are generated when cost is incurred and set up as a liability commitment. When payments are made, they represent cash disbursements and a reduction to the payable balance. The development of the formula used is to combine the projected beginning accounts payable balance with the forecast incurred costs for the period and deduct anticipated cash payments to obtain the ending payable balance. Noted below are two methods that can be used mechanically to develop payment forecasts and, at the same time, reduce payables.

(1) *Average Disbursement Method*
- Based on historical experience, it is possible to determine an average payment cycle for projection purposes.

- This statistic would be determined by dividing annual or annualized total operating costs (other than labor, asset acquisitions) by 365 days to obtain the average cost incurred per day.
- Next, total the ending accounts payable balances for the year and divide this value by 365 to obtain the average accounts payable balance per day. Dividing the average cost incurred per day into the average accounts payable balance will result in the number of days of costs unpaid.
- To derive the percentage of unpaid costs to accounts payable balance, divide the number of days of unpaid costs by the number of calendar days within the month to obtain a decimal factor.
- To obtain a projected ending payable balance, combine the beginning payable balance with the period's projected incurred cost and multiply this total by the percentage factor developed above.
- The combined beginning balance and incurred cost less the ending balance will result in projected cash payments.

An arithmetical illustration of the processes follows:

- Annual or annualized sales of \$730,000 ÷ 365 = \$2,000 average costs per day.
- Average payable ending balance of \$40,000 (based on history) ÷ \$2,000 equals 20 days of unpaid costs in the payable balance.
- The percentage of unpaid costs (payables) is obtained by dividing the 20 days by the number of calendar days in the month (30) and the result is a factor of .6667.
- The projected beginning payable balance (\$30,000) plus the estimated costs to be incurred (\$45,000) totals \$75,000, and the application of the factors results in an ending payable balance of \$50,000—liquidation of the payable.
- The \$75,000 less the \$50,000 equals \$25,000, representing the forecasted cash payment for the period.

(2) *Disbursements as Percentage of Cost Projections*

- Establish a statistical correlation between disbursement of payables and costs based on historical experience.
- Apply the developed formula (regression analysis) to anticipated incurred costs to obtain cash disbursement values.
- Combine the projected beginning payable balance with the forecasted costs and reduce this value by the cash disbursements above to obtain the ending payable balances—another form of payable liquidations.
- To be most realistic and effective in planning, the historical experience factors should be developed from monthly data.

WEEKLY CASH FORECAST

The primary objective of a weekly mechanical system is to develop detailed cash forecasts for short-term cash planning by week and month, by contract and summary, and compare each period's current forecast to the prior period's plan and current actuals. The anticipated receipts are also compared to the projected disbursements in order to determine the net gain or loss forecasted for the cash balance account. The report information is segregated into fixed-price, cost, and other types of contracts or sales orders.

Mechanical System Input

Exhibit F represents the weekly format to be used in making the various projections required. As displayed on this exhibit, Column 1 is used to indicate the time period as defined under "period code" (X through 5) in the upper left side of the form.

- Column 4 reflects the code designation of the type of disbursement that is being projected such as material and payroll, as shown on the chart.
- Columns 7 and 8 reflect identifiers as to whether specific payments to vendors are over or under \$250K. This value is dependent on an organization's requirements. It permits management the opportunity to make pay-or-delay decisions on major disbursements during critical times of cash shortages or other constraints. As indicated on the input format, the "B" code is for the various payroll projections and "C" represents corporate payments.
- Columns 11-28 require a vendor's name entry. There are separate input sheets for the over- and under-\$250K anticipated payments.
- Columns 31-34 indicate the due date for payment (month and day). Management has the capability of changing the payment date if so required for control purposes.
- Columns 37-41 contain the amount to be paid to the nearest thousand dollars.
- Column 44 identifies the collection to the type of contract. A contract designation will be reflected in Columns 47-50 for contract reporting.
- Column 53 indicates the type of collection anticipated—delivery of a product or performance of a service, progress payments, or cost reimbursement. The projected amount of the collection is reflected in Columns 56-60 (in thousands).
- Columns 61-80 are available for other input as required.

Input Processing

The major processing activities are concerned with the following mechanical functions.

- Sorting of data to achieve the type of reporting required.
- Inclusion and retention of weekly and monthly actuals (performance measurement) by contract or other descriptive classifications on exhibit.
- Summation of actuals and forecast data into monthly totals by contract.
- Comparison of current period's forecast to prior period and generating the variances.
- Comparison of actual collections to disbursements by contract in order to obtain the cash gain or deficit by period.

System Developed Output

Various sorted and summarized output is generated from this system which permits data interpretive analysis, provides a means to determine the differences between the current week's projected plan and the prior week's, and highlights the specifics of plan deviations. There are five outputs from this system that will be briefly described below.

- *Material Disbursements.* This report will include the current week's forecast of vendor payments over or under \$250K and their comparison to the prior week's projections with the variance computed. The report is by weekly time periods and will include to-date

CASH FORECAST PROGRAM

Weekly Input Format

JOB NO. ______ SHEET NO. ______

BY ______

DISBURSEMENTS					COLLECTIONS				
PCD	DCD	DES CD	VENDOR NAME (OVER $250,000)	DATE PMT	AMOUNT	CCD	CONTR NO.	CCD	AMOUNT
1	4	7 8	11–28	31–34	37–41	44	47–50	53	56–80

DISBURSEMENTS

Col. 1 -- Period Code (PCD)

Code	Description
X	To-date actuals for the current month
1	Forecast for the current week
2	Forecast for the second week
3	Forecast for the third week
4	Forecast for the fourth week
5	Forecast for the fifth week

Col. 4 -- Type of Disbursement (DCD)

Code	Description
A	Material
B	Payroll Forecast
C	NY Disbursements
D	Other

Cols. 7 & 8 -- Detail Disbursement Description (DESCD)

Code	Description
A	Material
	01 -- Payments to Vendors under $250,000
	02 -- Payments exceeding $250,000
B	Payroll Forecast
	01 -- Pomona Net Payroll
	02 -- Navajo Net Payroll
	03 -- Bonds
	04 -- Terminations
	05 - Union Dues
	06 -- Contrib Club
	07 -- Management Club
	08 -- Allotments
	09 -- Executive Payroll
C	NY Disbursements
	01 -- Group Insurance
	02 -- Retirement Plan
	03 -- Savings Plan
	04 -- Payroll Taxes

CCLLECTIONS

Col. 44 -- Type of Contract Code (CCD)

Code	Description
A	Fixed Price
B	Cost Type
C	Other

Col. 53 -- Type of Collection Code (CCD)

Code	Description
1	Delivery
2	Progress Payments
3	Cost Reimbursement

EXHIBIT F

monthly actuals. The report will also include the title—Explanation of Major Changes—which information will be entered manually.

- *Payroll Forecast.* As in the case of material disbursements, this report will be prepared for similar comparative time periods. It will segregate corporate office payments from other payroll disbursements.
- *Cash Collection Projections.* The collection forecast will display the contract identification number and type of collection in the same time periods as above. The type of collection will be segregated first by contract type. For fixed-price contracts, a further segregation is made as to whether the collection resulted from a delivery or progress payment.
- *Cash Collection and Disbursement Summary.* This report will contain a summary of the total collections and disbursements and the net cash gain or loss. The prior week's forecast gain or loss will be compared to the current week's and the difference shown.
- *Collection Comparison by Contract.* The report will show the variances between the prior and current week's data by contract.

The above represents a comprehensive computerized program that will be timely, cost effective, and permit a tie-in to the mechanical billing system.

CASH BUDGETING

A cash budget includes the detail and summary projections for cash receipts and disbursements and reflects the increases or decreases to the cash balance over future periods of time. It is developed from operating budgets, the data of which is converted from an accrual to a cash basis by using experience lag factors.

Cash receipts are developed from anticipated revenues in terms of forecast product/service sales, liquidation of receivables, interest/royalty income, and outside investments. Cash disbursements are calculated from operating budgets which indicate direct and indirect production costs. Other disbursements involve capital expenditures; general, administrative, and selling expenses; and interest expense.

Cash budgeting is the process of translating income and cost factors into collections and disbursements through the use of lag factors that have been historically experienced between the occurrence of a given transaction and its reflection as cash inflow or outflow.

Effective Cash Requirement Management

When it has been determined through the development of a cash budget (if realistic) that funds will be required to meet future obligations because it is anticipated that sufficient receipts will not materialize, arrangements are tentatively made with banks or other lending institutions to cope with this problem. The budget therefore serves as a basic supporting document to negotiate with the lender a line of credit in advance to meet its anticipated cash needs. Demand loans (floats) are negotiated for daily fluctuations and others on a thirty- to ninety-day time basis.

Cash needs can also be met by issuance of capital stock, delaying purchases and capital asset investments, making arrangements with the vendors to delay payments, introducing and enforcing a stringent cost-control program, selling obsolete or surplus capital assets, and possibly accelerating production activities for increased sales.

Centralized Control

Centralized management control of cash transaction can be highly advantageous in meeting cash requirements. This is particularly true in large segmented organizations. This process would entail the following, which is common practice in some organizations:

- Each day, the individual organizations advise central management by telephone or telefax of the amount of funds deposited that day and anticipated for the next day. They also advise of their cash requirements. This provides central management with knowledge as to what will be available at each location and the payouts anticipated. One organization may be faced with a surplus and another with a deficit.
- Central management establishes and maintains a depositary account with a bank located in the area of segmented operations.
- Surplus funds are drawn into the corporate central account where they are redistributed as required to meet interorganizational needs. If the funds are insufficient to meet the needs, then the corporate office must borrow.
- The central management makes the decision as to delays in vendor payments when it is deemed necessary. The main advantage of centralized control is that it provides the opportunity to distribute excess cash surplus and/or invest it for the period of time availability.
- Centralized control affords maximum utilization of cash for the greatest return and provides the opportunity for effective cash management.

Criteria for Controlling Cash

The prime objective is to exercise effective and strong control over all cash transactions. It involves the following basic but very important considerations:

- Making timely collections and immediate deposits
- Processing disbursements on the last day possible to minimize loss of discounts
- Making realistic projections of cash excesses or demands to meet organizational needs
- Taking advantage of weekend and holiday cash floats
- Increasing organization profitability by intelligent investment and productive utilization of cash surpluses—also, to reduce cost of borrowings
- Establishing the necessary arrangements with lenders so that cash requirements will be available when needed
- Placing emphasis on and enforcing cash conservation policies and procedures
- Coordinating and reconciling organizational cash needs with the overall operating plan objectives
- Establishing cash balance limits in organizations to meet immediate needs
- Establishing centralized control for cash management

The above goals can only be achieved by a cash-oriented top management involvement in day-to-day cash activities, delegating appropriate responsibilities and taking immediate corrective action when deviations occur from the plan or when the organization is unresponsive to management's edict on effective cash-conservation practices.

SIMULATION TECHNIQUE FOR CASH FORECASTING

For the decision-making process, a supplemental computerized simulation model can be programmed that would save much time and effort in deriving dynamic information for management review and action resulting from testing alternate courses of cash operations. A simplified overview of this model is displayed on Exhibit G.

As shown on the exhibit, the following processes are illustrated:

- Cash disbursements include product costs; capital expenditures; general, administrative, and selling expenses; and other liability payable payments.
- Cash receipts result from sales billings, interest income, borrowings, royalty income, subsidiary disposals, and investments.
- Receipts less disbursements results in the period's increase or decrease in the cash balance.
- The net cash balance is derived by combining the cash receipts with the beginning cash balance and reducing this value by the period's disbursements to obtain the ending cash balance which is reflected on the balance sheet.
- At this point in the computerized system, the developed cash balance is compared to a predetermined cash balance required for day-to-day operations. The minimum cash balance requirements should provide for normal fluctuations of income versus disbursements within the budget periods.
- If the developed and anticipated cash balance is greater than the foreseeable requirements, management must decide on the usage of this surplus in terms of possible new investments, product market expansion, decreasing outstanding short- or long-term debts, dividend payouts, and/or capital acquisitions.
- If, however, the anticipated cash balance indicates that it will be less than the minimum required, the question then arises as to the source of the additional fund requirements —borrowing, possible acceleration of customer billings, delay of projected purchases, or delay of vendor payments. The decision may be to take action on more than one possibility indicated above.

The major advantages of this type of model capability are that it provides instantaneous data from various alternatives for management's assessment, automatically adjusts the cash balance that flows into the balance sheet statement, and permits more intelligent planning supported by basic data on which decision actions have been based.

UTILIZATION OF SURPLUS CASH

Examples of short-term investments would include, but are not necessarily restricted to, the following productive income opportunities.

- Bank certificates of deposit
- Short-term market securities
- U.S. Treasury bills

SIMULATION MODEL

Cash Receipts & Disbursements

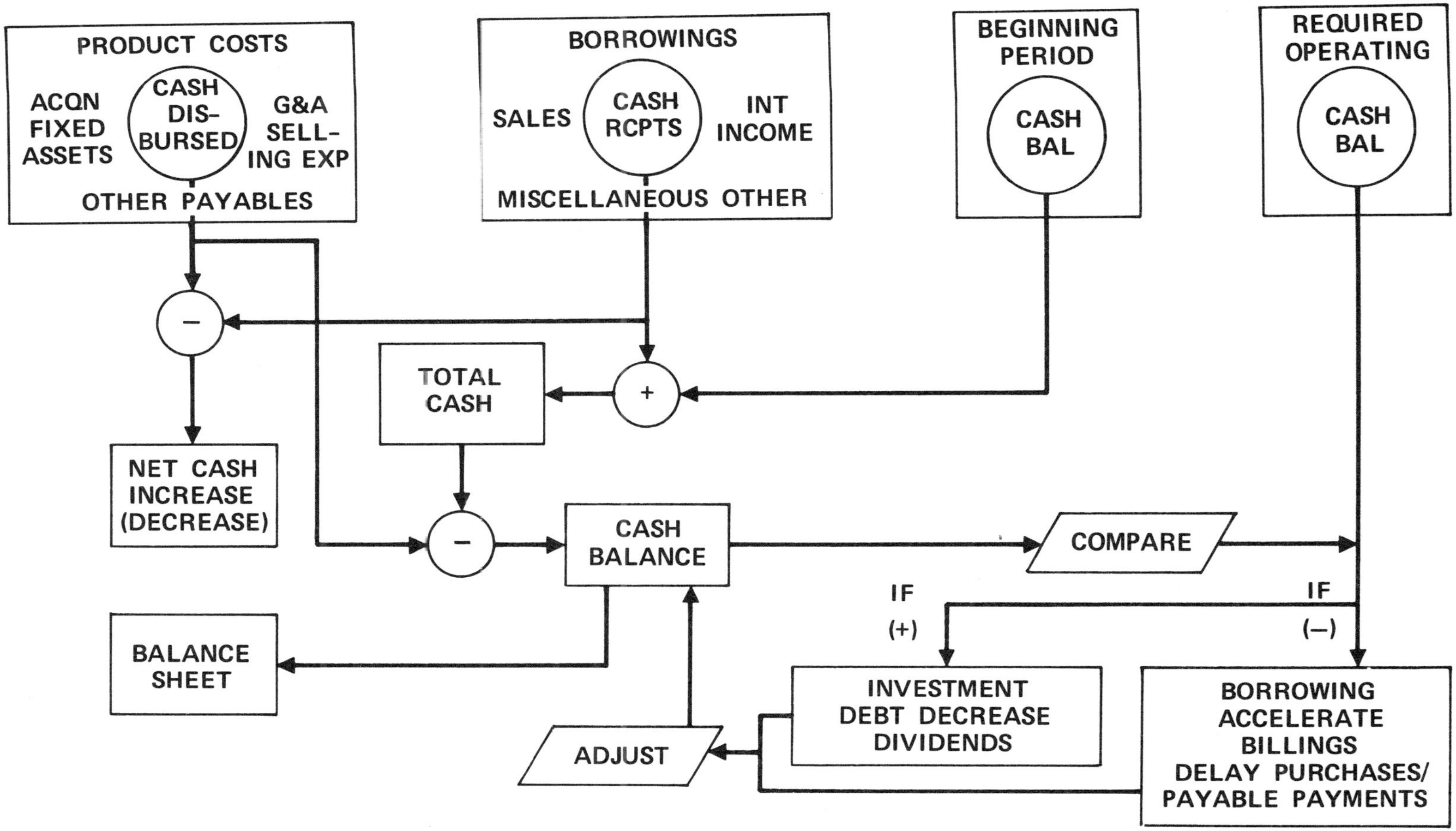

EXHIBIT G

- U.S. government or municipal bonds that will mature on or close to the anticipated date of cash needs
- Near-term loans to other industrial organizations
- Loans to lending institutions

All of the above proposals provide cash liquidity, collateral for low-rate bank loans (if required in the interim), and generally safety of principal. Some of the above recommendations also permit investment over weekends which could prove to be of substantial return. The main thrust of effective cash surplus utilization in investments is to improve an organization's profitability rather than have the surplus remain idle and nonyielding for any length of time.

For long-term investments, the following possibilities could lead to increased profitability and return on investment—

- Purchase of the organization's capital stock, thereby reducing stockholder's equity
- Development of new products and/or services
- Acquisition and/or upgrading of an organization's capital asset resources to improve operational efficiency
- Investment in or purchase of subsidiaries
- Creation of reserves for future contingencies
- Decrease of long-term debts

Efficient and realistic planning should determine when excess funds may be available for appropriate investment as discussed above. Planning and controlling are the key words in rewarding cash management results. An alert management has many options to effectively utilize their cash resources to improve the return on investment.

SIGNIFICANCE OF ACCURACY IN CASH FORECASTING

One of the prime motivating criteria that should be acknowledged by an organization in expending resources for improving its forecasting techniques is concerned with resolving the degree of accuracy required versus the cost of errors that could be committed. This is a necessary venture in order to identify and quantify the trade-offs of expenditures for improvements as opposed to projection inaccuracies.

Naturally, greater accuracy requires a larger investment in resources to accomplish because of the greater research and analysis of historical data plus the adoption of computerized scientific aids and techniques. Based on cash management objectives, costs and risks involved in a successful cash flow evaluation can be quantitatively defined as to accuracy potential and utilization. The relationship would be unique to each organization since the forecast for large-volume cash activity is more significant than that for a relative low cash organization. Further, short-term forecasts must be more realistic than long-term forecasts because of the greater immediate pressing problems to be faced.

In the short-term forecast of cash gain or loss, concentration is directed on the ability to effectively predict cash flow resulting from operational activity and the analysis of variances from plan. Another approach is its use as a cash management plan wherein emphasis is specifically directed to managing and controlling net cash results to a predetermined plan.

This approach is more difficult to achieve in that cost trade-off parameters must be well defined. The key parameters involve the cost of deviation from plan (how bad the projections were based on resultant cost exposure) such as loss of discounts, credit rating jeopardy, overexpenditures with need for borrowing, and so on.

APPROACHES TO ACHIEVING FORECAST EFFICIENCIES

There are two common methods used in improving the forecasting process. In the first instance, correlations are established based on relevant historical data and/or by making adjustments predicated on a detailed assessment of differences between the actuals and forecasts.

The correlation technique is only as valid and realistic as the availability of reliable historical data indicating that true relationships exist between two sets of data. If this is so, reliance on feedback corrections is reduced. Conversely, absence of appropriate historical data increases the reliance on feedback corrections in order to obtain accurate forecasts.

If it can be justified by trade-off analyses of cost versus value of accuracy, an ongoing process should prove to be profitable. Short-term (daily, weekly) and long-term (annual) forecasts should be projected by detailed item element so that a continuous tracking and evaluation of variances can specifically identify the problem areas that require attention in forecasting improvements.

SUMMARY CASH COLLECTION PROCESS

Exhibit H displays an overall summary of the processes involved in calculating and determining the collections in a mechanical system. As shown, cost-type contracts pose little problem as to the complexity involved in predicting cash receipts. Incurred costs lagged are lagged to the unreimbursed category of receivables and the assumption is that they will be collected within a two- to three-week time span.

Fixed-price collection processing is far more complicated. Progress payment limits and funding constraints on cost collections require many more calculations, as described previously. Relative to deliveries, a holdback percentage constraint is imposed by the customer and the full collection is not received until the complete delivery has been made and there is an acceptance on the part of the customer. The objective of this display is to provide the reader with a graphic view of what is involved in the overall cash collection cycle.

In summary, the dynamics of cash flow planning require constant surveillance of the detailed influx and outflow of funds. An operation's effectiveness is governed by having sufficient funds to meet day-to-day operational expenditures. Periodic cash surpluses must be profitably utilized through short-term investments. Cash forecasting provides management the means to assess their cash requirements in advance of need and establish a source for on-demand cash. Centralized management control offers many advantages in that cash requirements in one organization can be met by surpluses from another. Simulation of various alternatives assist management in resolving their cash needs with the overall objectives. Emphasis must be directed toward cash conservation policies and their enforcement to achieve ultimate cash management effectiveness.

SUMMARY CASH COLLECTION PROCESS

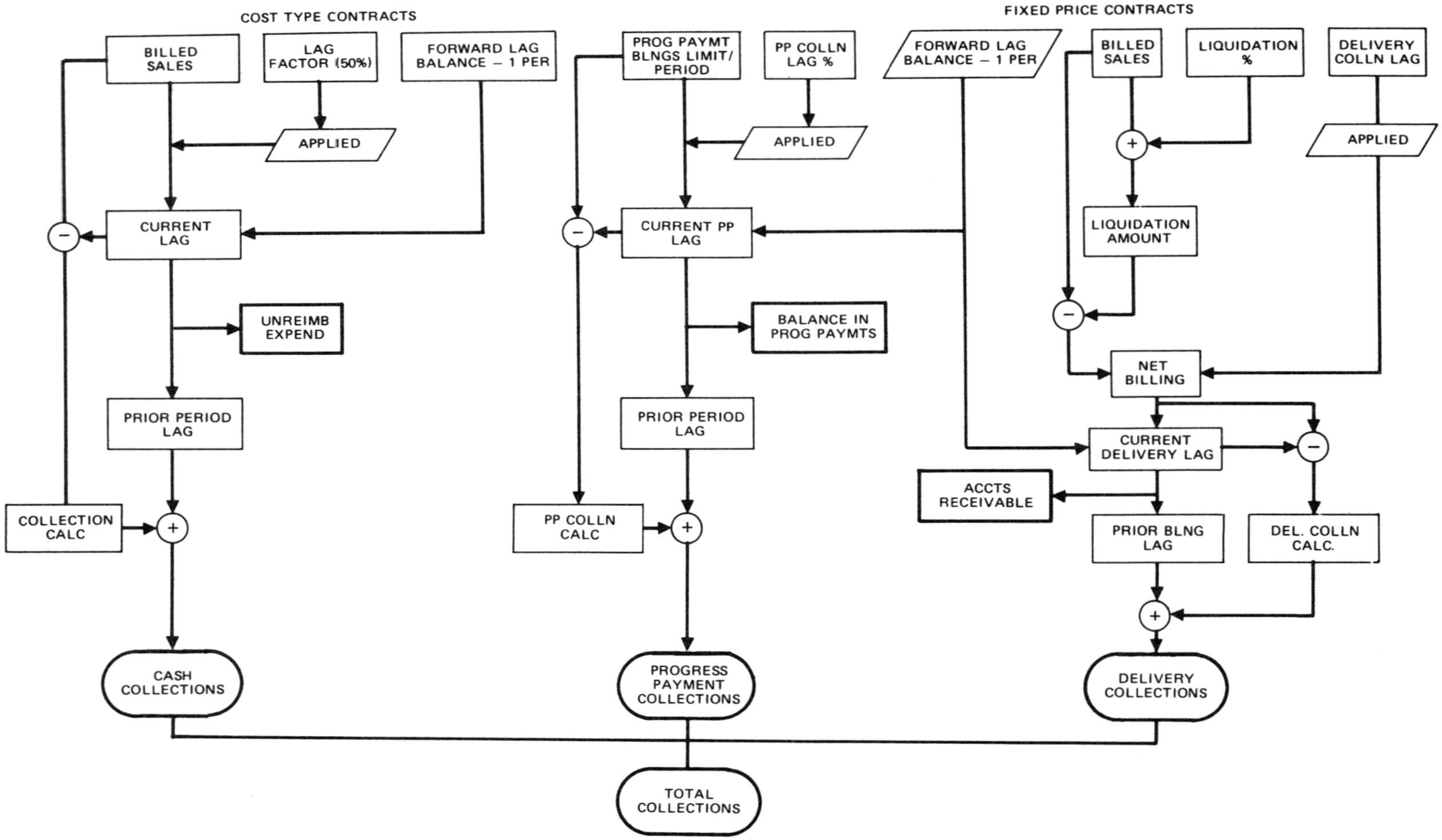

EXHIBIT H

9

Computerizing Inventory Planning, Control, and Management for Big Savings

There are various interpretations and definitions of the term "inventory" depending on the type of organization and its business environment. For example, retailers and wholesalers consider inventory to mean available merchandise on the shelf or in transit for customer sales. In the production climate, however, inventory is the organization's investment in a product (individual or a series of items) in terms of raw materials, level of effort, work in process, and/or finished goods. Organizations of all types should be concerned with the kind of inventory that is subject to obsolescence, deterioration, price fluctuation, and the requirement for constant surveillance, assessment, and control.

VALUE OF PHYSICAL INVENTORIES

Inventory represents a substantial investment in material purchases (and/or labor costs), financing, storage, and handling; therefore, it is important that appropriate attention be given to its constant management and control. Without inventory and production, sales could not be achieved, profitability would not materialize, and the organization could not survive.

Purpose of Physical Inventories

As has been experienced by countless organizations, what is disclosed by a physical inventory is often far different from what is shown in the accounting records. There may be over- and underdiscrepancies, items that could not be located, obsolete and/or unsalable material, shrinkages, and poor or nonexistent inventory management practices. The purpose, therefore, of a physical inventory is to verify that inventory exists and reflects the accounting records. The records are the bases for production/sales potential planning and replenishment planning, and also provide vital data to express the financial status of an organization because of its inclusion in the financial balance sheet reporting. Further, in some organizations, inventory records are not maintained, which makes the physical inventory mandatory in order to determine quantities and types of items that are available.

A physical inventory provides for the determination and correction of deviations from accounting records (if accurate) that may have occurred because of errors in recordkeeping, shrinkage, pilferage, or misplacement. It permits the opportunity to segregate material that has deteriorated and/or is obsolete with the appropriate adjustment to the official inventory status records. It is particularly essential in organizations where the unit of measurement at the time of raw material receipt could differ from that at the time of material issuance. For example, if raw materials are purchased in bulk quantities (by the ton) and issued by unit or size quantity, the same number of units available may not be the same and therefore a physical count is required.

Physical Inventory Criteria

The actual inventory process, depending on the product, involves counting the units; weighing, measuring, listing, and pricing of the raw materials, work in process, finished goods, factory supplies, perishable tools, and so on. It should also include goods in transit and the material received during the course of the inventory process.

Planning for the Physical Inventory

The planning process involves the establishment of the date for the inventory and the time to be allotted for its completion; the selection and organization of the personnel involved and definition of their functions; proper classification of items to be inventoried; development of appropriate instructions and forms to be used; preparation of the material for counting and/or measuring quantities; establishment of pertinent controls in the conduct of the inventory; and designation of appropriate responsibilities for accomplishing the task. All items and raw material/supplies, work in process, and finished goods on hand must be considered. Assessing work-in-process inventory is by far the most difficult task because each task must be identified and a determination made of the number of units in each operation and stage of completion.

The most appropriate time to conduct a physical inventory is at the end of the year when presumably inventory is minimal and up-to-date information is required for year-end financial reporting. The task must be done when there will be minimal effect or disruption on operations.

Types of Physical Inventories

There are generally two types of inventory-taking processes—continuous and periodic. In the continuous process, which is characteristic of larger organizations and multiple locations, a trained staff takes inventory. They conduct continuous counts or measures in rotation among the various sections of the stockrooms. This process allows minimum disruption to operations through the use of experienced staff and results in stock records that are continually adjusted and updated.

In the periodic process, the inventory is conducted at year-end or during slack operation periods. The record updates are not timely, the people used are generally untrained, and therefore the effort and results are not as accurate or efficient as in the use of a trained inventory control group.

In summary, physical inventories are valuable because they permit:

- Verification of items and quantities reflected in accounting records.
- Opportunity to determine condition and status of the inventoried items in terms of deterioration and/or obsolescence for record correction adjustments and disposal.
- Realistic reflection of the true inventory in financial status reporting.
- Assurance to management that the proper procedures are being followed in inventory control and management.

WORK-IN-PROCESS (WIP) COST PLANNING

The WIP inventory process flow basically involves the effort (labor), material, and support cost flow into the WIP cost collection and inventory systems; then, upon product completion, the cost is transferred into the finished goods inventory. When a sale is consummated, the finished goods inventory values are relieved to the cost of sales. On cost-type contracts, however, as costs are incurred and paid, they are billed to the customer with the applied fee percentage. A simplified mechanical flow of data into inventory is shown on Exhibit A.

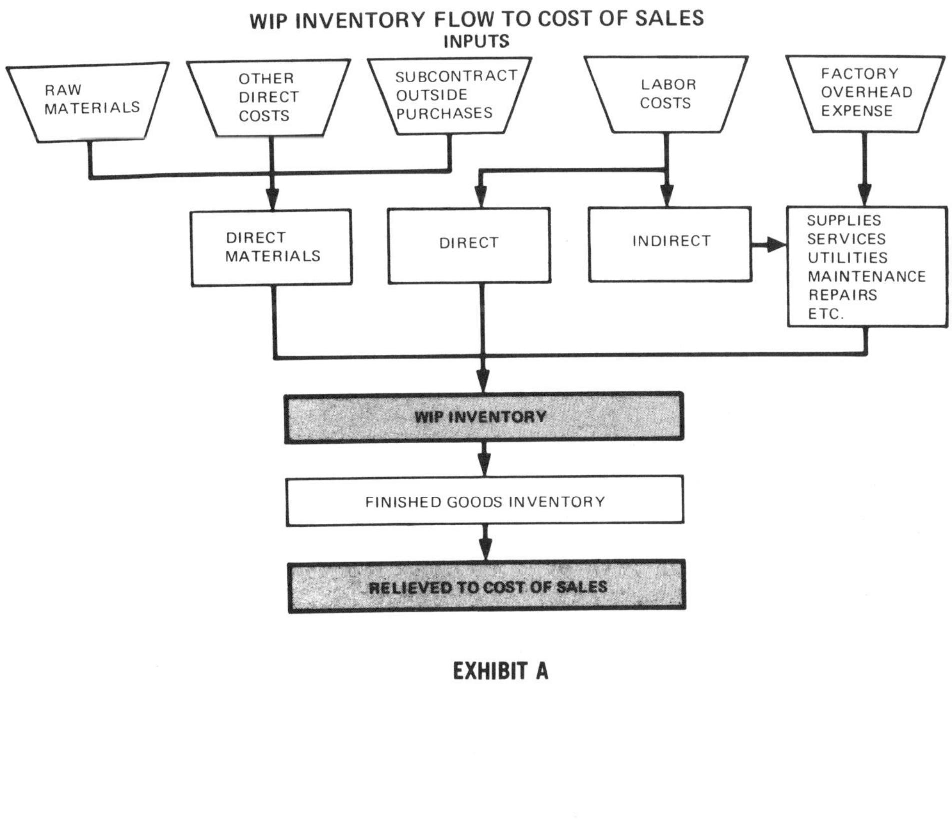

EXHIBIT A

Operations WIP Control

In actuality, the complete processing cycle is far more complex than projection of data. Cost incurrence is associated and controlled by the organization (cost center to hierarchy summary) in much greater depth through subsidiary record surveillance and reporting by detailed element of cost relative to the following requirements;

- WIP—account segregation
- Contract code, item, and task
- Manufacturing—part, item, and shop order numbers
- Test equipment—item and unit numbers
- Tooling—tool order and serial numbers
- Engineering—work order, work assignment plan, and group
- Manufacturing technology—manufacturing development work assignment
- Quality assurance—work assignment
- Manufacturing control—project budget center's functional responsibilities

Cost Incurrence Projections

Operating organizations and the appropriate management utilize much time and effort in operating plan preparation that will realistically reflect the direct cost of future operations. Starting with the basic objectives, data is developed at the contract level by each element of cost. Exhibit B displays an overview of the process.

Direct Material. As shown on the left side of the exhibit, material and other direct cost requirements, based on projected product needs, are assessed by the Material Control Group in terms of their availability in current inventory. If they are not in inventory and budget is available, purchase orders are initiated to procure the requirements. Subcontract effort needs are also reviewed and arrangements made to obtain these services to meet production scheduled dates.

Labor Activity. Based on manpower requirements, which are discussed in detail in chapter 5, direct and indirect labor hours are developed and expressed in terms of dollars. The direct labor dollars flow directly into WIP projections and the indirect factory labor dollars are reflected in the overhead forecast.

Overhead. Indirect expense is developed by individual expense accounts within the organization. Factory indirect support costs become a part of WIP inventory projections. The other overhead (such as general and administrative, corporate office, research and development), although a part of total costs, is reflected as a reduction to gross profit on the income statement both in actual and projected reporting.

Inventory Control Reporting

As period actuals of the direct WIP costs become available, they are mechanically matched by contract, organization, and cost element to the projected plan and previous

MANPOWER AND COST ELEMENT DEVELOPMENT

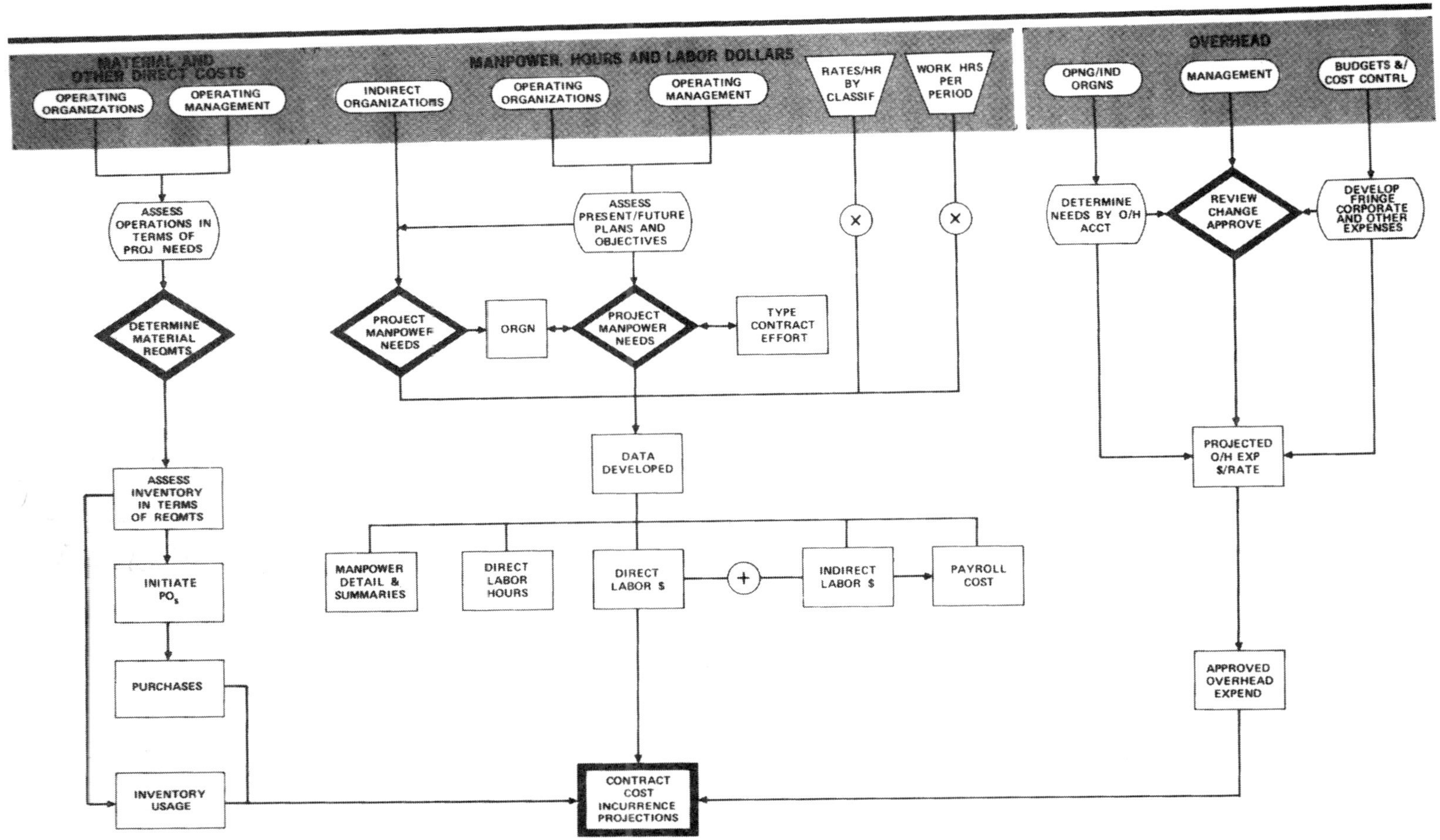

EXHIBIT B

period results. Variances are then derived for analysis and corrective action decisions. Common report formats, but not necessarily restricted thereto, that have proved successful in performance evaluation by contract, product, sales order, organization, and element of cost are illustrated below.

PERFORMANCE CONTROL REPORTING BY CONTRACT

Contract/ Product Identity	TOTAL WIP COSTS BY PERIOD			TOTAL WIP COSTS YEAR-TO-DATE		
	Prior	Current	Variance	Actual	Planned	Variance

PERFORMANCE CONTROL REPORTING BY ELEMENT OF COST

Contract/ Product Identity	CURRENT PERIOD DIRECT WIP COSTS*				Planned Effort	Variance from Plan
	Labor	Overhead	Material & ODC	Total		

*Similar format for year-to-date.

ELEMENT OF COST ANALYSIS BY CONTRACT*

Element of Cost	CURRENT PERIOD DIRECT COSTS			YEAR-TO-DATE DIRECT COSTS		
	Actual	Planned	Variance	Actual	Planned	Variance
Labor Overhead Material						
S/Total						

*Similar format by organization and summarized to project budget centers.

PERFORMANCE CONTROL REPORTING BY OPERATING ORGANIZATIONS*

Operating Organization Identity	TOTAL WIP COSTS BY PERIOD			TOTAL WIP COSTS YEAR-TO-DATE		
	Prior	Current	Variance	Actual	Planned	Variance

*Summarized to project budget centers.

The above reporting provides the basis for isolating problem areas to which attention can be directed. The reports are of sufficient variety that variances can be readily identified to specific areas requiring further analysis such as contract, organization, and element of cost. Under the computerized system, the output is rapidly achievable with minimal clerical effort.

It is noted that WIP inventory costs have been particularly stressed since they represent direct charges to the contract/product and are generated by the responsible operating organizations. The G & A expenses are excluded from this type of control analysis since their assessment and control fall under different functional entities.

AUTOMATED INVENTORY PRICING METHODS

Inventory cost flow procedures are predicated on the basic assumption that there will be unit lot utilization in sequence (FIFO, LIFO) or simultaneous use of all lots at the same relative rate and price (average method). There are various methods employed in pricing actual inventory costs for sales and/or inventory balance value development. The major ones utilized are classified as specific identification; first-in, first-out (FIFO); last-in, first-out (LIFO); and average price. Each has its own peculiar advantages and disadvantages. The organization selects the one most appropriate or desirable for their type of operation and needs. A description of each follows.

Specific Identification

In this type of costing, the items in inventory are costed based on reference to the actual costs on the purchase order and/or vendor invoice. This cost determination is a tedious method because of market price fluctuations and constant requirement for referral to the invoice to obtain the various cost data. It can be used for high-price, low-volume items or those where the inventory is purchased for a specific job and the material is physically segregated and designed for a specific project. The application has limited value on high-volume items.

FIFO

As the name implies, pricing is done on the basis of first-in, first-out. It is assumed that material issued into production is the first purchased and will be used first. When that lot is depleted, usage and price is made of the second, third, and so on. This method can be used successfully if this inventory can be readily identified as high-price-per-unit, slow-moving, or fairly large in size. Also, it is desirable if there exists a time problem associated with deterioration or obsolescence. This method is in conformance with sound principles of economics since the data used reflects accounting records and purchase/invoice data. Unrealized income or loss is not reflected in the inventory price. However, this method is undesirable for low-cost, high-volume items due to the complexity of the bookkeeping tasks and inflated profit results.

LIFO

The inventory pricing used under this method reflects the price of the latest lots being purchased last and used first in the production process. It is assumed then that the inventory balances would reflect the oldest lots and their costs, and the current cost of sales would reflect the more recent purchases. This method is similar to replacement cost in that the latest purchase price and inventory value is identical to the replacement cost at time of issue.

The LIFO method has a more important influence on profits, particularly if there are large inventories involved and the production process utilizes a lengthy time interval for product completion (this would be an indicator of a high volume of work-in-process inventory).

The LIFO method provides more realistic and stable data for the income statement from year to year and does not reflect false inventory profits during inflationary periods of higher costs. In other words, profits are more conservative which results accordingly in a reduction of income taxes. Further, this method is more desirable from management's point of view; the product sales price decisions are based on the most recent costs of inventory acquisition rather than on the historical lower costs.

The major disadvantage of LIFO is that it tends to confuse the issue of income measurement and utilization; the lowest purchase price items remain in inventory and, at some point in time, profit reporting will be distorted. LIFO costing, however, is particularly desirable where there is a definite relationship between selling price and current costs, which generally is the situation, and profit is dependent upon replacement costs. It is noted that the LIFO method cannot be used for income tax reduction purposes unless the information is also reflected in other financial statements such as the balance sheet.

Average Price Method

Under the average price method, all of the quantities and costs are combined and the average price per unit of measure is determined by dividing total costs by quantity. This method eliminates a great deal of clerical effort and is desirable for process-type industries. It has limited usefulness for job order operations.

The major disadvantage of this method is that pricing must be done at the end of the accounting period, particularly when there are continual purchases at varying prices during the period. This creates a heavy workload when time is of the essence in closing the books and issuing financial reports.

Comparative Illustration of Inventory Pricing

The methods described above in pricing inventories will yield varying profit results. FIFO would reflect the highest profits and, in turn, it would be followed by average price and LIFO (most conservative). An illustration of the above statement follows for a more comprehensive view of what happens under the three major methods of pricing. It will be assumed that 12,000 units will be sold and the markup for the sales will be 10%.

INVENTORY PRICING

Lot	Inventory & Purchases			Pricing Methods Reflecting Cost of Sales (C/S)					
				LIFO		FIFO		AVERAGE	
#	Units	P/Unit	Cost	Qty	Cost	Qty	Cost	Qty	Cost
1	2,000 @	$5.00 =	$10,000	—	—	2,000	$10,000	1,500	$ 9,187.50
2	4,000	5.50 =	22,000	2,000	$11,000	4,000	22,000	3,000	22,968.75
Beg. Inv.	6,000		$32,000	2,000	$11,000	6,000	32,000	4,500	$32,156.25
3	3,000	6.00 =	18,000	3,000	18,000	3,000	18,000	2,250	13,781.25
4	5,000	6.80 =	34,000	5,000	34,000	3,000	20,400	3,750	18,375.00
5	2,000	7.00 =	14,000	2,000	14,000	—	—	1,500	9,187.50
Total C/S	16,000		$98,000	12,000	$77,000	12,000	$70,400	12,000	$73,500.00
Summary									
Average Price		6.125		6.417		5.867		6.125	
10% Gross Margin					7,700		7,040		7,350
Sales					$84,700		$77,440		$73,500.50

The above illustrates dramatically the results of applying different price methods to inventory. The highest sales and profits are reflected under the LIFO method, next comes the average, and the lowest is FIFO. It is noted that once the pricing method selection has been made, it cannot be changed without the concurrence of the Internal Revenue Service.

Computerizing the Pricing Methods

Mechanization of the three processes illustrated above would greatly simplify the pricing process, particularly in volume lot and quantity purchases. The process is described as follows.

- Upon receipt of the invoice, the pertinent data would be entered in the system (invoice number, item description, lot identifier, quantity, and total cost). Price per unit would be calculated since it would have to include all associated costs.
- The computer program would contain the necessary instructions to perform the processing calculations for each method, which is a matter of associating quantity sold to the appropriate lot based on the pricing method.
- The gross margin percentage would be a direct input to calculate sales.
- Upon designating the method to be used, the computer would perform the above illustrated processing to derive sales, profits, ending inventory quantity, and cost balances by lot.
- The sales and cost of sales would be linked to their respective mechanical programs and would provide the basis for financial projections.

Computerizing this system would provide management with rapid data for inventory planning, results from using alternate methods of pricing, and impact of the methods on profits due to price-method decisions. It is an expedient tool for inventory and profit planning.

COST OR MARKET PRICE IMPLICATIONS

The decision as to the method to be employed in assessing and pricing inventory can have a major effect on financial reporting. The use of cost or market price, whichever is lower, reflects a combination of both actual and replacement costs. Cost represents the actual price paid for the merchandise as reflected on the purchase order and/or vendor invoice. The market price is regarded as the prevailing current price of the goods at the time that the inventory is being costed. Therefore, the inventory cost to be used will reflect the lower of the above two price comparisons.

The implication of the above price utilization for inventory is that, if the market price is less than actual cost, an adjustment will be required in the sales price in order to meet competitive bidding for business. At the same time, consideration should be given to the acceptance of probable realizable losses in the future. This is a conservative approach to inventory valuation in that effect is given to unrealizable losses but not to unrealized profits. The use of this theory of valuation varies among organizations in the same industry, as well as among industries.

The objection to this type of inventory valuation is that it does not completely satisfy either the organization's financial or operations reporting. On the one hand, the balance sheet should accurately reflect the solvency of the organization, which implies the use of the lower price as reflected by the market or cost. However, the income statement should report the exact results from operations, which are based on the true costs, since this is the criterion for judging operational performance. This valuation dilemma indicates that using the lower of cost or market distorts the current period's income statement results; however, by using the cost basis, the balance sheet reflects misleading solvency data even though the profit or loss is reported in the period that it is realizable.

A solution to the above problem would be to reflect in the income statement the estimated unrealizable profit or loss from merchandise that is sold and included in the sales price which resulted from the use of cash realizable valuation. If a profit is indicated, it would be reflected in the net worth account on the balance sheet; if a loss is anticipated, it would be included in the surplus account. On the balance sheet the inventory valuation cost value would be converted to a cash realizable basis; that is, if the cash value is anticipated to be greater, it would be added to the inventory cost valuation or deducted if realizable cash value is lower.

OBSOLESCENCE

When products are redesigned for improvement or replaced by a new product, an assessment must be made as to whether the inventory on hand still reflects the obsolete material. The lower of cost or market valuation also applies to obsolete or even damaged material. As soon as the obsolescence situation has been resolved and the material so classified, it is actually no longer applicable for inventory valuation purposes. To determine the value of the obsolete material, the process would be to estimate sales price less anticipated costs to consummate the sale to an outside source to obtain net realizable value or market price.

Continual inventory surveillance would reveal the presence of obsolete or damaged material in stock and, if the material could not be made salvageable, action would be taken to dispose of it. This could mean thousands of dollars in tax savings (depending on the size of the company's operation and the extent of obsolescence) because of the tax on inventory in possession of the organization at year-end.

INVENTORY RESERVES AND PLANNING

There are various reasons for creating raw material reserves somewhat similar to the depreciation reserve established for fixed assets. Some of the major considerations are:

- To recognize losses due to anticipated obsolescence, pilferage, shrinkage, damage, or slow-moving stock items.
- To reduce inventory cost values due to anticipated or realized declining market value to reflect a more realistic value in the accounting records.
- To minimize future losses because of the above with the reflection of the differences in the current period.

- To reflect anticipated or known differences between the accounting records and the actual physical inventory.

Using the reserve account makes the above process much simpler than attempting to associate the anticipated losses to individual stock accounts or specific units or lots. In reducing inventory valuation, the opposite side of the bookkeeping entry would be a charge to cost of sales if the cause of the reduction was the responsibility of an operating organization. If the cause was due to a general administration activity, the reflection of the reduction would be made against the income or loss account.

Types of Reserve Plans

There are three possible approaches to reflecting reserves. In the first instance, the inventory valuation price increases or decreases can be reflected in the income statement, excluded from the income statement, or they can reflect the information in surplus reserves as a liability or adjusting inventory value on the asset side of the balance sheet.

MECHANICAL INVENTORY PROCESSING

In the actual day-to-day environment, inventory control and management is best effected through mechanization. Literally hundreds of thousands (in larger firms) of items must flow through the system and be identified by various nomenclatures, component parts, locations, account descriptions, organization control responsibilities, and so on. Status must be maintained for acquisitions, transfers, usage, scrap, and resultant balances. Exhibit C displays various inventory items and the subaccount identification (numbers in the outer circle) within the major classification accounts of materials and advances, and raw materials and supplies.

As can be well imagined, the task of control and management is horrendous, involving a large number of personnel to perform the functions required.

Material Flow to Inventories

This process is initiated by a request to purchase (actual or forecast climate) to the Material Planning Group for various items that will be required to meet their operational needs. When approved (not in stock and budget available), the request is forwarded to Procurement to initiate the requisition action. A purchase order is issued to the vendor indicating item description, quantity, price, shipping instructions, delivery date, and other terms deemed necessary to establish the purchase agreement. Generally, the agreement is preliminarily resolved over the phone before the P.O. is issued.

Upon availability, the vendor ships the material to the receiving department, which inspects, verifies quantities, and issues a receiving memo. The material is then moved to a storeroom until requisitioned for use. Upon request from the production department, the material is issued, the transaction is recorded, and it is now designated as work in process. When the product has been completed, the various associated costs are assembled, recorded,

INVENTORIES - MATERIAL STORES

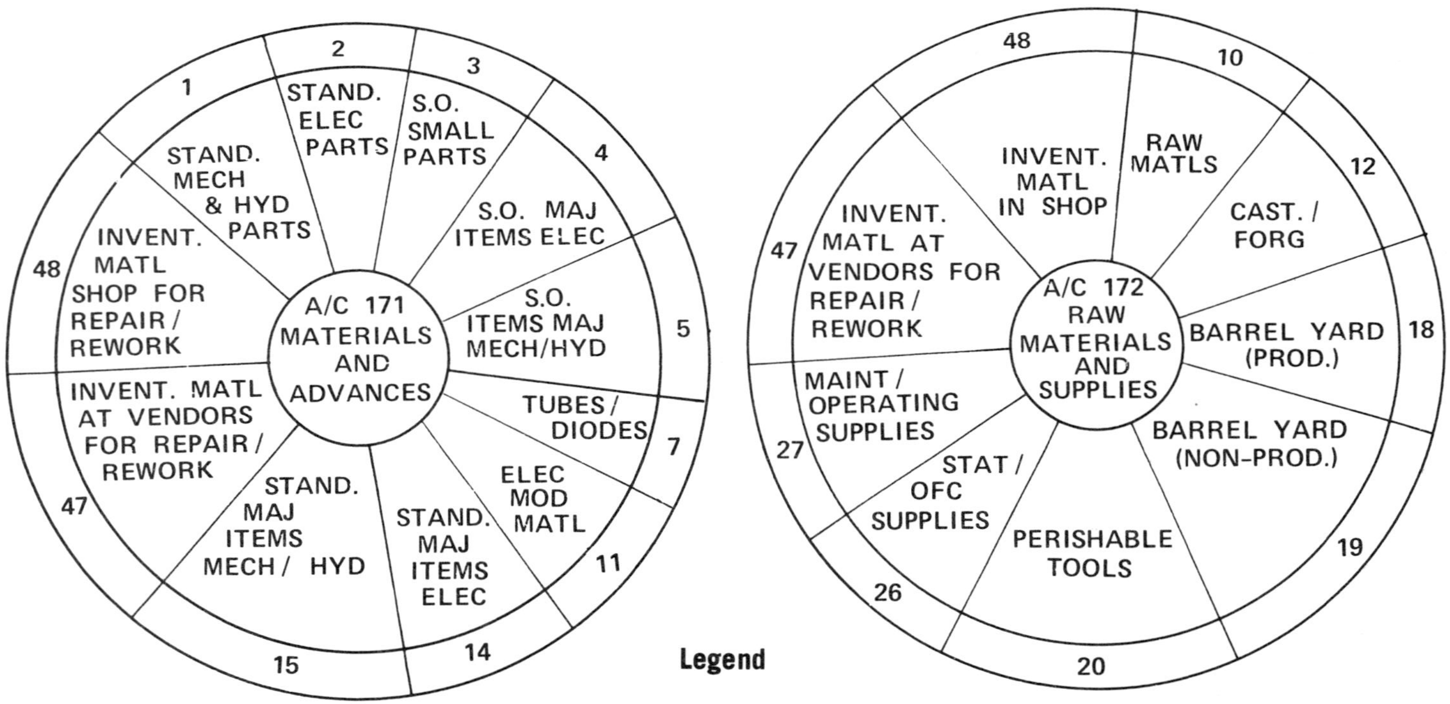

Legend

S.O.—Shop Order	**CAST—Casting**	**MOD—Modification**
STAND—Standard	**FORG—Forging**	**MATL—Material**
STAT—Stationery	**HYD—Hydraulic**	**MAINT—Maintenance**
OFC—Office	**MECH—Mechanical**	**PROD—Productive**

EXHIBIT C

and the product now is classified as finished goods and available for sale and delivery to customers.

Control Documents and Mechanical Records

To accomplish the above processing, various documents are required to record the transactions. Information for the mechanical system is inputted by the various responsible organizations. The input is initiated from purchase requisitions, purchase orders, receiving reports, change notices, stock ledger, and perpetual inventory computer file records relative to quantities, value of purchase, receipts, and disbursements. The mechanical system reconciles the data and derives inventory material quantities and costs by item identifications and their current status. Reports are issued to the organizations involved.

COMPUTERIZED INVENTORY PLANNING MODEL

As discussed under inventory processing, the development of realistic inventory data is significant in assessing the solvency and soundness of an organization's financial status. It also has an effect on a firm's operating position either as a gain or loss which reflects management's competence and success in operations. Although in the projection process the recording and reporting detail is not as horrendous as in the actual environment, nonetheless the data is planned by individual contract/product and represents a time-consuming task. Further, since this information is integrated with an overall financial model, it is necessary that this sytem be computerized to coincide with the other related mechanical systems.

An Overview of the Mechanized Process

Inventory planning for fixed-price contracts is quite similar to that employed for commercial products in terms of data development. On cost-type contracts, however, you have no inventory as such but you have residual costs classified as unreimbursed expenditures. These costs result from effort performed and are classified as accrued but unbilled or billed but payment has not been received. Exhibit D displays the process of inventory development on fixed-price contracts.

The mechanical process is described as follows:

- Work-in-process (WIP) projected direct costs to be incurred, which consists of the elements of cost, is combined with beginning WIP balance to obtain the total WIP inventory balance.
- Sales and gross profit are developed by contract and the difference between the two results in cost of sales (C/S); or C/S can be developed separately and, when deducted from forecast sales, results in gross profit.
- The WIP cost is deducted from the total WIP inventory to obtain the projected WIP ending balance as shown on the exhibit.
- The beginning material and supplies (M & S) balance is combined with the projected purchases to derive the total M & S inventory, which, when reduced by the usage, gives the ending M & S balance.

FINANCIAL DATA DEVELOPMENT

FIXED PRICE CONTRACTS

Inventories

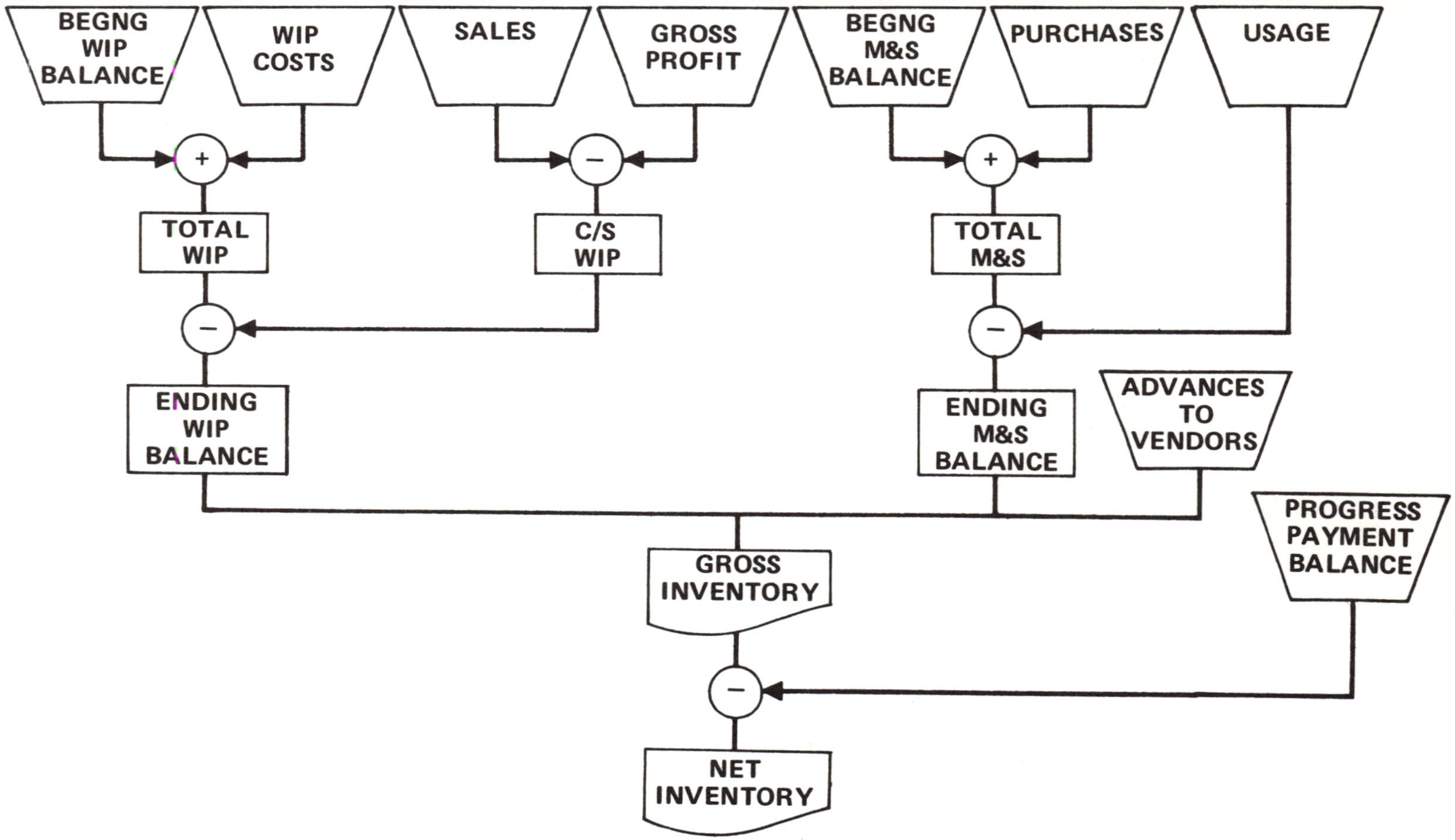

EXHIBIT D

- Advances to vendors is considered a form of inventory as it represents an investment in work being performed by the vendor for a specific contract/product. This inventory category is relieved when the work has been performed and the vendor costs equal the advances made.
- The sum of the WIP and M & S ending balances and vendor advances represents gross inventory.
- The progress or partial payment balance is deducted from the gross inventory to obtain the projected net inventory which is reflected on the asset side of the balance sheet.

The same process described above is performed for each contract and is summarized to a grand total for the organization. The mechanical process greatly simplifies the effort involved, accelerates inventory development, and gives accuracy in the calculation processes. The inputs into the system are derived from mechanical file records.

Inventory Status Development

A more detailed, but slightly different, version of the above planning process is reflected on Exhibit E, which represents the aggregate mechanical process. The object of this display, which is self-explanatory and was previously discussed in segments, is to provide an overview of the interfaces among the inventories and the income statement development. It is noted that the cost of sales is deducted from the total WIP costs to derive the ending WIP balance. The progress payment balance is combined with the decrement balance (difference between cumulative sales and billings) and deducted from the gross inventory to obtain net inventory. The loss reserve balance is a projected contingency (a pessimistic approach but could be a realistic assumption) and is added to the WIP balance to adjust the gross inventory accordingly.

This type of mechanical model can save countless hours in reconciling projected data that interface to obtain end results. The major advantage is the ability to change input (developed by contract) and immediately observe the effect from the simulation process change. Further, the data bank files provide the opportunity to compare and evaluate operation performance results when actuals become available and are inputted into this system.

ASPECTS OF INVENTORY CONTROL

The control of inventory is one of management's most difficult problems since it involves an intelligent determination of the level at which inventory should be maintained. The resolution must be based on the premise that inventory must be large enough to meet the demands of business (sales). However, it must be maintained conservatively small to avoid excess. Inventory levels above the demand of sales result in increasing expenditures for storage space and handling; interest on borrowed funds to finance purchases; problems with cash flow and physical control; higher property taxes; and deterioration and obsolescence.

Another aspect involved in the inventory control process is its valuation that can fluctuate and affect profit or loss as well as the organization's financial status as reported on the balance sheet. This situation can result from uncontrollable price and volume influences.

INVENTORY STATUS DEVELOPMENT

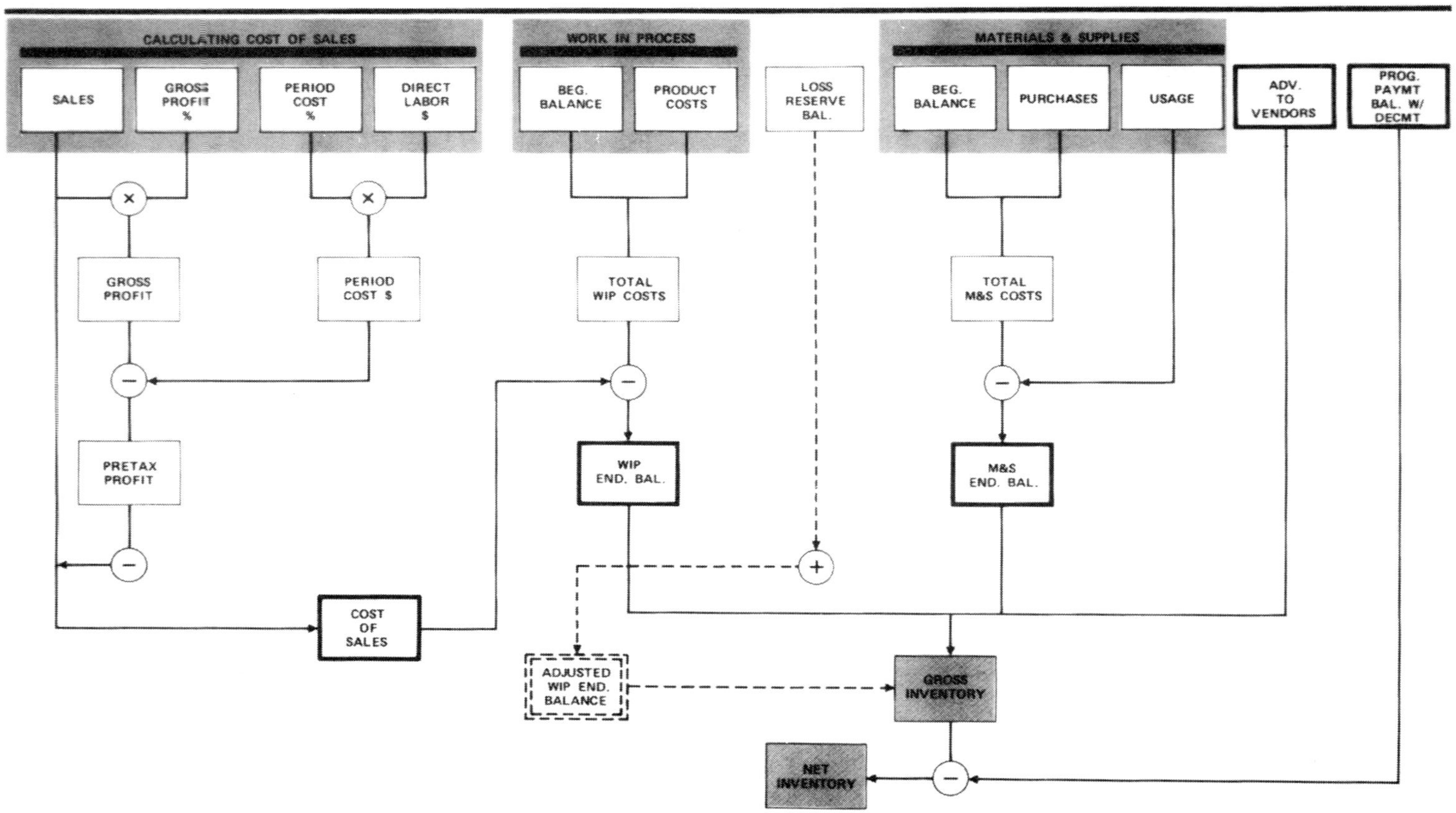

EXHIBIT E

The price level at the date of acquisition can differ substantially from a subsequent market replacement cost, which could be minimized by the extent of inventory at a given point in time. Commodity volume variation is dependent upon customer demand and the projection of future requirements.

Objectives of a Mechanical System

Computerization of an inventory control and planning system would achieve the following advantageous objectives:

- Provide more timely advice as to current or potential shortages.
- Give a capability of reporting inventory at the part, product, and contract levels.
- Afford visibility as to excess usage resulting from scrap, shop loss, waste, deterioration, inventory gains or losses.
- Provide an updated status of inventory in stock versus projected requirements by items or groups of items.
- Make available detailed inventory for improving control and material management.
- Fulfill the requirements for contractual status reporting.
- Be cost effective and considerably reduce clerical effort in manual transaction recording, reconciling, and reporting.
- Provide for selective and exception reporting.

Use of Ratios for Analysis and Control

Ratios can often be used as an effective means of inventory status measurement and progress, which in turn provide criteria for management decisions to improve planning and control. They can also be misleading if certain influencing factors are not considered in the data analysis. Evaluating considerations are concerned with the relative events that may have affected the organization's inventory status during the year, the trend of ratios in successive periods of time, and a recognition of the typical and comparative behavioral pattern of the common industry as a whole.

The prime ratios for analysis and investigative control are noted as follows:

(1) *Inventory turnover*—Calculated by dividing the annualized cost of sales by the average inventory—indicates the number of times inventory had to be replenished to fulfill the requirements of the cost of sales.

(2) *Relationship of inventory balances to cost of sales*—Computed by dividing average inventory for sale by the total average cost of sales—indicates the proportionate inventory value included in the cost of sales.

(3) *Inventory to current assets*—Calculated by dividing the inventory balance by the total current assets—determines the inventories' proportionate contribution to the total current assets.

(4) *Average days of cost of sales in inventory*—The most realistic method of calculating this statistic is to sum the ending inventory balances for the year (or annualize) and divide by 365 to obtain the average daily inventory. Follow the same procedure for cost of sales. Then divide the average daily inventory by the average daily cost of sales. Determines the number of days of cost of sales in inventory.

Decreases in turnover with increases in the number of days of cost of sales in inventory indicate a problem that should be investigated and corrected. It signifies that a buildup of inventory is occurring that may be due to lack of sales, mismanagement, or possibly a buildup of unsalable or obsolete merchandise—any of the three situations is a problem.

INVENTORY MANAGEMENT

Inventory management is concerned with all aspects of this asset's utilization. It is applicable to all phases of material acquisition, inventory shortage forecasting, allocation issues, and cost control. Inventory management planning involves the cycle of events displayed on Exhibit F.

INVENTORY MANAGEMENT PLANNING

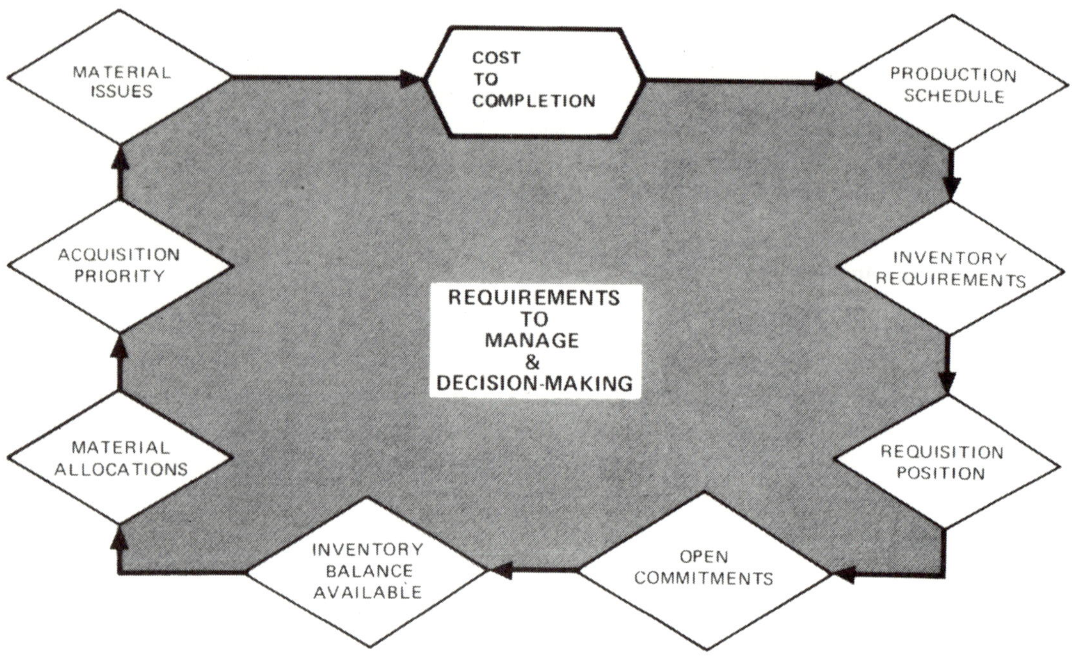

EXHIBIT F

Computerized Inventory Management

In order to properly manage inventory and provide planning criteria, management must be provided with various types of information for their decision-making process. This is most effectively accomplished through a computerized system the objectives of which, in terms of output, would include the following capabilities:

- Provide accurate cost-to-complete information relative to program status, excess inventory, open commitments, requisition requirements, and inventory value by program.

- Inactive material reporting and measurement.
- Centralize material issue control.
- Reconcile accounting and inventory records.
- Properly allocate material to meet production schedule requirements.
- Provide data for the make-or-buy decisions.
- Project inventory requirements by period.
- Forecast material shortages by time period based on inventory/purchase availability and requirements.

Establishing the above reporting requisites in a computerized system will greatly reduce the effort involved in managing inventory successfully and providing the appropriate data support to operational organizations.

In summary, the importance of managing, planning, and controlling inventory cannot be overemphasized. There is much interface between cost accumulation and inventory status. Physical inventories are necessary to verify accounting records and provide a periodic means to isolate and dispose of obsolete and damaged material as well as to assess inventory management procedures. Setting up inventory reserves should definitely be a consideration in the planning process. Inventory valuation methods should be carefully evaluated in order to select the one that is most appropriate for an organization's operations due to financial statement effect. Computerization is most cost effective and recommended for successful inventory planning control and management.

10

Computerized Methods and Control of Accounts Receivable

A basic practice in the business environment is the sale of a product or performance of a service on credit terms, whether it be to an individual, another business enterprise, or a government agency. When this situation occurs, upon delivery of the product or service, a receivable is automatically created.

Overextension of credit or selling to poor-risk customers can cause a catastrophe to the organization's operations adversely affecting cash flow and working capital. This could lead to complete impairment of an organization's ability to function due to lack of purchasing power to buy goods and the means to pay their bills. Many examples can be cited to prove this point which can occur in any size organization. The cause for this dilemma is generally attributed to overzealous sales activity at the expense of strict credit policy precautions, cash insufficiency to support operations, and lack of receivable controls.

In order to preclude this situation, it is very important for an organization to be totally cognizant of the interactions among credit policy and sales, customer appraisal, receivable controls, bad debt estimation and consequences, and the collection cycle. Lack of understanding of any of these considerations could unfavorably affect the results and veracity of instituting the appropriate control measures.

PRODUCT COST AND SALES DATA FLOW

An actual credit sale or its projection involves many facets of an organization's transaction activity. A simplified version of the data flow relative to sales, receivables, and collections is displayed on Exhibit A.

This exhibit represents a mechanical projection model in which the elements of cost (requirements) are generated through subsystem models in order to determine the cost of

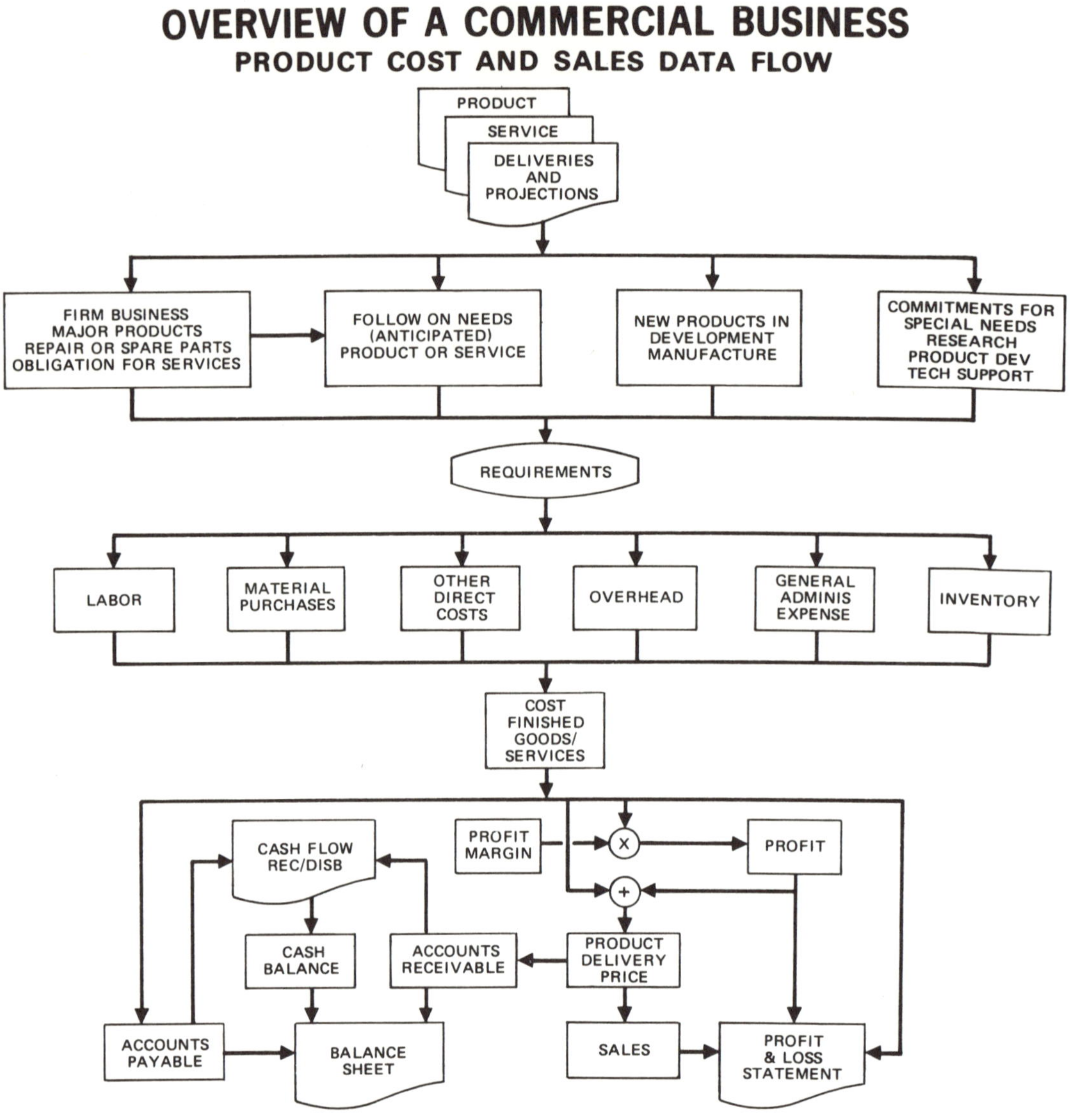

EXHIBIT A

finished goods or services performed. A similar type of process is involved in the actuals environment.

A predetermined profit margin percentage (actual or projected) is applied to the total costs to obtain the profit dollars; this is added to the costs to determine the product/service delivery price which represents sales. Costs, profit, and sales are then reflected in the income statement.

Upon delivery and invoicing, a customer accounts receivable is created. When a customer payment is made, a cash receipt results that is reflected in the cash flow schedule as well as the balance sheet. Converse to sales, costs or purchases are reflected in the accounts payable account and, when paid, a cash disbursement entry is created that affects both the cash flow and balance sheet schedule. A by-product of this system is a listing of projected sales by customer and period, receivable balances, and collection status.

ASPECTS OF CREDIT SALES

Since credit sales govern receivable values, there are certain pertinent facts that should be considered relative to sales for a better understanding of the receivables balance account.

Terms and Conditions

Before a sales order is consummated, the agreement will specify certain terms and conditions relative to the product being purchased such as description, quantity, price, delivery date, shipping instruction, and cash or credit sale terms.

As an incentive to cash sales, the seller will generally specify a discount in terms of some percentage being deducted from the purchase price if the account is paid within the time limit, generally ten days. The majority of transactions are net within thirty days.

Another common provision of most sales contracts is that, if the product does not meet certain specifications as agreed upon, it can be returned to the seller and the appropriate allowance or credit will be given to the buyer. This is a good practice on the part of the seller if he wants to maintain an amicable relationship with the buyer, particularly in terms of future sales and reputation for fairness.

When the above situation occurs, the sales value is reduced by the amount of the return and, if the sale was for cash, the appropriate amount is refunded to the buyer. Credit sales returns or allowances are also a reduction to the receivable account.

Sales Order Entry

A sales transaction is accomplished by several different methods: purchase order received directly from the customer, salesman's order forms (direct contact) which are signed by the customer, letters of inquiry as to a sale price quote which subsequently culminate in a sale, and through the contract which is a formal agreement of a commitment for services to be performed or deliveries made. The contract method is the most common way of doing business, particularly with government agencies.

For effective internal control over the sales order entry, certain verifications are required such as: catalogue number and description, price, credit authorization, quantity, a numbering system to assure the organization that all of the sequential sales numbers are accounted for in the records, and the reporting of all open orders for action and disposition.

Customer's Ledger

As deliveries are made to a customer, an invoice is prepared showing the customer's name and address, his record identification number, date, terms of the sale, quantity being delivered, unit sales price, and total price. This information is entered in a customer's subsidiary ledger.

When transactions occur such as payments, additional purchases and returns, and allowances, this information is added to the ledger record so that the account is continually updated. At the end of a given period, all of the customer's account balances are summarized to the total receivable balance account for journalization.

Under the mechanization process particularly, a series of subledgers is maintained for more refined analyses such as: receivables by type of customer, by product line or program, sales territory, salesman, risk grouping (very important), and aging. Categorization is an indispensable tool to analysis and more precise monitoring of receivable accounts for control purposes.

CRITERIA FOR CREDIT SALES DECISIONS

Continual surveillance is required not only of the credit and collection policies, but also of the specific customer's payment performance. At any point in time, a customer's risk status may change from good to bad and vice versa depending on many circumstances. Examples of what could happen are noted as follows:

a. Changing business climate—The customer's position in the competitive market lessens due to new and better products and methods presented by his competition.
b. Changes in customer's credit rating by credit agencies—There may be some reversal of his business in the offing that had not yet become public knowledge such as anticipated losses or a traumatic change in the cash flow position or working capital.
c. Major changes in the organization management—This could affect payment policies such as delaying payment of their bills to conserve cash or delays in decision-making policies because of their newness with the organization.
d. Problems encountered by the customer in obtaining proper financing for business operations, expansion plans, or new product development—This could result in a serious situation detrimental to their business.
e. External forces' effect such as high interest rates on borrowing money, new government regulations on environmental controls that would increase costs and jeopardize operations, and possible restrictions on expansion—Any of these could influence the customer's operation.

Credit Account Appraisal

Most companies generally use credit agencies to obtain data as to a customer's ratings through financial statement analysis, investigation of a customer's past history relative to his payment record, trade relationships, delinquency record, and any other pertinent information that might be helpful in assessing the customer's ability or creditability to pay for his purchases.

Larger organizations usually maintain their own credit and collection resources which are the responsibility of the treasurer or controller. This setup is highly desirable when there are a large number of accounts that have to be continually monitored in order to preclude the lack of attention to possible account delinquencies and/or changes in customer credit ratings or status.

TYPES OF RECEIVABLES

A receivable can be defined as an informal agreement to pay a debt or obligation which results from a delivery of a product or performing a service. They are classified and segregated in the financial records as to the type of customer involved and defined as follows:

- TRADE—This group is generally identified as ordinary business accounts, commercial in nature, and involved in a similar industry or complementary type of operations.
- NONTRADE—This group includes nonprofit organizations and other types of businesses that do not fall into the typical trade or government account groupings.
- GOVERNMENT—This group includes both military and civilian agencies. When the contract is for a total negotiated price, the receivable is classified as "Fixed Price." If the contract is negotiated for costs plus fixed or incentive fee, then the receivable is classified as "Unreimbursed Costs and Estimated Profits."
- INTERDIVISION/INTERCOMPANY—This type of receivable results from internal suborganization sales or purchases.

ASPECTS OF BAD DEBTS

When a credit sale is made to a customer, the amount due represents the accounts receivable owed. For various reasons, not all of the receivables are collected or collectible. The customer may have gone into bankruptcy since the sale was made, his business may have suffered adverse problems such as increased competition, technological changes, or major redirection of the organization's operations.

To cope with this kind of situation, the seller has reconciled himself to the fact that bad debt expense should be reflected in their planning and financial reporting. This is part of accounting's conservatism in recordkeeping. This is an accepted and good procedure to follow in order to avoid surprise of potential losses that could greatly influence the cash flow position and future commitments.

Bad Debts Versus Depreciation

Uncollectible receivables can be compared to a depreciation reserve for capital or fixed assets. Both are valuation accounts and reflect the anticipated value of the asset on the books. Both are based on judgment, experience, and management decision in estimating the values to be projected or recorded.

Bad debt expense and depreciation are reflected in the income statement as a reduction to profit. In the balance sheet, the accumulated depreciation reserve is shown as a reduction to the gross cost of property acquired to derive the net property value reflected under assets. Estimated uncollectibles are reflected as a reserve for doubtful accounts, which is a reduction to the accounts receivable asset.

Direct Write-Off of Receivables

When it has been determined that an account is no longer collectible due to the various reasons discussed above, many organizations consider it advisable to write off the account as a total loss. To achieve this in the accounting transaction, the entry would debit bad debt expense and credit the customer's receivable account. This transaction, in effect, offsets profits with the loss and removes the receivable from the records and total receivable balance.

Worthless Account Write-Off

If an organization has been projecting aggregate allowances for doubtful accounts and it has just cause to believe a specific customer's account is now worthless, the bad debt transaction would be recorded as a debit to allowances for doubtful accounts and a credit to the customer's receivable account. Since, in the aggregate, the loss was written off in prior periods, the bad debt expense is not debited as shown under the direct write-off procedure above.

Collection of Accounts Written Off

There are occasions when an account has been written off to allowances for doubtful accounts (or uncollectibles) and, later, the customer pays his debt. When this situation occurs, an adjustment must be made to the records to reflect this change. The accounting transaction entry would debit accounts receivable and credit the allowance for doubtful accounts, which would, in effect, reverse the previous write-off of the receivable.

Another entry is also necessary in order to properly reflect this change in events; that is, to debit cash for the payment received and credit the receivable account. It is true that the receivable debit in the first entry offsets the credit in the second entry, but the customer's account should be adjusted so that the records do not show him to be delinquent. This could influence future sales to this customer based on his credit history record.

The above changes are readily accomplished in the computerized system through a transaction input entry which would result in a simultaneous adjustment to all records. Also, the mechanical output status of a customer's account would reveal all types of data differences such as under- or overpayments, over- or underdeliveries, age of account balances, date of last sales order, deduction of unentitled discounts, failure to take a discount, last payment date, and type of purchase. All of this data makes up the customer's history record on file.

PROJECTING UNCOLLECTIBLE RECEIVABLES

There are any number of methods that can be used successfully in projecting uncollectible receivables. The aging process is one typical example in which the receivables are classified according to the uncollected value of the receivables by time period. An assessment is made of each period's receivables and amounts are segregated as to under 30 days, 30-59 days, 60-90 days, and over 90 days. This method will be discussed in detail under "Receivable Balance Analysis and Control."

Percentage of Credit Sales

This method uses a rate application to credit sales based on historical statistics to project bad debt expense. The total average uncollectibles for given periods divided by the sales volume average results in a projected percentage that will indicate the additions to be made to the doubtful account balance. An example of this method is reflected below:

Year	Total Sales	Total Uncollectibles	%
19X1	$ 50,000	$ 750	1.5
19X2	70,000	1,260	1.8
19X3	80,000	1,600	2.0
Total (3 years)	$ 200,000	$ 3,610	1.85 (average)
Total (2 years)	$ 150,000	$ 2,860	1.91 (average)

If the projected sales for year 19X4 were $85,000, the most realistic average percentage would be the last two-year average, since data analysis indicates that as sales volume increases, the uncollectible percentage increases relatively. However, the more conservative approach would be as follows:

a. Sales between 19X2 and 19X3 increased 14% and the percentage of uncollectibles increased .2%.
b. The projected sales for 19X4 of $85,000 is an increase of 6% over 19X3, which would indicate a .1% increase in uncollectibles or 2.1% total (19X3 uncollectibles of 2.0% plus .1% for increase in sales).
c. The projected uncollectibles for 19X4 would be estimated at $1,785 ($85,000 × 2.1%).

Careful analysis of historical data and exercise of judgment will provide the best basis for projecting uncollectibles relative to sales volume. It is noted that if sales returns and allowances are also projected, they must then be deducted from the projected sales before the percentage of uncollectibles is applied to the sales amount.

Percentage of Receivable Balance

This is another means of projecting uncollectibles that may be more appropriate in some organizations. In this method, the total uncollectibles are divided by the average receivable to obtain a percentage that could be used to estimate bad debt expense. The procedure for generating this statistic is reported as follows:

Year	Average Receivables	Average Uncollectibles	%
19X1	$ 50,000	$ 2,000	4.0
19X2	45,000	1,890	4.2
19X3	55,000	2,090	3.8
Total	$ 150,000	$ 5,980	3.99 (use 4.0%)

If the projected average receivable for 19X4 is $46,000, the estimated uncollectibles would be $1,840 ($46,000 × 4.0%), which represents the total allowance need for 19X4. If, however, there is a balance in the allowance account, then that amount would be deducted from the estimated uncollectibles of $1,840. If we were to assume that the balance was $500, then the transaction entry at year-end would be a debit to bad debt expense and a credit to allowances for doubtful accounts of $1,340 ($1,840 − $500).

RECEIVABLE BALANCE ANALYSIS AND CONTROL

In addition to the precautions that can be taken prior to making a credit sale, such as credit agency investigation, bank checks, other supplier or buyer information, and the purchaser's previous history records, the seller must perform constant surveillance of customer accounts after the sale agreement has been consummated and deliveries effected.

Internal Controls

In order to provide adequate internal control of receivables, the following criteria should be observed:

1. Appropriate action should be taken to ensure the least possible risk in extending credit. A thorough investigation must be made of all potential customers. The terms and limits of the account should be carefully defined.
2. The individuals responsible for receivables should not, in any way, be associated with cash receipt activity in order to preclude tampering with account balances; otherwise, this would endanger the existence of the very necessary double-check process.
3. Delinquent accounts should be reviewed and analyzed periodically in order to minimize the possibility of additional sales being made unknowingly, which would aggravate the situation of further bad debt expense incurrence.
4. Bad debt write-off authorization procedure should be carefully followed as defined by management edict so that the proper authority is providing the decision-action in each case.
5. The detailed customer account balances should be reconciled to the total receivable balance on a periodic basis to assure that the records are in balance.
6. The billing department's records and statements should properly reflect the customer account balances in the subsidiary ledger.
7. The terms and conditions of the sales agreement should be strictly adhered to.

Centralization Versus Decentralization Receivable Control

In organizations with multi-plant locations and suborganizations, the question often arises whether to centralize or decentralize accounts receivable and cash collection control. There are pros and cons to this determination that can best be resolved by individual situation assessment. Some of the considerations involved in the judgment decision are noted below.

Advantages of Centralized Control

1. Economy exists in maintaining centralized records, particularly when using computeriza-

tion. Data entry is by suborganization, which receives customer status reports as a by-product of the aggregate receivable summary.

2. Standardized procedures are utilized for all units within the parent organization.
3. Receivable information is on a continual up-to-date basis for central management's review and decision-making when problems of delinquency are starting to arise.
4. Centralization serves as a control over suborganization's operations relative to sales, collections, and receivable status.
5. Computerization of receivables and collections could be more practicable at the centralized level.
6. More competent personnel, with greater experience, generally prevails on the central organization level with greater authority to make immediate decisions.

Disadvantages of Centralized Control

1. Less personal knowledge of a customer's specific problems could negatively influence decisions on credit extension or resolution of problems.
2. Reporting to the decentralized organization could be slower, which could impede important decision-making on the lower level.
3. Future planning may not be truly representative of the decentralized organization's needs or desires.
4. It could be a deterrent to the initiative and progress of personnel in the decentralized atmosphere.
5. Many relative facts of an impending problem may not be available at the time of need to the suborganization, thus preventing prompt customer service.

Aging Process

Periodically, generally monthly, all open account balances should be classified as to their billing dates. This is done by segregating the accounts as to under 30 days, 30-59 days, 60-90 days, and over 90 days. The following simplified table illustrates how two time periods are compared to indicate the trend of the time delay in making collections.

	3/31/X1		6/30/X1		6/30 Inc. (Dec.) 3/31/X1	
Age of Billing	Amount	% Total	Amount	% Total	Amount	% Variance
Under 30 Days	$ 10,000	55.6	$ 15,000	55.6	$ 5,000	—
30-59 Days	5,000	27.8	8,000	29.6	3,000	1.8
60-90 Days	2,000	11.1	3,000	11.1	1,000	—
Over 90 Days	1,000	5.5	1,000	3.7	—	(1.8)
Total	$ 18,000	100.0	$ 27,000	100.0	$ 9,000	—

It is noted that, in spite of the dollar variance in the first and third aged groups, the percentage of the total remained the same with no variance percentage. Further, a favorable variance percentage occurred in the fourth group and an unfavorable one in the second group. This indicates that attention must be directed to an analysis of the second group in detail in order to ascertain the reason for the increase. A detailed computerized run of the past-due accounts in this category would provide the answer in a matter of seconds.

Analysis of Current Versus Past-Due Accounts

Another means used to determine what controls should be established is through an assessment of the individual customer account balances as a supplement to the above aging process. This type of analysis shows the beginning period balances plus the customer's purchases during the period as well as the payments and the ending receivable balance categorized as to invoicing age. The following example illustrates this method:

	Customer			
Beginning Balance	A	B	C	Total
Under 30 Days	$ 3,000	—	—	$ 3,000
30-59 Days	—	$ 2,000	—	2,000
60-90 Days	—	—	$ 1,000	1,000
Total Beginning Balances	$ 3,000	$ 2,000	$ 1,000	$ 6,000
Current Period Billings	6,000	4,000	2,000	12,000
Current Period Payments	2,000	1,000	1,000	4,000
Ending Balances	$ 7,000	$ 5,000	$ 2,000	$14,000
Aged Group Detail:				
Under 30 Days	$ 6,000	$ 4,000	$ 2,000	$12,000
30-59 Days	1,000	—	—	1,000
60-90 Days	—	1,000	—	1,000
Total	$ 7,000	$ 5,000	$ 2,000	$14,000

In the above analysis, you can see a trend in which Customer B's account is getting more delinquent whereas Customer C is improving his status. This analysis indicates a need for closer surveillance of the future status of both Customer A and Customer B accounts relative to credit risk.

Other Common Ratio Analyses

The collection ratio to credit sales every three months would provide a moving trend as to whether the receivable is increasing, decreasing, or remaining static. Particular attention, however, is required that the appropriate payment lag has been reflected in this analysis. Collection and sales averaging should overcome this reservation on the lag period.

The delinquency ratio is often used to test an organization's credit and collection policies. This is a comparison of the total delinquencies to sales volume for given periods of time. It could also provide an indication as to whether the organization's customer sales policies are too loose or too strict, which, in turn, would be a determining criterion in establishing future credit policy.

Under the proper circumstances, the bad debt ratio can be used as a standard for receivable balance measurement and control. This is a ratio of bad debts to sales for a given period of time. Its major disadvantage is that the bad debts may have been from a prior period that may not necessarily reflect the current operations and decisions.

REPORTING FOR CONTROL PURPOSES

In order to effectively analyze and control the status of the receivable accounts and monitor customer payments, certain output reports from the mechanical system are necessary to highlight the various pertinent transactions occurring during a period and their effect on the customer's account. The following reports typify the information required for the customer's account status review:

1. *Accounts Receivable Detail*
   This report shows the billings, collections, and balances by individual sales order/contract number and customer for the current time period and year-to-date.
2. *Unpaid Invoice Summary*
   This report displays all invoices unpaid by the customer and total unpaid. Its purpose is to highlight the open balances for analysis and possible action. The summary of the unpaid invoices represents the accounts receivable balance on the books.
3. *Age of Receivable Balances*
   This report lists all of the open balances by sales order and customer for the current period, 30-59 days, 60-90 days, and over 90 days. The purpose of this report is to determine the age of the receivables and why these balances exist.
4. *Composite Customer Record Report*
   This report shows a summary of total billings and collections by customer for the period and year-to-date. It provides a means of determining how much was actually billed and collected from each customer. The billings reflect outstanding receivables and the collections represent cash receipt values for the period and year-to-date.
5. *General Ledger Reconciliation*
   This report displays total billings and collections by account classification reconciled to customer totals in order to make sure the general ledger accounts tie in with the customer's subsidiary ledger.
6. *Individual Customer Record*
   This report is segregated into individual customer listings that display the detailed month-by-month transactions in terms of sales, billings, collections, and balances. It provides a means for a detailed analysis of the customer's account.

TRANSACTION DATA FLOW

Sales or Services

An overall view of sales or services performance data flow is displayed on Exhibit B. As shown on this exhibit, deliveries are invoiced to outside organizations and to other internal suborganizations such as divisions and subsidiaries. The delivery represents a receivable for collection. There is a lapse of time between the invoicing and the cash receipt. This time lag varies in different organizations and with the type product involved but the general terms are payment within 30 days. Extenuating circumstances, such as a change in

TRANSACTION DATA FLOW
SALES OR SERVICES

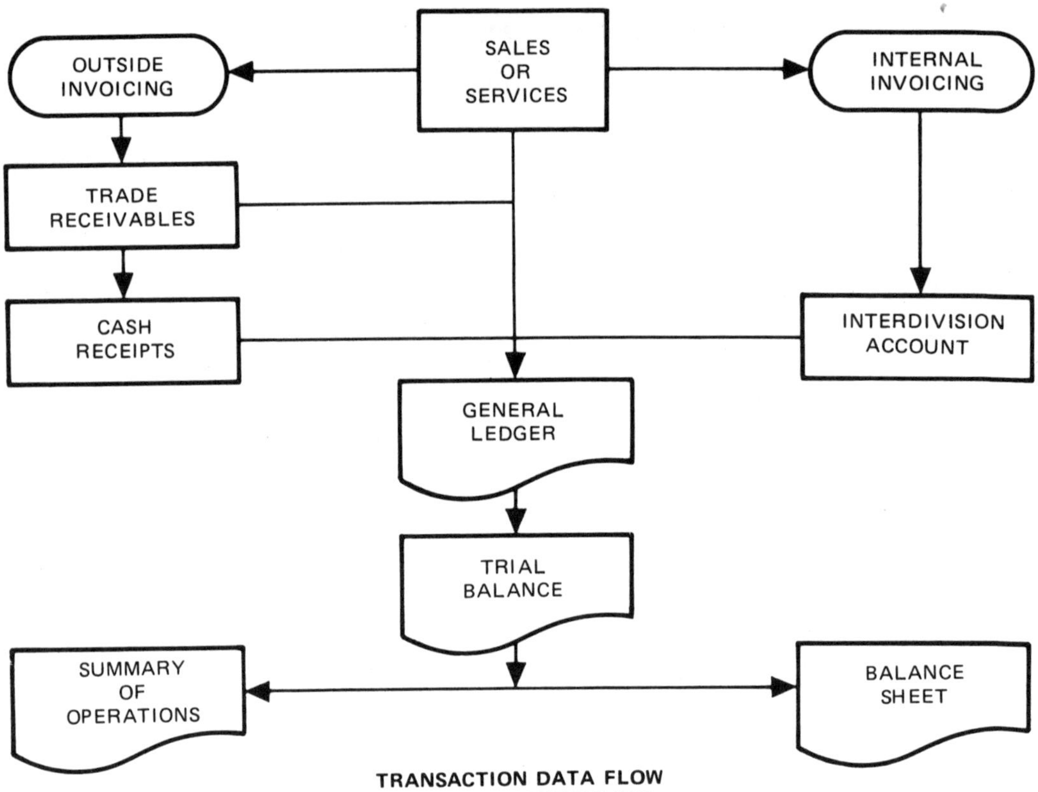

TRANSACTION DATA FLOW
INVENTORY PURCHASES

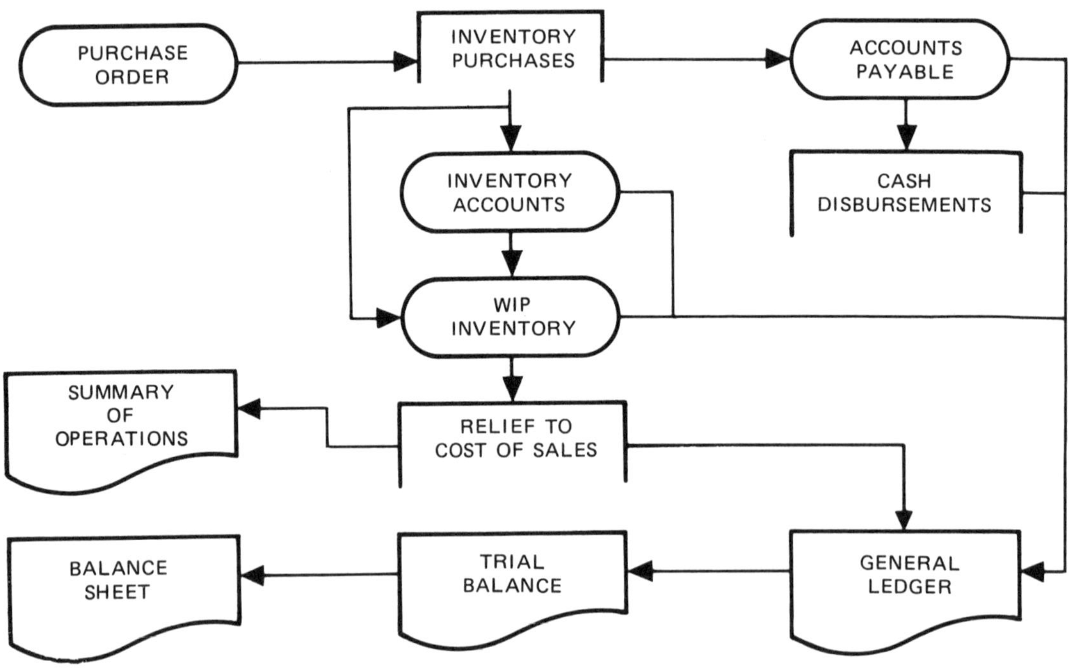

EXHIBIT B

the customer's cash flow, could delay payment for a much longer period of time. In government business, it is not unusual to experience long delays because of contract definition, funding, or contract changes.

The initial sales transaction is journalized by a debit to receivables (customer) and a credit to the sales account. Upon receipt of payment, cash is debited and the account receivable credited. The journalized data is next entered into the general ledger from which a trial balance is drawn.

The trial balance is the basis for preparing the financial schedules. All sales (including cash) are reflected in the income statement: receivables in the balance sheet and cash receipts in the cash flow schedule.

Inventory Purchases

Conversely to sales above, the inventory purchase cycle is reflected at the bottom of this exhibit. In brief, the procedure is as follows:

a. The purchase order activates the actual purchase action and, upon delivery, an invoice is received from the seller which is the basis for setting up the accounts payable liability account which is reflected in the balance sheet.
b. The purchase costs become part of the basic raw material inventory account and, when placed into the production environment, the inventory is reclassified to work-in-process (WIP) inventory.
c. As the product is completed, the WIP inventory becomes part of the finished goods cost.
d. Upon delivery of the product to the customer (sales transaction), the inventory costs are relieved to cost of sales through a transaction entry: a debit to cost of sales (reflected in the income statement) and a credit to the inventory account, which become part of the balance sheet reporting.
e. When the account payable is paid, the transaction entry is a debit to accounts payable and a credit to the cash disbursement account.

Receivables Versus Payables

Exhibit B also reflects the difference between the creation of the asset receivable account and the liability accounts payable account. Receivables result from credit sales whereas the payable accounts reflect the cost of purchases. The receivables eventually become a cash receipt whereas the payables become a cash disbursement. Sales and costs are both reflected in the income statement and the receivables and payables are reported in the balance sheet.

PROJECTION OF ACCOUNTS RECEIVABLE

Projecting receivable balances is very important because of their effect on the anticipated cash flow position. Receivables are based on sales deliveries and/or services performed, and the timing of the collections influences the receivable balance. The relationship, therefore, is very significant among sales, collections, and receivables.

Another important factor in projecting receivables is reference to the credit and collection policies. Changes in payment practices can significantly influence collections due to time lag of the receipts.

Consideration should also be given to prevailing and anticipated economic conditions. In a period of price increases, expanding economy, and strict credit controls, the tendency is to conserve cash and thus receivables will be larger and, of course, cash collections slower. Contrarily, in a period of easy credit and lower prices, the tendency is to pay debts and take advantage of cash discounts and debt reduction.

Receivable Balances and Collections

The first step in determining the projection of receivables is to determine the correlation between receivables and collections. For purposes of illustration, let us assume the following experience factors (refer to the aging process above for their determination):

a. 60% of the unpaid receivables (beginning balance plus period sales) is collected in the first 30 days.
b. 30% is collected within 60 days.
c. The balance, or 10%, is collected within 90 days.

Data Input. The following information is inputted into the system in order to calculate the ending receivable balances and collections:

1. The actual beginning receivable balance.
2. Projected sales by period.
3. The factors assumed above and associated with the collection periods.

Processing. As shown on Exhibit C, the beginning receivable balance is added to the sales ($2,000 + $5,000 = $7,000). The program applies the 60% to the $7,000 to obtain $4,200, which represents the collections in 30 days; 30% is applied to obtain $2,100 estimated for collection in 60 days, and $700 anticipated in 90 days.

At the end of the period, the receivable balance would be the sum of the 60- and 90-day periods of uncollectibles, or $2,800. This value then becomes the beginning balance of the next period, and so on through the projections. Totals for the 60- and 90-day columns are irrelevant since they represent ending receivable balances with the collections being reflected in the 30-day column.

Some useful statistics derived from this aging process are noted at the bottom of this exhibit.

Receivables as a Percentage of Annualized Sales

Based on historical data, receivable balances can be projected on the basis of their relationship to annualized sales. Under this method, the sales are annualized each period and the percentage relationship is established to the average receivable balance. A four-period example of this procedure based on actual data follows on page 204.

RECEIVABLE PROJECTIONS

(Based on Aging Process)

Periods	Beginning Balance Receivables	Sales	Total	30 Days (60%)	60 Days (30%)	90 Days (10%)	Ending Balance Receivables
1	$ 2,000	$ 5,000	$ 7,000	$ 4,200	$ 2,100	$ 700	$ 2,800
2	2,800	5,600	8,600	5,160	2,580	860	3,440
3	3,440	5,800	9,240	5,544	2,772	924	3,696
4	3,696	5,200	8,896	5,338	2,669	889	3,558
5	3,558	5,400	8,958	5,375	2,687	896	3,583
6	3,583	5,600	9,183	5,510	2,755	918	3,673
7	3,673	5,800	9,473	5,684	2,842	947	3,789
8	3,789	5,800	9,589	5,753	2,877	959	3,836
9	3,836	5,700	9,536	5,722	2,861	953	3,814
10	3,814	5,900	9,714	5,828	2,914	972	3,886
11	3,886	6,000	9,886	5,932	2,966	988	3,954
12	3,954	6,000	9,954	5,972	2,986	996	3,982
Totals	$ 42,029	$ 67,800		$ 67,028	$ 33,009	$ 11,002	
Average	$ 3,502	$ 5,650		$ 5,587			

Statistics resulting from above calculations:

Average receivables as a percentage of annual sales	5.2%	(3,502 ÷ 67,800)
Collections as a percentage of sales	99.0%	(67,028 ÷ 67,800)
Ending balance as a percentage of sales	5.8%	(3,982 ÷ 67,800)
Average receivables as a percentage of average collections	62.6%	(3,502 ÷ 5,587)
Average receivables as a percentage of total collections	5.2%	(3,502 ÷ 67,028)

EXHIBIT C

Period	Period Receivables	Average	Period Sales	Annualized	Average Receivables % of Sales
1	$ 2,760	$2,760	$ 5,000 × 12	$60,000	4.65 (2,760 ÷ 60,000)
2	+2,970		+6,000		
	$ 5,730 ÷ 2	2,855	$11,000 × 6	66,000	4.33 (2,855 ÷ 66,000)
3	+3,102		+5,500		
	$ 8,832 ÷ 3	2,943	$16,500 × 4	66,000	4.46 (2,943 ÷ 66,000)
4	+3,111		+5,800		
	$11,943 ÷ 4	2,986	$22,300 × 3	66,900	4.49 (2,986 ÷ 66,900)

If an organization has definite major seasonal period variations, it would be more suitable to use period average receivable percentage factors rather than the annual average applied monthly.

Knowing sales and receivables, collections can be easily determined based on the following formula plus or minus any unusual knowns anticipated in the future that could not reasonably be reflected in the formula.

BEGINNING BALANCE ACCOUNTS RECEIVABLE + PERIODIC SALES
— ACCOUNTS RECEIVABLE BALANCE = COLLECTIONS

Sales and Collections as a Basis for Projections

Receivable balances can also be obtained if projections for sales and collections are available. The first step in this process is to obtain the correlation of collections to sales based on historical experience. The next step is to apply the collection factor to sales to obtain the projected collections. The formula to obtain the receivable balances would be as follows:

BEGINNING BALANCE ACCOUNTS RECEIVABLE + SALES (PROJECTED)
— COLLECTIONS (PROJECTED) = ENDING RECEIVABLE BALANCE

This becomes the beginning balance for the next period and the procedure above is repeated for the number of periods required.

Average Collection Period Projections

The average collection period for a business is the number of calendar days of sales that are represented in the accounts receivable balances. This statistic is developed by dividing the annual or annualized credit sales by 365 (days in year) to ascertain the average sales value per day. The average receivables for the year (less the reserve average) is next divided by average sales per day to obtain the average collection by period.

In most businesses (excluding government contracts), the average collection period will approximate ⅓ more days than the net selling terms. If the terms were 2% in 10 days and net in 30, the reasonable average collection period or lag should be 40 days.

The above developed statistic can be utilized to analyze collections or make cash projections based on the sales lag.

Estimating Receivables Based on Sales Weeks

To determine receivables in terms of sales weeks based on historical experience, the following procedure would be followed:

a. Divide monthly sales by the number of workdays in the month to obtain the average daily sales. In the 4, 4, 5 week accounting periods (common in most organizations, particularly aerospace), the number of days would be 20 and 25 respectively.
b. Divide the accounts receivable balance by average daily sales to obtain the number of days of uncollected receipts.
c. Divide the number of days of uncollected receipts by the number of days in the week to obtain the sales weeks represented by the receivable balance.
d. Divide the results in (b) above by the days in the month to determine the percentage to apply to projected sales to obtain an estimated receivable balance.

The above procedure is very useful in projecting sales lags and receivable balances or as a means of testing the validity of projections made by other methods.

LAG FACTOR UTILIZATION FOR PROJECTIONS

Lags are defined as the delay or retardation of the development of a portion of the whole data. In other words, it is the time span between two events such as the time frame between cost accrual and cash disbursement, or between invoicing the customer and receiving payment.

The lag percentage is developed by dividing the length of the lag period by the number of weeks (in some cases, days) in the accounting period. Noted below is a lag factor table:

	Month		
Periods*	(5 weeks)	(4 weeks)	Quarter
1	.20	.25	7.69
2	.40	.50	15.38
3	.60	.75	23.08
4	.80	1.00	30.77
5	1.00	1.25	38.46

*Period of time between accrual and disbursement or between disbursement and reimbursement.

MECHANICAL BILLING PROCESS

To expedite the invoicing process and improve controls, file updating, and reporting, computerized billing is most desirable. Further, it could be effectively utilized as a common linkage between the sales order entry and reconciliation to deliveries, open order status collections, accounts receivable, and individual customer history records.

Exhibit D reflects an overview of a mechanical billing system and the considerations involved in its development.

A description of this system and its operation is noted as follows:

1. An Individual Customer History File contains such relevant data as the customer's name, address, identification number, purchase description, sales order number, dates, quantity, price, payments and dates, deliveries and open order status, outstanding receivable balance aged, and credit rating. As additional purchases are made by the customer, his file would be updated to show current and year-to-date summary of his purchases, deliveries, and payments. The output from this file serves as a tool to analyze each customer's account in depth as to possible lack of sales bookings, payment record, and undelivered purchases.
2. The Invoice Billed Sales file reflects all of the deliveries made to all customers or services performed in terms of quantity or hours, price, data, invoice number, customer name and address, item description, sales order number reference, and shipping date. This file is updated as deliveries are made and the invoices are prepared mechanically. Outstanding order balances are adjusted to reflect the deliveries. The output from this file serves to record the billed sales for the period and year-to-date.
3. An Open Order Status file includes a complete listing of the sales orders by customer in terms of quantity and price, dates, undelivered balances, and sales order reference. The output from this file serves as a means to query undelivered sales, which could highlight possible problems in production scheduling, oversight, or nonavailability of sold product. The open orders also represent the backlog of business to be delivered, which is reported on the financial statements and also used in future planning.
4. A Receivable Balance file contains all of the receivable balances by customer and receivable. The aggregate receivable balance is aged by time period and dollar amount. The output from this file is used to review the organization's overall receivable status with particular emphasis on the balances that are outstanding in excess of sixty days. The total receivable balance is reported on the balance sheet.
5. The Collection file includes all of the cash receipts by customer for the current period as well as year-to-date. The summary of the receipts is used in the cash flow schedule and the cash balance is reflected in the balance sheet.

The automated billing system produces the customer's invoice mechanically which eliminates the tedious clerical effort involved in this chore. Billing is a major effort, particularly in larger organizations where hundreds or possibly thousands of invoices have to be prepared daily.

Receivables serve as a short-term financing vehicle to the customer. Some customers abuse or misuse this privilege. In order to minimize the risks concerned with credit sales, the seller must be constantly vigilant in appraising the status of the individual customer receivable accounts to ward off or reduce potential losses. This is done by following a strict, but flexible, policy of credit extension and collection. Projection of uncollectibles and receivable balances are necessary for realistic short- and long-term financial planning. Computerization of receivables and the billing process permits timely analysis and rapid assessment of customer outstanding balances, which can result in preventing thousands of dollars of losses due to bad debts.

MECHANICAL BILLING SYSTEM

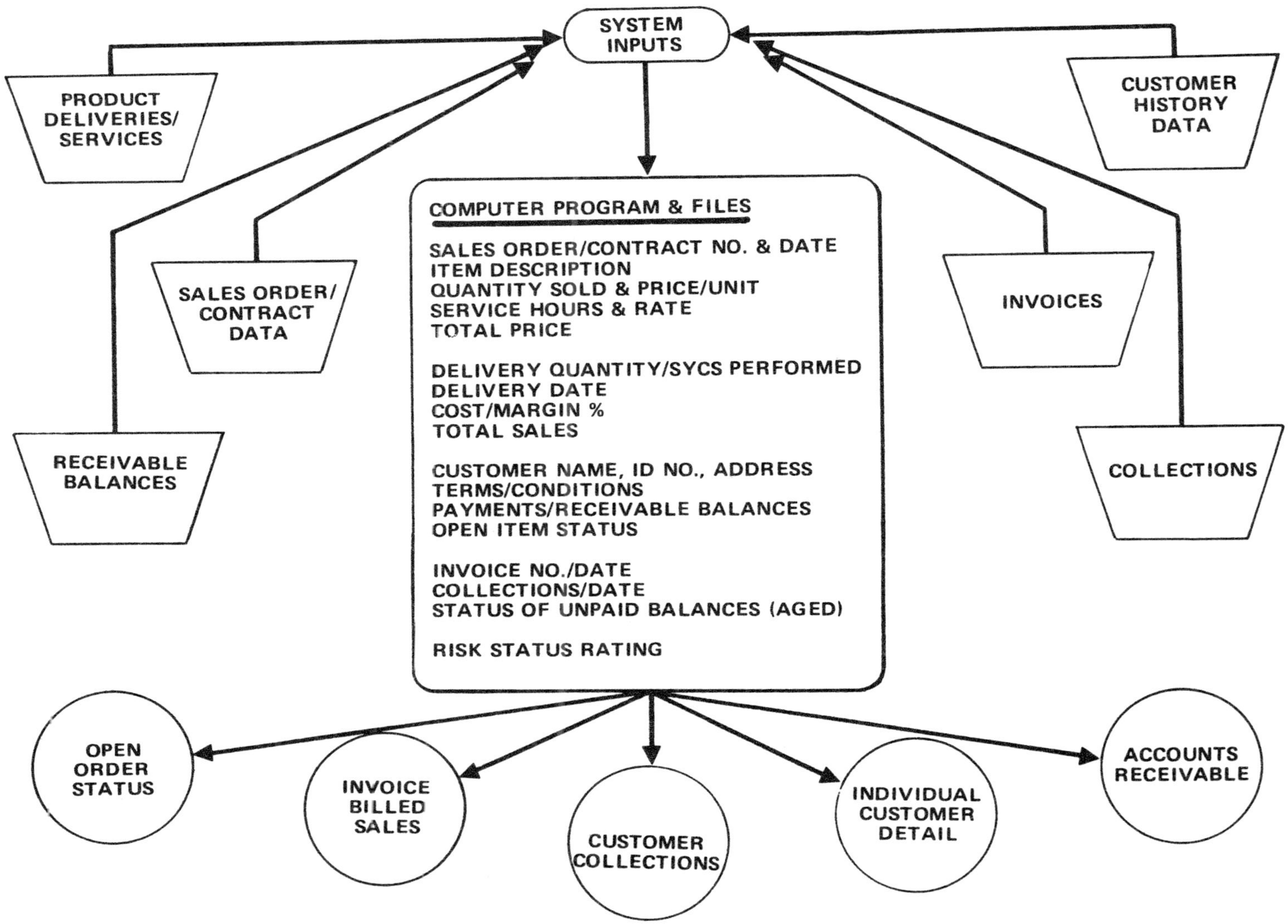

EXHIBIT D

11

Controlling Aspects of the Computerized Accounts Payable Function

Accounts payable represent creditor obligations or commitments incurred as a result of various purchases of goods and/or services. Purchases include such items as raw materials, product components, indirect supplies and services, real property, or equipment.

Accounts payable are captioned under "current liabilities" on the balance sheet and are unsecured since their liquidation is anticipated to occur within a relatively short period of time.

One very important goal in creating an accounts payable liability is to purchase goods or services on credit with the objective of selling them rapidly enough to obtain funds to liquidate this liability. In this process, an inventory is created which is really financed by creditor money; in other words, it is possible, under certain circumstances, that a company can operate on the creditor's equity.

INTERNAL CONTROL OBJECTIVES

In effecting control of accounts payable processing and the appropriate subsequent cash disbursement, the following considerations are relevant and paramount.

1. *Prior to initiating the request to purchase,* the vendor's history file should be checked to determine his record in terms of past performance, financial stability, and his ability to meet product specifications or service requirements and commitments on scheduled dates.

2. *The receipt of goods or the performance of services* should be achieved in accordance with the terms of the contractual agreement or purchase order relative to price, quantity, quality, delivery, and performance criteria.
3. *If there were discrepancies* in (2) above, they should be properly resolved. Verification of terms and conditions involves the initial requester of products/services, the authorizing organization, receiving department, purchasing agent, and the accounts payable function.
4. *The required records of the transaction* should be accomplished with respect to an organization's established accounting policies and procedures: For example, direct purchases identified to specific contracts sales orders, if applicable; purchased capital assets reflected in the appropriate asset accounts; expense identification to overhead accounts and cash payouts substantiated by a cash disbursement journal entry.

All of the above controls must be adhered to if the accounts payable function is to operate effectively and efficiently in their delegated responsibilities.

CENTRALIZED VERSUS DECENTRALIZED CONTROLS

All organizations should analyze their operations to determine the type of controls that should be established for their accounts payable function. This is necessary so that effective procedures can be established as guidelines to achieve the required control objectives.

Two basic control segregations are identified as *centralized* and *decentralized*. The characteristics of each type are outlined in the following discussion.

Centralized Controls

This type of control is usually characteristic of small and uncomplicated organizations for the following prime considerations.

1. *More effective utilization* of cash funds since the overall cash requirements are better known by the control organization than by its subordinate offices.
2. *Decisions on cash availability* can be made at the executive management level.
3. *Relieves the operating units* of the responsibility for recordkeeping in order that their time and efforts can be concentrated on operational tasks as opposed to bookkeeping endeavors.
4. *Prevents possible collusion* between the requester or buyer of goods or services since the amounts paid are accomplished by the main office; a source other than the originating individual or group.
5. *Summary data reporting* and financial statements are developed at the central office which precludes misunderstanding and misinterpretation of data requirements by the subordinate organizations in their reporting process to the main office.

Actually, there are very few disadvantages to centralized control if appropriate to an organization's operations. The purchasing department is still provided with a vendor invoice, has a control on the receipt of deliveries, and performs its control of the functions involved except for payments. It is kept apprised of payments by the central office but is somewhat relieved of the function of making disbursement decisions and physical transfer of payments.

Decentralized Control

In the decentralized control environment which, generally, is representative of far-flung operations or those of considerable size, it appears to be more advantageous to have the control monitoring delegated and the accounts payable function responsibility vested in the individual subordinate organizations. The reasons are cited as follows:

1. *Referral of all invoices* for payment from many subordinate organizations to the central office would entail a tremendous clerical effort and burden on the central organization whose prime activities are concerned with the overall operational control, direction, planning, and decision-making.
2. The subordinate organizations are generally *self-sustaining* and can perform the accounts payable function more capably and effectively since they are closest to the scene of the action.
3. The decentralized organization's *internal controls* enable them to more efficiently perform their tasks and exercise care and judgment in the decisions they make relative to commitments and liability payments.
4. The central organization would still maintain *their appropriate control* by management edict as to the cash position and other constraints that have to be maintained by the subordinate organizations.
5. The main office is apprised daily of the suborganization's cash position which allows them the opportunity to make a *pre-advance decision* on large payouts of cash. Funds are deposited to the suborganization's accounts or they have access to bank draws to the extent permissible by the central office. One very large West Coast firm practices the procedures outlined above and has been very effective in its cash flow and conservation activities, which is one of the paramount problems facing organizations in this troubled economy.

The assessment relative to centralized or decentralized control can only be determined from an analysis of the individual situation and/or specific objectives of an organization. It could be that some sort of compromise between the two types of control would be the appropriate direction to take. The results of the review, pro and con, would then govern the type of functional/operational control most desirable for that organization.

EFFECTIVE CONTROLS TO PRECLUDE COLLUSION

Although collusion to defraud has occurred in many organizations, as commonly reported in newspapers, adequate precautions are still lacking to alleviate this threat. This is verified by the author's experience in one very large organization.

In this situation, highly respected veteran employees in each of the purchasing, receiving, and accounts payable functions organized a dummy firm and established an office in a distant city as home base. Purposely, the vendor organization was established as a small business in order to avoid undue publicity and investigation. The proposed commodity was of the type that the large organization could use and would buy. Because the firm was small-business oriented, it had an advantage in its solicitation of business from large firms whose main contracts were with the government. Nondiscriminatory practices, which favor small business in many cases, helped the dummy firm gain business from government-oriented business organizations.

After disclosure of the facts, it was learned that the fictitious organization had bilked its customer of hundreds of thousands of dollars. Their operation was quite simple: The buyer in the large organization, a partner in the fictitious firm, would issue the purchase order based on a fraudulent request to the dummy organization. His cohorts were alerted to the action and the data was entered in the mechanical procurement system. After a reasonable period of time, the receiving employee acknowledged the receipt of the shipment and issued the appropriate documentation to Accounts Payable. In Accounts Payable, the other trusted employee and a partner in the bogus firm performed the document-matching process and authorized payment of the vendor invoice that was fraudulently provided. The invoice was subsequently paid to the dummy firm.

This firm operated in this manner for about two years before the fraud was discovered by accident. A young, aggressive auditor was performing a routine test audit of one representative purchase order flow through the system. In trying to audit trail the purchase request to delivery receipt and the item usage or location, he discovered that no such item was ever received, used, or in existence. The rest became history as soon as the appropriate authorities began a thorough investigation. Although the perpetrators of the crime paid with prison terms, most of the thousands of dollars involved were never recovered.

The above case illustrates one of the many incidents that happen and, in some instances, are never detected. Some of the major controls required to safeguard an organization's interests in the procurement/payment operation are noted below:

1. There must be a *separation of authority and responsibility* for the various functional areas of purchasing, receiving, authorizing approval of payment, and the actual payer (check signer).
2. The *vendor history* must be thoroughly screened through reputable sources before an organization's selection as a vendor participant.
3. The *action documents* must be filed together by vendor in order to provide an audit trail to the transactions if the need should so arise. The action documents should indicate the responsible action personnel in the transactions.
4. Although the checks are produced mechanically, the *authorizing signature* should be that of a person other than the one either approving an invoice for payment or associated directly with the accounts payable function.
5. *Frequent audits* should be performed and large invoices particularly scrutinized thoroughly even to the extent of verifying the need, quantity, and receipt. Further, a spot check should be made as to the cash disbursed versus the vendor balances as shown on the computer report. This would verify the reconciliation between cash and the commitment balance records.
6. Functional employees in the procurement/payment process *should be forced to take their periodic vacations* so that they are replaced during this period with other personnel not thoroughly familar with the daily routine who would question any unusual situation that connotes collusion.
7. The procurement/payment system should be developed with *overlapping control points* or double-checks so that it would be impossible or at least very difficult for people to be dishonest or careless.

8. An *efficient voucher system* must be required in which incoming invoices are reviewed and approved by *various* assigned personnel in order to assure the validity of the charges for preclusion of fraud, collusion, or any other form of misrepresentation.
9. Adequate controls must start at the *point of cost incurrence*. It is generally too late to start controlling cash disbursements after a liability has been authorized and approved for payment.

INCURRED COST DATA FLOW

The two primary and recurring types of cost obligations resulting from purchases are the direct costs, which are identifiable to an end product, and indirect expenses, which are not directly associated but rather represent general support items or services that are allocated to the product based on an overhead application.

Direct Cost Flow

Direct labor, transfers in, direct material, overhead, and other direct costs are all representative of costs that are identifiable to the end product. These costs are processed through the accounts payable system as displayed on Exhibit A. As further shown on this exhibit, the costs are reflected in the accounts payable and accrued salaries and wages accounts and become part of the cost ledger for product costing and the general ledger for financial reporting.

Indirect Expense

Overhead expenses are generally classified into three major categories, depending on their activity support association, and are identified as product, general and administrative, and selling expenses. As shown on Exhibit B, the indirect labor flows to accrued salaries/wages and the other expenses are reflected in the accounts payable processing. The product expenses also flow to the expense ledger and are allocated to the product/contract through an overhead application rate to direct labor hour or dollars. The general administrative expense, research and development, corporate office allocation, proposal, and bidding expenses are also allocated on the basis of direct labor. Selling expenses represent marketing costs, which are reflected in a separate expense pool.

Similarly to the direct costs discussed above, various ledgers and financial statements are affected by overhead transactions.

A TYPICAL PROCUREMENT/PAYMENT CYCLE

The functions involved with purchasing, receiving, and vendor invoicing are all interrelated. Each activity is dependent upon the other for certain pertinent information in order to complete the cycle from the initial point of request to purchase to the physical cost disbursement activity.

TRANSACTION DATA FLOW
DIRECT COSTS

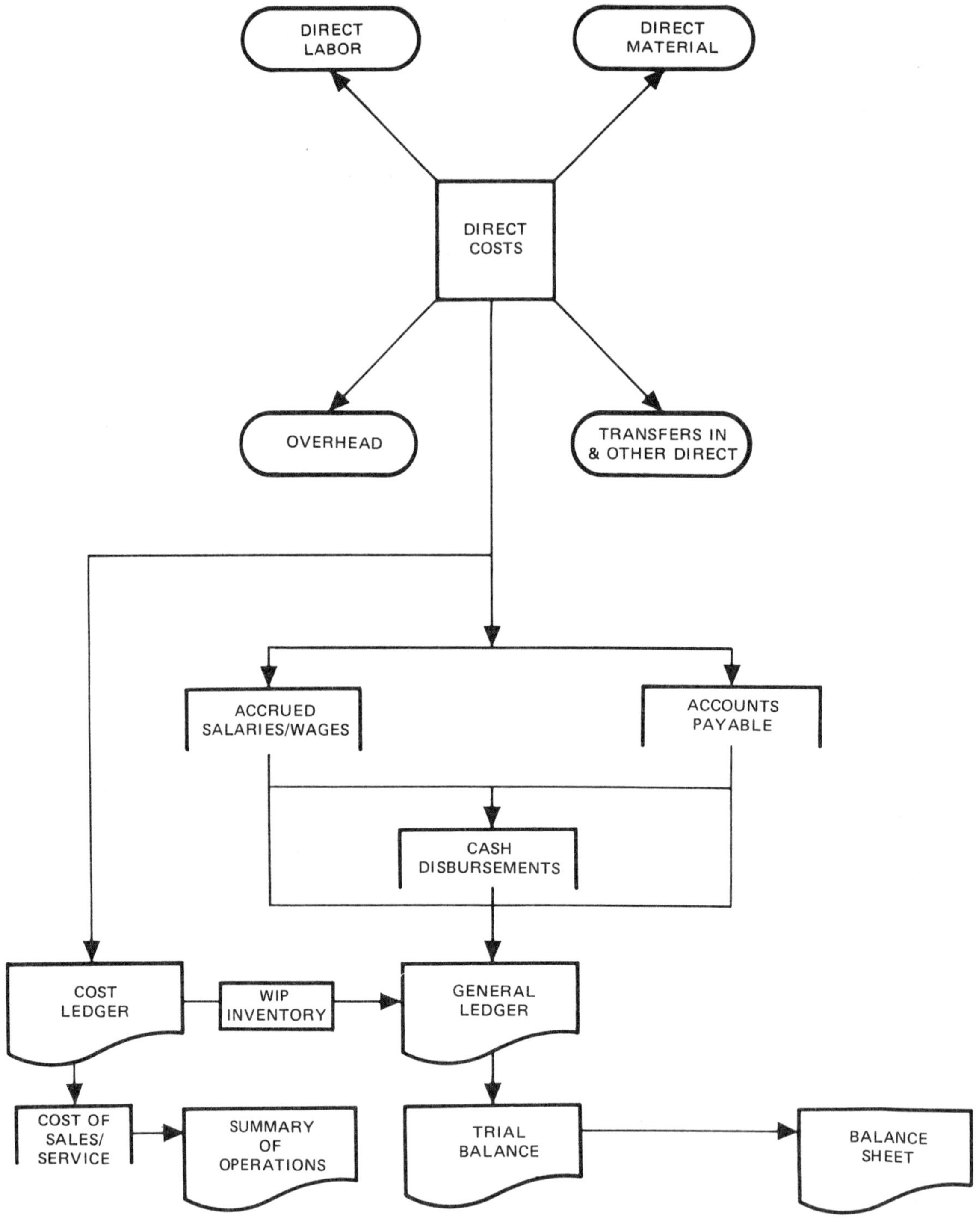

EXHIBIT A

TRANSACTION DATA FLOW
OVERHEAD

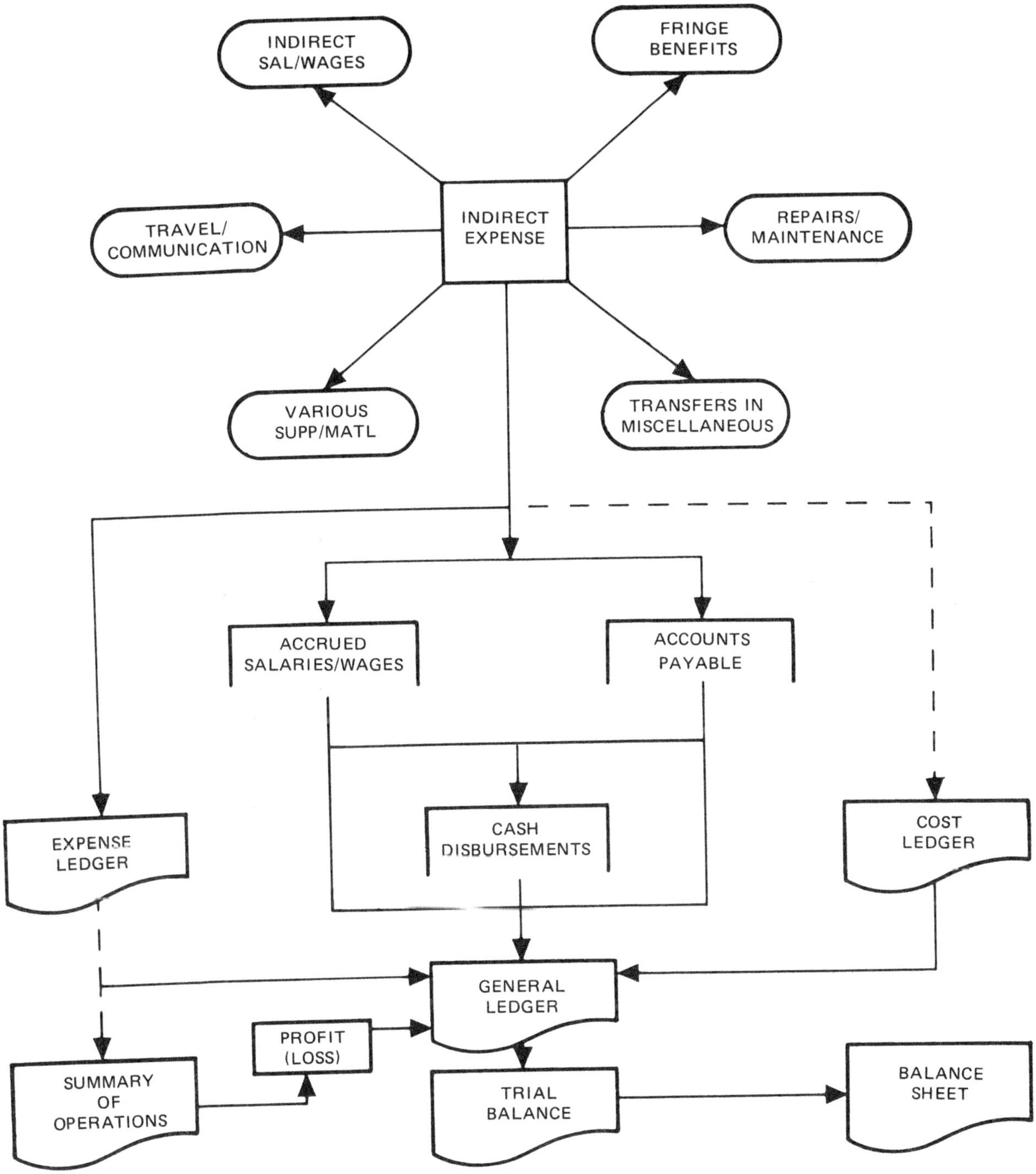

EXHIBIT B

Procurement

Procurement is charged with the responsibility of initiating the effort required to purchase, lease, or otherwise acquire materials, supplies, and services necessary for Engineering and Manufacturing to produce a product. They also have the responsibility of obtaining the capital assets required to achieve the objectives of the organization. A copy of the purchase order is forwarded to the requesting organization, Receiving, and Accounts Payable.

Receiving

This organization receives delivery of purchases, inspects for quantity and quality, and stores or forwards the shipment to the requesting or using organization. Inadequate inspection and control can lead to thousands of dollars of losses in inventory or end-product performance or salability. A copy of the receiving memo is forwarded to the requesting organization, Accounts Payable, and the purchasing function.

Invoicing

This activity is performed by the vendor organization upon their shipment of a product or performance of a service. The invoice contains a purchase order reference and other pertinent data such as quantity, price, description, and shipping destination. The invoice is directed to accounts payable for matching with other documents and the delivery packing sheets are used by Receiving to support and verify the shipment received.

Matching Process

Accounts Payable has the responsibility of ensuring that similar data contained in the purchase order, receiving memo, and the vendor invoice is reconciliable before payment is effected. This is a horrendous task in an organization that has a high volume of purchases. In the computerized process, to be discussed later in the chapter, this activity is performed mechanically and any discrepancies are outputted in the exception reporting.

Processing Controls

Throughout the processes described above, various control points are in evidence as displayed on Exhibit C. These asterisked checkpoints ensure, if properly exercised, the validity of purchasing, receiving, and paying activities. If each responsible functional unit performs its audit and checkout activities properly, the procurement/payment process will be an effective operational control system.

REQUISITES FOR A MECHANICAL VOUCHER REGISTER

A mechanical voucher system is used as a means of achieving processing control and its data is supported by Purchasing's documentation, Receiving's verification, vendor's payment,

CONTROLS IN "PURCHASE REQUIREMENT TO PAY" PROCESS

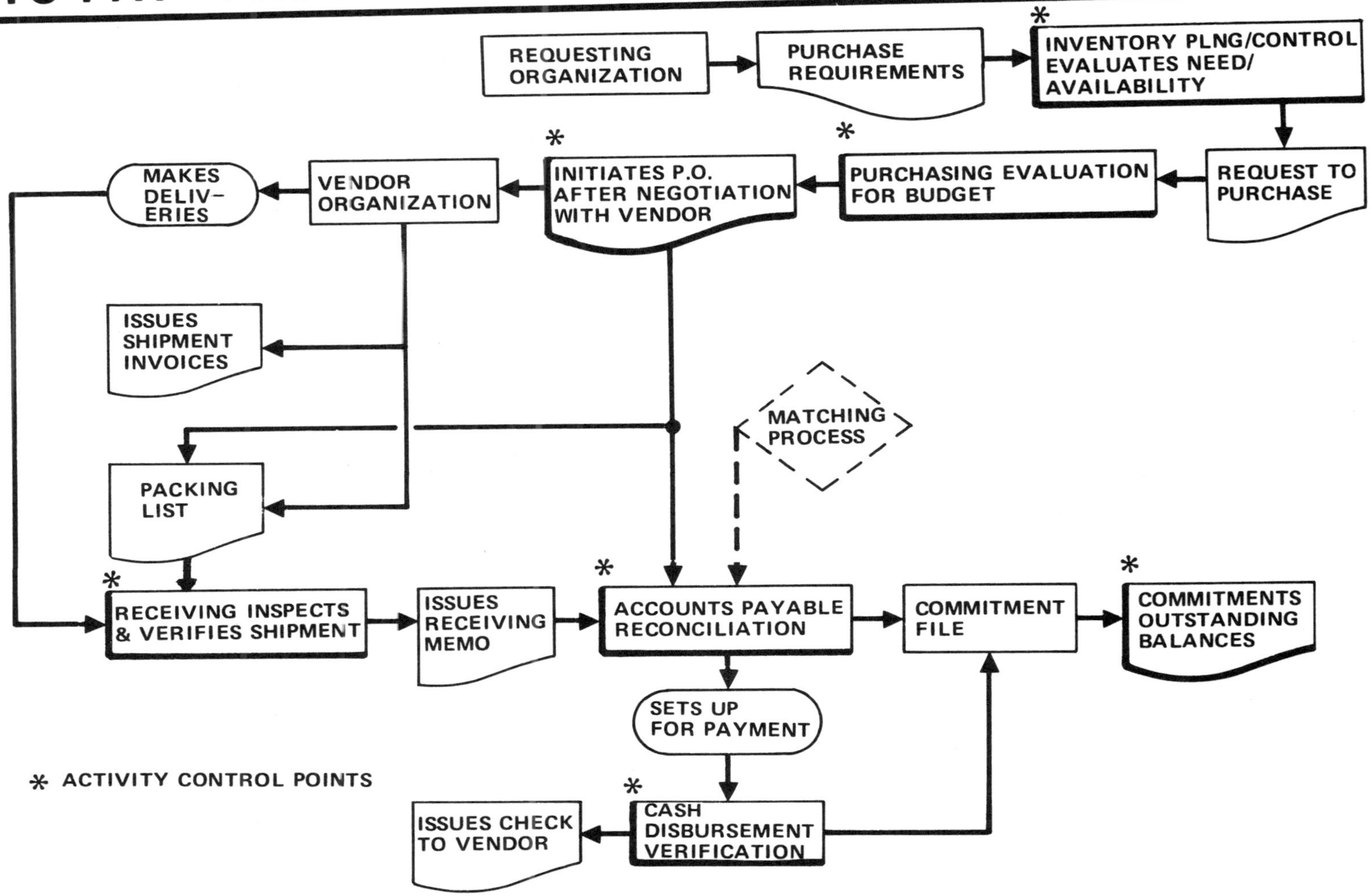

EXHIBIT C

and the check disbursement record. All of the data manipulation and formal records development is a function of the computerized process. The voucher system includes account distribution, purchase order and invoice identifications, item descriptions, quantity, price, discounts, returns and allowances, due dates, and payments.

In order to achieve an effective voucher control system, the following prerequisites should govern its establishment and operation.

1. *Responsibility for data input validity* must be assigned to specific designees. The purchase order is the responsibility of the procurement organization, the shipment receipt input is a function of Receiving, and the invoice information is provided by Accounts Payable. *No* other organization is permitted to make any type of input or changes to the responsible group's data files.
2. Relative to the *matching process*, it is the responsibility of the accounts payable function to monitor and verify that the invoiced quantity and price meet the purchase order terms and conditions and, if they do not, initiate the required action to resolve the discrepancies with the vendor.
3. *Discounts and returns and allowances* must be considered before payment is effected.
4. The *liabilities must be aged* in order that payments can be met on due dates to protect discounts and credit rating. The aging process also permits instant longevity analysis of unpaid commitments and a means of projecting future payable balances based on volume activity.
5. The *proper account distribution* must be made before data inputs are introduced into the system since this identification directs the flow of information to the proper ledger files such as direct cost, indirect expense, and/or the general summary ledger.
6. The internal mechanical control automatically checks the amount to be paid to determine *if it is in excess* of the agreed-upon purchase price. If this situation occurs, a special report is outputted for analysis action.
7. *Daily reports* must be available to indicate cash disbursements and requirements as well as outstanding commitment balances.

ON-LINE PROCUREMENT/PAYMENT SYSTEM

The traditional procurement/payment process involves much time, paper work flow, and clerical effort. Some organizations have developed, and others are seeking, an effective means to overcome this dilemma. Practically every successful solution for the manual process, as well as incorporating new innovations, has involved some form of mechanization. A very comprehensive and efficient application is described below.

Specific Problems with the Traditional Approach

The historical procurement/payment cycle is today an obsolete process since it has as its shortcomings the following:

a. Excessive paper work flow and processing
b. High cost of administration
c. Responsibility for higher than necessary inventory levels
d. Clerical errors in records

e. No immediate visibility on procurement status
f. No realtime input, inquiry, and reporting capabilities

In order to alleviate the above situation, a computer-oriented system was developed.

The On-Line Operation

This system involves all purchase orders *under $500* and other purchases against *established* annual contracts irrespective of dollar values. The reason for the under-$500 limitation is that the Uniform Commercial Code currently stipulates that a contract for $500 or more must be in writing. It is noted that, in many organizations, 75-80% of their purchases fall into the under-$500 category.

Input information is captured mechanically and combined with other data in the files so that buyers can exercise their *buying* prerogatives; Receiving can *receive and record* the vendor shipments; and Accounts Payable can *pay* without a large volume of traditional paper in the purchase/payment cycle. A display of this process is reflected in Exhibit D. A discussion of the functions performed by the involved organizations relative to the on-line operations displayed on the exhibit follows.

Inventory Planning and Controls

This function is to receive material requirements from the user organizations and establish the need in terms of item and quantity. It makes a determination as to whether the requirement is in inventory or if purchases are required. If a purchase is necessary, it initiates a purchase order request (POR) to Procurement and enters the data into the mechanical system file.

Procurement (Eliminating the PO)

This organization receives the request, evaluates it in terms of budget constraints, and contacts the vendors involved by phone for price quotes on the proposed requirement to be purchased. When the decision has been made as to the successful bidder, the vendor is telephoned and the terms established relative to PO number, quantity, price, shipping instructions, and payment conditions. Procurement then enters the above data into the system file. A printed PO will be requested by the buyer for those vendors who have not agreed to accept verbal orders. Formal standard terms and conditions of an agreement are in the computer file and could, if required, be entered mechanically on the output-generated PO. It is noted that procurements cannot be split to obtain the $500 value.

Changes in the Receiving Operation

Receiving receives the delivery which is accompanied by a vendor packing list and interrogates the computer through a PO identifier for a video display of the purchase order. This is done in order to verify that the terms of the agreement have been met. The receipt data is inputted into the computer and a receiving memo is mechanically generated.

ON-LINE PROCUREMENT/PAYMENT PROCESS

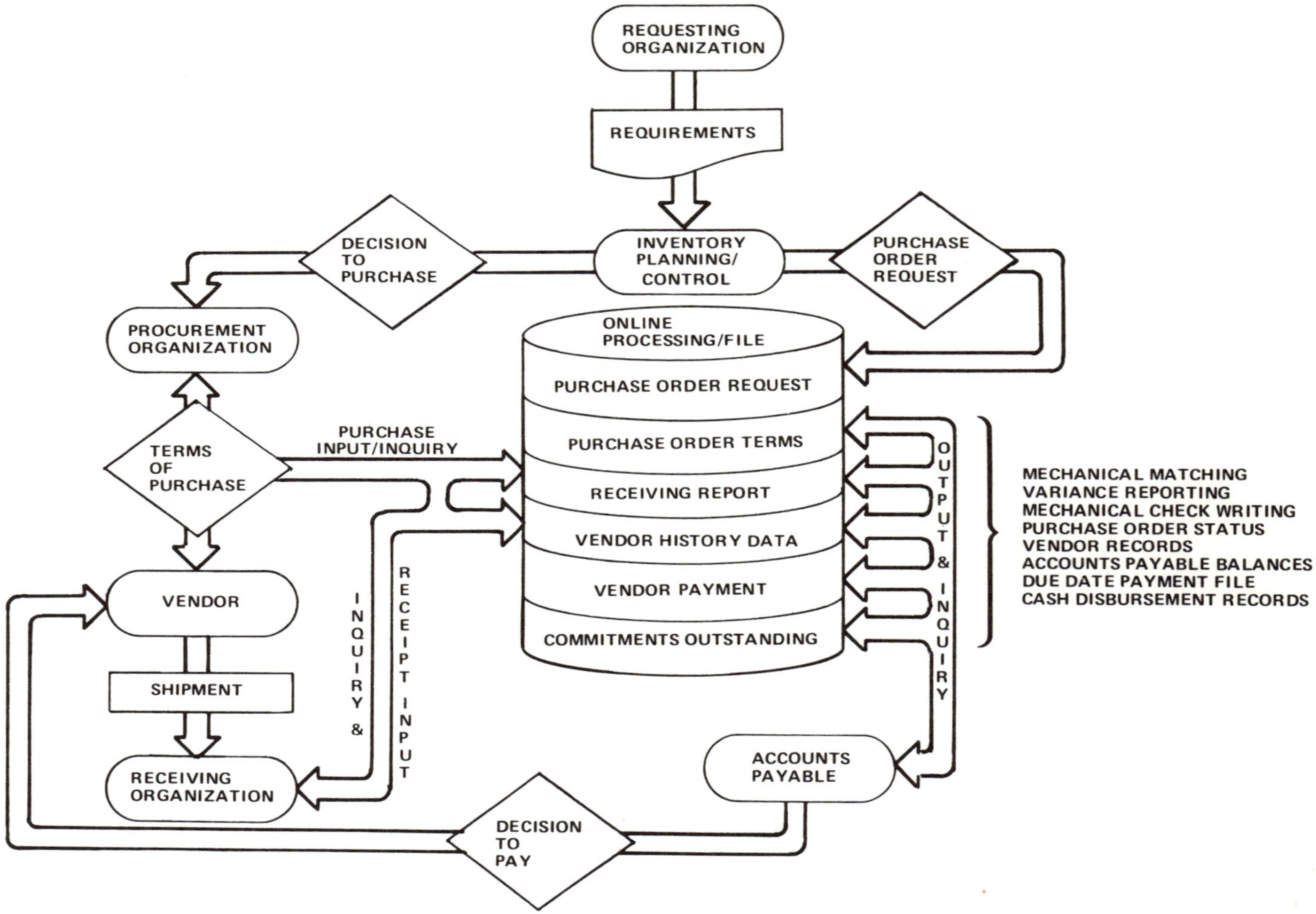

EXHIBIT D

Accounting (Eliminating the Vendor Invoice)

Payment checks are prepared mechanically and Accounts Payable releases them when it has been verified that payment is in order. No vendor invoice is required to release the payment. A remittance statement accompanies the check reflecting the purchase numbers for each amount paid. Accounts Payable also maintains records and performs the verification process on all other transactions not covered by the under-$500 mechanical system.

Other Notable Capabilities of This System

a. *Closing Out the PO.* After six months, the PO is automatically closed out when the records show deliveries to be complete. A microfilm record of the data is sent to Material Planning and Control and Procurement.

b. *Over/Under Shipments.* The program tests for quantity and price tolerance. A manual entry is made to adjust PO data and, in the case of overshipments, a notice to that effect is produced. If the overshipment is not returned and is under $500, a new PO is processed.

c. *On-Line Inquiries.* Instant retrieval is a major advantage of this system relative to bid history by part numbers or material stocking numbers, listing of open orders, payment history, receiving report changes, purchase order summary, and due dates.

d. *Security Features.* A knowledge of the correct password is necessary to activate the system. Mechanical locks are used on the input/inquiry terminals. Only designated personnel can enter specific data such as purchase order requests (PORs), POs, and receiving information. Inputting personnel are required to have identification numbers for access to specific data.

e. *Audit Capability.* Inputs are internally edited for alphanumeric field sizes and master file contents such as account number and catalog number.

System Benefits

A number of organizations have claimed the following specific benefits in using this type of system:

a. Elimination of the matching process for this type of purchase order
b. A 75% + reduction in the purchase order and receiving files
c. Reduction in inventories since procurement can be quickly and effectively accomplished
d. A 90% reduction in PO issuance and its attendant clerical effort
e. Forms standardization with a 35% reduction in costs
f. Greater visibility of the procurement and payment processes
g. Automatic purchase order closeout with no manual effort
h. The handling of a double volume of purchase requests with half the number of processing personnel.

This system goes a long way toward reducing clerical efforts and costs in the traditional process involving voluminous paper work and processing activity.

Two Known Users of the On-Line Technique

Two very well-known organizations have been successful in implementing the above computerized processes—Lockheed Missiles & Space Division with their "Paperless Procurement" and General Dynamics, Fort Worth Division, with their VOCOL system (an acronym for Verbal Order Control On-Line).

DISBURSEMENT BUDGET PREDICATED ON PAYABLES

An analysis of accounts payable and accrued liabilities should reveal a pattern of payments that can serve as conducive criteria for projecting cash disbursements. Considerations involved in this process are as follows:

1. *Segregate vendor payments* into several categories so that a determination can be made as to the type of purchase and whether it is: (a) of consistently recurring nature such as supplies and materials; (b) a one-shot situation such as capital asset acquisitions; (c) a periodic assessment such as government taxes and insurance premiums, and (d) dependent on production/sales volume, which would indicate the need for raw materials/component parts. This is a very important evaluation since it provides the capability for time-phasing anticipated payouts by future period.
2. The *recurring purchases*, such as material and expense items or services, should next be charted to determine the peaks or valleys in particular time periods and to further determine the causes of deviation from a normal period. Based on a given assumption that an organization's activity will be approximately the same, greater, or less, comparable values or volume compensations are then projected for the anticipated commitments. The actual cash disbursements for this type of purchase are analyzed to determine the time-lag interval between purchase and payment. Generally, this time cycle is 30 days; therefore, the disbursement is projected for the following month on purchases projected for the current month.
3. In the case of *unusual or nonrecurring purchases*, a determination has to be made as to whether such purchase action will occur during the forecasted time period. Major purchases such as capital assets can be obtained from the Capital Expenditure Budget, which would also reveal the anticipated date of purchase request initiation and the time interval that will elapse before delivery is effected and payment made.
4. In the *period assessment classification,* there are included such items as insurance which could be paid semiannually; property rent which could be paid quarterly; dividends paid either quarterly or annually; federal income tax installments paid quarterly, and so on. This type of expense payment is projected on an accrual basis and paid at the time specified. This is a fairly simple projection process based on historical accounts payable records.
5. The *sales/production category* of needs cited above is probably the most difficult to predict since changes in sales philosophy, increasing material prices that were unanticipated, new products development that could change the mix in types of purchase, or change in vendors dramatically affect the requirements. These considerations make this type of forecast an unwelcome but necessary task.

   The most common approach to take is to base the quantities to be purchased at specified times on the production schedule predicated on anticipated sales volume. A relationship chart should be constructed to display the trend of purchases as they relate to production volume. Further, accounts payable balances related to this type of purchase should be included to indicate the time interval between the purchase, the payable balance, and the payment. Generally, the time lapse between the receipt of goods and payment follows a 45-day cycle, but this is dependent on the type of industry and its practices.

6. The above analyses should effectively provide the purchase and payment projections. The payable balance is determined by adding the purchases anticipated during the period to the beginning balance and reducing this value by the projected cash disbursements.

The above procedure is a natural for mechanization because the segregation of purchases could be made automatically by unique identity inputs. Relationships of purchases to payable balances and payments could be statistically derived through a computer program application.

Evaluating the Debt-Paying Capability

A rewarding policy to follow is to occasionally evaluate the effects of possible organization liquidation. This type of analysis could very well avert a calamity to a company's resources, particularly if the company were overextended on its commitments to vendors or vice versa.

In order to do this type of evaluation, pertinent data must be developed relative to the maturity of receivables versus payables in order to determine the capability of liability payment. The standard practice is to measure current assets against current liabilities; however, this is not always a good criterion due to inventory value uncertainty and price fluctuations on the asset side, and the salary/wage accruals in the current liabilities.

Accounts Receivable to Accounts Payable Approach

The liquidity of the receivables is a valid criterion for the assessment of debt-paying capability. The following illustration demonstrates this approach:

Time Frame	Accounts Receivable	Accounts Payable
Under 30 days	$15,000	$10,000
30-60 days	9,000	7,000
61-90 days	4,000	5,000
Over 90 days	2,000	3,000
Totals	$30,000	$25,000

The receivable to the payable ratio then is calculated to be 1.2. On the surface, this ratio does not appear to be a good situation; however, other factors must be taken into consideration before a judgment can be made as to the capability of liability payment. The considerations to be viewed in the assessment are noted as follows:

a. Planned new products to be marketed and their sales potential
b. Actual asset liquidation status

c. Unusual or extraordinary income anticipations (sale of capital assets, issuance of stock, etc.)
d. Projection of future sales volume of current products
e. Revision upward of product sales price

The above represents some of the criteria that could be used as guidelines for assessment and decision-making as to whether an organization is capable of meeting its obligations or, on the other hand, receiving payments.

STATISTICAL ANALYSES FOR CONTROL

Since the accounts payable balance in product-producing organizations represents the bulk of the current liabilities (about 80%), a good indicator of its general stability is the generally accepted current ratio of current assets divided by current liabilities. Depending on unusual circumstances, a 2 to 1 result is considered an adequate consideration in determining the paying ability status. This statistic varies, however, among different types of industries.

Adjusted Current Assets to Accounts Payable

A more appropriate method than the current ratio would be a variation of the formula in which current liabilities, other than accounts payable, would be subtracted from the current assets and the result divided by accounts payable to obtain the ratio. The rationale for this is that the other current liabilities primarily represent accrued salaries and wages, which would have first priority of payment over the accounts payable liability. This assessment of ability to pay the vendor is a more realistic approach to judgment criteria.

Adjusted Liquid Assets to Accounts Payable

The quick or acid ratio analysis provides another means of testing the ability to pay an organization's debts. In this case, the current monetary assets are divided by the current liabilities. The logic of this is that some current assets, such as inventories, cannot be readily transformed into a cash position due to the disposal time factor. Further, the valuation of the inventory may have been based on cost rather than the market price which could be misleading as to the amount for which it could be sold. Then, too, there are the factors of often ignored obsolescence or spoilage.

Prepayments also cannot be directly transformed into ready cash since they represent advance payments for specified obligations such as taxes, insurance, rentals, utility deposits, and so on. Monetary assets are those that represent cash or its equivalent such as interest and accounts receivable, marketable securities, or bonds.

Using the same rationale as discussed under "Adjusted Current Assets to Accounts Payable," the more realistic approach to determining ability to pay is obtaining the ratio of accounts payable to the monetary current assets less the other current liabilities. This affords a valid assessment criterion for analysis and control.

Cash Receipts to Accounts Payable

A recently accepted technique is to measure accounts payable against projected cash receipts. This type of analysis permits the establishment of a ratio that indicates whether or not an organization is extending its debts too far when compared to the cash inflow. With an adequately developed ratio, the limit of accounts payable commitments relative to the anticipated cash receipts could then be projected. This serves as a control on purchasing expenditures and the time framework in which they are to occur.

Summary

The procurement/payment cycle and function is one of the most important activities involved in an organization's stability and success. It is an operation that must be closely monitored and controlled to avoid internal collusion and protect debt-paying ability. This, in turn, assures sources of supply to conduct its operations. An on-line computerized system enhances the various control processes, simplifies the voluminous processing activity, permits projections of cash disbursements and commitment balances, provides statistics for evaluating financial position, and mechanically pays the bills on schedule.

12

Computer-Aided Property Management Planning and Decision-Making

Capital or fixed assets are nonmonetary in nature in that they are not readily convertible into cash as are accounts receivable, for example. They represent physical items, such as land, buildings, machinery and equipment, furniture and fixtures, that contribute directly or indirectly to the production of a product. Their major characteristic is that their usefulness is projected over a longer period of time than are expense charges against current periods of operation. Actually, they can be considered as deferred charges since the cost is spread over the life of the asset and only a certain amount of write-offs (depreciation/amortization) occurs within a given operating period.

Capital assets involve new acquisitions, replacements, and enhancements to property resulting from improved technology. Included in the total cost of the asset are the acquisition costs, freight, installation, and so on.

CAPITAL VERSUS REVENUE EXPENSE

It is often difficult to assess and classify an expense item as capital or revenue. The rules of demarcation generally differ among organizations. There is no problem of classification relative to the major items such as machinery and equipment, vehicles, or building. In the case of low-cost items, a $100 expenditure could be classified as either capital or revenue expense depending on utilization, useful life, and future benefits. An operating expense in one organization, such as a pocket calculator, could be carried as a capital asset in another organization.

The general guideline for determining cost capitalization is whether benefits will be derived in the future or whether its value is in the current period, which would infer an expense to be charged against operating revenue. Another test is to judge whether or not it is of recurring nature; if it is, it is classified as an operating expense.

Maintenance and repairs are considered to be operating expense since they represent costs required to maintain the plant and machinery in good operating condition without increasing the plant's productive capacity or increasing the life of the original asset beyond the time initially established. It is noted that absorption of costs (through depreciation) reduces current income and taxes but will penalize future profits.

CAPITALIZATION OF ORGANIZATION EXPENSES

The costs involved in organizing an organization are capitalized like any other fixed asset. These costs are generally in the nature of fees to the organizers, promoters, and attorneys. They include such other expenses as obtaining stock subscriptions, cost of the certificates to be issued, and meeting security exchange regulations. The initial organization costs represent start-up expenses and are not associated with operating revenue since there is generally no income being earned during the period of organization. These costs represent capital expenditures and are usually written off rapidly as soon as revenue becomes available. If similar costs are incurred after the organization is in operation, they are then considered to be operating expenses.

ASPECTS OF DEPRECIATION

Depreciation expense represents a predetermined period allocation of capital asset costs over the life of the asset based on historical experience, organization policy, judgment of valuation experts, and possibly Internal Revenue guidelines. Since capital assets are used to produce revenue or income, the devaluation of an asset's usefulness is charged against revenue over a designated period of time. The service life of an asset is primarily predicated on its efficient performance usefulness over a period of time.

Depreciation reserve represents accumulated depreciation write-offs or booked charges over a given period of time. It is the total estimated loss value of the property between the period of acquisition and date of the valuation. Setting up a depreciation reserve provides a means to set aside funds or allowances as a hedge against future asset replacement and/or upgrading.

Criteria for Establishing Depreciation Factors

The service life of an asset is based on obsolescence, normal wear and tear factors, deterioration, advancing technology efficiencies, anticipated negligence (experience factor) in utilization or inappropriate maintenance, intensity of usage, and product demand changes. A brief description of some of these causes follows.

- *Inadequacy* can result from physical development and growth of a business enterprise that can cause changes in operating conditions and thus make the asset inappropriate for further utilization. Increased production requirements may dictate new equipment since the old cannot satisfy the new needs.

- *Obsolescence* results from reduced valuation of an asset because of corrosion, new developments in product processing, and change in product mix or demand. This situation may result from major changes in operations or a number of small changes over a period of time that diminishes asset value.
- *Deterioration* is generally associated with exposure of the asset to adverse weather conditions (moisture, heat, snow). It can also occur from poor or nonexistent preventive maintenance.
- *Wear-and-tear* conditions occur over a period of time of asset usage. This could be due to mechanical or natural causes attributed to the actual operating climate (vibration, oxidation) or just plain old age.
- *Technological advancements* in equipment efficiencies and capabilities can also be a major factor as, for example, in the computer industry where new innovations are constantly occurring.

Common Methods of Computing Depreciation

There are a number of methods, or combinations thereof, that can be used in calculating depreciation. The method selected is contingent upon company policy and an assessment of its relevance and objectives. A brief description of some common methods follows.

- *Straight Line*—Equal amounts are charged off by period over the designated life of the asset.
- *Declining Balance*—A fixed percentage of depreciation is applied to the *net* asset value at the end of each accounting year. A five-year asset life would mean 20% application each year to net asset value. Generally, the straight-line method would be used for the last two years in order to avoid infinity in asset write-off.
- *Double Declining*—An accelerated depreciation in which you double the straight-line depreciation and apply a factor to net asset value each year.
- *Sum of the Year's Digits*—The number of years are totalled and divided into each year with the last year being first, next to last, second, and so on, to obtain the rate to be applied to the same total acquisition cost each year.
- *Production Methods*—This depreciation is based on units of output, time utilization, jobs, sales, and the like. It is used in those industries where this type of assessment can be readily determined.

In the computerized environment, depreciation is mechanically developed from an input of the estimated life of the asset and the formula method of calculation.

Importance of Depreciation Planning

The type of method used in calculating depreciation is very important to an organization. Excessive depreciation can affect product costs (making them higher) and thus possibly result in loss of sales to competition. If the depreciation criterion is too low, the product cost is accordingly lower, and the result is an increase in profit subject to a greater tax exposure. Further, the actual value of the capital asset will be understated which can create future problems in replacement financing. Then, too, overstatement of profits might result in a declaration of higher dividends. This situation could affect an organization's financial position when the time arrives for asset replacement.

Another aspect of depreciation planning concerns the volume of productivity. It is assumed that in periods of high volume of output, the profitability is greater and the intensity of asset usage (wear and tear) is greater. Depreciation expense should be greater when usage is high versus a low-volume situation.

An inherent problem in depreciation planning is that the write-off, although eventually matching the asset acquisition cost, may not be sufficient to meet the replacement cost due to higher prices in the future. Some organizations have turned to the establishment of a sinking fund which is invested and the interest proceeds added to this fund with the objective that the combined total will equal the future replacement value.

ASSET LEASE VERSUS BUY CONSIDERATIONS

Long-term leasing of plant and equipment is preferable to buying if it can be proven that it is in the company's benefit to do so. This is particularly so on certain government contracts where lease rental costs are allowable and recoverable. Interest cost associated with purchase is unallowable on facility investments. Generally, the organizational policy dictates that if machinery and equipment, for example, is expected to be used until worn out, the decision favors the purchasing route. In situations where the above criterion is not specifically applicable, a study should be undertaken to determine which of the two alternatives is most advantageous.

Determining the Lease/Buy Decision

The basic criterion revolves around comparing the sum of the rental payments (less maintenance costs included in the rental), plus a reasonable carrying charge versus the amortization of the asset at the going discount rate. The basic procedure is to compare costs of ownership as opposed to leasing, allowing for the fact that a dollar profit now is worth more than the dollar profit that will materialize sometime in the future. An example of the assessment to be made relative to lease versus buy follows:

Cost Advantage Assumptions—An airplane is to be purchased at a cost of $110,000 cash. Money would be borrowed on a three-year basis at 4% (improbable) with a down payment of $10,000. The plane is expected to be worth 25% of its purchase price at the end of three years, or $27,500. Monthly lease of airplane services is $2,900 with no down payment. All other costs will be borne by the organization, in both cases, thus removing their impact from the comparative consideration. Dollars invested in this organization's operations earns 10%

Calculations—From statistical tables, the monthly payment required to amortize a loan of $100,000 (total price less down payment) at 4% is $2,952.40. A cost table comparison is noted as follows.

	Annual Payments		Annual Cost Advantage
Year	Purchase	Lease	to Buy
1	$ 45,428.80	$ 34,800	$(10,628.80)
2	35,428.80	34,800	(628.80)
3	35,428.80	34,800	(628.80)
Total	$116,286.40	$104,400	$(11,886.40)

The cost (dis)advantage of buying is discounted at the rate of earnings of the business at 10% (above assumption). The present value (discounted cash flow) factors are taken from statistical tables and used as follows.

	Annual Cost Advantage to Buy	Present Value Factor	Present Value of Cost Advantage to Buy
	$(10,628.80)	.9091	$(9,662.64)
	(628.80)	.8264	(519.64)
	(628.80)	.7513	(472.42)
Total	$(11,886.40)		$(10,654.70)

The salvage value of the plane is also worth less than the face amount to the organization currently because it will be unavailable for three years. Using the third-year present value factor, the discounted calculation is as follows:

$$\$27{,}500 \times .7513 = \$20{,}660.75$$

In Summary—

Present value of investment cost (dis)advantage to buy	$(10,654.70)
Present value of salvage amount	20,660.75
Total advantage to buy	$ 10,006.05

Effect on Cash Flow—In order to accomplish this assessment, additional assumptions relative to depreciation allowances are required. It will be assumed that the plane has a five-year life for tax purposes and a salvage value of $10,000 at the end of that period. The double-declining method of depreciation will be used. The effect of the purchase on cash follows:

Year	Cash Payment	Less Depreciation	Annual Cash Drain
1	$ 45,428.80	$ 40,000	$ 5,428.80
2	35,428.80	24,000	11,428.80
3	35,428.80	14,400	21,028.80
4	—	8,640	(8,640.00)
5	—	5,144	(5,144.00)
Total	$116,286.40	$ 92,184	$ 24,102.40

Adjustment is then made for disposal at the *end* of three years.

Year	Cash Payment	Less Depreciation	Write-off at Salvage	Proceeds from Salvage	Annual Cash Drain
1	$ 45,428.80	$ 40,000	—	—	$ 5,428.80
2	35,428.80	24,000	—	—	11,428.80
3	35,428.80	14,400	$ 21,600*	$ 10,000	(10,571.20)
Total	$116,286.40	$ 78,400	$ 21,600	$ 10,000	$ 6,286.40

*$110,000 less $10,000 (salvage) = $100,000 less $78,400 = $21,600

Since lease expense is entirely recoverable through overhead in the year in which incurred, the above represents the effect of purchasing on cash flow. The results above therefore indicate that the purchase of the plane is the most advantageous direction to take based on the effect of less cash outflow.

Advantageous factors in leasing (however):

- Cash flow benefits if surplus capital can yield greater profitability from alternative investment.
- Under government contracts, it is assumed that lease expense is reimbursable.
- Less detailed recordkeeping and control which is so essential to purchased fixed asset.
- Renewal options are generally on a lower rental basis.
- In situations where changing product requirements make machinery and equipment subject to early obsolescence.
- All benefits of performance, guarantees, and/or warranties are available to the leasing party.

MAKE-OR-BUY DECISION

In a number of situations, a decision must be made as to whether a capital asset will be designed and manufactured internally rather than obtained through outside purchase. There could be various reasons for this such as: unavailability from the vendor, unique requirement, depressed business conditions that make time and material available and justify maintaining manpower levels, less expensive to make rather than buy, vendor delay in delivery which would exceed utilization requirement date, and more profitable use of the investment internally.

Factors Relevant to the Decision

Before action is initiated to make or buy a certain asset, an evaluation should be made of the comparative cost supplemented by the nonmonetary considerations discussed above. Since fixed costs remain constant, the main emphasis should be directed to the effect on variable costs. Comparative cost estimates should reflect the following relevant factors:

- Design, drawing, and detailed specifications of the requirement must be known.
- Raw materials and/or completed parts must be purchased and these should be based on the anticipated price at the time of their requirement.
- Production methods should be explored as to how the task can be accomplished, facilities required, and estimated cost of manufacture.
- Determination has to be made as to whether the appropriate manpower skills are available and their costs.
- Overhead has to be evaluated in terms of different indirect support variables (manpower, supplies, etc.) to accommodate the needs of different requirements (asset fabrication versus the standard product production).

After the above data has been determined and documented and cost estimates assembled, a comparison of make price to the anticipated purchase price is made to provide cost effectiveness results; however, as stated previously, other reasons, as described above, might overrule the importance of the cost aspects.

COMPUTERIZED CAPITAL EXPENDITURE BUDGET

In conjunction with the development of the annual operating plans and long-range forecasts, appropriate attention must be given to the preparation of the proposed capital expenditures. This is necessary in order to provide adequate facilities to meet production requirements on a timely scheduled basis, which is the basis for achieving the sales delivery programs. Underestimating the needs can create havoc with the schedule, and overexpenditures can result in costly investments that would affect an organization's profitability. Therefore, careful planning must be exercised to evaluate all proposals deemed essential for capital expenditures. Capital budgeting decisions are concerned with acquisitions, replacements, modernizing, make or buy, initiation of new projects, or termination of those in existence.

Planning Objectives

More specifically to the above, the following provides the criteria for evaluating capital budgets through appropriate planning considerations:

- A thorough analysis and economic justification must be established for all proposed capital asset projects.
- Proposed expenditures must reflect needs to meet management goals and objectives.
- To ensure compliance for adequate control, the necessary procedures must be prepared and disseminated to the involved personnel.
- Property records must be evaluated to preclude the existence and availability of the proposed asset somewhere else in the organization.
- The make-or-buy aspects must be properly assessed.
- Assurance must be determined that the proposed capital expenditures are within the limits of available resources.
- The necessary approvals must be obtained to authorize the acquisition of the proposed assets.
- An effective reporting system must permit continual follow-up monitoring of actual results against the approved expenditure plan.

Capital Expenditure Requests

Before the capital expenditure budget can be formally resolved, all organizations are requested to submit their expenditure request to the appropriate management for review, resolution, approval, and consolidation. The following information is required by individual proposal relative to new acquisitions, replacements, improvements, or rearrangements:

Description of the project and submitting organization
Justification and purpose of the requirement
Date required for project completion or asset acquisition
Estimated cost (in-house or external by time period)
Projected life of the asset
Forecasted savings by period
Make-or-buy evaluation results

Identification as to capital asset ledger number
Listing of machinery or equipment to be retired—age, book value, salvage value, removal costs, and so on

Each request should also be categorized as essential (to meet development, production, and customer requirements, or to improve profitability) or desirable (to enhance internal operational efficiencies or information security).

Mechanical Request Consolidations

After the review and approval of each request, the data is inputted into the computerized system which basically contains the information shown above. The history file thus created affords the opportunity of summarizing data by asset number within the organization with grand totals and also lends itself for comparison to funds authorized and actually expended.

It is noted that before any funds are actually spent, even though the request has been approved for the budget, an authorization request to expend funds must be submitted to management for approval. There are two reasons for this procedure: First, it allows the approving management to review once again the expenditure request budget and make a determination as to whether funds are available; second, it permits management to verify the priority at the time of the anticipated fund commitment. It might be that prior projects have cost (or are costing) more than previously estimated with an adverse effect on cash flow, or the expenditure priorities may have changed due to new operational requirements.

Performance and Control Reporting

In order to be continually apprised of the status and control of appropriations versus expenditures, periodic reports are required by management to assess their position because of the impact on cash flow and possible deviations from the budget plan. Two sample key reports that effectively provide the status insight required are illustrated on pages 235 and 236. In the computerized system, the annual budget data is in the computer files, actuals are derived from a separate mechanical program, and the current estimates and approved appropriations to date are direct inputs.

PROPERTY MANAGEMENT DATA BANK

For planning visibility, accountability, management, and control of all of the customer and organization property transactions and records, a mechanically oriented data bank is a powerful tool that should be given its appropriate emphasis. In some organizations, it was found that over a quarter of a million dollars in annual savings were achieved by the installation of this type of system which integrates all property records into data file banks. Adding an on-line capability further enhances the timeliness of charges and selective data retrieval. It would provide specific data to all concerned organizations such as Accounting, Property Control and Administration, Plant Engineering, operating organizations and the customer (if appropriate). It would meet the requirements of the new ASPR (Armed Services Procurement Regulations) reporting needs.

APPROPRIATION/EXPENDITURE STATUS

APPROPRIATIONS			EXPENDITURES		
Annual Budget	Approved to Date	Description	Annual Budget	Spent to Date	Current Estimate
		Approved This Year			
		Board Approval Listing			
		Appropriations Approved by Corporate Management			
		Appropriations Approved by Division Management			
		TOTAL APPROVED			
		Appropriations to Be Approved This Year			
		Appropriations Submitted to Corporate Office			
		Other Appropriations to Be Approved			
		Total Appropriations to Be Approved This Year			
		Carry Forward from Prior Years			
		TOTAL			

SUMMARY OF APPROPRIATIONS AND EXPENDITURES

APPROPRIATIONS	Annual Budget	Actual to Date	Current Estimate
Expansion Replacement Modernization Cost Reduction Other			
TOTAL			
DEPRECIATION			

	APPROPRIATIONS	EXPENDITURES
ANNUAL BUDGET Major Additions (list) ALL OTHER Reduction of expenditures on prior year open projects Reduction of expenditures on current year appropriations Deferment of projects requiring approval		
CURRENT ESTIMATE		

Organization of the Data Bank File

The file would be organized in a manner that would provide the capability to access at random any specific data without sequential searching. The data would be stored on disk since there are continual input, changes, and requirements for data retrieval. The field file records would contain the following essential information, as appropriate, by property number identification and organization:

Organization-assigned property number and description
Date of acquisition
Quantity, unit price, and total acquisition cost (including freight and installation)
Accounting work order number (if contract related) for charging purposes
Work authorization number (if costs are to be collected at the detail level)
Journal voucher and general ledger asset account numbers
Estimated life, depreciation method, and rate
Journal voucher and general ledger depreciation account numbers
Period, year-to-date, and cumulative-to-date asset addition costs, depreciation expense/reserve, and book values
Department designation for charging depreciation expense
Investment tax credit group identifier to indicate percentage cost factor (3-5 years is 2.33% cost; 5-7 years is 4.67%; 7 or more years is 7%)
Identifier to designate whether asset is qualified for tax credit
Month and year-to-date investment tax credit amount
Period, year, and cumulative-to-date labor and material costs for repair, maintenance, and calibration (includes outside vendors)
Manufacturer's code (Federal Supply Code Handbook) name, model and serial numbers, and year of manufacture
National stock number (government-owned facilities) and standard commodity code (plant equipment)
Ownership code (organization, customer, leasing organization)
Facility code and location (building number, floor, column, room)
Department-assigned custodial responsibility or employee number in the case of personal-use items (radios, cameras, calculators)

With the above data in the files, practically any type of reporting can be accomplished. It represents an ambitious undertaking. It is noted, however, that many organizations will *not* require all of the data indicated above. The requirements are contingent upon the individual organization's needs for managing property, controlling, and planning. Certain of the above data is basic to all organizations such as recording acquisitions, providing data for depreciation calculation, and general and property ledger requirements.

Mechanical Functions for Financial Reporting

The following manipulations are performed in the computerized system:

- Transaction data is used to update file records and a listing of the input is outputted.
- Property items are sorted and summarized within subaccount, control account, major category, annual classification, and facility.

- Depreciation expenses are calculated by line item for the current period within the subaccount, and year and cumulative-to-date totals are updated.
- Depreciation data are sorted and summarized similar to the procedure for property assets above.
- Book values are calculated for the various sorts and summaries of fixed assets and depreciation.
- Qualified property is segregated for investment tax credit, and the tax is calculated.
- Batch reports are structured for output, and on-line capabilities are provided.
- Fixed asset and depreciation journals are automatically prepared for entry into the general ledger system, which reflects beginning balances.
- A fixed asset, depreciation reserve, and book value analysis schedule is provided, which reports beginning balances, additions, deletions, and ending balances—actual, budget, and variances.

On-Line Processing

The sequence of events in the processing cycle are displayed on Exhibit A. After the historical records have been entered into the data bank files, the sequential procedure involves keyboarding the subsequent transactions from basic documentation into the computer via an on-line terminal device, or the input process can be accomplished by utilizing card input. The computer teleprocessing monitor collects the data in predetermined and specified formats. It is edited and audited to verify the validity of the input in terms of account and code identifiers. If, for some reason, certain data is lacking and/or incorrect, it will be rejected and relayed back through the monitor to the on-line terminal for analysis, correction, and resubmission.

Valid data is processed in accordance with the program instructions and entered into the master file records for updating the data bank (storage depository) for batch reporting or on-line retrievals as shown on the exhibit. A listing of the accepted transaction input is reported on the organization's terminal device for review and file record reference.

The property transactions are captured only once in this system, and, through the appropriate sorting and updating process, the information is reflected in all of the pertinent file records. Property management and control, through the use of computerized data banks and formalized fund authorization and expenditure budgets, is increasing in importance to advanced management in the current business environment. This is only natural in light of the continuing emphasis on an appropriate return on investment of which capital assets represent the major share. Then, too, there is the impact on cash flow that could adversely affect an organization's operational capabilities.

In order to achieve an effective capital budget, management should be provided with a number of alternatives on which to base decisions to determine the most efficient utilization of their resources. Other considerations discussed in this chapter should also be given due emphasis to ensure that appropriate action and concern are accorded to capitalization versus expense, and that lease or make-versus-buy advantages have not been ignored in the planning process.

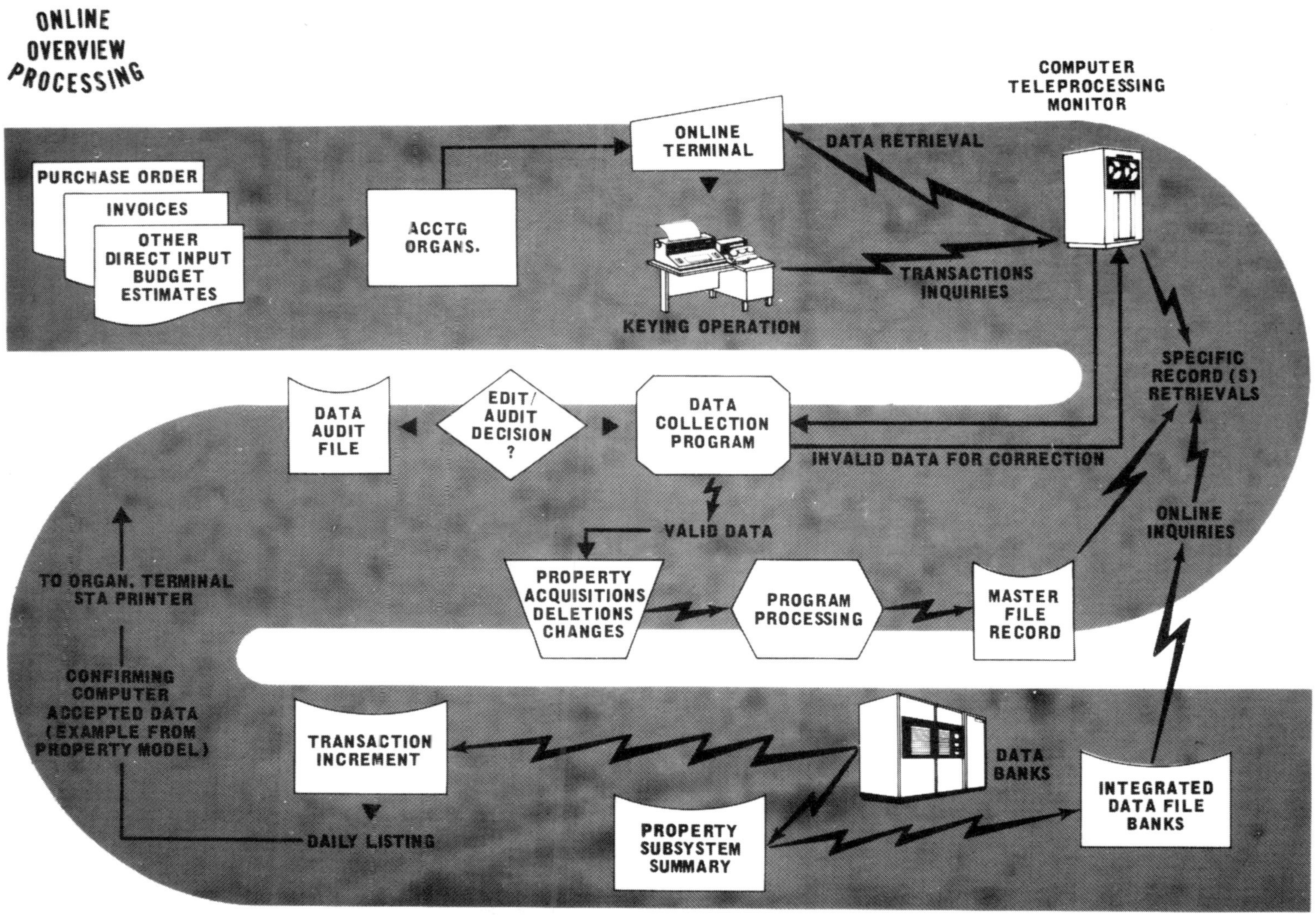
ONLINE
OVERVIEW
PROCESSING
PURCHASE ORDER
INVOICES
OTHER
DIRECT INPUT
BUDGET
ESTIMATES
ACCTG
ORGANS.
ONLINE
TERMINAL
KEYING OPERATION
DATA RETRIEVAL
TRANSACTIONS
INQUIRIES
COMPUTER
TELEPROCESSING
MONITOR
SPECIFIC
RECORD (S)
RETRIEVALS
DATA
AUDIT
FILE
EDIT/
AUDIT
DECISION
?
DATA
COLLECTION
PROGRAM
INVALID DATA FOR CORRECTION
VALID DATA
ONLINE
INQUIRIES
TO ORGAN. TERMINAL
STA PRINTER
PROPERTY
ACQUISITIONS
DELETIONS
CHANGES
PROGRAM
PROCESSING
MASTER
FILE
RECORD
CONFIRMING
COMPUTER
ACCEPTED DATA
(EXAMPLE FROM
PROPERTY MODEL)
TRANSACTION
INCREMENT
DAILY LISTING
DATA
BANKS
PROPERTY
SUBSYSTEM
SUMMARY
INTEGRATED
DATA FILE
BANKS

EXHIBIT A

13

Controlling Costs and Increasing Profits Through Computerized Financial Planning and Measurement Methods

The motivating force for achieving success in business is profits. Some may deny this, but it is noted that profits make business enterprise survive and grow. Profits provide the basis and the incentive, through dividends and success, for outside sources to invest in an organization. Profits make business expansion possible through investments in various new product development pursuits, purchase of additional facilities and equipment, and attraction of more and higher calibre personnel and management. A dismal profit picture does not attract working capital through stock issuance or improve the organization's posture in borrowing money from banks and other lending institutions. Losses do not promote vendor confidence in extending credit since ability to pay bills on time becomes questionable.

ASPECTS OF PROFITABILITY

A definition of profit may take a number of forms depending on its source. The prime source in a business enterprise is the difference between product sales/service revenue and costs associated with producing the product or performing the service. Profits are also generated by royalty/interest income; sale of surplus capital assets; investment in other organizations or in internal projects that improve efficiencies in production output, enhance production characteristics for a wider market, or create new products or services through research and development activities.

Project Profit Planning

Since successful organizations are continually evaluating opportunities for increasing profitability, the objective then is to make a determination of how capital can be employed most lucratively to achieve the highest rate of return on investment. Project profit planning involves the detailed evaluation of each proposed project in quantitative financial terms so that a proper assessment can be made and also to provide data comparability in measuring the anticipated rate of return on resource investment.

In the review of two or more projects, a decision must be made as to the relative return on each, particularly when there is a limitation on fund availability. Future costs and sales revenue are the two major determinants in the planning process that provide the major bases for making decisions relative to project selection and initiation. It is noted, however, that there may be other valid extenuating reasons for investment such as obsolete equipment, requirement for expansion, or new product needs. The final determination is concerned with the assessment of alternative proposals for capital investment. Although this criterion is not absolute by any means because of future intangibles, it does provide the most logical way, all other things being equal, of selecting the project with the greatest return potential. The selection process also includes consideration of the timeliness of payback; short-term payback represents a more profitable return than long-term payback.

The mechanical process is appropriate for evaluating the alternative proposals because the same type of procedures are uniformly employed in the inputs and processing, the data is readily computed, changed, and recomputed with the results being in comparable output. Computerization also provides for comparison of future actuals with minimal clerical involvement.

Project planning employs estimating techniques in deriving projected financial data rates. Assumptions must be quantified in future monetary terms for proper assessment. Project data must further be integrated with other operational/financial data of the organization so that the overall planning results can be evaluated in terms of sales, costs, profits, cash, and the like.

Product Profit Planning

This type of planning is similar to project planning, but it is generally on a higher plane because it encompasses high-volume or costly production; it is assumed that products represent the bread and butter of the organization's business. Similar product lines usually share in joint expenses where costs such as heat, light, power, or maintenance cannot be practicably assigned to a specific product. The distribution of these costs is often based on activity or usage factors such as a rate per direct labor hour or space utilization.

Determining Sales Price and Profitability Decisions

As previously stated, profitability is based on the magnitude of relevant costs and sales revenue from a project and/or product/service that are related to accounting periods. Historical costs and sales are generally useful determinants of future activity; however, due consideration should be given to certain cost escalations projected to occur as a result of union negotiations, shortages arising from unusual conditions (weather, strikes, competition, war), cost of borrowing money, or product enhancements. Consideration is also directed to the rate of return required to perpetuate business operations. Another key determination of sales price is likely to be what the traffic will bear, yet with price competitive in terms of the consumer.

There are a number of methods that can be employed to make these kinds of projections. The most logical means to be used is based on previous experience. Computerization of the procedures greatly simplifies the task involved and provides alternatives for selecting the most relevant results and further affords the opportunity for changing costs, sales, and profit plans if the situation so dictates.

It is noted that the projection of costs should be segregated in detail as to direct elements of cost, research and development, allocations, selling expense, and general and administrative expenses. They should also be detailed into the fixed and variable classifications. This permits a more finite assessment of specifically where changes can be effected. Further, it highlights the variable expenses that are under the individual manager's control with the responsibility to authorize, monitor, and justify.

Characteristics of Profitability Evaluation

In order to evaluate most effectively the characteristics influencing profits as a result of fluctuations in sales, cost, and volume, an efficient tool often used is the profitgram. It is also called profit-cost-volume relationship, profitgraph, or breakeven point, all having essentially similar objectives. The name "profitgram" is used to emphasize the primary concern of this technique which is to assess profit fluctuations in terms of causal factors from other relevant data associations.

PROFITGRAM

There are actually two analytical aspects to the profitgram tool: First, you have the cost-volume-profit relationships that indicate what happens to costs and profit when volume changes; second, there is the criterion of why costs change.

A further basic procedure in the profitgram approach is that costs can be classified as fixed or variable, and are either influenced significantly or to a lesser degree by the fluctuation of production and/or sales volume. Of less consequence in some organizations, but very useful in a more detailed analysis of expense identification, is the semivariable classification. In this category, costs are segregated as to those that vary with volume but not in direct proportion as would be the case of the true variable expense. It is noted that expense changes are relative to total costs rather than to the individual units of cost such as labor and material.

Fixed and Variable Cost Effect on Profitability

Fixed costs have little or no relationship to volume or quantities (produced or sold) and generally include such items as insurance, taxes, depreciation, and rentals. For this expense category, it is stated that certain costs are required to maintain operations irrespective of volume fluctuations. Generally, little can be done to effect changes

Variable costs usually fluctuate with the activity volume. As volume increases or decreases, the effect influences higher or lower manpower, supplies, or power requirements.

Continual evaluation and control of these expenses is one of the most effective means of increasing profitability.

Other Major Influences on Profitability

There are a variety of factors that influence profitability such as sales volume, product mix, product obsolescence, competition, and higher than anticipated costs for production. The volume of productivity is also a major influence, particularly if the projected learning curve results do not materialize and there is increased scrap loss, idle time, inefficient operating methods and equipment, material shortages, and even inefficient control by management relative to manpower utilization and production operations.

Essentials of Profitgram Development

In developing the profitgram model, the following steps characterize the procedures employed:

- The vertical axis reflects the cost trend by volume segregated into fixed and variable costs.
- The horizontal axis reflects the sales volume in either percentage of capacity, unit output, or sales dollar trend.
- The profit line is the difference between the total cost and sales lines.
- The breakeven point is represented by the intersection of sales and costs where costs equal sales.

Graphic illustrations of breakeven point development is provided in depth in chapter 2.

Characteristics of the Profitgram

- The sales trend line indicates the average unit price and is calculated by dividing price by volume.
- Unit costs decrease gradually with volume increases.
- Fixed costs remain constant irrespective of volume increases (usually), whereas variable costs fluctuate with volume.
- The breakeven point is calculated through the use of the formula: Fixed Costs divided by 100% less (Variable Costs divided by Sales).
- Profit generally varies with volume.

From the above, it is evident that a thorough analysis of a profitgram display will reveal a number of varied facets of cost and revenue impact on the profit position. Varying the data plot points for projection purposes provides a valuable tool in viewing alternate courses of action for more effective profit planning and control.

PROFITABILITY PROJECTIONS

Through the study and experimentation with the profitgram technique in terms of cost-volume and other pertinent considerations, future profitability can be projected mechanically using mathematical formulae. There are a number of possibilities that could point to increased profit. Some basic actions that can be considered would include the following: increasing sales volume through new market penetrations or developing new products or services; increasing the sales price with possible minor enhancements on current products; changing product mix (eliminating marginal or loser products); and seeking ways to reduce costs. Noted below are two simplified examples of what happens to profitability when sales/cost changes are made.

Increasing Sales Volume and Costs

As indicated above, sales can be increased in a number of ways by initiating certain appropriate actions. With increased sales, there is generally a rise in costs but usually not in the same relative proportion. Based on the assumptions below, the effect is shown on profits when changes are made to sales and costs.

Assumptions	Before Changes		After Changes
20% Increase in Sales	Sales	120	144
15% Increase in Costs	Costs	80	92
No change in Sales Price	Profits	40	52
Values in 000s$			
	Profit % Sales	.333	.361
	Profit Increase		.30

Although the profit shown above increased 30% due to greater sales, actual experience might prove that it could be higher if there were mass production efficiencies, lower material costs due to volume purchases, or improvement in the learning curve. Conversely, the costs could be higher than assumed above due to additional costs for initiating changes in production methods, requirement for new machinery, or expanding facilities.

Increasing Sales Price but Decreasing Volume

It might be possible to increase the sales price/unit, particularly if the organization is the sole source of the product or service, if product improvement can be made at a relatively insignificant additional cost, and/or due to inflationary economic conditions. It is quite conceivable that an increase in the sales price would probably produce a decrease in sales volume but not in the same relative proportion. Illustrated below is an example of what happens to profitability based on the above assumptions.

Assumptions	Before Changes		After Changes	
20% Increase in Unit Price	60 units @ \$2	120	\$2 × .20 = .40 + 2.00 = 2.40	
10% Decrease in Volume	Costs	80	60 units × .10 = −6 + 60 = 54	
Costs Remain Same				
Value in 000s$	Profits	40	Sales	129.60
	Profit % Sales	.333	Costs	80.00
			Profits	49.60
			Profit % Sales	.388
			Profit Increase	.24

As shown above, the profit would increase 24% even at the 54-unit volume level. This indicates that an increase in unit price generally offsets an anticipated decline in volume.

REDUCTION IN PRODUCT COSTS

A detailed evaluation of the individual cost accounts may reveal that there is hidden "fat" in the expenditures that could be drastically reduced or eliminated through initiated management control actions.

In the direct product cost area, it has been found that often material substitutions could be made that would not impair product efficiency or utilization and the result would be a significant reduction in the cost per unit. In some instances, it might be even more advantageous to do so, as in the case of plastic soling being substituted for leather in some shoes (provides longer shoe life). Then there is the substitution of inexpensive paper and plastic containers for the more costly glass, and other similar substitutions that lower cost.

In other cases, it has been revealed that the industrial engineer's close scrutiny of methods being used in production activities led to changes that resulted in increased volume at a lower cost. Improved production controls decreased and, in some instances, totally eliminated defective products, which led to a dramatic decrease in overall product costs. More modern and efficient equipment, particularly with computer monitoring control capability, will definitely lead to increased production output at a lower cost.

Runaway Costs

An excellent example of runaway cost in one organization's overhead was excessive travel. It was found that a number of people in the organization were attending the same seminar in distant places. After travel was computerized, a capability became available to perform various data sorts by traveler, destination, and trip reason. The report revealed that, in a particular week, eight people traveled from the West Coast to the East Coast to attend the same three-day seminar. Various other statistics came to light, such as a number of people visiting the same city at the same time to perform individual chores. Management action was immediately initiated to establish strict controls authorizing only one individual to attend a seminar and, upon his return, permitting him to conduct an in-house seminar for those who had an interest. Further, individuals visiting a location would perform a number of tasks (if at all possible) to reduce one-function trips. The corrective action resulted in a 50% decrease in travel expenditures, which increased profitability accordingly.

Other Expenses Requiring Close Surveillance

Through thorough analysis, overhead reductions were achieved in such areas as entertainment, supplies (volume purchases and effective lower cost substitutes), supervisory salaries (increasing ratio of the number of workers per supervisor and/or combining functions), and paid memberships/expenses in professional organizations for employees.

CHANGING PRODUCT MIX FOR INCREASING PROFITABILITY

In the above discussion, profit analysis and performance emphasis has been concerned primarily with those products that are similar in nature and their cost characteristics (for example, a product line). When the situation exists where the products are of dissimilar types, then cost and profit evaluation should be by individual product. The procedures described above are also appropriate for individual product analysis in order to determine the relative profitability and problems concerned with each. Decisions should be made as to which should be eliminated, reduced, or increased in production volume, and/or corrective action taken to resolve profitability problems.

Considerations in Changing Product Mix

- Have all means been explored and detailed cost analyses made to determine if costs can be decreased in order to achieve higher profitability?
- Has the sales market been tested as to the effect of product price increases and their influence on sales volume?
- Is there another source for (cheaper) raw materials and/or can material substitutions be made to lower costs?
- Are the most advanced techniques and equipment being used in product production?
- Are unrealistic sales commissions making the unfavorable impact on profits?
- Have overhead and other allocation distributions been analyzed to determine equitability of assignment to products?
- Have customer comments been solicited as to product improvements that might warrant making changes in product mix to increase profits?
- Are there extenuating circumstances as to why one product has a higher profit markup than the others?

As noted above, there are a number of considerations that must be explored before action is taken to change product mix. A cursory decision could lead to more problems in profitability than currently exist. Careful analysis of the facts is the key to increased profits.

MECHANICAL INCOME STATEMENT DEVELOPMENT

Exhibit A displays the processes involved in developing the income statement for two types of contracts. On fixed-price contracts, the total price is negotiated with the customer and the price includes a projected profit and rate. It is noted, however, that if there is a cost overrun on this type of contract, the profits are impacted by the amount of the overrun.

The gross profit percentage is applied to the sales to obtain gross profit dollars, which, when deducted from sales, yields the product cost of sales.

The period cost percentage is projected based on past experience and anticipations for the future. Period costs include anticipated expenditures for general and administrative expense, research and development, and proposal and bidding that are projected to occur in a given period. The application percentage is applied against the direct labor dollars to obtain

SUMMARY PROFIT (LOSS) DEVELOPMENT

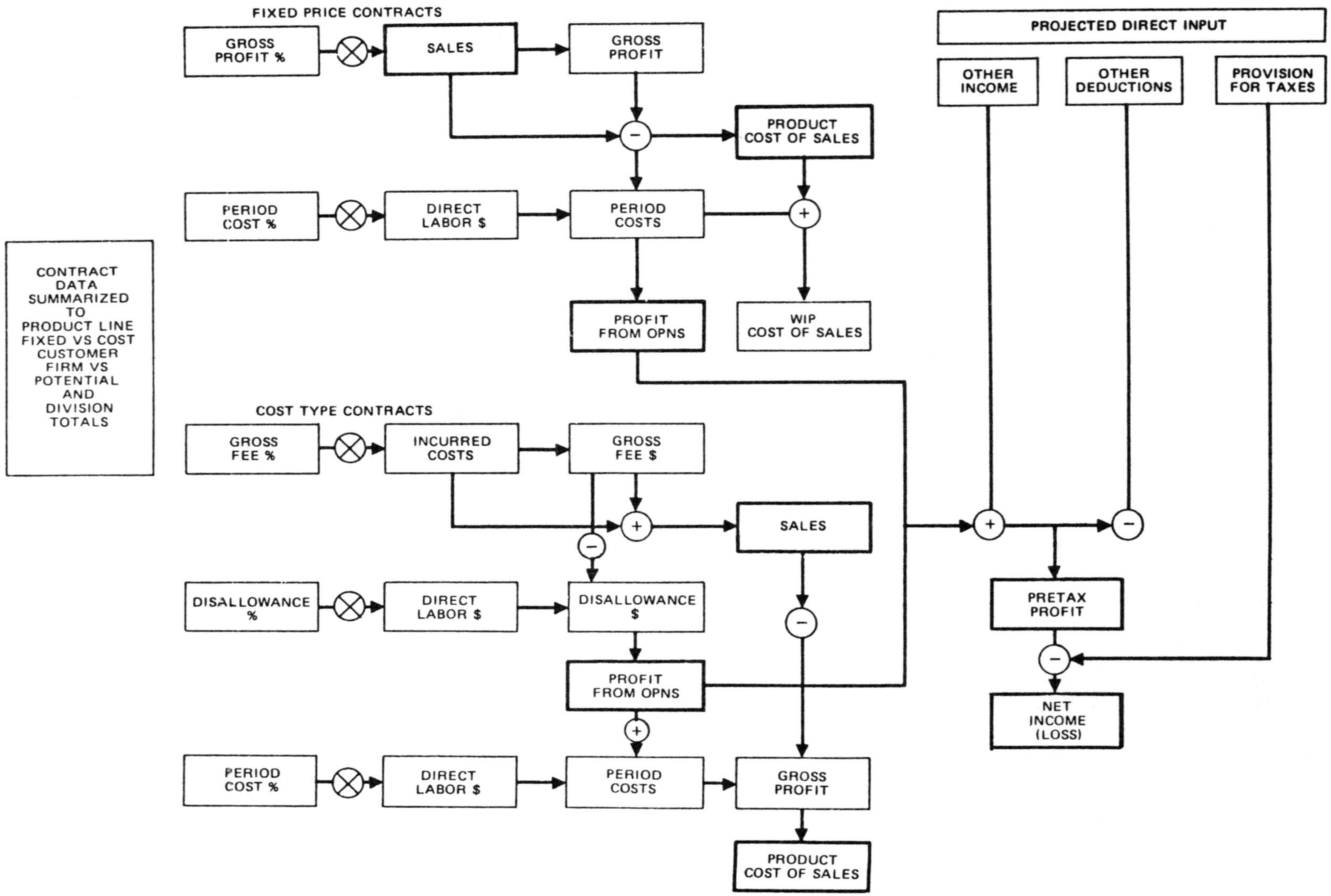

EXHIBIT A

period cost dollars. This value is subtracted from gross profit to obtain profit from operations. It is also added to the product cost of sales to derive work-in-process (WIP) cost of sales.

Other income is added to the profit from operations, and other deductions subtracted in order to obtain pretax profit. A provision for the tax rate is applied to that value; taxes are calculated and deducted from pretax profit to obtain the net income (or loss).

On cost-type contracts, the costs and fee rate are negotiated with the customer. The gross fee percentage is applied to projected incurred costs to obtain gross fee dollars, which are added to the costs to obtain the sales forecast.

Disallowances are based on historical experience plus anticipations. The disallowance percentage rate is applied to the direct labor dollars to obtain the disallowance dollars. The projected disallowances are deducted from the gross fee dollars to obtain profit from operations. Period costs are determined as indicated for fixed-price contracts above. The balance of the processes are similar to those discussed for fixed-price contracts. In the computerized process, similar data is summarized for organizational totals.

Although not displayed on this exhibit, commercial net income from operations represents the application of a markup percentage to the total costs involved in producing a product. This is generally at the quantity lot level; when divided by the number of units produced, the unit sales price is determined.

The mechanical process permits the changing of any projected assumption and rapid obtaining of new data for review, particularly the manipulation of profit factors. Maximizing profit through simulations has been found to be a rewarding technique for increased profitability and its cost effect on operations.

OPERATIONAL INCOME ANALYSIS

Another effective technique for income evaluation is to set forth relevant comparative data by product type or mix in order to determine the relative differences in the sales, cost elements of the product, and the resulting profits. This type of analysis provides a clue as to possible problem areas affecting profitability. An example of this type of evaluation is displayed below.

	Product A	% Sales	Product B	% Sales	Total	%
Sales	7,000.	100	4,000.	100	11,000.	100
Cost of Sales						
Labor	2,310.	33	800.	20	3,110.	28.3
Material	1,400.	20	1,200.	30	2,600.	23.6
Overhead	2,800.	40	1,800.	45	4,600.	41.8
Subtotal	6,510.	93	3,800.	95	10,310.	93.7
Operational Income	490	7	200	5	690.	6.3

From the above it is quite obvious that an analysis is required to assess the disparity cost element makeup as indicated by the differences in the two products, particularly in the relatively high overhead on Product B as compared to A. It appears that the overhead allocations are disproportionate to the labor activity and sales volume. Changes in the cost data would certainly influence the magnitude of the profits and the return on investment.

RETURN ON INVESTMENT

One of the more important criteria of measuring an organization's profitability is the determination of its return on investment. This is of particular interest to the external world such as stockholders and lending institutions who provide resources for an organization's operations. It is a financial evaluation statistic reflecting the stability of a business.

An overview of the aspects involved in developing the return on investment statistic is displayed on Exhibit B. The stockholders' net investment is the combination of preferred and common stock, with the investment in subsidiaries, plus earned and capital surpluses. The owners' equity can also be calculated by reducing total assets by total liabilities and adding to this value the beginning net investment as well as the changes in additions and reductions in investments that may occur during a particular time period.

Another means to ascertain the ending investment balance is displayed in the center of the exhibit where the beginning balance is combined with the other data elements as shown.

Return on Investment and Turnover

Return on investment is calculated by adding the prior period's investment balance to the current period's investment balance and dividing by two to obtain the average investment for the current period. As subsequent period data become available, it is combined with that of prior periods and divided by the number of periods involved to obtain the average. For example, December, January, and February balances would be combined and divided by three to arrive at the average balance for the end of February.

At any point during the year, the net income would be annualized and divided by the average net investment balance to obtain the return on investment at this point in time. Investment return is a measure of profitability indicating how well the organization utilized its assets and the magnitude of the return itself. A negative return indicates generally poor or negligent management decisions as well as operational problems in the conduct of the business.

Investment turnover is another critically important criterion for measuring investment performance. In this case, the emphasis is on how many times the average investment was utilized in producing the level of sales or revenue. This is accomplished by dividing annualized sales by the average investment. The turnover factor represents a useful statistic in determining investment utilization and provides a motivating force in the planning and operating process to achieve greater profitability—an index that is always a source of exploration and assessment by stockholders, lending institutions, and credit rating organizations.

Criteria for Investment Evaluation

In making decisions on investment proposals, a computerized assessment technique that is used is present value. This process is based on the assumption that a proposed project should not be accepted if the present value of its earnings are equal to or greater than the amount of the investment required since true earnings are representative of actual future cash flow. *Example:* If you were to invest $1,000 and you required a 10% return, the question

ASPECTS OF NET INVESTMENT

Development

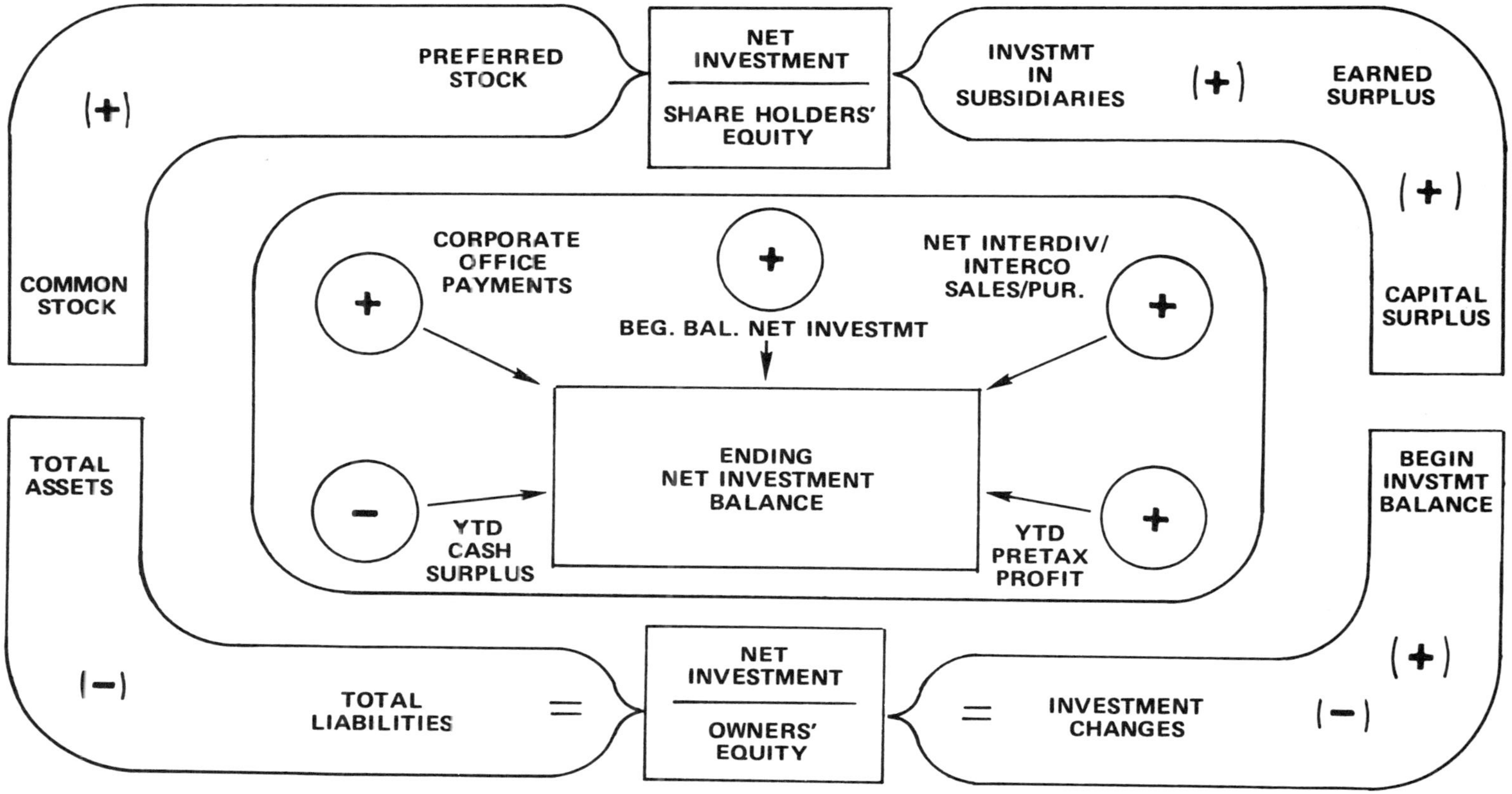

EXHIBIT B

arises as to the present value or earnings of the $1,000. The formula used to calculate this value would be: $1,000 ÷ ($1.00 + .10, or 1.10). The result is $909 present value, or a difference of $91 representing 9.1%.

The profit value of one project cannot be reliably measured with that of another unless the proposed investments in each case are of comparable value. If a $100 investment produces $150, or 150% of present value, the return on the project would be better than a $1,000 investment producing $1,200, or 12% of the present value. Higher earnings, therefore, should be the major indicative criterion for investment decisions; however, the risk factor of the investment as well as other relevant considerations should be carefully assessed before the final investment determination is made.

INCOME STATEMENT MANIPULATION

A representative computerized Summary of Operations (Income Statement) model is displayed on Exhibit C. As shown on this generalized chart, sales, cost of sales, and period costs are developed in the contract (CONMULT) program. Any changes to profit percentage period (G & A, R & D, etc.) costs, sales and/or direct cost elements would be reflected in the end profit results. Changes are made in the individual contract files or, as possible, in a separate program routine at the aggregate division level. The direct input (represented by the PLMULT in-file) provides data that is generally developed manually and/or is provided in the plan premises. Investment can be obtained from the balance sheet file (BSIN) or inputted directly if necessary.

All of the inputs are assembled in a file identified as "$PLPLAN." Any title can be assigned to this input providing it is incorporated in the program. The "@PLPLAN" is the name of the program that processes the data. The results from the processing take the form of not only a formal income statement projection but also output various statistical data (lower right of the exhibit) for assessment and determination of its appropriateness in the forecast plan. If management is dissatisfied with the profit results, then the "what if" gaming activity commences to develop revised data starting at the initial input. This is a highly versatile and advanced income model.

In conclusion, profitability is basically derived from the difference between revenue and costs. Historical experience plays a major role in projecting the future, but only intelligent planning and controls can achieve the objectives. Increasing profitability is a prime goal of all growing and successful enterprises. Management must always be on the alert to see that profit planning and measurement is accorded its proper importance and unique perspective relative to operating decisions. The use of the techniques discussed in this chapter should aid substantially in meeting or surpassing profit planned objectives. All levels of management must participate in profit planning and control if profitability is to be achieved.

DIVISION SUMMARY OF OPERATIONS

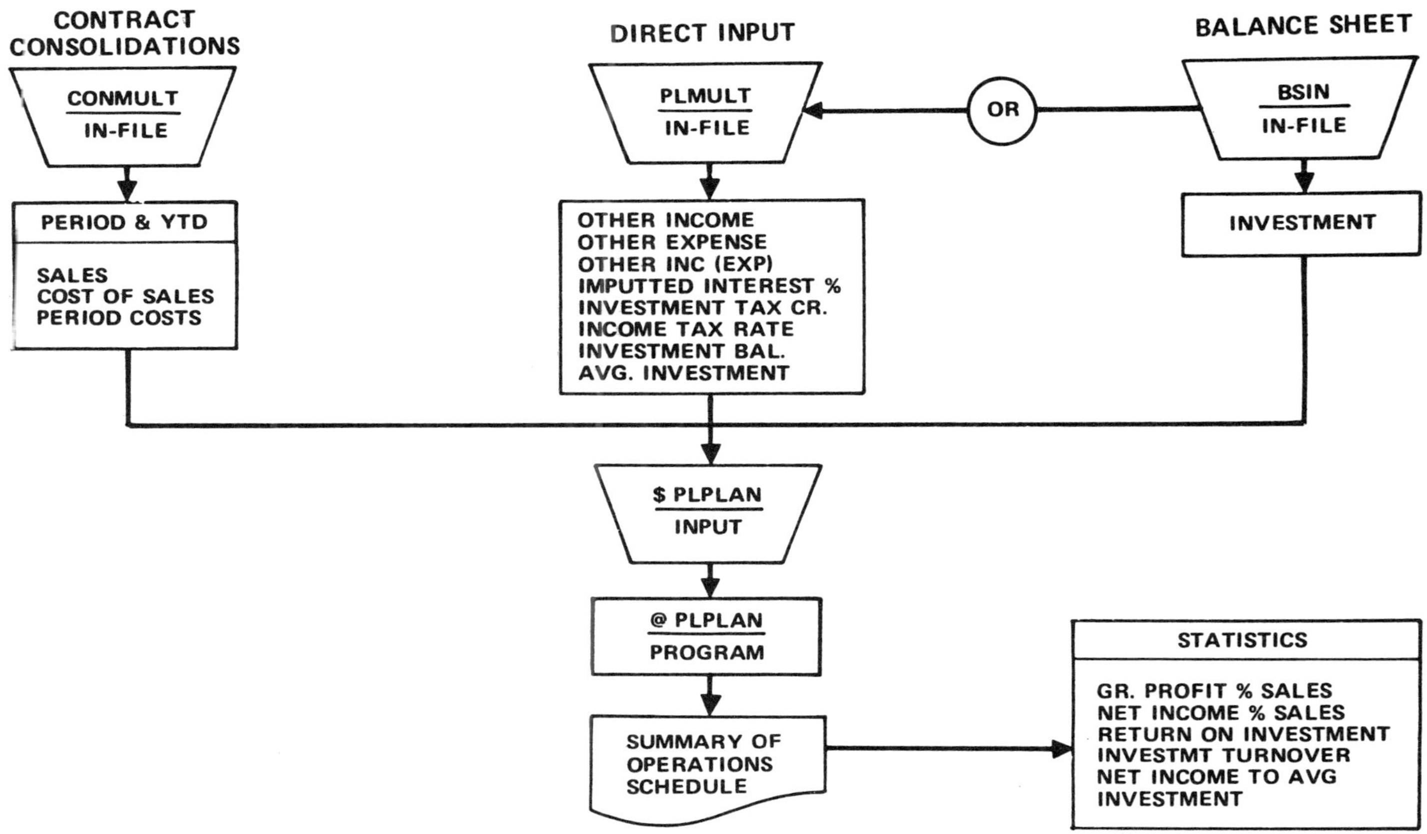

EXHIBIT C

14

Computerized Techniques for Strategic Financial Planning and Control

In order to effectively manage and control the various facets of its business, corporate hierarchy must be directly involved in the suborganizations' operations and planning functions. This does not mean involvement at the lowest level of operational detail, but rather at the point pertinent to its major function of strategic planning. Its concern is with sales volume and market penetration, profitability, economic indicators, effective utilization of resources, provision of sufficient working capital to achieve operational goals, cash flow, selection and assessment of investment opportunities, and isolation of present or potential problem areas that will require corrective action.

PLANNING REQUIREMENTS

Corporate management, like other levels, achieves its operational and financial direction and success through establishing achievable goals and objectives and closely monitoring progress through appropriate assessment of performance reporting. Financial ratios provide a quick overview to significant changes. Various statistical techniques are used to assist management in their decision-making process such as discounted cash flow, risk analysis, and centralized cash control. Models can be developed to aid them in their asset management resource planning. Simulation models permit the testing of various courses of action in their planning processes before finalized plans and decisions are made to proceed in one direction or the other.

This chapter will discuss the more important aspects of corporate planning through utilization of various computerized techniques relative to strategic planning and controls.

ACHIEVEMENT THROUGH PLANNING AND CONTROL DECISIONS

When a corporation or other entity is losing ground in sales, profits, and investment return, the first concern of the Board of Directors and stockholders is the effectiveness of the management team. In many instances, if their corrective actions do not succeed, a reorganization occurs and a new management team replaces the old. The new management comes in with a fresh outlook, they have no past employee loyalties to appease, and, generally, because of monetary benefits and prestige, they have a strong will to succeed and establish personal reputations as well as to face the challenge.

In one billion-dollar organization in which the author was exposed to the above situation, the new team chosen (executives from several top organizations) was young, aggressive, and seasoned. They were imbued with a sense of their opportunity to turn around the downward trend of this huge organization. Their initial task was concerned with assessing each operation's status, problems, direction, potential, and performance.

From their investigation, they found certain operations were unprofitable; if they were unable to correct the situation, they merely disposed of the operation by sale or other type of elimination. They discovered inefficient managers who had been allowed to continue in their tasks because of longevity or friendship. These executives were either demoted, retired, or otherwise replaced. They ferreted out inappropriate and unprofitable product mix and product lines within organizations. The situation was assessed in depth and corrective action taken. The team uncovered surplus manpower that was allowed to grow or remain constant in spite of a turnaround in the business environment from prosperity to recession. Manpower goals were established and controls initiated that resulted in a dramatic 40% decrease over two years (involving tens of thousands of people) with no effect on operational effectiveness. All investments in capital assets and new ventures were halted and could not be established without corporate involvement and approval. Cash flow was significantly improved. Old facilities were overhauled and modern machinery was purchased to increase operational efficiencies. Production and profitability increased. It was discovered that overhead was excessive and controls lacking. This was corrected and each organization was held accountable to a pegged rate as one of its prime objectives.

The result of the new team's action in one to two years was a dramatic turnaround in sales with a 35% increase ($350 million) over prior peak years. Profits increased 50% ($55 million) over past good years (the company was in a loss position when the team took over). Return on investment improved 45%; inventories and receivables were greatly reduced. Personnel morale improved tremendously because of the organization's successes. The corporation had once again become viable and a challenging threat to all of its competition.

This improvement and progress points up the inescapable need for a management that can effectively manage, plan, control, and make appropriate, sound decisions based on fact-finding and evaluation.

REPORTS FOR MANAGEMENT CONTROL DECISIONS

Management reports provide the means to assess the organization's progress status when past and current performance is measured against planned objectives. Some of the most important reports are noted below, although they are not described in depth, since their utilization is quite common in the business environment.

- Preliminary and Final Income Statement—Emphasis is on sales volume, costs, and profits.
- Manpower—Trend levels of growth or decline and the ratio of indirect to direct personnel.
- Cash Flow—Receipts, disbursements, ending balances, and future outlook.
- Receivable Status—Evaluation of increases/decreases, reasons for change, and assessment of age of receivable balances by customer.
- Sales Deliveries or Service Performed—Volume and profitability of individual products, contracts, and product mix.
- Source and Application of Funds—Source of receipts and fund disposition.
- Inventory Evaluation—Analysis of increases/decreases, turnover rate, and average days of cost of sales in inventory.
- Capital Expenditures—Amount authorized versus actually spent.
- Balance Sheet—Financial status of organization at point in time relative to assets, liabilities, and investment.

Operating data (sales, costs) is reported by period and year-to-date, also with a comparison to prior period and planned goals. Financial status data (cash, receivables) is for month-end balances compared to beginning of the year, previous period, and planned performance. Each reported data item has a purpose in assisting management to effectively analyze operations and make action decisions when required.

In order to successfully manage a business enterprise, management must be constantly on the alert as to the results from operations as compared to the objectives that reflect past experience and future anticipations—this is accomplished through the reporting media.

CORPORATE CONTROL THROUGH ASSET MANAGEMENT

Establishment of an asset management program is one of the most effective means of assuring an organization's progress and survival in the current business climate of competitive goals and objectives. Corporate management must take the initiative in organizing this type of effort so that proper emphasis and support is directed to achieving the requirements of performance measurement, planning, and control. This program is concerned with organizational statistics relative to a company's assets in terms of historical, current, and future trends. Proper utilization of resources is one of the key aims of this type of program. Historical performance is undoubtedly the best source of initial reference in establishing the guidelines to effect the necessary controls.

The following discussion is primarily concerned with inventories, unreimbursed expenditures, and accounts receivable.

CALCULATING ASSET CONTROL STATISTICS

Assessment of Inventories

A determination must be made as to how many days of cost of sales is reasonable in gross inventory. An unwarranted high gross inventory balance can indicate an overinvestment condition, which is a drain on an organization's resources, and ineffective inventory control policies and practices. Too low an inventory can lead to problems of adequate sales deliveries, which may lead to loss of sales and profitability. A reasonable determinant, therefore, must be established that will preclude either of the conditions above.

A proven approach to resolve the above requirement is through the development of factors that will serve as guidelines to the enforcement of compatible inventory balances. This is accomplished by a statistical analysis process in which historical inventory data is evaluated in terms of the following criteria:

- Average number of days of sales (or sales) in gross and net inventories. In most instances, cost of sales (C/S) is a more valid statistic to use than sales because it is net of gross profit, which is not generally reflected in inventory values.
- Turnover rates for both gross and net inventories.
- Net inventory as a percentage of gross.
- Average work-in-process (WIP) inventory as a percentage of gross.
- Average number of days of C/S in WIP inventory.
- Material, supplies, and purchases (MSP) inventory as a percentage of gross.
- Average number of days of C/S in MSP inventory.

Calculation Process for Above

Average days of C/S in gross and net inventory balances is calculated by dividing the average inventory by the C/S daily average. The first step is to divide the annual or annualized C/S by 365 (days in the year) to obtain the daily C/S. The next step would be to divide the resultant value into the average gross and net inventory balances to obtain the average number of days of C/S in those balances.

The above process should be done for a period of years in order to establish a representative value that is consistent with management's policy and objectives relative to the number of days of inventory that should be maintained. This factor will vary among organizations depending on the product, sales demand fluctuations, and the specific characteristics of the industry. It is noted that gross inventory includes both WIP and MSP inventories.

On government fixed-price contracts, net inventory represents the gross inventory values less progress payments. Generally, there are about 45 days of C/S in net inventory, but it is emphasized that this factor will vary among organizations.

Establishing the above factors from historical data analysis and judgment application provides the basis for determining realistic inventory levels. It further provides a tool to measure the reasonableness of future inventory values for control purposes.

Turnover rates are calculated by dividing the annual/annualized C/S by the average gross and net inventories. This statistic indicates the number of times inventory is absorbed into the C/S. It provides management with a tool for measuring actual and planned turnover rates against the goals that have been predicated on historical experience.

Gross inventory percentage of C/S is derived by dividing the average gross inventory by the annual/annualized C/S. This statistic provides management with the means of establishing a targeted goal based on past history in order to ensure control that the gross inventory will not be disproportionate to the C/S.

Net inventory as a percentage of gross is one indicator as to the status of progress payment balances. If the percentage is high, this would mean that the progress payment balance is low, which is an adverse situation for investigation. A low net inventory balance is more desirable since it indicates greater customer billings. This percentage is obtained by dividing the average net inventory balance by the gross value.

Average WIP inventory as a percentage of gross is determined by dividing the average WIP inventory by the gross average.

The remaining factor development follows the same pattern as that described above.

It is recommended that the inventory data be plotted graphically in order to demonstrate the direction of the trend line. Where the points are of wide divergence from the norm, an analysis should be performed to determine the reason. The results then provide additional judgment factors in establishing realistic goals.

In one organization that was evaluated, the above type of inventory assessment led to a management estimated reduction of approximately 20% in inventory balance values, which in turn reduced investment resources of *eight million dollars* annually. This figure did not include a substantial reduction in property taxes.

Unreimbursed Expenditure Guidelines

As costs are incurred on cost-type contracts and remain unbilled to the customer, this expenditure of resources is classified as unreimbursed on the balance sheet. It represents uncollected assets. In order to establish reliable guidelines for setting objectives and controlling the size of this account, the following analysis is made of the historical data:

- Determination of the average number of days of cost contract sales in the average unreimbursed expenditure balance.
- Turnover rate.
- Average unreimbursed expenditures as a percentage of sales.

Calculation Process

The average number of days of sales in unreimbursed expenditures is calculated by dividing the annual/annualized sales by 365 to obtain the sales per day. This value is then divided into the average unreimbursed expenditure balance to determine the number of days of sales in the balance. This statistic dramatically highlights the number of days of sales that have not been collected, which signifies tied-up resources.

The *turnover rate* is determined by dividing the annual sales by the average unreimbursed expenditures. This statistic indicates the number of times per year the balance has turned over. The turnover rate should be high since funding and progress payments do not pose the problems that they do on fixed-price contracts.

The *average unreimbursed expenditures as a percentage of sales* is derived by dividing the expenditure balance by the annual sales. This factor will be low if the billing process is accelerated to reduce the balances.

Based on the evaluation of the above historical statistics in one organization, it was determined that the days of sales in the unreimbursed expenditures was excessively high, which in turn was reflected in low turnover rates and a high balance as a percentage of sales. Management's investigation of the problem revealed that this was due to delays in the billing cycle and other problems. According to ASPR (Armed Services Procurement Regulations), the maximum billing cycle required for reimbursement was twenty days. Historical data indicated that unbilled sales were sometimes as high as seventy days. Corrective action was initiated that reduced expenditure balances outstanding by $2 million and the cash flow benefited by this amount. This further meant a reduction of the investment in uncollected expenses. This example illustrates that effective control and achievement of asset management can result in the savings of millions of dollars in resources through a thorough analysis of data and the establishment of target goals that are realistic and rewarding.

Accounts Receivable Performance Measurement

The accounts receivable historical data is also analyzed in a manner similar to that of unreimbursed expenditures discussed above. The calculation procedures are the same to obtain the statistics required. A careful analysis will reveal that improvements can be made in the billing to accelerate cash flow and also reduce the number of sales days in the receivable balances. Management, however, must initiate the necessary goals criteria to be followed. Accounts receivable representing fixed-price contracts have the added problem of funding limitations and progress payments.

The evaluation of the above factors in one organization resulted in establishing controls and targets that ultimately led to a reduction in receivable balances of 25% or $3.5 million. The reduction would vary among organizations depending on size of the organization and current controls in effect.

Another excellent means of measuring an organization's performance and status relative to receivables is to compare results to that of competitors in the same industry. This data is generally readily available from the annual financial reports, credit agencies, Moody's book of industrials, or stock market literature. This type of evaluation is healthy and could lead to greater profitability (particularly if there is a problem), better utilization of resources, and improvement of an organization's competitive position in the business environment. It could also reveal certain soft spots in operations that indicate the need for investigation and corrective action.

The comparative industrial analysis should include return on sales, solvency, age of receivables, inventory turnover, and various financial ratios that are indicative of an organization's progress.

Aspect of Computerization

Statistical analysis is conducive to the use of computers in performing the computations required to obtain the data required. Analytical factor development results from the use of various equations that can be readily programmed into a system where actuals would be fed, comparisons made, and performance variances generated.

FINANCIAL RATIOS FOR PERFORMANCE MEASUREMENT

Financial ratios play a significant role in assessing the results from operations in one period versus another. They indicate various trends that assist management, as well as external organizations (banks, credit agencies, stockholders), in determining the progress and stability of an organization. Ratios are also utilized as comparative statistics with other external organizations. Some of the most common ratios used in the business world for analysis and planning purposes are displayed on Exhibit A. As shown on this exhibit, the significance of the ratio is indicated, such as operation/management efficiency, profitability, investment utilization, receivable turnover, measure of solvency, and stock earnings per share. A mechanical program to calculate and provide this type of data would be of invaluable aid to management in rapidly assessing the results from operations and highlighting problem areas for attention.

CAPITALGRAPH PROJECTION MODEL

An effective concept that has rapidly gained recognition and use in recent years is the projection of balance sheet data elements through the establishment of their relationship to the fluctuation of sales volume. This method of forecasting is primarily concerned with the major items on the balance sheet that are required to develop the total operating capital, including cash, receivables, inventories, and net capital assets. The model permits gaming at the division or corporate level to ascertain the impact on the balance sheet at varying sales volume. It also provides a rapid test of the reasonableness of detailed projection submissions as well as the resulting summary.

The basic assumption of this model's concept is that the sales volume fluctuation has a decided effect on the financial status of an organization. As has been verified in some organizations that have experimented with it, the status of the receivable balance, inventory requirements (greater sales resulted in higher inventory and receivable balances), and current liabilities are influenced because of larger cost commitments (labor, material, overhead) involved in producing the sales products to meet demand. Capital assets may have to be increased relative to facility expansion and/or additional machinery and equipment to support the operations effort. Working capital is also affected through changes in current assets and liabilities in order to finance operations on a sound, sustaining basis.

Development of the Model

The process involved in developing the balance sheet projection model requires reference to and analysis of historical data (two to three years) and establishment of the relationships as to what effect sales fluctuations in the past had on balance sheet items. The processes involved are described as follows:

- The regression analysis technique is employed to establish and/or determine the nature of the association between variables (sales versus cash, receivables, etc.). The results represent historical facts translated into a formula. Of course, reasons as to why a relationship does or does not exist are not revealed by the formula but must be determined by a detailed analysis of the data.
- Scattergraphs are used to plot the sales data on a monthly (but annualized) or annual basis against monthly average year-end balances. The monthly (annualized basis) data provides a more realistic approach to establishing the existence of data relationship. Based on the plot points, a regression line is drawn and the projection equation calculated.

SIMULATION MODEL

Financial Statistics For Gaming Process

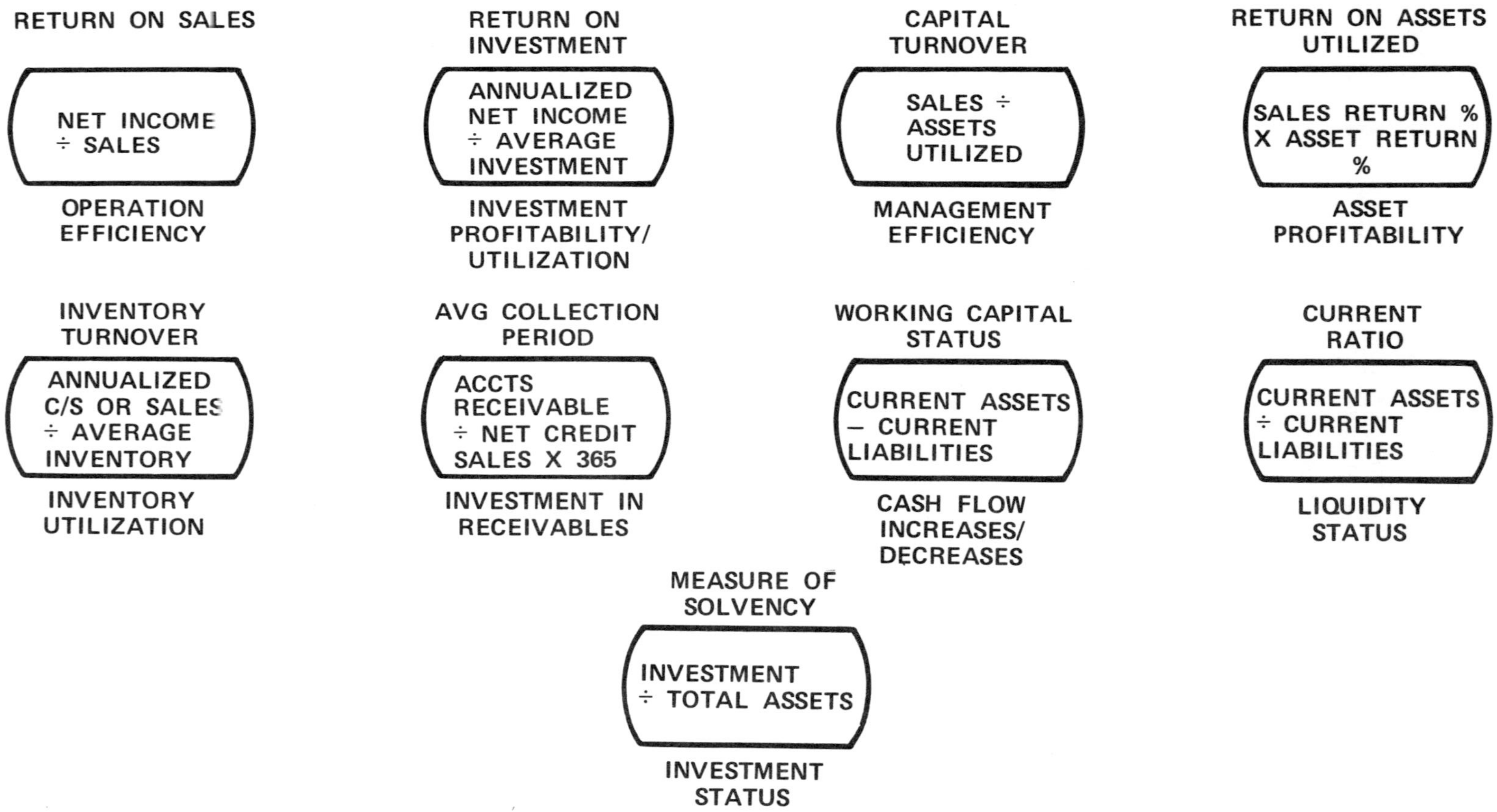

EXHIBIT A

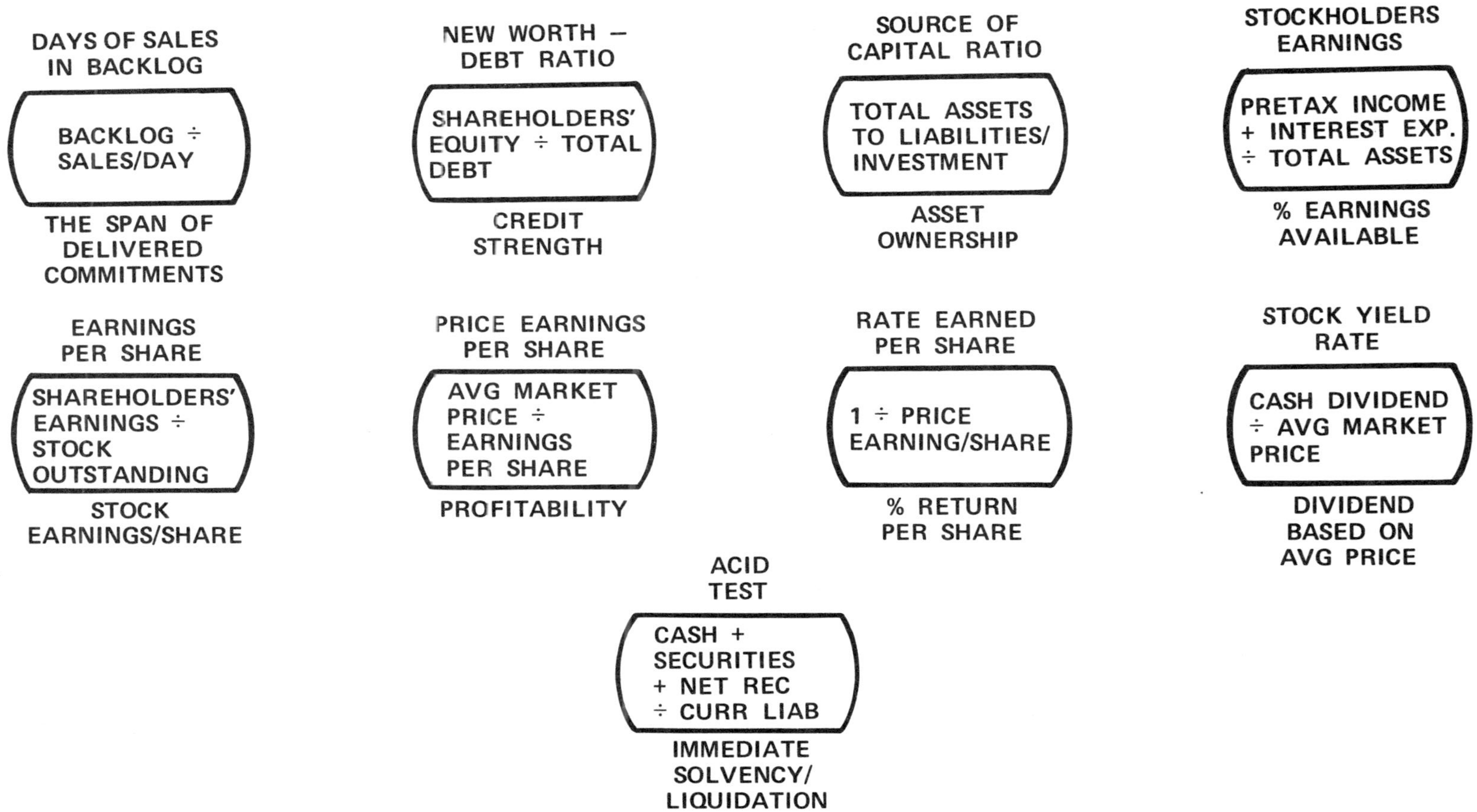

EXHIBIT A, continued

Based on the performance of the operations above, minimum standby or fixed and variable capital factors are derived for application to sales volume for asset balance projections. It is noted that fixed capital requirements represent an arithmetical description of a portion of the total capital requirements that are necessary to operate a business.

Operating Capital Projections

Using the capitalgraph technique, Exhibit B displays the trend line approach to fixed and variable factors. The line intercept on the "Y" axis indicates a minimal capital requirement of $800K, which represents cash, beginning balances, and investment in plant, property, and equipment. At zero sales, there are no receivables but they are generated as soon as sales deliveries and invoicing occur. It is noted on the exhibit that at a volume of $5.2 million sales, the total operating capital required is $1.806 million. The total operating capital required less the fixed portion of $800K results in $1.006 million variable. The variable portion divided by the sales results in a variable percentage of 19.36.

Using the above procedure in an actual business environment, the following data was developed to reflect the detail of the fixed and variable factors above. A comparison is also made between an actual sales volume of $3.0 million versus the projections at that volume based on the formula application.

	Actuals at $3 Million	Capital Factors Fixed	Variable %	Capitalgraph Projections (based on volume)		
				$3.0	$4.0	$6.0
Cash and Equivalent	145.0	50.0	3.37	151.1*	184.8	252.2
Receivables	282.0	50.0	8.05	291.5	392.0	533.0
Inventories	550.0	150.0	12.60	528.0	654.0	906.0
Current Assets	977.0	250.0	24.02	970.6	1,210.8	1,691.2
Current Liabilities	302.0	75.0	7.04	286.2	356.6	497.4
Working Capital	675.0	175.0	16.98	684.4	854.2	1,193.8
Capital Assets	710.0	625.0	2.38	696.4	720.2	767.8
Operating Capital	1,385.0	800.0	19.36	1,380.8	1,574.4	1,961.6

*Calculated by multiplying sales volume ($3.0 million) by variable factor (3.37%) plus fixed portion ($50.0) = $151.1.

All other projections are calculated on the same basis of factor application to sales volume as described in the footnote above.

Observations from Data Manipulation

- The capitalgraph projections are fairly compatible at $3.0 million with the actuals.
- To derive working capital at any sales volume, you would apply a variable factor of 16.98% to the sales volume plus the fixed capital value of $175.0. Other data elements in the above illustration are obtained using the same procedure.

CAPITALGRAPH FORECASTING OF OPERATING CAPITAL

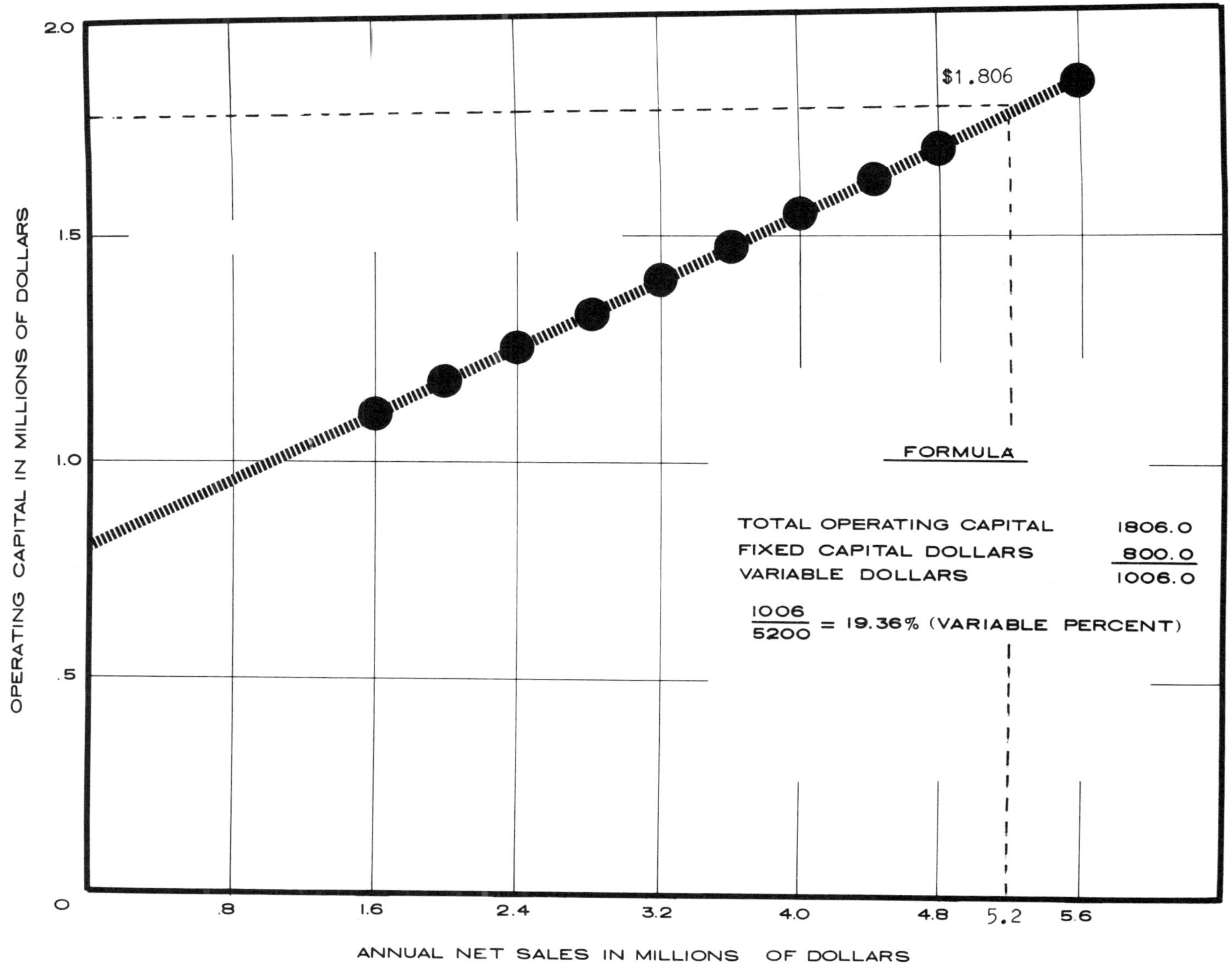

EXHIBIT B

- Upper and lower limits of the regression line factors will vary more from actuals because the formula is based on average trends.
- The projections must be tempered with judgment and any known or anticipated major deviations from norm should be reflected as adjustments to the projected data derived by formula and/or changes made to the formula itself.
- The above projection process is rapid, lends itself to mechanization, and provides an analytical planning tool to assess the results of detailed projection development.

Capitalgraph Model Use

This technique, like many others, may not be appropriate for all organizations as a planning tool, but this determination can only be made by a detailed evaluation and testing of historical data as to its applicability. It may be that it would be suitable in projecting the aggregate operating capital but not the detailed items (could be percentaged). If it can be utilized and proven as effective as demonstrated above, then the capability provides management with a technique to simulate balance sheet results from varying sales volume levels.

CORPORATE CASH DISBURSEMENT DECISIONS

A major problem at the corporate level is the capability to maintain an adequate overall cash flow position. This means sufficient cash receipts to meet liability commitments on schedule and hopefully to use any excesses as short-term investment opportunities. The validity of projecting cash receipts is usually effectively accomplished based on sales deliveries, level of effort, services rendered, and progress payments. Based on historical experience, the time lapse in the billing cycle is readily determinable and cash collections are fairly accurately projected, particularly for the immediate future.

The forecast of cash disbursements is the problem area. Cash outlays, primarily, consist of two major expenditure classifications—payroll and accounts payable. The timing of payroll disbursements poses no major problem since the time period for accrued salaries and wages payment is stable—weekly, semimonthly, or monthly. Payable disbursements are far more difficult to predict, particularly for future periods. Payables represent a conglomerate of varied liability commitments for overhead expenses, direct materials, subcontracts, and asset acquisitions. Delivery schedule of purchase receipts is highly variable and due dates for payment differ among the large volume of invoices.

To provide corporate management with the kind of visibility required for immediate cash planning and decision-making to pay, hold, invest, or borrow, a mechanical process is recommended which will be described below. Although the proposed systems were developed for a multi-organization corporation with varied locations, the concept can be adjusted to an organization of any size. The main purpose of the proposals is to provide ideas for improving cash flow projections.

Objectives

Development of an overall accounts payable reporting model will provide the corporate office with daily projected cash payment data over a specified amount (depending on the size of the organization—$10K to $50K), with advanced due dates (five days recommended), by vendor, which will permit corporate management to make the necessary pay/delay decisions based on the daily overall cash flow position.

Assumptions

- Each organization involved currently has a basic mechanical accounts payable (A/P) reporting system.
- There exists a central data processing center (DPC) or designated responsible organization to whom will be transmitted daily A/P data for sorting and summarizing the information in such a manner that it is conducive to management's decision-making process. There could be more than one DPC.
- Each organization and/or DPC has the capability of transmitting data in accordance with a predesignated format that will be compatible for sorting and consolidating (data identifiers).

Overview of One Approach

Exhibit C displays the proposed data flow processing involved in this approach. Under the DPC (Data Processing Center) concept, the organizations would provide the centers with vendor transactions daily. These would be processed at the centers to update the individual division commitment files. The centers will sort and summarize the data into prescribed formats that will meet the needs of the reporting requirements. After the data is developed, it will be transmitted over communication network lines to a central or designated center for corporate-specified consolidations.

The responsible summarizing organization will transmit the data to the corporate office on a daily basis for their review and action. The reported information will be sorted by day for five consecutive workdays in advance of the reporting day. Each day, the data will be updated by dropping the first day and adding the extra day.

When a delay payment decision is made, the checks will be held and records adjusted at the designated center to reflect the new pay dates. The information is communicated back to the concerned divisions by the responsible center.

An alternative approach is also a possibility in that the Exhibit C proposal is quite involved due to the need for establishing the necessary communication linkage and more complicated programming. The substitute approach, which is more suitable to low-volume, large payments, will be discussed subsequently.

System Input

Exhibit D shows the format of data extracted from the files for transmission. Division detail is sorted into various combinations and the totals reflected accordingly. This type of report affords detailed analysis and reference capability. The lower portion format on the exhibit includes only those projected vendor payments over $50K (if that is the limit) on which the decisions will be made.

Exhibit E shows the type of data that will be required from the corporate office relative to the delay payment decision, which will have to be communicated back to the center indicating that all other payments can be made and the action and file adjustments can be made accordingly.

CORPORATE CASH DISBURSEMENT PLANNING/DECISIONS
Proposed Data Flow Processing
DAILY

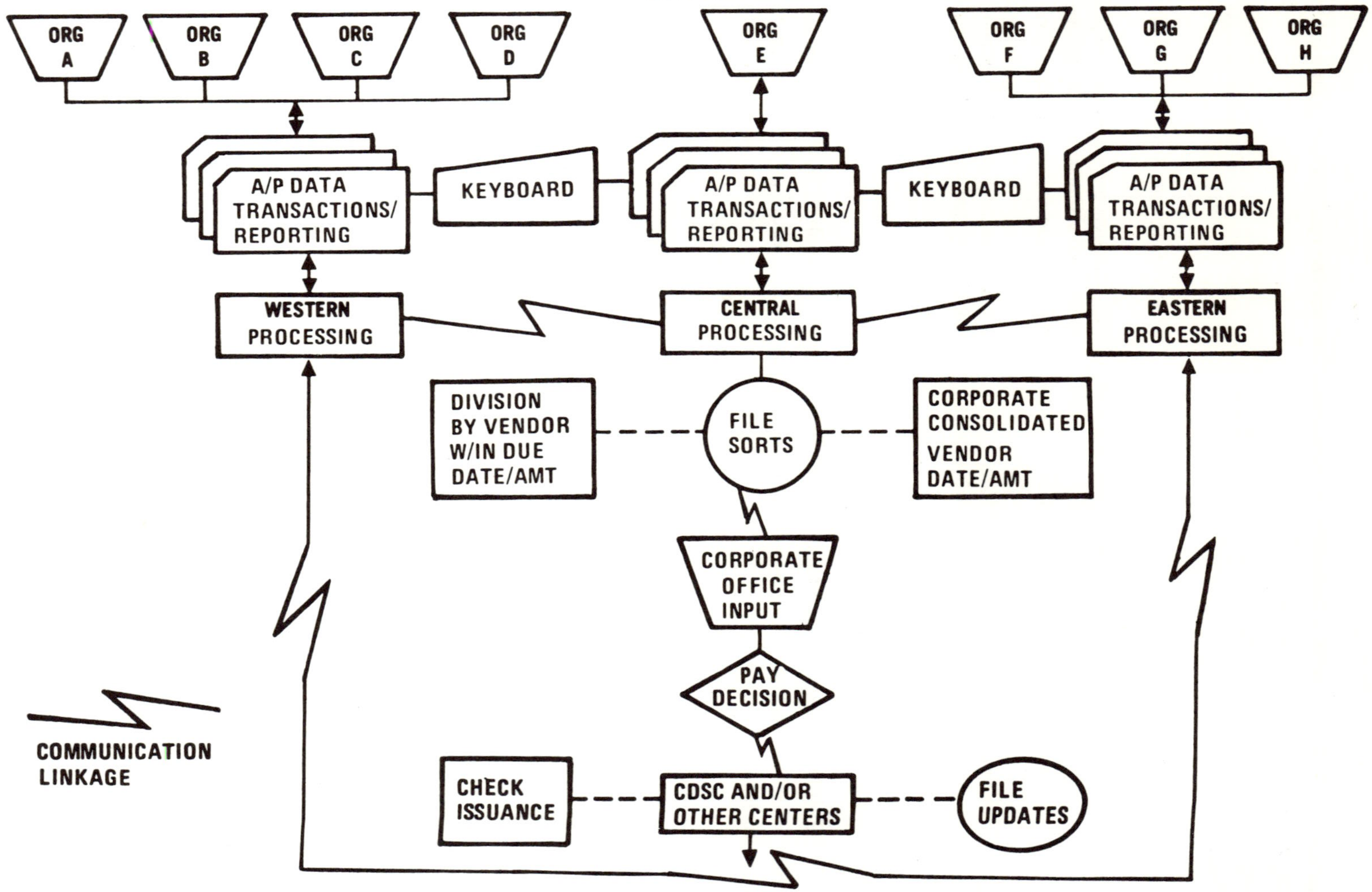

EXHIBIT C

CORPORATE CASH DISBURSEMENT PLANNING/DECISIONS
Proposed Daily Reporting to Corporate

VENDOR DETAIL WITHIN DIVISION FOR REFERENCE

*DIV CODE	*CENTER CODE	*DUE DATE	VENDOR		*PAYMT CDE $50K & OVER	BANK		*DAYS CHK CLEARANCE	INVOICE				DISC AMT
			*CODE	NAME		*LOCATION	NAME		NO.	DATE	AMT	TERMS	

*SORT CAPABILITY

SUBTOTALS VENDOR WITHIN DIVISION & DUE DATE
VENDOR WITHIN BANK LOCATION & DUE DATE

TOTALS BY DIVISION WITHIN CENTER & DUE DATES
BY CENTER WITHIN DUE DATES

IDENTIFY WITH SYMBOL – VENDOR TOTAL DUE PAYMENTS $50K OR OVER WITHIN DUE DATE

CORPORATE CONSOLIDATED VENDOR PAYMENT DUE REPORT

*DUE DATE	*DIV CODE	*VENDOR		*BANK		$DAYS – CHECK CLEARANCE	INVOICE				DISC AMT
		CODE	NAME	LOCATION	NAME		NO.	DATE	AMT	TERMS	

*SORT CAPABILITY

ONLY DUE PAYMENTS OF $50K OR OVER BY VENDOR WILL BE INCLUDED IN THIS REPORT

SUBTOTALS VENDORS WITHIN DUE DATE (5 CONSECUTIVE DAYS) & DIVISION/CENTER – OVER $50K
BANK LOCATION & NAME, AMOUNT & VENDOR WITHIN SPECIFIED CHECK CLEARANCE DAYS & DUE DATE

TOTALS ALL VENDORS, TOTAL WITHIN DUE DATE
ALL BANK LOCATION TOTAL WITHIN DUE DATE

EXHIBIT D

CORPORATE PAY EXCEPTION REPORT

*CENTER CODE	*DIV CODE	*VENDOR NO.	*INVOICE NO.	DELAY PAY DATE	AMOUNT

*SORT CAPABILITY
INPUT FROM CORPORATE OFFICE TO CDSC OR DIVISIONS
FILE RECORDS OF DIVISION ARE ADJUSTED FOR PAYMENT DELAY

EXHIBIT E

Implementation Considerations

This system is more appropriate for a high volume of large vendor payments. It lends itself to a central center's complete involvement in the process from the point of other centers' (or divisions') input, processing and transmitting data to the corporate office, making the nonpay decision adjustments, updating the files, and transmitting results to the other centers (if appropriate), which, in turn, relay the data to the divisions. Checks could be produced at the central center or issued at the other centers or divisions. This would have to be a management decision as the most effective procedure. Bank clearance lapsed time is very important since it is an indicator as to the actual date when issued checks will require funding. Implementation of this procedure would require more time and cost than the alternative proposal.

ALTERNATIVE DISBURSEMENT APPROACH

Objective

The purpose of the alternative disbursement approach is to establish an expedient computerized method of providing the corporate office with projected cash payments to vendors that exceed $10K over a daily five-day workday period; further, to segregate the data within due dates into the time lapse between check release and bank clearance. The data process flow is reflected on Exhibit F.

Input

Division vendor transactions are transmitted to the appropriate center on a daily basis. Division delay payment date and related vendor ID number/invoice are communicated back to the originating organization.

CORPORATE CASH DISBURSEMENT PLANNING/DECISIONS
Alternative Daily Processing Proposal

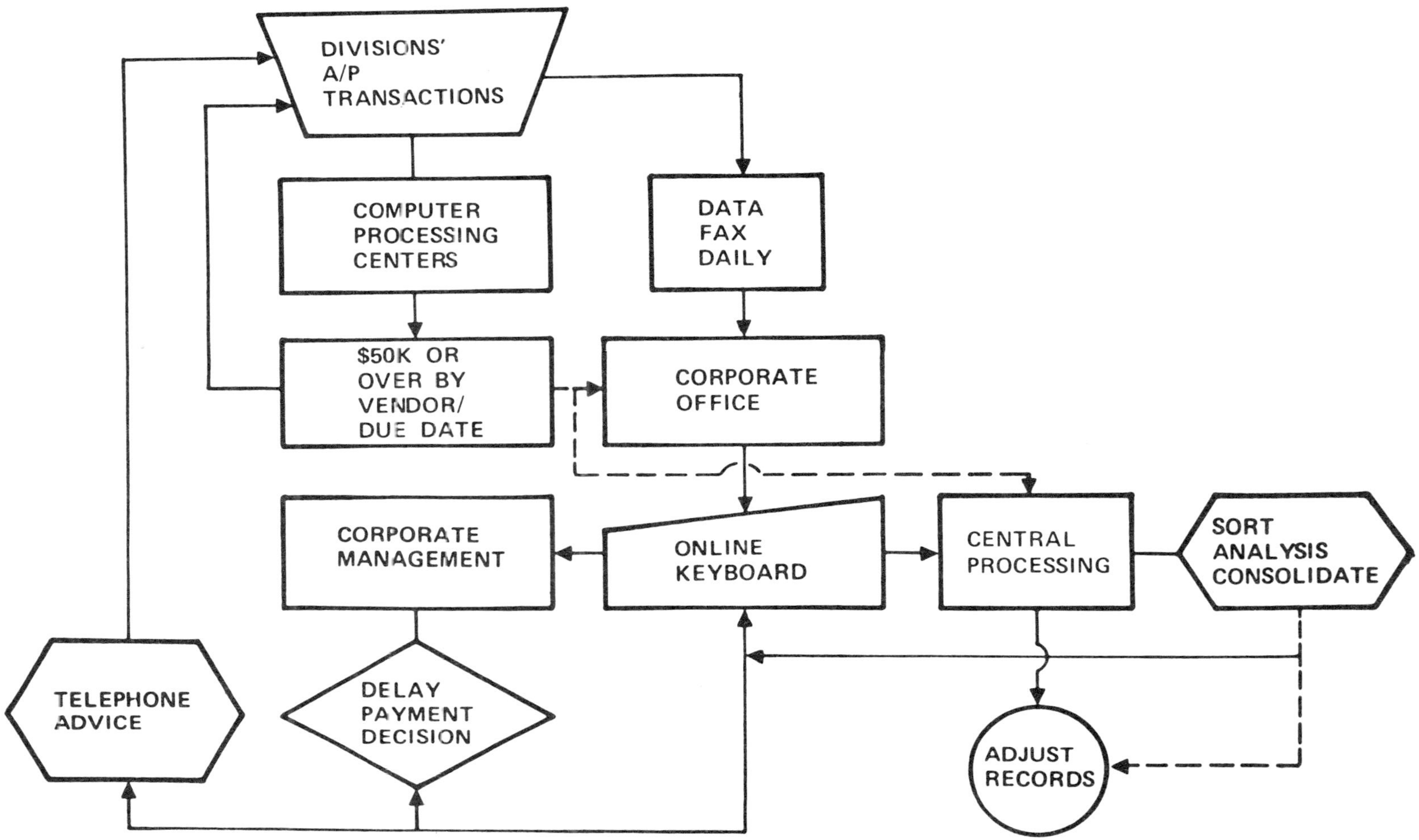

EXHIBIT F

Processing

Division transactions would be processed at the appropriate center. Records are updated and the division would be provided daily with a listing of vendors to whom amounts are to be paid in excess of $10K.

Divisions will individually datafax the information to the corporate office in order to ensure their direct involvement in the cash-flow process. This could also be accomplished directly from a center (which handles more than one division) on a composite division basis to the central center. If the divisions (or centers) datafax this information to the corporate office, it is then keyboarded for sorting by bank location. There would be a table file identifying vendor payment destination to location and time lapse between check release and bank clearance.

The consolidated listing within due date is transmitted to the corporate office for review, and the delay-pay or pay-all decision would be relayed via telephone to the divisions. The decision is also communicated to the central center so that their file records could be adjusted accordingly. If the delay-pay decision is transmitted directly to the divisions, they would have to re-input the new pay data into the system.

Output

This would be a listing of the paid amounts to the vendors and a pay-delay listing showing the revised pay dates.

Implementation Considerations

A procedure would have to be issued describing division/center responsibilities and action. A small program would have to be written at the central center or responsible consolidating organization to perform the sorts, analysis, and summary processes. A determination would have to be made as to whether inputs would be direct from the divisions to the corporate office or from centers. This procedure could be readily implemented to provide the data required by the corporate office in a timely manner.

Implications of Centralized Control

This type of centralized control would enable corporate management to make intelligent decisions on all major vendor disbursements on a daily basis for five days in advance. They would have the opportunity to assess their daily cash position for all organizations based on anticipated receipts versus projected cash disbursements. Due consideration would be afforded to taking advantage of discounts versus the possible borrowing required in terms of the cost of money. Visibility would be available, in advance, as to the need for borrowing and making the necessary arrangements for fund availability. When cash surpluses were anticipated, investment possibilities would be sought. Depending on the size of the organization, thousands of dollars, if not hundreds of thousands, can be saved in interest charges or earned from investments through effective and timely cash planning achieved by appropriate reporting, analysis of data, centralized control, and decision actions. There is the added advantage that the surplus in one organization can be planned to meet anticipated deficits in other organizations.

DISCOUNTED PRESENT VALUE

In making venture/capital investments, an organization is primarily concerned with the amount of return that will materialize in the future plus the extent of current investments to achieve the desired future amount. The investment decision must be predicated on the ability to calculate these values and determine if the results will fulfill the future return requirements. Present value tables are available that provide the factors to be used at varying interest rates for a given number of period-end dates.

For example, if the investing organization wants to accumulate $100,000 in four years and it can currently negotiate a 9% interest, the question then is how much of an investment it must make now to achieve this goal. The statistical table indicates a factor per $1.00 of .7084. This value times $100,000 indicates a current investment requirement of $70,840. To develop and verify the factor obtained from readily available present value tables, the following calculations would be required.

Factor Development

PERIOD	INTEREST CALCULATION	PERCENT INTEREST	INTEREST VALUE	INVESTMENT PLUS INTEREST
1	100,000.00	.09	9,000.00	109,000.00
2	109,000.00	.09	9,810.00	118,810.00
3	118,810.00	.09	10,692.90	129,573.90
4	129,573.90	.09	11,661.65	141,235.55

FACTOR: 100,000 ÷ 141,235.55 = .7084

Factor Verification

PERIOD	INTEREST CALCULATION	PERCENT INTEREST	INTEREST VALUE	INVESTMENT PLUS INTEREST
1	70,804.00	.09	6,375.60	77,215.60
2	77,215.60	.09	6,949.40	84,165.00
3	84,165.00	.09	7,574.85	91,739.85
4	91,739.85	.09	8,265.59	100,005.44

As noted above, the discounted cash flow indicates that an investment of $70,840 made currently at 9% for four years would yield the desired $100,005. Before cash outlays are made, the above processing should be made as an alternative check against other types of investments being considered to obtain future yields; however, it should be noted that there could be other important determinant criteria involved in the decision such as risk, time length of investment, compatibility of the venture with organizational objectives, or operational requirements.

Importance of Discounted Cash Flow

Management must be constantly on the alert for investment opportunities in order to achieve maximum profitability from resource utilization. Proposed investments in projects are ranked in descending order relative to their rate of return. This ranking permits management to exercise judgment in selecting the investment choice of greatest return. This assessment reflects constant dollar returns in the early years of the investment life.

RISK ANALYSIS TECHNIQUE

This technique bases its usefulness on the development of data indicative of varying future probabilities and the risks involved in the selection of various alternatives. The results from risk analysis facilitate and improve the decision-making process.

Criteria for Model Construction

The risk analysis model involves the following procedural processes, which lend themselves readily to computerization:

- Identification of variables necessary for the analysis task.
- Determination of the best estimate of each variable that can occur, or be exceeded, in the ranges of 90%, 50%, or 10%.
- Estimation of the probability distributions in terms of practical upper and lower limits for data set values.
- Division of the range between extremes into segments and assignment of a probability to each.
- Determination of the possibility of the values occurring for each segment.
- Assignment of the estimated probability to a representative point.
- Determination of the mean and standard deviations.

After the values have been determined, they should be graphically plotted. At this point you can determine visually the relative frequencies for midpoints at each interval and calculate the probability distribution. Examples of the graphic displays are shown in Exhibit G.

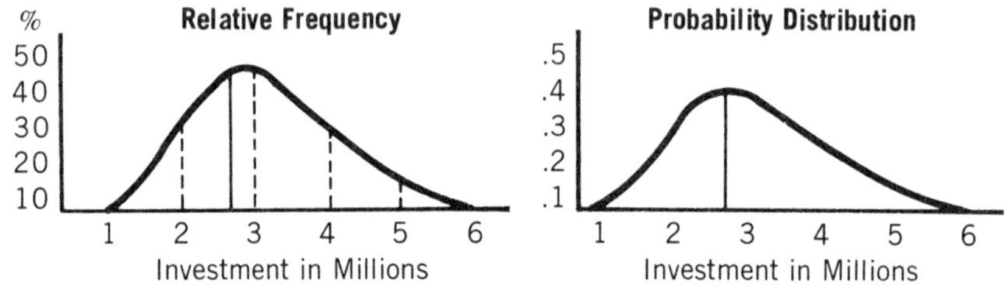

EXHIBIT G

Use for Cash Management

The risk analysis simulation lends itself to cash management because of its dependence on factors and events anticipated in the future. Based on the sales budget, cash receipts are predicated on deliveries, invoicing, and the timing of the receivable liquidations. Extenuating circumstances can cause delays in cash receipts or possibly result in uncollectible receivables (bad debts). The occurrence of these events may necessitate borrowing, decreased expenditures, and/or delays in the payments to vendors—each action may have a significant penalizing effect on the organization.

Relative to cash disbursement probabilities, a determination must be made as to the level of accuracy in data projections and what happens when the level of cash outflow cannot be achieved due to insufficient receipts from customer receivables. In the cash management procedural process, the cash balance and projected cash receipts from operations are classified within various range probabilities. Correlated to this data are the anticipated cash disbursements. The difference between the two sets of data will result in cash surplus or deficit values.

For utmost utilization, risk analysis calculations should be computerized because of the extent of manual effort involved to reflect varying changes to receipts, disbursements, or both. Mechanical programs provide greater flexibility in the simulation process of testing the results from a multitude of varying input factors, which is practically impossible in the manual environment on a timely basis.

The risk analysis model would be used to produce quantitative measurement values of risks involved in each proposed investment opportunity. It provides a basis for decision-making that could prevent costly errors. This is also a sound technique for sales and profit determination, capital investment, business diversification possibilities, and new product development assessment. Using risk analysis provides management with greater visibility as to future probabilities and helps to resolve the differences that are major among various alternatives and thus improves planning.

SIMULATOR MODELS FOR PLANNING

The development and use of mechanical corporate models has increased significantly in the past few years and is expected to continue in the future as complexities grow in managing a business enterprise. Since all organizations are involved in the overall corporate objectives planning, masses of data have to be assimilated and consolidated into meaningful financial data summaries. The comprehensive data manipulation required for evaluating various plan ning alternatives is a horrendous task that generally cannot be effectively accomplished within the time frame required and therefore important and viable considerations in plan resolution may be detrimentally neglected.

Characteristics of a Planning Model

Planning models consist of a series of equations that are used to mathematically calculate and derive the end-result data in varying degrees of relative detail as required. They are constructed to reflect the manual budget development process but are effective in accomplishing the task because of the inherent computer accuracy and flexibility. In developing the model, careful attention must be directed to the needs of management. Their requirements should be thoroughly explored, resolved, and incorporated within the program, which forces the establishment of precise and fixed ground rules for achieving planning needs. Without management's involvement and interest, a computerized planning model cannot be successfully achieved.

Corporate planning objectives can be effectively evaluated in the mechanical model based on predesignated parameters established by management. As actual performance data becomes available, it will be compared to the planning goals, and deviations from the plan will be outputted for analysis and corrective action decisions. This comparison is done in summary and by individual organization so that the proper assessment can be made to pinpoint responsibility.

Integration of Variable Gaming

This process involves a sophisticated form of computerized planning in which several sets of data are changed and reflected in other data classifications and different financial schedules. One job stream program controls and directs the transfer of data through various files, manipulations, and summations. Exhibit H illustrates basic gaming files that are used and the subsequent data that is revised when changes are made. As shown on the exhibit, there are four major summaries that are affected when there are revisions to sales, costs, or profits.

Effect of Current Asset Changes

Exhibit H indicated the results of changes to basic files. Proceeding a step further, changes to the data elements included in current assets have a subsequent effect on financial ratios and turnover rates as shown on Exhibit I.

In a well-constructed simulator model, management is not restricted to the detailed file simulations but also can play the ''what if'' game at a higher level of management data (cash, receivables, inventories) as shown on Exhibit I. It may be that before changes are made to the basic files, management might want to know the effect on end-resulting financial ratios when changes are made to current asset data. Or, it could be possible that they would want to do the simulation at that level of information to resolve the kind of ratios that were acceptable before the detail was revised. In any instance, the gaming model provides this capability.

In summary and throughout this book, the author has referred a number of times to planning and control capabilities that are available for improving operations. A corporate model enjoys similar advantages to those discussed for other mechanical systems. A summary of the simulator model attributes in effecting more realistic planning and controlling is reiterated below.

SUMMARY

- Feasible & Desirable
- Reduced Clerical Effort to Effect Changes
- Rapid & Selective Manipulation of Data
- Immediate Results (Detail/Summary)—Review & Analysis
- Testing Alternate Courses of Action
- Effective Planning & Decision-Making Tool
- Ideal for On-Line Activity
- Future of Financial Operations Success

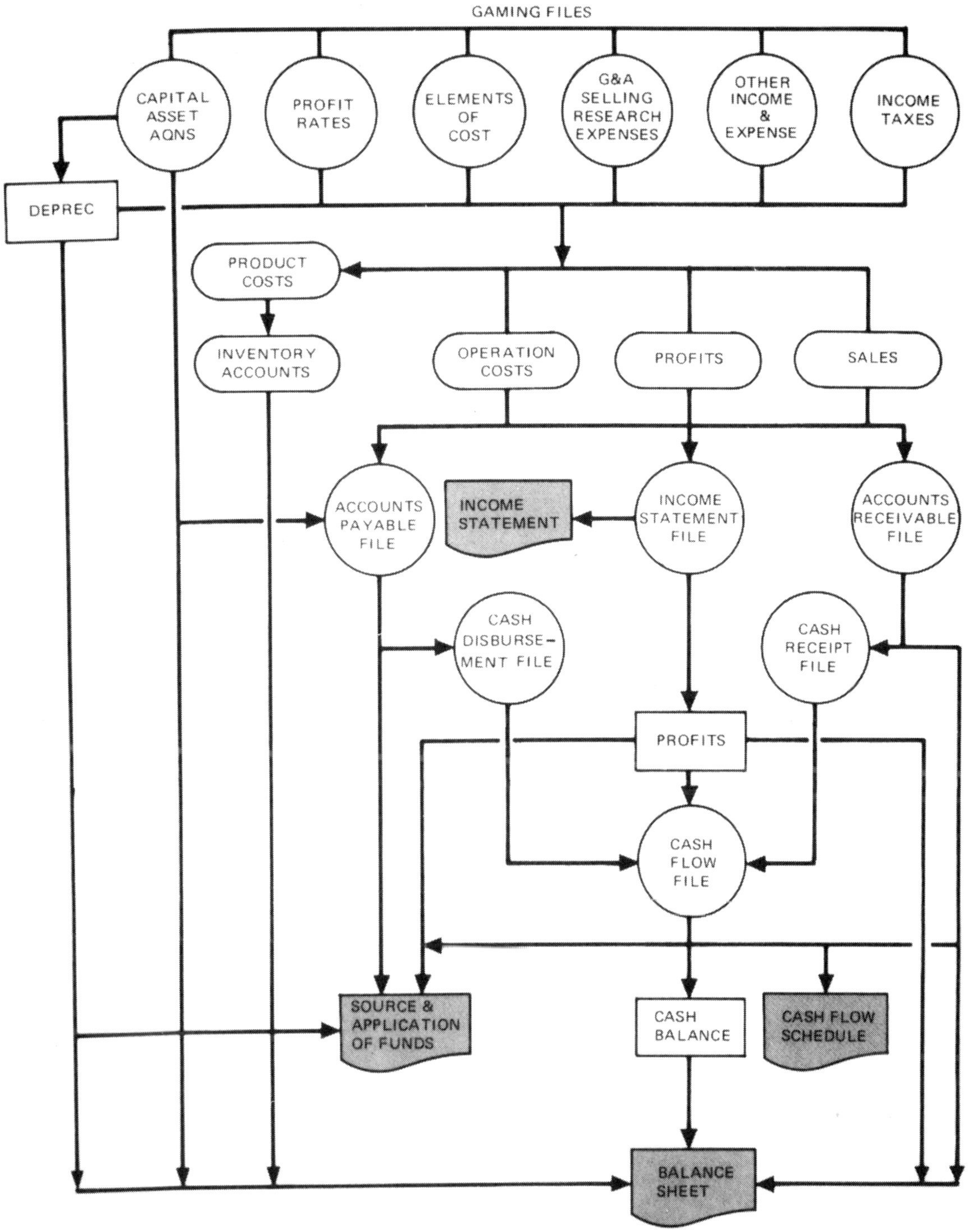

INTEGRATED GAMING MODEL OVERVIEW

EXHIBIT H

EFFECT OF CHANGES TO PROJECTED DATA

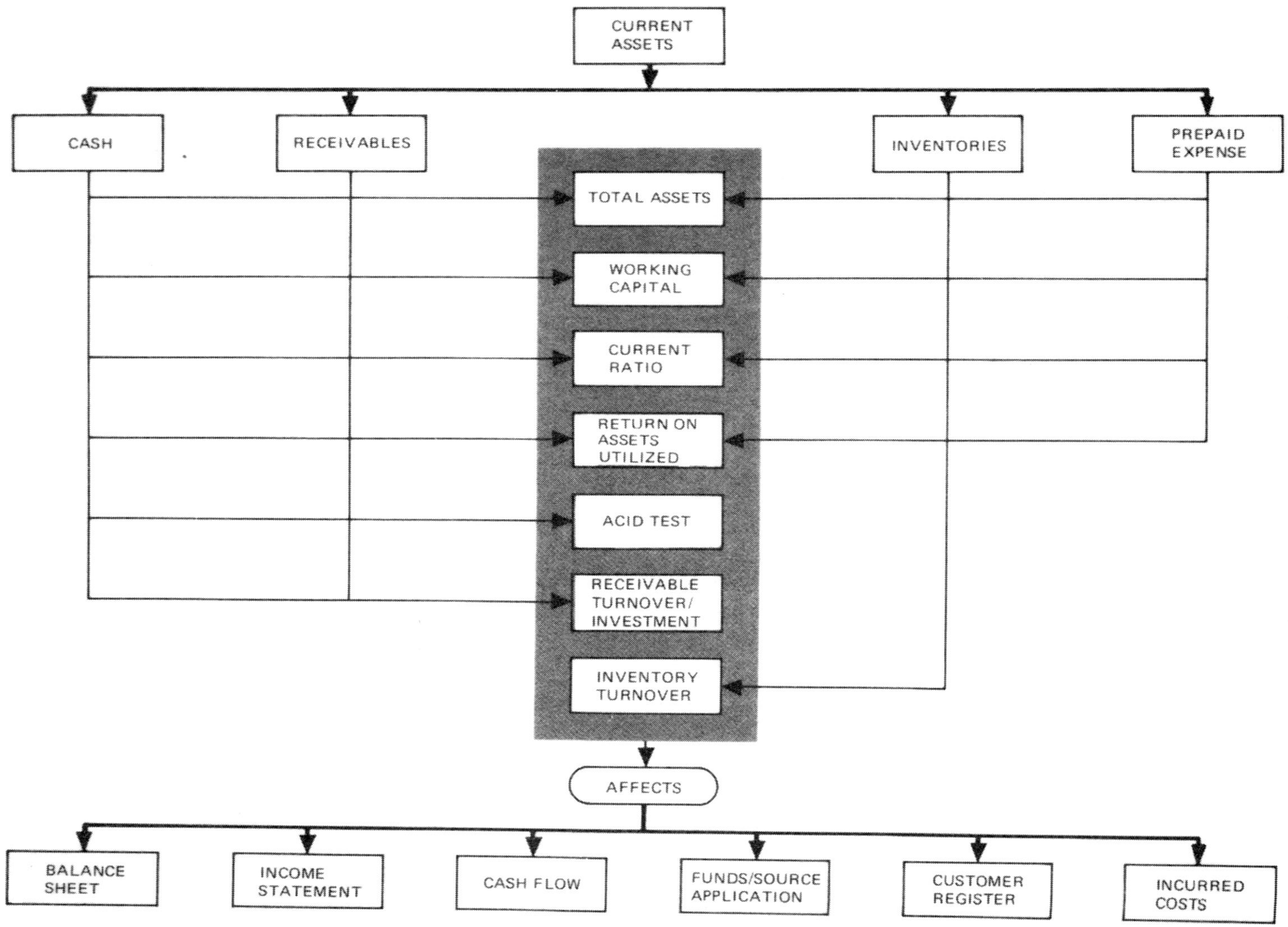

EXHIBIT I

The greatest value of simulator models is that they provide a rapid and efficient means of testing various alternatives, which provides management with a means of resolving their operating plans. The models are most effectively used in projecting sales, cost, profits, cash flow, and the fund statement.

Corporate financial planning, control, and reporting will be greatly enhanced through the evaluation and use of the tools described in this chapter relative to the capitalgraph capability, centralized cash control, utilization of financial ratios for measuring an organization's progress, and the establishment of an effective asset management program.

Index